D1571199

ARGUING THE APOCALYPSE

ARGUING
THE
APOCALYPSE

A Theory of Millennial Rhetoric

STEPHEN D. O'LEARY

New York   Oxford

OXFORD UNIVERSITY PRESS

1994

Oxford University Press

Oxford   New York   Toronto
Delhi   Bombay   Calcutta   Madras   Karachi
Kuala Lumpur   Singapore   Hong Kong   Tokyo
Nairobi   Dar es Salaam   Cape Town
Melbourne   Auckland   Madrid

and associated companies in
Berlin   Ibadan

Copyright © 1994 by Stephen D. O'Leary

Published by Oxford University Press, Inc.
200 Madison Avenue, New York, New York 10016

Oxford is a registered trademark of Oxford University Press, Inc.

Library of Congress Cataloging-in-Publication Data
O'Leary, Stephen D.
Arguing the apocalypse : a theory of
millennial rhetoric / Stephen D. O'Leary
p. cm.   Includes bibliographical references and index.
ISBN 0-19-508045-9
1. Apocalyptic literature—History and criticism.
2. Rhetoric.
3. Discourse analysis.
I. Title.
BL501.044   1994   291.2'3—dc20
93-17563

1 3 5 7 9 8 6 4 2

Printed in the United States of America
on acid-free paper

Acknowledgments

Many people contributed support and encouragement to the development of this study. First and foremost, I thank my wife, Mary Rose, who patiently supported me through years of writing and rewriting and tolerated my quirks and demands when it must have seemed as if the end would never come. To her I dedicate these words of another student of prophecy who sought to understand its proper place in our lives: "Love will never come to an end. Are there prophets? their work will be over. Are there tongues of ecstasy? they will cease. Is there knowledge? it will vanish away; for our knowledge and our prophecy alike are partial, and the partial vanishes when wholeness comes" (1 Cor. 13:8–10). This book is for Mary Rose, for our children, Lucy and Rachel, for our children's children, and for all those yet to be born.

My parents, Paul and Helen O'Leary, provided me with every kind of support from earliest childhood through the most difficult days of graduate school. Without their love and guidance, this project would never have been begun, let alone completed.

A great debt of gratitude is due to my teacher, mentor, friend, and critic, Tom Goodnight, who guided me through a critical portion of my education and introduced me to many concepts that are incorporated in this study. Though the conclusions are my own, the whole work bears the stamp of his creative insights and suggestions. This book would not have been possible without him.

David T. Arthur, curator of the Orrin Roe Jenks Collection of Adventual Materials at Aurora University, Aurora, Illinois, provided invaluable assistance with the Millerite periodicals quoted in chapters 4 and 5. I am grateful for his historical insights and encyclopedic knowledge of early Adventism, which contributed immeasurably to my work.

I wish to thank Henry and Vergilia Dakin and Susanna Dakin, whose material and technical support, in the form of computer equipment and grants for travel and study, facilitated the production of the manuscript and made possible some of my most fascinating research.

My teachers and colleagues at Northwestern University and the University of

Southern California have provided all kinds of assistance. Among those who helped me work out key portions of my analysis, provided expert editorial guidance and proofreading, or simply were willing to listen as I talked incessantly about the Apocalypse, are Walter Fisher, Stephen Toulmin, Bernard McGinn, Robert Jewett, David Zarefsky, and Leland Griffin. Finally, there are many other friends, teachers, colleagues, and critics who cannot be named here, but to whom I owe a hearty "Thank you!" To all of you I say, with a sigh of relief, "The end is here. What shall we do next?"

Los Angeles   S. D. O'L.
May 1993

Contents

A Note on Sources
and Translations

When analyzing and discussing scriptural texts, I have generally employed the New English Bible (NEB); however, since this is a study of biblical interpretation, I have also frequently referred to the translations selected by the authors under scrutiny. Chapters 4 and 5 use the King James Version (KJV) exclusively, since this was the text used by the Millerites; chapters 6 and 7, which deal with Hal Lindsey and other contemporary apocalyptic arguers, employ at various points the New International Version (NIV), the Revised Standard Version (RSV), and occasionally other translations, since Lindsey switches back and forth between these at will. I apologize for any confusion this may cause the reader, but internal consistency seemed to me to be less desirable than fidelity to the authors and arguments analyzed here. Abbreviations are used to indicate the source of the translation in question; if a text is otherwise unmarked, the reader may assume the NEB as the source unless it is found within a direct quotation from another author.

The bibliography provides complete reference information for all substantive works mentioned in the text or in footnotes. However, for the sake of brevity, I did not attempt to list every article from prophecy newspapers or magazines. Sources not listed in the bibliography will usually include complete reference information in a footnote. The Millerite periodicals and newspapers quoted in chapters 4 and 5 are all located in the Jenks Collection at Aurora University; Hal Lindsey's *Countdown* newsletter, quoted in chapter 7, is available from his ministry, located in Palos Verdes, California.

ARGUING THE APOCALYPSE

This world is a comedy to those that think, and a tragedy to those that feel.
                                                            Horace Walpole

Only our concept of Time makes it possible to speak of the Day of Judgment by that name; in reality it is a summary court in perpetual session.
                                                            Franz Kafka

The imagination stands always at the end of an era.
                                                            Wallace Stevens

ONE

Toward a Rhetorical Theory
of Apocalypse

The approach of the year 2000 is already anticipated with excitement in various circles of American culture. Commissions of experts have been established to project developments in the economic, cultural, and political spheres;[1] artists have produced films, paintings, songs, and novels depicting a breathtaking variety of utopian and dystopian scenarios for the future;[2] fundamentalist Christians and New Age seers have joined a host of secular prophets in declaring that the dawn of the new millennium heralds a change of cosmic significance.[3] New translations of the quatrains of Nostradamus crowd the shelves of mass market chain bookstores,[4] alongside dozens of other works seeking to unlock the mysteries of the upcoming decades. It seems safe to predict that humanity's passage beyond the year 2000 will be imagined, celebrated, and memorialized in literally thousands of ways during the next decades. Our time provides a fertile ground in which both optimistic and catastrophic predictions of the future proliferate.

In recent years, popular interest in biblical prophecies of Armageddon has been a highly visible (and sometimes controversial) trend. Fascination with apocalyptic predictions, whether from the Bible, from new interpretations of the writings of ancient seers, or from New Age "channelers," seems likely to increase dramatically as the turn of the millennium draws nearer. The purpose of this study is to offer a theoretical framework for understanding the millenarian and apocalyptic discourse that will inevitably be generated as we approach and move beyond the two thousandth year of the Christian era. My foundational assumption is that the discourses of apocalypticism and millennialism can usefully be viewed as rhetoric.

The wide variety of meanings this term has acquired renders an explanation of my own usage necessary. In ordinary use, *rhetoric* often refers to ornate or flowery speech, to speech that is clever but lacks substance, or to manipulative language, deception, and propaganda. Literary scholars, on the other hand, often use the

3

term to refer to the formal devices and techniques of composition. As a method of textual criticism, rhetoric has recently sparked a revival of interest among biblical scholars, social scientists, and literary critics.[5] The steady growth of modern scholarship in this area has contributed to an expanded conception of rhetoric that rejects both the popular understanding of "mere rhetoric" as empty talk and the purely literary view of rhetoric as formal technique.[6] As understood by its most astute interpreters from Aristotle to Kenneth Burke, rhetoric is a social practice of "public, persuasive, constitutive, and socially constituted utterance";[7] it is a discipline located at the intersection of aesthetics, politics, and ethics;[8] it is a method of inquiry whose object is to discover how audiences are moved or persuaded through the interplay of style, form, content, and context in texts both spoken and written.[9] Throughout this book, then, I have employed the term *rhetoric* in this expanded sense, to refer to the texts of persuasive discourse and to the method of investigating such texts, while the related term *rhetor* is used to denote authors or orators self-consciously engaged in the task of public persuasion.

There is a considerable body of scholarship that focuses on the stylistic features and social contexts of apocalyptic discourse.[10] While these dimensions are necessary to any rhetorical analysis, I have tried in this book to go beyond previous studies by paying close attention to the specifically argumentative dimension of apocalypticism. This is to say that when a prophet or prophetic interpreter proposes that the world is coming to an end, or that a period of millennial peace is about to begin, he or she is offering an argumentative claim—a statement that is designed to gain the adherence of an audience and that must be supported by reasons and proofs. In simple terms, then, I have attempted to provide a framework for comparing and classifying the types of claims most prevalent in the Christian apocalyptic tradition, and the various reasons and proofs offered to support these claims. Some readers may find that, in pursuing the trail of apocalyptic logic over the centuries, I have lingered too long on the intricacies of arguments that neither require nor deserve such scrutiny; these readers are invited to skip to the summary and conclusions offered in the final chapter. However, I make no apologies for having taken this discourse seriously enough to subject it to close analysis and critique. Apocalyptic arguments made by people of good and sincere faith have apparently succeeded in persuading millions; it is unfair and dangerous to dismiss these arguments as irrational and the audiences persuaded by them as ignorant fools. In a world where bright utopic visions compete with increasingly plausible scenarios of global catastrophe, it seems imperative to understand how our anticipations of the future may be both inspired and limited by the ancient logic of apocalypticism.

The End of the Age through the Ages

From the beginning of time, humanity has attempted to imagine and predict the end of time. Every culture that has developed a myth of its divine and cosmological origin has sought to peer ahead toward its own ending. The mythologies of Hinduism, Zoroastrianism, Buddhism, Judaism, and Christianity all offer evidence that the desire to fix humanity in a divinely instituted order of cosmic time has played a significant role in the formation of cultures. Though there are significant differences between the Hindu myth of the Kali Yuga, the Teutonic legend of *Ragnarok*, and the Judeo- Christian vision of the Last Judgment, these traditions exhibit a common concern: to understand the successive human ages and their culmination in a catastrophic struggle between the forces of good and evil.[11]

This eschatological understanding can be seen in the age-old lament that describes the decline of morals in society: young people no longer respect their elders, while war and all kinds of immorality increase in direct correlation with the growth of humanity's knowledge and technical skills. For the Greeks of classical antiquity, this decline was explicable in terms of the cosmic progression from an Edenic golden age through successive ages of silver, bronze, and iron. Plato's reimagination of the myth of cosmic decline in the *Statesman* shows the ancient roots of the doctrine:

> It is from God's act when He sets [the universe] in its order that it has received all the virtues it possesses, while it is from its primal chaotic condition that all the wrongs and evils arise in it—evils which it engenders in turn in the living creatures within it. When it is guided by the Divine Pilot, it produces much good and but little evil in the creatures it raises and sustains. When it must travel on without God, things go well enough in the years immediately after He abandons control, but as time goes on and forgetfulness of God arises in it, the ancient condition of chaos also begins to assert its sway. At last, as this cosmic era draws to a close, this disorder comes to a head. The few good things it produces it corrupts with so gross a taint of evil that it hovers on the very brink of destruction, both of itself and of the creatures in it.
>
> The God looks upon it again, He who first set it in order. Beholding it in its troubles, and anxious for it lest it sink racked by storms and confusion. He takes control of the helm once more. Its former sicknesses He heals; what was disrupted in its former revolution under its own impulse He brings back into the way of regularity, and, so ordering and correcting it, He achieves for it its agelessness and deathlessness.[12]

Plato's myth of a corrupted universe set adrift from the guidance of its creator, where evil has achieved such strength that only divine intervention can set things right, strikingly parallels the early Christian vision of "the whole creation groaning in travail" (Rom. 18:22). The hope or expectation of God's regaining control over the helm of the universe that Saint Paul held in common with Plato testifies to the enduring power of eschatological myth as a way of understanding the problem of evil.

The particular type of eschatology that is the subject of this book is apocalyptic. Eschatology, from the Greek *eschatos*, meaning furthest or last, is the 'logos' or discourse about the last things, the furthest imaginable extensions of human and cosmic destiny.[13] *Apocalypse*, a Greek word meaning revelation or unveiling, is thus that discourse that reveals or makes manifest a vision of ultimate destiny, rendering immediate to human audiences the ultimate End of the cosmos in the Last Judgment. Apocalyptic eschatology argues for the imminence of this Judgment, in which good and evil will finally receive their ultimate reward and punishment.[14]

Apocalypse is, of course, only one of many ways in which history may be represented as a dramatic contest of good and evil. As Richard Hofstader noted in his famous analysis of "The Paranoid Style in American Politics," conspiracy theories offer a similar view of history as a gigantic clash of occult forces. Hofstader identifies an affinity between the apocalyptic mentality and that of the conspiracy theorist.[15] Expanding upon Hofstader's essay, Earl Creps argues that human communities tend to develop foundational narratives that define the relationship of the social order to the perceived evils of the universe.[16] In conspiracy argument, the source of evil is seen in an Other, defined as foreign or barbarian, though often appearing in our midst disguised as the innocent and upright. Such discourse can function both to motivate people to political action and to create an understanding through which evil is explained and thereby tamed. The primary orientation of conspiracy argument, however, is spatial: as Creps puts it, the source of evil is defined as outside the "true community." When conspiratorial discourse calls its adherents to action, they are generally meant to seek out and eliminate or neutralize the locus of evil, the cabal. The unique feature of apocalyptic myth is that it offers a temporal or *teleological* framework for understanding evil by claiming that evil must grow in power until the appointed time of the (imminent) end. In Norman Cohn's words, apocalyptic myth proposes a salvation that is collective, terrestrial, imminent, total, and miraculous.[17] That this salvation, like the conspiracy argument, functions as a rhetorical and mythic solution to the problem of evil is shown by the frequent appearance of conspiracy and apocalypse in the same discourse. In fact, the conspiracy argument often appears intact within the larger structure of apocalyptic myth as it is interpreted by many communities. The demonic conspiracy of the Antichrist of the last days has served as the prototype for political conspiracy arguments in the United States since before the American Revolution.[18]

The discourses of conspiracy and apocalypse, therefore, are linked by a common function: each develops symbolic resources that enable societies to define and address the problem of evil. While conspiracy strives to provide a spatial self-definition of the true community as set apart from the evils that surround us, apocalypse locates the problem of evil in time and looks forward to its imminent resolution. Conspiracy argument may also take a historical perspective and advocate the eradication of the evil cabal, but in its extreme form (when the conspiracy is imagined as all-powerful) it may also call for withdrawal from communal life to avoid the taint of evil. At such times, belief in divine intervention in the historical process may appear to be the only alternative to utter despair. This study thus seeks to develop an understanding of how the form and symbolism of apocalyptic discourse are shaped by, and in turn help to shape the collective behavior of, its historical audiences. The story of the apocalyptic tradition is one of community building, in which human individuals and collectivities constitute their identities through shared mythic narratives that confront the problem of evil in time and history.

Apocalypse has been a dominant theme in Christian culture for over two thousand years. The German New Testament scholar Ernst Käsemann wrote that "apocalyptic was the mother of all theology."[19] Whether or not this sweeping claim is strictly true, the central place of apocalypse in Western religious history can scarcely be denied. In addition to the importance of apocalyptic myth in Judaism and the early Christian church, the rhetoric of apocalypse has been used by such diverse communities as the imperial and papal parties struggling for power in thirteenth-century Europe,[20] by Luther and the German Protestants in their battle against the papacy,[21] by the English Puritans as they fought against the Anglican church and the royalists,[22] and by modern evangelists arguing against ecumenism, pacifism, and the nuclear freeze movement.[23] The attention paid to apocalyptic prophecy by these various historical communities, and their use of apocalyptic rhetoric in political struggles, suggest that apocalyptic discourse has a persuasive appeal that can outlast the communities themselves. Though the apocalypse has been predicted time and time again through the centuries, the disappointment created by the failure of these predictions has not lessened the appeal of this discourse to its believers.

The appeal of apocalyptic prophecy has endured through the ages; but its popularity has undergone a remarkable resurgence in the latter half of the twentieth century. America's most prominent exponent of apocalyptic prophecy, Hal Lindsey, has been declared by the New York Times the best-selling author of the 1970s. His books have sold many millions of copies, while the apocalyptic messages of preachers such as Jimmy Swaggart and Jerry Falwell have found increasingly wider audiences through the media of radio, television, and film. Two events that have provided powerful evidentiary support for the arguments of these modern exponents of the apocalyptic doctrine are the development of atomic weapons and the establishment of the state of Israel in 1948. The nuclear threat in particular seems to have fundamentally altered our religious situation by making the threat of planetary destruction credible to a much wider audience. As church historian Ray Petry notes, "[T]he emergence of the atomic threat . . . has posed anew the problem of man's future and his end. . . . [A] number of religious enthusiasts now find sudden and unprecedented support for their most frenzied contentions. More than one person not of their persuasion asks whether these wildest predictions may not shortly be translated from the realm of shadowy aberration into the blaze of stark actuality.[24]

The increasing popularity of apocalyptic predictions beyond the circles of fundamentalist Protestantism, and the growing sense of a need to re-examine apocalyptic myth in light of the current nuclear situation, has helped to rekindle an interest in the topic among scholars in different fields. Studies by writers as diverse as Carl Jung, Robert Jay Lifton, Amos Wilder, and Frank Kermode have attempted to place the current preoccupation with a technological Armageddon into psychoanalytic,[25] religious,[26] and literary[27] contexts; historical scholars such as Paul Hanson and Nathan Hatch have traced the origins and persistence of the apocalyptic mentality in early Palestine and revolutionary New England.[28] What is lacking in these studies is a coherent rhetorical approach to the problems posed by apocalyptic discourse. What are the reasons for the persistent appeal of apocalypse? What problems in the minds of its audiences does it seek to address? How does it function rhetorically to solve these problems? In what ways does apocalyptic discourse shape or reinforce the world view and the behavior of individuals and communities? Finally, what impact have visions of the End had on the broad visions of society's future that appear in the practices of public discourse?

My purpose in this study is to answer these questions by proposing a rhetorical theory of apocalyptic discourse, a theory which accounts for both the internal logic of apocalyptic speculation and the public logic of apocalyptic advocacy. The second and third chapters develop this theory through a detailed examination of the internal topical logic of Christian eschatological discourse. Chapters 4 through 7 present historical case studies that illustrate how this internal topical logic is developed into an external, public logic of apocalyptic persuasion. The task of this first chapter is to summarize some of the controversies in apocalyptic scholarship in order to explain how a rhetorical study will address these issues and depart from previous methods of treating them. Two controversies figure prominently in the studies performed so far: the problem of explaining the appeal of apocalyptic belief, and the problem of understanding and predicting the social and political consequences of such belief. These questions will be treated separately in order to justify the claim that they are properly conceived as problems that demand a rhetorical analysis.

The scholar who searches the extensive secondary literature on apocalypse in order to discover the secret of its appeal will find a variety of disparate explanations offered. Most historians and sociologists realize that an adequate answer to the question begins with audience analysis; that is, before we can find out how and why the discourse wins adherents, we must first discover who its adherents actually are. Virtually all scholars of apocalypse have attempted to define the audience in terms of factors that predispose converts to accept apocalyptic claims. Thus, for example, Frank Kermode speaks of an "apocalyptic set—a state of affairs in which one can discern some sociological predisposition to the acceptance of apocalyptic structures and figures."[29] The factors that are said to define this set vary widely. Hobsbawm and Worsley look for economic explanations of apocalyptic movements, finding in them a primitive response to material deprivation and the social dislocation of modern industrial life.[30] Accordingly, the audience for apocalyptic discourse, according to Hobsbawm, is composed of "small struggling peasants, agricultural craftsmen, village artisans, and the like."[31]

Such characterizations may be adequate for the Italian peasants or native cargo cults examined by Hobsbawm and Worsley, but are of little use when we attempt to generalize from these examples. In much the same vein, Norman Cohn's well-known work *The Pursuit of the Millennium* offers both material and psychological reasons for the appeal of apocalypse, seeing the apocalyptic fantasy as a "paranoid" response to economic deprivation and political persecution.[32] Economic and psychological factors may well be sufficient to account for the medieval apocalyptic movements with which Cohn's book is mostly concerned; but his extrapolations into modern political and religious history certainly seem suspect. Cohn's conclusions are worth reproducing here because they exemplify the circular explanations prevalent in much recent scholarship on apocalypticism:[33]

> Industrial workers in technologically advanced societies have shown themselves very eager to improve their own conditions. . . . But emotionally charged phantasies of a final, apocalyptic struggle or an egalitarian millennium have had much less attraction for them. Those who are fascinated by such ideas are, on the one hand, the populations of certain technologically backward societies which are not only overpopulated and desperately poor but also involved in a problematic transition to the modern world, and are correspondingly dislocated or disoriented; and, on the other hand, certain politically marginal elements in technologically advanced societies—chiefly young or unemployed workers and a small minority of intellectuals and students.[34]

It seems apparent that the millions who have bought Hal Lindsey's books or watched Jerry Falwell, Jimmy Swaggart, and their cohorts on television cannot be adequately described as either "young or unemployed workers" or "a small minority of intellectuals and students." Nor can they truthfully be labeled as "politically marginal" in the America of the 1980s. A brief survey of the history of apocalyptic discourse shows that its appeal has historically cut across class lines. The audience of those receptive to prophecy and its interpreters has included emperors, peasants, merchants, farmers and factory workers, the educated and the uneducated alike from Isaac Newton to Ronald Reagan. The mechanistic theories of apocalypse's appeal based in economic circumstance that prevail in much current scholarship fail to account for this wide variety of class and education in apocalyptic audiences.

An alternative explanation for the appeal of apocalyptic rhetoric is offered by political scientist and social historian Michael Barkun. His *Disaster and the Millennium* attempts to document the thesis that the main predisposing factor determining the apocalyptic set is the common experience of natural and man-made calamities. Barkun analyzes apocalyptic movements in many cultures and historical eras, compiling much evidence to support his claim that "disasters serve to predispose individuals to millenarian conversion." His argument is weakened, however, by his own admissions that disaster "is to some extent in the eye of the beholder," and that "if the world has no disaster to offer, then one must be constructed."[35] I argue that both these observations indicate the necessity of rhetorical analysis; for even if we allow that events such as earthquakes, wars, and depressions are experienced as disasters by virtually everyone, not every event of this kind is accompanied by an increase in apocalyptic conversion. Some occurrences, on the other hand, are viewed as disasters because a rhetor succeeds in persuading an audience with this definition; and only rhetoric can turn any disaster, real or perceived, into a sign of the imminent end. Only a discourse- centered theory can account for the the role of disasters in apocalypse. The issue is not whether audiences are predisposed by such experiences to accept apocalyptic arguments, but how apocalypse contextualizes disasters as a "rhetorical use of calamity."[36]

Theories of apocalyptic persuasion based on the predisposing factors of socioeconomic status or experience of disaster are clearly inadequate. The theory of relative deprivation offered by some sociologists is somewhat more sophisticated in that it seeks to account for the role of perception in predisposing audiences to apocalyptic conversion.[37] David Aberle defines relative deprivation as "a negative discrepancy between legitimate expectation and actuality";[38] seeking to ground the theory in measurable factors, he classifies the relative experience of deprivation into categories of possessions, status, behavior, and worth, and argues that deprivation in one or more of these areas may result in adherence to apocalyptic belief. But, as Ernest R. Sandeen has noted, "[T]he ease with which relative deprivation can be documented has had the effect of devaluing the concept."[39] This study does not seek to take issue with Aberle's theory, but rather to expand upon it by pointing out the discursive and rhetorical foundations of relative deprivation. Possessions may be material and nondiscursive, but expectations can be fostered and legitimated only through discourse, and social systems of status, behavior, and worth have their origins in language and symbolic communication.[40]

A recognition of the need to account for apocalypticism in terms of the inter-action of symbolic communication and social structures has prompted some scholars to propose that apocalyptic believers suffer from psychological conditions of anomie and absence of meaning.[41] The anomic condition is offered to fill the gaps left by theories of disaster and economic or relative deprivation. Typical of such expla-nations is Barry Brummett's contention that "apocalyptic has a 'hard-core' audience that suffers from an unusually strong sense of anomie or disorientation. This anomic audience is motivated by the *perception* of disasters which cannot be explained by received systems of meaning."[42] Brummett's acknowledgment of the role played by perceptions of disaster indicates the need for a thorough rhetorical analysis that would not assume an audience molded by prior conditioning, but he fails to pursue his own insight. Ronald Reid has offered a similar explanation for the appeal of apocalyptic rhetoric: "Apocalypticism has been accepted widely only during periods when substantial numbers of people were dissatisfied deeply with their present and faced an uncertain future."[43] Such a formulation is of questionable usefulness. One might ask the critic to point to a time when substantial numbers of people were *not* deeply dissatisfied with the present, or when the future has not seemed un-certain.[44] The omnipresence of such emotions as anxiety, apprehension, and dis-satisfaction presents an inherent difficulty to those who attempt to account for the appeal of apocalypse by linking fluctuations in its historical popularity to intangible societal moods. The evidence presented in McGinn's *Visions of the End* (to name only the best of a host of recent studies) indicates that apocalypticism cannot be understood only as a series of movements with discrete and identifiable causes in historical events, but must also be seen as a tradition, a textually embodied com-munity of discourse founded in the accepted canon of Western sacred Scripture and occasionally augmented by the production of new revelations and interpretive strategies.

The problem of explaining the appeal of apocalyptic discourse is thus a complex one. Critics are confronted with a continuous textual tradition, maintained and embroidered by a discourse of exegesis and commentary fostered in learned and elite circles, which at various historical intervals has erupted into more mainstream popular discourse through movements inspired sometimes by new prophecies and sometimes by new interpretations of canonical texts. Apocalyptic rhetoric has always found an audience, though this audience has varied greatly in its size and composition over the centuries. No simple explanations will account for the increased popularity of apocalypticism that historians have documented in medieval Europe, in Renaissance England, or in the United States during the early nineteenth and late twentieth centuries.[45] Even if it were possible to prove that people during these periods experienced identifiable disasters that led to conditions of anomie, this would still not explain why anomie was expressed in the particular form of apocalypse. While it is clear that anomie and apocalypse are somehow related, the appeal of apocalyptic argument cannot be explained by fluctuations in an imaginary anomic indicator. If anomie is caused by experiences of disaster, which in turn are defined as events that cannot be explained by received systems of meaning, then we have not really added anything new to our conceptual vocabulary; having defined disaster in terms of symbolic communication, anomie becomes endemic to the human condition and so loses its explanatory power.[46] For all symbolic systems, all hierarchies of terms, find their limit in the inevitable confrontation with the anomalous event.[47]

It comes as no surprise that sociologists and historians, lacking the perspective of rhetorical studies, should expend so much energy in trying to explain the appeal of apocalyptic discourse by discovering audience predispositions based in conditions of social and economic class, in experience of calamity, or in psychological anomie. It is curious, however, that even those rhetorical scholars who attempt to account for the appeal of apocalyptic never seriously entertain the hypothesis that people are actually persuaded by apocalyptic arguments; that is, that the nature of apocalyptic's appeal should be sought in transactions of texts and audiences.[48] The rhetor who announces that the world is nearing its end is making a predictive claim; it should surely be the province of the rhetorical critic to discover how such claims are advanced and supported, and the dynamics of audience responses to them. I do not intend to argue that no predispositions exist among converts to apocalypticism, or that concepts such as calamity, anomie, deprivation, or oppression (whether economic or psychological) are utterly useless in the analysis of apocalyptic rhetoric; rather, I intend to argue that previous analyses have ignored the specifically rhetorical nature of these concepts. The early Christians who responded favorably to the book of Revelation were, by most historical accounts, subject to intense persecution that included execution and public torture. If the largely middle-class group of fundamentalist Christians in the United States who today form the core of Hal Lindsey's readership believes itself to be similarly persecuted, this is surely a rhetorically induced perception; for there is an obvious difference between being torn apart by lions in front of cheering crowds and being forced to endure media onslaughts of sex, violence, and secular humanism. As one critic puts it, "the crucial element is not so much whether one is actually oppressed as whether one feels oppressed";[49] and this is always a subject for persuasion. Dissatisfaction with the present and fear of the future are not simply existential facts that the discourse must address; analysis of the discourse itself reveals that much effort is often expended at developing the sense of dissatisfaction and fear.

A complete understanding of the appeal of apocalypse, then, requires a theory of rhetoric. In the same way, we cannot hope to describe how apocalyptic beliefs are turned into political and social commitments (or into withdrawal from such commitments) without a rhetorical analysis. Norman Cohn's identification of structural similarities between medieval apocalyptic sects and modern revolutionary and totalitarian movements provides a strong incentive for studying the political implications of apocalypse.[50] Whether or not Cohn's comparison ultimately proves sound, and whether scholars study apocalyptic movements as antecedents of modern political phenomena or simply for the terms they have contributed to our cultural vocabulary, the necessity of studying apocalyptic politics in its many forms is clear. In American studies, historical scholars are divided on the role played by apocalyptic themes and the political consequences of such beliefs in the eighteenth, nineteenth, and twentieth centuries. In the words of historian Ruth Bloch, apocalyptic "has been interpreted as a spur to action, as a source of comfort, and as a rationale for passivity. . . . Ideologically it has been judged inherently radical, 'progressive,' and conservative."[51] Many scholars rely on the terminology of "premillennialism" and "postmillennialism,"[52] arguing that the premillennial interpretation of apocalyptic has led to a passive role in public affairs, if not to actual withdrawal from the public sphere, while the more optimistic postmillennial interpretation has encouraged social activism and eventually been subsumed into progressivism and American civil religion.[53] Some, however, notably James West Davidson in his *The Logic of Millennial Thought*, are beginning to question this typology;[54] and the recent entry into the political realm of such committed premillennialists as Jerry Falwell and Pat Robertson certainly calls for a more sophisticated analysis.[55]

The problem of premillennial believers engaged in political activism is addressed by historian Timothy Weber, who devotes the last chapter of his study *Living in the Shadow of the Second Coming* to examining political arguments in the writings of Hal Lindsey and Jerry Falwell. Weber concludes that there is an inherent contradiction between religious belief and political practice that these rhetors never resolve successfully. In the field of rhetorical studies, Daniels, Jensen, and Lichtenstein likewise assume an inherent contradiction between fundamentalist doctrine and practice.[56] The academic controversy over the social consequences of apocalyptic belief cries out for resolution; but in attempting to resolve it, I will not simply endorse a position that apocalypticism (whether of the premillennial or postmillennial variety) naturally leads to a particular public stance. Rather, I shall argue that a dramatistic and argumentative analysis is necessary to understand how and why mythic texts support apocalyptic beliefs and are interpreted by rhetors and audiences to justify a range of active and passive stances in the social realm.

A full appreciation of the significance of apocalyptic discourse cannot be reached without attention to specific argumentative and interpretive practices. For it is through argument and interpretation that the symbolic content of any myth is appropriated by a given audience. Examining the discourse of most modern apocalyptic evangelists, one finds that their claims are founded not on the charismatic authority of the prophet granted a divine vision, but on the (ostensibly) rational authority of one who interprets canonical scripture. Analyses that fail to recognize the distinction between prophetic and interpretive discourse therefore miss the principal strategy at work in modern apocalyptic; a focus on interpretation is necessary for an understanding of how the discourse operates rhetorically by linking the 'rational' with the 'oracular' voice. Such an analysis has the potential of casting new light on the age-old debate over the the relationship of logical to mythic thought.[57]

The potential contribution of rhetoric to the study of apocalypse should by now be obvious: the rhetorical perspective offers the possibility of resolving problems that previous studies of apocalyptic discourse have raised but failed to address successfully. Equally significant is the potential contribution of apocalyptic studies to the field of rhetoric. The rapidly growing literature on the rhetoric of temporality[58] will be enriched by critical study of apocalypse in all its manifestations, since the historical influence of this discourse is achieved precisely through its symbolic constructions of time: apocalyptic succeeds or fails with its audiences to the degree that it persuades them of their situation within the particular historical pattern of temporal fulfillment represented in its mythic imagery. Thus, developing a rhetorical theory of apocalypse will assist scholars in developing a more sophisticated temporal theory of rhetoric. Such a theory must conceive of time not only as an external fact to which discourse must adapt itself, but as an experience that is perceived through symbols, and hence is subject to discursive manipulation.

Michael Leff's recent efforts in textual criticism present communication scholars with a model that effectively addresses this problem. Leff hypothesizes that "Time as experienced in the text becomes the vehicle for transforming time as experienced in the world to which the text refers."[59] J. Robert Cox's application of this insight to Martin Luther King's "I Have a Dream" speech argues that the address "reconstitutes public time" in terms of the eschatological vision of the biblical prophet Isaiah.[60] Cox's study, along with the work of historians such as Ernest Tuveson and Ruth Bloch, shows how the recurring mythic forms of eschatology have shaped American perceptions of national destiny and political possibility. Such studies imply that critical attention should be turned to the direct examination of apocalyptic texts as a means of discovering the symbolic resources through which the discursive structuring of public time is accomplished. Since it explicitly takes the structure and significance of time as its subject, apocalyptic discourse offers a unique opportunity to verify Leff's hypothesis. As argument, apocalypse seeks to situate its audience at the end of a particular pattern of historical time; to the extent that people adhere to apocalyptic claims, their perception of time is altered. The study of apocalyptic thus enables us to approach an enduring problem, the relationship of time and rhetoric, in a way that accounts for both the effect of time's passage on discourse and the effect of discourse on our phenomenal, social, and historical experiences of time.

The justification for this study, then, is fourfold. First, the historical significance of humanity's apparently universal tendency to imagine its own end, from the beginning of the Christian era to the nuclear age, is apparent. Second, the paucity or inadequacy of specifically rhetorical analyses of apocalyptic discourse necessitates such a study. Third, the potential that such a study holds for a fresh perspective on the relationships of religious belief to social and political practice, and of rational to mythic thought, is considerable. Finally, the study of apocalypse should lead to valuable insights on an issue of increasing significance in recent rhetorical scholarship, the constitution of public time through rhetoric and symbolism.

Hypothesis and Method of the Study

The central contention of this book is twofold: that apocalyptic functions as a symbolic theodicy, a mythical and rhetorical solution to the problem of evil, and that its approach to this problem is accomplished through discursive construction of temporality. I do not claim that these conceptions are entirely new; they have been anticipated in many previous studies of the apocalyptic genre. However, the theory of literary or rhetorical genres is flawed as a critical method by its emphasis on discourse as form over discourse as action, which tends to diminish the importance of situation by reducing a dynamic temporal process to a static model. Genre theory may aid understanding of texts, but tells us little about how and why the audiences for these texts behave as they do. This limitation is evident in much of the scholarly literature on apocalypticism. Sandeen, a respected historian of American millennialism, expresses frustration over the inability of historians and critics to move beyond the generic labels of "premillennialism" and "postmillennialism":

> These terms correspond, for example, to the vocabulary of the late nineteenth century monetary controversy—gold standard, bimetalism, and free silver or to categories of contemporary rock music—soft rock, acid rock, and punk rock. They are names of parties which are not necessarily useful in figuring out the behavior of Populists or rock musicians. It is surprising that historians have so generally utilized this theological vocabulary instead of developing more dynamic categories.[61]

Apart from the inability of genre theory as currently formulated to account for the dynamics of behavior in apocalyptic sects or movements, the generic labeling of texts can itself blind critics to formal and substantive differences between these texts. Apocalyptic literature in Western and non-Western cultures has exhibited such an astonishing variety of style and content that one should be cautious of claiming, as does Barry Brummett, that "apocalyptic is a genre of discourses which address one *type* of perceived situational exigency with consistent forms of rhetorical style and substantive argument."[62] No reference is made here to the debate among biblical critics regarding the essential features of the apocalyptic genre.[63] Various laundry lists of generic characteristics have been compiled, including pseudonymity, dualistic views of history, and claims to secret knowledge, and various arguments put forth as to the primacy of this or that theme in apocalyptic discourse.[64] Such formistic approaches to these texts frequently lead to seemingly arbitrary classifications; in the field of biblical criticism, for example, we find one critic arguing for a sharp distinction between genres of prophecy and apocalypse and classifying the original Christian Apocalypse, the book of Revelation, as prophetic and not apocalyptic at all![65] Within the field of rhetorical criticism, the generic method has had similar results. Brummett's conception of the genre leads him to classify Revelation as an example of apocalyptic—alongside General Sir John Hackett's *The Third World War*. To view such dissimilar texts as responses to the same type of perceived situational exigency, or to claim that they exhibit identical features of style and argument, yields insights of such broad generality that one must question their utility. This is not to discount the value of critical attempts to discover the ways in which the recurring forms of apocalypse have been secularized in our culture; it is merely to say that our critical method should be able to take account of the important differences between these texts. As a root metaphor for critical method, formism cannot account for variations in style, substance, and situation.[66] Critics guided by formistic assumptions will tend to ignore such variations as they develop categories that either exclude too much, or include too much, in proportion to the specificity of their definitions.

This study will, therefore, reject the generic method in favor of a dramatistic and argumentative analysis guided by the root metaphor of contextualism.[67] Rather than judging texts by their success or failure in meeting generic standards that are inevitably problematic, the analysis seeks an understanding of apocalyptic discourse not as a text embodying archetypal and timeless formal principles, but as an event "alive in its present,"[68] attempting to discover how it influences and is influenced by the discursive practices that surround it. Apocalyptic discourse unfolds in the context of changing cultural assumptions and presumptions about rationality, about the nature of time and history, and about the purpose and destiny of human collectivities. The root metaphor of contextualism allows us to comprehend apocalyptic as part of these larger patterns while at the same time accounting for particularity in the discourse.

In the previous section I argued that critics should view apocalyptic discourse as argument that is intended to persuade, focusing attention on specific interpretive practices. This emphasis on logic and rationality might seem misplaced to those disposed to view apocalypticism as an outbreak of irrationality or mass hysteria. However, a brief survey of the history of apocalyptic interpretation shows that its long tradition of scriptural exegesis and chronological calculation includes such figures of the Enlightenment as Joseph Priestly and Isaac Newton, and that such discourse often exhibits intense concern with the appearance of rationality and a tendency to build tightly constructed sequences of 'logical' argument. Such concerns and tendencies illustrate the necessity of examining argument practices for a contextual understanding of apocalypticism. Argumentative analysis by itself is insufficient, however, for this discourse is produced by human beings who view themselves not only as rational creatures, but as actors in a cosmic drama. The 'logical' form of the discourse thus takes shape within the structure of the participants' dramatic world view. Insofar as rhetors and audiences perceive history and human action in terms of the dramatic narrative of myth, their discourse will exhibit dramatic, as well as argumentative, form.

Accordingly, this study offers an analysis that draws from the terminology of both modern argumentation theory and Kenneth Burke's dramatism. It will be organized as a comparative study in American religious public address, focusing on the systems of interpretive apocalyptic argument developed by William Miller and Hal Lindsey. The analysis will demonstrate that time, evil, and authority are the principal topoi of apocalyptic argument.[69] The strategies of proof in each system will be described and compared in order to demonstrate the rhetor's evocation of these topoi as a function of an audience-centered "psychology of form." I will show that in their resolution of the topical questions of time and evil, these argumentative systems exhibit dramatic form rooted in the "tragic frame."

The centrality of the themes of time and evil in apocalyptic discourse have been noted by other critics. Bernard McGinn's discussion serves a cogent summary of the best of current scholarship and an excellent departure for this inquiry: "Apocalyptic texts from various religious backgrounds and different ages display family resemblances in key areas that include: first, a sense of the unity and structure of history conceived as a divinely predetermined totality; second, pessimism about the present and conviction of its imminent crisis; and third, belief in the proximate judgment of evil and triumph of the good."[70] The discursive structuring of temporality and the relationship of such structures to doctrines of redemption from evil are evident in McGinn's summary; the purpose of the present study is to reconceive his insight in terms of rhetorical theory, and to expand our knowledge of both rhetoric and apocalypse by studying the discourse as it evolves in history. Apocalyptic discourse is *about* time; it places the rhetor and the audience (and by extension, the whole human community) into a context of cosmic time where the judgment (*krisis*) of history is revealed as imminent. It therefore seems appropriate to examine the ways in which this discourse develops *in* time, to see the effect of time's passage on individuals and communities whose discourse aims to modify their perception of temporality. The study will thus focus on the historical development of two systems of apocalyptic argument: that of William Miller and his nineteenth-century followers, who in the early 1830s predicted the end of the world and second coming of Jesus Christ in 1843; and that of Hal Lindsey, who has produced a number of books from 1970 to the present in which he has made the same predictions, arguing that these events will transpire before the end of this century.

The choice of William Miller and Hal Lindsey as examples for this study is both appropriate and necessary for several reasons. First, as Sandeen observes,[71] American apocalypticism seems not to fit the historical and anthropological models of millennialism developed through studies of medieval and non-Western cultures. A study of the peculiarly American forms of eschatological expectation therefore seems necessary before any theory can be developed that accounts for other cultures and historical eras. Second, circulation and publication records indicate that both Lindsey and Miller succeeded in reaching a wide audience, gaining large numbers of followers and provoking considerable public controversy over their views.[72] The examples are thus comparable in terms of historical impact and significance. Third, the success of these rhetors in reaching wide audiences through the public media of their times allows us to study apocalypse not only as a phenomenon of a marginalized fringe, but as a way of thinking that both draws upon and contributes to mainstream social thought. Studying these two moments when apocalypse has succeeded in finding a large audience in the United States will afford the opportunity to reach some conclusions about how forms of discourse are able to move from the fringes of culture to its center by appropriating and reformulating its base of social knowledge.

Finally, the choice of discursive examples similar in form but separated in time by a century and a half enables the study to take an evolutionary perspective. By examining and comparing religious argument over time and across time, the study seeks to discover how conceptions of time, history, and ultimate meaning change through the course of American history, and the different social consequences that result from choices between these varying temporal conceptions. In particular, the later chapters of the study will argue that the public failure of Millerite discourse in the 1840s has influenced American religious discourse down to the present by serving as a cautionary example that demarcates the line between "orthodox" and "heretical" apocalyptic argument. Hal Lindsey's modern rearticulation of apocalypse thus provides the critic with an excellent opportunity to study how, in Thomas Farrell's words, "arguments within history are able to repeat and reinterpret themselves,"[73] and to achieve success through this reinterpretation. For if apocalyptic arguments are again salient in today's public discourse, it is surely not because they have proved their validity by withstanding the test of time; rather, they have managed to survive the repeated disconfirmations of time's passage by a process of discursive reformulation that continually ties apocalypse to the present by reconceiving the relationship of past and future.

Scope, Limitations, and Plan of the Study

Many recent studies in American religion have attempted to relate the apocalyptic theme to a secularized faith in progress and a uniquely American national destiny.[74] Though I will address some of the issues raised by these studies, including the consequences of apocalyptic belief systems for their adherents' stance toward political activism and the public sphere, I will not attempt a comprehensive evaluation of millennialism in American civil life. To do so would involve the study in a time-consuming effort to trace the uses of apocalyptic discourse through a variety of sermons and political speeches where it appears not as a central theme but simply as another resource for rhetorical invention. In a recent essay on millennial scholarship, James Moorhead argues that these apocalyptic themes appear in American

discourse "in both systematic and allusive forms."[75] This study will bypass the
allusive use of apocalyptic (although an examination of these forms would provide
powerful support for claims concerning the importance of this discourse in American
history) in order to concentrate on the attempts by William Miller and Hal Lindsey
to develop a systematic understanding of the significance of the Apocalypse within
their particular historical contexts. Such a focus means that the majority of the
secondary sources on American apocalyptic will not be drawn on for this study
(except insofar as they have useful comments on the primary literature analyzed),
since most of these works paint in such broad strokes that significant details and
distinctions are missed. This limitation does not mean that I will shy away from
larger conclusions about the place of apocalyptic discourse in American civic life;
rather, my assumption is that broad conclusions are best supported through careful
analysis of the systematic logic of apocalypse as it develops through theological and
public controversy.

Logic and argument have not been entirely neglected by historians of American
apocalypticism. Two recent studies that provide an excellent foundation for this
analysis are James West Davidson's *The Logic of Millennial Thought* and Ruth
Doan's *The Miller Heresy, Millennialism, and American Culture.*[76] Davidson's
sensitive analysis of the internal and public logics of apocalyptic discourse in the
Colonial era and his clearly articulated perception of the theodicical function of
apocalyptic schemes of history provide a useful starting point for the present study,
which seeks to trace this logic into the nineteenth and twentieth centuries. Doan's
study is a thorough and thoughtful account of the public controversy over Millerism,
and provides a wealth of data that can be used to develop an understanding of the
relationship of apocalyptic as argument to social canons of logic and rationality.
The discourse of modern apocalypticists has as yet received no thorough analysis;
nevertheless, some excellent studies are available. Weber's *Living in the Shadow
of the Second Coming* does much to place current trends in American religious
thought in a historical context, while Paul Boyer's *When Time Shall Be No More*
is an able exploration of the landscape of contemporary prophecy belief. The
historical accounts provided by these scholars will assist my effort to develop a
rhetorical theory of apocalypse and demonstrate the contributions of this discourse
to social thought and practice.

The study is divided into eight chapters. The present chapter introduces some
of the problems in millenarian scholarship identified by previous authors, argues
for a rhetorical approach to these problems, and specifies the research hypothesis
and methods that guide the study. The second chapter develops a rhetorical theory
of the problems of theodicy, temporality, and authority. After presenting a topical
theory of human social knowledge grounded in classical and modern rhetorical
theory, the chapter turns to an examination of evil, time, and authority as recurring
topoi in the Christian traditions of cosmological discourse. The classical, logical
formulation of the problem of evil is presented in order to show how mythic
narratives of apocalypse function as temporal resolutions to the apparent contradiction created by the experience of evil within a framework of theistic belief. The

development of time as a topos of Western apocalypticism is illustrated through a discussion of chronology and epochal discourse that demonstrates the power of temporal symbolism. The problem of authority is addressed through an examination of Christianity's uses of charismatic, traditional, and rational legitimations, and of positive and negative uses of the eschatological symbols of authority. Chapter 3 moves through the apocalyptic narrative toward its modes of interpretation, using Kenneth Burke's conception of the tragic and comic "frames of acceptance" as developed in *Attitudes toward History*. I argue that while the Christian eschatological myth has historically allowed for both tragic and comic readings, the premillennial interpretation of apocalypse and of history is based in the tragic frame of acceptance. The topical theory of eschatology developed in the second chapter is refined by studying the topoi as they function in apocalyptic argument through the interaction of rhetor and audience according to Burke's "psychology of form."

The fourth through seventh chapters apply the topical theory developed in chapters 2 and 3 to the discourse of two historical communities that appropriate the apocalyptic myth by arguing for its continuing relevance. Chapter 4 presents a rhetorical history of Millerism, showing how persuasive strategies and themes varied as one man's biblical speculations grew into a movement with tens of thousands of followers. Chapter 5 turns to a close textual analysis of Millerite apocalyptic argument, focusing on the persuasive pamphlets, books, letters, and newspapers produced and disseminated by William Miller and his followers in the years 1832–1848. The analysis demonstrates how the pattern of Millerite arguments addresses the apocalyptic topoi of authority, time, and evil, and how this pattern was itself affected by the flow of historical time. I then move from the nineteenth century into the twentieth, focusing on the apocalyptic discourse of modern fundamentalists and the movement that came to be called the New Christian Right. Chapter 6 offers a close textual analysis of Hal Lindsey's bestseller *The Late Great Planet Earth*, showing how the rhetorical strategies of America's most prominent evangelist for the apocalyptic doctrine both drew upon and helped to define current "mainstream" apocalypticism. Patterns of argument in this modern discourse are analyzed, with a particular focus on the use of nuclear weaponry as a powerful new warrant for apocalyptic claims. Chapter 7 demonstrates how Lindsay's reformulation of the apocalyptic topoi in his later book *The 1980s: Countdown to Armageddon* enabled a more activist political commitment, and compares his rhetoric to that of other prominent figures in the fundamentalist movement.

The concluding chapter compares and contrasts the arguments of the two apocalyptic systems and reaches some critical judgments on the similarities and differences between them. The comparison provides support for the thesis that authority, time, and evil constitute the three essential topoi of apocalyptic argument as it has appeared in this country, while illustrating the different possibilities for political and social enactment that attend the topical choices made by rhetors and audiences. Finally, I argue that Burke's "comic frame" provides a fresh perspective on the rhetoric of apocalypse that affords new insight into the significance of apocalyptic belief in American history and in the nuclear age.

TWO

Time, Evil, Authority

The previous chapter advanced the claim that the essential topoi of apocalyptic discourse are authority, time, and evil, and that this discourse functions as a symbolic theodicy, a mythical and rhetorical solution intended to "solve" the problem of evil through its discursive construction of temporality. To support and explicate this claim, it is necessary to define what is meant by the term *topoi* in the context of this study, and to examine the problems of authority, time, and evil as they appear from the perspective of topical argument. The first section of this chapter will set forth elements of a topical conception of human social knowledge drawn from Aristotle and recent rhetorical theory. The second section will utilize this topical conception as an analytic tool to discover the contributions of cosmological discourse to social knowledge. The essential topoi of the cosmological myth of apocalypse are shown to develop from the phenomenal experience of evil and time by individuals and collectivities. I argue that evil and time are omnipresent and interrelated conditions of human existence, factors that constitute the "rhetorical situation"[1] for all symbol systems that attempt to make ultimate sense of humanity's role in the cosmos. The third and fourth sections will elaborate these topoi into the symbolic forms of theodicy and chronology, and the relationship of these forms to the discourse of apocalypse. Finally, the chapter will conclude with an examination of the problems of charismatic, textual, and interpretive authority, and the politics of interpretation as revealed in apocalyptic symbols of legitimation and subversion.

The mode of topical analysis employed here does not purport to be a definitive approach to time, evil, or apocalypse. Rather, the topical method is intended to complement previous efforts and to open up the study of apocalyptic discourse to fuller and richer interpretations. Most analyses have located the power and rhetorical effectiveness of this discourse primarily in its imagery of the grotesque and fantastic;

few have focused on the logical structure of apocalypse and its contributions to social knowledge. While the potent metaphoric images generated by apocalypse over the centuries are indeed a significant resource for religious and public argument, the claim of this study is that apocalyptic metaphor cannot be understood apart from apocalyptic logic. The study of these metaphors in the context of the topical logic that formed them provides an opportunity to examine the way in which "topics partake of ideas and images,"[2] and thereby to modify our understanding of the role of metaphor in argument. For while mythic imagery forms our original stock for metaphoric invention, such imagery can itself be viewed not only as a predecessor to logical thought, but also as a product of a certain kind of logic. Such a sophisticated conception of logic, myth, and metaphor is well articulated by Paul Ricoeur in his recent study of the problem of evil:

> [M]yth's function of providing order, thanks to its cosmological import, has as its corollary—and its corrective—the profusion of explanatory schemes it has produced over time. The realm of myth . . . is a vast field of experimentation, or even of playing with hypotheses in the most varied and the most fantastic forms. Within this immense laboratory, it appears as though no conceivable solution to the order of the whole cosmos, and hence to the enigma of evil, has not been essayed at some point or another. These solutions oscillate between the level of legends and folklore, close to the demonic dimension of the experience of evil, and that of metaphysical speculation.[3]

The purpose of the analysis that follows, then, is to trace the patterns of oscillation between myth and speculative thought in order to demonstrate more clearly the social consequences that follow from certain experimental solutions to the cosmological problems that face all human societies. The study of cosmological speculations on the end of time, the origin and future of evil in the universe, and the destiny of humanity will enable critics to identify the premises, expressible in propositional as well as narrative form, from which religious arguments are derived and constructed. Examining myth in regard to its argumentative form, and argument as mythic enactment, this study of apocalypse aims to show how hierarchies of ultimate terms are placed in time as they define an epoch, an age coming to its fulfillment or completion, and how these hierarchies are then modified as they are forced to account for the particularities of experience.

Topoi as Propositions of Human Social Knowledge

The history of topical theory offers no single definition of the term *topos* satisfactory for the purposes of this study. From the time of the Sophists to the present, the function and significance of the topoi has been debated by rhetoricians. As Michael Leff notes, "The term 'topic' is notoriously ambiguous, and even in its technical uses, its meaning ranges from recurrent themes appearing in a certain kind of discourse to abstract patterns of inference."[4] The spatial metaphor implied by the original sense of *topos* as "place" has added to this confusion; thus, Weaver defines topics as " 'places' or 'regions' where one can go to find the substance for persuasive argument . . . the seat of an argument."[5] Topoi, then, have been variously understood as the themes or subject matters of rhetorical argument, as locations or inventional resources where themes can be discovered, and as the patterns, forms, or analytic categories by which argument is conducted. Frank D'Angelo provides some order to this multitude of definitions by arguing that the development of the topoi follows the pattern of the development of consciousness: "[T]he analytic *topoi* begin in an undifferentiated state in oral poetic narrative where they are imbedded in the narrative continuum, and they emerge historically in stages of increasing abstraction, differentiation, and hierarchic integration."[6] From this evolutionary perspective, the various definitions and catalogues of the topoi produced by rhetorical theorists over the centuries is somewhat less bewildering: these conflicting conceptions represent different stages of abstraction and different ways of portraying the activity and possible avenues of inventional thought.

This study aims to make productive use of these ambiguities in the tradition of the topics. I will use the term *topoi* in more than one sense—to indicate both recurring themes in discourse and patterns of reasoning—but to avoid confusion some attempt is made to disentangle these topical conceptions and determine how they are related. A brief review of Aristotelian conceptions will serve as a starting point for the analysis. As Thomas B. Farrell has pointed out, however, "Aristotle had no theory of history."[7] Since "classical rhetorical forms required stable and static assumptions about the nature of the world and its possibilities,"[8] assumptions that have since proved mutable, classical theory by itself is ill-fitted to a study of modern historical argument, and most especially of argument that seeks to revise our assumptions about the nature of the world. It will, therefore, be necessary to make use of Leff's revision of the tradition of topics in developing a theory applicable to modern discourse.

Aristotle distinguishes between two basic categories of topoi. The common or universal topics "apply equally to questions of right conduct, natural science, politics, and many other things that have nothing to do with one another," while the special topics "are based on such propositions as apply only to particular groups or classes of things. Thus there are propositions about natural science on which it is impossible to base any Enthymeme or syllogisms about ethics."[9] Translating this conception into modern argumentation theory, the common *topoi* are field invariant, while the special topoi are field specific.[10] Applying equally to all forms of knowledge production (that is, discourse taking place in the context of any discipline or practice), the common topoi can be described as basic categories of human practical reasoning. Designated by Aristotle with a word or phrase, they include "the possible and the impossible," "past fact," "future fact," and "the more and the less," or the topic of degree.[11] In specifying two of the four common topoi in terms of temporal reference, Aristotle seems to indicate that some essential categories of practical reasoning are based on time. The decision that the rhetor requires of the audience in the present can be argued for by relating judgment in the present to what has gone before or what may come after. It should be noted that Aristotle's designations for the common topoi do not describe actual reasoning processes, but are terms for categories into which these processes can be grouped.[12]

Common topoi are rooted in modes of thought pervasive among all human beings: the questions of what is, what has been, what can or might be, and of comparisons between these, are constituted through the very existence of any linguistic or symbolic system. The special topoi, on the other hand, are rooted in the more relativistic realm of opinion [doxa], or what modern rhetorical theorists call "social knowledge."[13] This connection is evident in Aristotle's Topics, which "proposes to find a line of inquiry whereby we shall be able to reason from opinions that are generally accepted about every problem propounded to us."[14] In the Rhetoric, these topoi are identified as "elementary classes of enthymemes."[15] Enthymeme is a term used by Aristotle to indicate a special form of rhetorical reasoning that parallels the syllogism in dialectic. Kathleen Hall Jamieson provides a concise explanation of its significance: "A speaker creates an enthymeme by suppressing premises in an argument on the assumption that the audience will invest the argument with them. Enthymemes gain their power from their reliance on unexpressed beliefs and information."[16] The special topoi are thus basic building blocks for enthymemes, in that they derive their substance from communally accepted opinion and function as warrants or connective principles in rhetorical argument.[17]

Aristotle gives a number of examples of special topoi for deliberative or political rhetoric. Since deliberative is concerned with the question of whether a given course of action is good or bad, advisable or unadvisable, these special topoi are expressed as propositions relating to political goods and the good in general. The character of these propositions is of interest here in two respects. First, they are intended to be self-evident: statements such as "That is good of which the contrary is bad" would seem to require no demonstration or proof. Second, they are often expressed in contradictory pairs. Thus, the proposition "What is rare is a greater good than what is plentiful," seems intuitively obvious, or is intended as an example of a statement that would seem obvious to an Aristotelian audience. But the proverbial force of such a statement, its apparently self-evident truth, is not negated by the fact that its converse serves equally well as a topical proposition for enthymematic proof: "Reversely, it may be argued that the plentiful is a better thing than the rare, because we can make more use of it." Similar pairs illustrate further the contradictory nature of such topical propositions: "[T]he hard thing is better than the easy, because it is rarer: and reversely, the easy thing is better than the hard, for it is as we wish it to be."[18] Leff notes that these contradictions reveal the essentially incoherent nature of social knowledge: "Common beliefs, attitudes, and values are mutable and volatile, and they take clear form only as they come into contact with particular situations."[19]

Such contradictions in social knowledge indicate the scope of the problem of cultural relativity. Competing notions of truth exist not only between cultures, but within a single society, and even within a single divided mind. A proposition that appears self-evident, so obvious as to be hardly worth stating, even tautological,

to some individuals, can seem prima facie absurd or false to others; a single individual can occasionally be caught arguing both sides of a value proposition. These
dialectical opposites, which can be characterized as the antinomies of practical
reason, are rooted in the phenomenal world of direct experience. This is to say
that beliefs and values only assume propositional form as individuals and groups
confront specific lived situations; differing situations seem to call forth opposing
statements of value. For example, it is easy to imagine how, if faced with a division
of labor involving tasks of varying degrees of pleasantness, one might argue to a
coworker that the hard thing is better than the easy, while justifying one's own
laziness on the principle that the easy thing is better than the hard. Social knowledge,
then, is formed through a common experience of phenomenal situations; it can
assume antinomic forms because social knowledge propositions are articulated differently as human beings shift between vantage points and define situations with
different terminologies (such as those of self-interest or altruism).

These antinomies of practical reason arise from the experience of ordinary
deliberative situations. The purpose of this analysis, however, is to study not the
deliberation that occurs in everyday contexts, but mythic and argumentative forms
with transcendence as their avowed purpose, as Burke defines transcendence: the
adoption of a point of view in which what is initially perceived as disjunction
appears as unity.[20] The next step in this analysis is to consider the antinomies of
transcendent reason that result from the attempt to surmount those in the practical
realm. This requires an examination of the complex relationship of cosmological
myth and social knowledge.

The Topoi of Cosmology

Any attempt to discover an internal logic in the discourse of cosmology encounters
a difficulty first raised by Immanuel Kant in his *Critique of Pure Reason*. Kant's
carefully reasoned attack on "rational theology" dismissed all eschatological and
cosmological speculation as language without any objective referent, and therefore
with no valid claim to truth. Summarizing this positivistic view, Glenn Tinder
writes:

> Internally consistent discourse is possible only in regard to entities within the world;
> the world as a whole, and being-in-itself, cannot be treated scientifically and ob-
> jectively. Thus in such a sphere as eschatology one is forced to speak metaphorically
> and symbolically. Some will conclude that in these circumstances one should not
> speak at all and indeed that one should not concern himself in any way with "realities"
> which cannot be dealt with objectively and rationally.[21]

To take the Kantian position seriously is, therefore, to assume the burden of
demonstrating the rationality of what is assumed to be irrational. In this section, I
will develop a response to Kant based on the following assumptions. First, the
object of this study of eschatological discourse is not the End of the world as an

objective fact, but the empirical reality of people's speculation on the End.[22] Second, the positivistic way of making sense of the world is itself a mode of symbolization (and an incomplete one at that); rhetoric and narrativity constitute an alternative way of knowing with different conceptions of rationality, which even the positivist philosopher can never escape entirely. As Tinder puts it, "[T]he detachment advocated by positivists . . . is a mere intellectual option and not one which is available to the entire, living person. The latter must, at least tacitly, have conceptions of the world and its encompassing being. Nothing is gained by leaving these conceptions unacknowledged."[23] My purpose in this section is, therefore, to demonstrate the rationality of cosmological speculation within the terms of a logic that is narrative and rhetorical—a logic not only of the intellect but of the "entire, living person." The demonstration will proceed by setting forth the relevant elements of this logic as they appear in the works of Kenneth Burke, Walter Fisher, and David Carr.

Peter Marston's recent study of rhetorical forms in cosmological discourse demonstrates that cosmology has historically been expressed in the narrative form of myth and the propositional form of argument.[24] In its narrative form, cosmology has the essentially religious function of "establishing solidarity within a society or culture through a common vision of humankind's relationship with the cosmos."[25] In presenting a coherent, narrative account of the origin and destiny of the universe, cosmologies function as highly elaborated "terministic screens": symbol systems that name and define the acts, agencies, and agents (divine, diabolical, and human) that establish the cosmic "scene" and that will ultimately bring it to its conclusion.[26] As narrative, cosmology establishes a group ethos through a vision of shared origin and destiny that implicitly represents a culture's beliefs, attitudes, and values. In its argumentative form, cosmology offers propositions both descriptive and normative, intended to depict and explain the universe as it is and to orient human beings toward right action. This study is concerned with apocalyptic eschatology as a particular type of cosmology. Through the study of apocalyptic narrative and argument, I hope to show that mythic discourse both furnishes premises of social knowledge and derives its narrative and propositional structure from social knowledge grounded directly in experience. Put another way, myth is a second-order source of social knowledge propositions, establishing a particular type of *doxa* or received opinion by which people come to believe that the earth is flat or round, or is surrounded by crystalline spheres, or that the universe will end six thousand years after its creation. A close examination of eschatological conceptions will illustrate the way that myth both borrows from and contributes to social knowledge.

In *A Rhetoric of Motives*, Burke discusses traditional cosmological speculation on origin, along with eschatology, under the rubric "the temporizing of essence." Contrasting the two, he argues that "a history's end is a formal way of proclaiming its *essence* or *nature*. . . . [I]f there is this ultimate of *beginnings*, whereby theological or metaphysical systems may state the essence of mankind in terms of a divine parenthood or an originating natural ground, there is also an ultimate of *endings*, whereby the essence of a thing can be defined narratively in terms of its *fulfillment* or *fruition*."[27] Eschatologies and cosmogonies, myths and speculations about ultimate endings and origins, are therefore strategies of transcendence, in which the seemingly contradictory realities of phenomenal, practical experience are unified through the temporizing of essence in relation to the future or the past. When the cosmological conceptions of a given cosmogony and/or eschatology are adopted by large numbers of people, they become part of a culture's reservoir of strategies or "coping mechanisms." People draw upon such terministic screens as necessary, as conceptual "maps" to help them navigate their daily lives.[28]

As Kant noted, however, such efforts at transcending the dualities and contradictions of everyday life bring conceptual thought to yet another level of opposition. In the *Critique of Pure Reason*, Kant presents a "System of Cosmological Ideas" in the form of a series of conflicting propositions that embody the various cosmological concepts.[29] Only the first of these "transcendental antinomies," in which Kant articulates a dialectic of cosmological ideas on time and space, is of immediate interest to this inquiry.[30] The antinomic propositional form of this dialectic bears an evident resemblance to the Aristotelian topical oppositions:

> Thesis: The world has a beginning in time, and is also limited in regard to space.
> ... Antithesis: The world has no beginning, and no limits in space, but is, in relationship both to time and space, infinite.[31]

Kant then presents parallel arguments for thesis and antithesis that show the self-contradictions that result from the denial of either proposition. Since these arguments serve the purpose not of establishing the truth or falsehood of either proposition, but of demonstrating the impossibility of such proof, there is no need to analyze them here. This study is solely concerned with the propositional form of the cosmological ideas and their relationship to topical logic. It will be immediately noted that Kant's propositions are descriptive, while the previously cited Aristotelian deliberative topoi are normative, in their intent. The apparent discrepancy can be ignored at this juncture, for, as Marston demonstrates and as will be shown in the following chapters, cosmologies serve rhetorical functions when normative or prescriptive propositions are derived from descriptive or narrative accounts of the universe. However, some adjustments must be made to Kant's antinomy before it can be used as a model of the topical logic of eschatology and apocalypse.

Since this is a study of eschatological conceptions, it should come as no surprise that this analysis will find it necessary to add to Kant's antinomy (which is concerned exclusively with limitations of time and space in terms of origin) a brief statement regarding the end of time, thus: "The world has a beginning *and an ending* in time, and is also limited in regard to space." This thesis is now opposed to its antithesis, "The world has no beginning *or ending*, ... but is, in relation both to time and space, infinite." Such an addition is explicitly rejected by Kant himself, who dismisses eschatological considerations from his study of cosmological argument: "But as regards time future, which is not the condition of arriving at the present, in order to conceive it; it is quite indifferent whether we consider future time as ceasing at some point, or as prolonging itself to infinity."[32] This dismissal of eschatology can be set aside for two reasons. First, it may be granted from the rhetorical perspective that the problem of eschatology is "an arbitrary, and not a necessary problem";[33] but the concern of this study is not the logical validity of these doctrines, nor their claim to objective truth, but what people actually do believe (however arbitrarily) and what use they make of these beliefs. From the point of view of "pure reason," one may remain indifferent to the question of whether time will end or will extend into infinity; but cultural norms are not formed from this perspective, and cosmological speculation of this type can foster decidedly different understandings of policy choices.[34] Throughout history, the question of whether future time is finite or infinite has not failed to excite the interest of many excellent minds.[35] From a Kantian perspective, of course, this is simply confirmation of the errors or "impurities" to which pure reason is subject. Kant's rejection of eschatology is, after all, only a prelude to his ultimate rejection of the entire transcendental dialectic[36] as composed of "sophistical assertions"[37] of which the thesis and antithesis are but examples:

> Nothing seems to be clearer than that, if one maintains: the world has a beginning, and another: the world has no beginning, one of the two must be right. But it is likewise clear, that, if the evidence on both sides is equal, it is impossible to discover on what side the truth lies. . . . There remains, then, no other means of settling the question than to convince the parties, who refute each other with such conclusiveness and ability, that they are disputing about nothing, and that a transcendental illusion has been mocking them with visions of reality where there is none.[38]

Since the present study is not concerned with logical validity or objective truth, an initial response to Kant's dismissal would be to reiterate the thesis of the first chapter, and argue that the "transcendental illusion" of cosmological (and specifically, eschatological) argument has led enough people astray that the critic's task of untangling the nuances of this argument form is all the more urgent. A defense of this project based only on this argument, however, would accept the fundamental assumptions behind Kant's dismissal of transcendent reasoning, and ultimately relegate the study of eschatology and apocalypse to a freakish sideshow in the carnival of history. A second response could be made based, not on an argument for the historical importance of this "illusion," but on an alternative understanding of human knowledge and perception as constituted through narrative.

Summarizing Kant's solution to the problem of temporality, Donald Wilcox claims, "Things exhibit an order not because of the way they are in themselves but because our minds contain the notions of time and space and apply these notions to experience as a necessary part of the act of perception. Time and space are thus not derived from the outside world; before all experience they exist in our minds as *a priori* intuitions."[39] Kant held that the error of transcendental dialectic lay in its illegitimate generalization from the phenomenal realm of experience to the noumenal realm of 'reality,'[40] from time and space as a priori intuitions by which we organize perceptions to statements that treat time and space as empirical realities rather than as categories through which reality is perceived. Recent theories of narrativity have adopted Kant's insight regarding time as an a priori intuition and extended it in directions of which he would certainly disapprove. Walter Fisher, for example, proposes a definition of human beings as *homo narrans*, the storytelling animal.[41] Fisher's position seems to be that the narrative conception of time and temporality is an essential category of human perception, an a priori structure without which we cannot perceive, much less make sense of, events in the world. In his book *Time, Narrative, and History*, David Carr argues that "narrative is . . . a 'primary act of mind,' " and that the form of narrative "is not a dress which covers something else but the structure inherent in human experience and action."[42] Kant would certainly find these narrative theorists guilty of an illegitimate generalization from phenomena to noumena; and given his rejection of dialectic as a mode of knowledge production, there is no doubt that Kant would reject Fisher's claim to narrative rationality as a valid form of human knowledge.[43] It is hardly necessary to mount a defense against all such projected critiques; others are better equipped than I to defend rhetoric and narrative against the attacks of analytic philosophy. Here I will only say (in defense of narratology), that the human activity of making sense of the world through the temporal structure of narrative is itself a noumenal fact that must be empirically accounted for.[44]

From the perspective of "pure reason," eschatology is an arbitrary and not a necessary idea. From the perspective of narrative rationality, as defined by Fisher and Carr, the idea of an ending is logically implied by the idea of beginning. Narrative time is constituted through "a beginning, a middle, and an end"; while "[a] sequence, a series, or a process can theoretically be endless, . . . an event, an experience, or an action is something that begins and ends."[45] In Frank Kermode's words, "Men, like poets, rush 'into the middest,' *in medias res*, when they are born; they also die *in mediis rebus*, and to make sense of their span they need fictive concords with origins and ends, such as give meanings to lives and to poems."[46] The cosmogonic narrative of Genesis thus implies the eschatological resolution of Revelation.

To say that beginnings imply endings, according to the logic of narrative, is not necessarily to endorse a narrative epistemology. One may make use of narrative theory without accepting its claims to totality; thus, whether or not critics accept Fisher and Carr's arguments for the universal importance of narrative form in human perception and action, the study of the logic of eschatology can still be grounded in Burke's notion of form as the psychology of the audience. Form, according to Burke, is "the creation of an appetite in the mind of the auditor, and the adequate satisfaction of that appetite."[47] The arguments for narrative rationality offered by Carr and Fisher may in the end prove to be no more than an extension of Burke's theory of form from the realm of purposive symbolic communication into epistemology, whereby appetites are created not only by intentional stimulus but by the very acts of perception and cognition. The validity of such an extension is not an issue that I propose to address here. For purposes of this study it is enough to say, with Carr, that "narrative may be only *one* way of confronting time and its inherent threat," but "it is *our* way."[48]

From the narrative perspective, then, the idea of eschatology or cosmic endings is (contrary to Kant) necessarily entailed by (rather than arbitrarily derived from) the accounts of origin offered by cosmological speculation. How can these insights into the nature of temporality be integrated into a topical theory of human social knowledge? In the first place, Aristotle's universal topoi of 'past fact' and 'future fact' are temporal categories that begin to imply narrative structure at exactly the moment they are brought to bear on present considerations. A fact (whether past or future) is only an arbitrary single point in temporal sequence until it is placed on a continuum with present conditions or exigences. Put another way, using the topoi of past and future fact in argument requires that a story be not only told, but entered into. The cosmological speculations of cosmogony and eschatology represent the perfection of the past and future as motives of human communication: time is extended backward or forward to a 'sacred' point of origin or ending, widening the scope of temporal considerations to include that which is at the limits of human understanding. Thus, what might ordinarily be a routine issue of rhetorical invention is transformed into terms of ultimate significance. When discourse is produced within the temporal frame provided by eschatology, then, the stakes of the universal topoi are raised to their highest level.

One effect of cosmological speculation about time is, therefore, the reformulation and expansion in significance of the universal topoi of temporality. Cosmology is also, however, a discrete field of discourse with its own special *topoi*, or propositional truths, that provide syllogistic and enthymematic warrants for speculative arguments. Kant's antinomy as amended above can be understood in this sense as one formulation of a principal topic in cosmological argument. The world is eternal, *or* the world is not eternal. There was a moment of creation, when all things came to be, *or* creation is forever repeated, and all things have always been. Time must have a stop, and come to its fruition in a point of ending beyond which is eternity, *or* time is infinite, and will continue on through the unending cycle of eternal return. Such are some of the antinomic forms assumed by the propositions of cosmological argument.

Mythological narratives are not reducible to such propositional statements; they are speculative enactments of them, attempts to realize their implications by "playing with hypotheses" (as Ricoeur puts it) in narrative form. The cosmological antinomies cited above illustrate the hypothetical propositions that can be abstracted from the mythic narratives of a wide variety of cultures, or (to reverse perspectives) from which these narratives are derived. Mircea Eliade's comparative review of eschatological doctrines in *Myth and Reality* illustrates the range of narrative solutions that the world religions have produced as they play with the hypotheses of cosmology.[49] His summary of the cosmic cycle of Hindu mythology will serve as "representative anecdote" for a systematic resolution of these topical issues very different from that of the Jewish and Christian traditions:

> The complete cycle is terminated by a dissolution, a *pralaya*, which is repeated more intensely (*mahapralaya*, great dissolution) at the end of the thousandth cycle. According to the Mahabarata and the Puranas, the horizon will burst into flame,

seven or twelve suns will appear in the heavens and will dry up the seas and burn the Earth. The Samvartaka (the Fire of the Cosmic Conflagration) will destroy the entire Universe. Then rain will fall in floods for twelve years, and the Earth will be submerged and mankind destroyed (Visnu Purana 24, 25). Sitting on the cosmic snake Sesa on the surface of the Ocean, Visnu is sunk in Yogic sleep. . . . And then everything will begin over again—*ad infinitum*.[50]

Eliade argues that this Vedic doctrine of cosmic regeneration and destruction bears a structural similarity to, and may even have influenced, the mythologies of Babylon, Iran, and classical Greece.[51] Elements of these theories of cosmic aeons and the degeneration toward universal conflagration are evident in Hesiod and the pre-Socratic philosophers, such as Empedocles and Heraclitus, and were popularized by the Stoic, Pythagorean, and Platonic schools.[52] As a possible solution to the cosmological problem, then, the cyclical doctrine competed with Christianity for followers in the world of late classical antiquity. Compare this doctrine, as articulated above, with Augustine's forceful argument for a linear conception of time in *The City of God*:

> The Physicists, for their part, considered that there was only one possible way of solving this difficulty; and that was by the postulate of periodic cycles. They asserted that by those cycles all things in the universe have been continually renewed and repeated, in the same form, and thus there will be hereafter an unceasing sequence of ages, passing away and coming again in revolution. These cycles may take place in one continuing world, or it may be that at certain periods the world disappears and reappears, showing the same features, which appear as new, but which in fact have been in the past and will return in the future. And they are utterly unable to rescue the immortal soul from this merry-go-round, even when it has attained wisdom; it must proceed on an unremitting alternation between false bliss and genuine misery. For how can there be true bliss, without any certainty of its eternal continuance, when the soul in its ignorance does not know of the misery to come, or else unhappily fears its coming in the midst of blessedness? But if the soul goes from misery to happiness, nevermore to return, then there is some new state of affairs in time, which will never have an end in time. . . . And so we may escape from these false circuitous courses, whatever they may be, which have been devised by these misled and misleading sages, by keeping to the straight path in the right direction under the guidance of sound teaching. [53]

In this argument, which artfully exploits the spatial metaphors of linearity and circularity, the topical question of time is resolved by appeal to another enduring issue in cosmological speculation: the topos of evil. In other words, Augustine's argument boils down to, "Time must have its conclusion in some new state redeemed from present suffering: for who could bear an eternity of such misery?" Or, as an editorial in the Millerite newspaper *The Advent Herald* restates the theme, "Shall to-morrow be as to-day—shall the antagonism of Good and Evil continue as heretofore, forever?"[54] The relationship of time and evil will be presently be addressed at greater length; the purpose of these quotations is merely to demonstrate the intermittently controversial nature of the resolutions to the topical issues of

cosmology.[55] Augustine's words in particular are evidence that the systematic formulation of Christian doctrine was undertaken in deliberate opposition to the
cosmological hypotheses of Greco-Roman culture.[56] The contributions of the cosmological antinomies to social knowledge must be assessed with this in mind. In
a relatively homogeneous society unused to competition from other symbolic systems, the topical formulations of myth (whether propositional or narrative in form)
may be unquestioned and even unquestionable, so that discourse cannot take place
unless based on these assumptions. As John Angus Campbell notes, however, all
symbol systems must eventually break down when confronted with events that their
symbolic resources cannot encompass;[57] depending on the circumstances, such
failures of a prevailing mode of symbolization may result in the articulation of new
"epochal symbols" or the reformulation of the old.[58] Thus, during certain historical
periods, a variety of symbolic systems may strive against each other, each offering
an alternate set of terms with which to describe the cosmos and characterize
its epoch. When this occurs, as it has in pluralistic societies such as those of the
late Roman empire or twentieth century America, the incommensurability of
social knowledges may be heightened to a remarkable degree. In such situations,
the various cosmic narratives and their propositional correlatives can contribute to
the topoi of social knowledge without ever attaining dominance. For example, the
scientific study of cosmology has recently added such concepts as entropy and the
"big bang" to our cultural vocabulary, so that these now exist alongside the archaic
terms of Christian cosmology as resources for understanding.[59]

With this review of topical theory and cosmological discourse, it is now possible
to speak with clarity when referring to time and evil as the topoi of apocalyptic
eschatology. Defining the topoi in their broadest sense, time and evil are the
recurring themes of all eschatology (of which apocalypse is a particular type); in a
more restricted sense, as propositions of social knowledge that describe the world
as it is or is believed to be, time and evil appear in eschatological discourse as
statements about the universe that are assumed to be true (though in a pluralistic
society they may have to be defended) and that provide warrant for rhetorical
arguments. The specific version of the topos of time that forms the basis of Christian
eschatological discourse has already been presented: in its propositional form, this
topos can be expressed in the words, "Time must have a stop."[60] As this study will
demonstrate, it is but a short leap from this proposition to the apocalyptic positions
that "It is possible to know when time will end," and "The End is near." The only
remaining task of this section is to refine social knowledge about evil into its similar
propositional forms. This requires a brief examination of the grounding of social
knowledge in the intertwined phenomenal experiences of evil and time.

To study the problem of time leads one invariably into contact with the problem
of evil, for the phenomenal experience of time as ineluctable sequence is bound
up with the concrete realities of chance, change, death, and decay. Paul Ricoeur
has noted, in The Symbolism of Evil, the process through which events in the
natural world come to embody a "matrix of symbolic meanings as words."[61] Applying
Ricoeur's "phenomenology of the symbol" to the experience of death, it can be

seen that as one encounters the death of others and imagines one's own, this most terrible and irreversible event becomes a potent symbol of both the passage of time and the corruption of the universe. Just as the experience of time forces individuals to ponder the meaning of death and decay, and thus inevitably to partake of the symbolism of evil, so too does a historical and social consciousness of time force members of any society to imagine and anticipate its end. As Carr notes, "Every . . . community is faced . . . with the constant possibility of its own "death"; if it is not threatened with destruction from without, it must deal with its own centrifugal tendencies toward dissolution or fragmentation from within. . . . The prospective death of a community, like the death of an individual, is usually an open eventuality of uncertain date."[62]

The prospect of cultural death is most readily understood through the symbolism of evil, for the negation of communal ideals comes about either through the actions of a demonic Other or through the living community's own moral failure. Evil is thus intimately linked to our individual and social experiences of time; its symbolism is already present within any construction of temporality. In every culture's representation of its past origins and imagination of a future destiny, the "open eventuality" of its prospective death is implicit. So long as the date of this eventuality remains distant and uncertain, the death of culture appears as no more than a shadow or possibility; when the date is perceived to be imminent, visions of the end can develop fearful potency.

A certain view of time is also assumed in the concept of moral choice between good and evil; for, like death, such choice is seen as irreversible. Following Ricoeur's tripartite division of the symbolism of evil, it is evident that to describe evil in terms of defilement, sin, and guilt is to depend on the language of temporality. For sin and guilt imply both wrongful choice and the possibility of redemption, and the awareness of defilement points to a time of cleanliness and offers the hope of restoration. Evil is most readily imagined as one element of a narrative structure; the dialectic of good and evil is the means by which societies give meaning to historical time, the terministic screen that rescues time from the destructive chaos of mere sequence.[63] Time and evil, therefore, contain and imply each other. The repeated perception of evil and suffering as experienced directly ("Why me?") and vicariously ("Why the Jews?"), and the compounding of this perception through the ineluctable experience of time and death as conditions of human existence, form the occasion or "rhetorical situation" not only for eschatology and apocalypse, but for all human communication.[64]

Some might argue that such a broad definition of "situation" in terms of the existential dilemma of all human symbolization so widens the scope of this concept as to deprive it of any explanatory power. In response to such anticipated objections, I would argue that Lloyd Bitzer's definition of the rhetorical *exigence* as "an imperfection marked by urgency . . . a defect, an obstacle, . . . a thing which is other than it should be"[65] implicitly characterizes *all* rhetoric in terms of the problems of evil and time. The apparent omnipresence of such "defects" furnishes humanity with endless exigences for deliberative rhetoric. This book is concerned with the discourse that results when an entire cosmos (and not just its individual elements) is perceived as "other than as it should be." A world seen as inherently imperfect invites discourse that makes sense of imperfection by reasserting the *principle* of perfection, locating the cause of the flaw, positing some mechanism of redemption, and orienting human beings in some fashion so that they may participate in (or at least take a proper stance toward) cosmic renewal. Such discourse is always urgent, given the shortness of the human life span and the magnitude of evils to overcome; in times of perceived historical crisis, the urgency of this perennial "ultimate exigence"[66] can be multiplied ad infinitum. As a topos of social knowledge, this ultimate cosmic exigence is addressed in the eschatological proposition, "Evil is or will be justified and made sensible in the ultimate destiny of the cosmos." By combining this topos of eschatology with the topos of time, apocalyptic rhetoric constructs its present and immediate future in terms of an imminent divine response to the ultimate exigence.

The antinomic reversal of the eschatological proposition, which could be expressed in the form, "There is no possible justification for evil," is one that is rarely upheld in its pure form, since no human society can maintain its cohesiveness in the face of such nihilism. The strategy of opposition more often takes the form of redefinition, according to which one argues not that there is no evil, or that evil is utterly beyond the human ability to make sense of the world, but that the prevailing mode by which evil is symbolized is inadequate. For example, Ricoeur notes about Kant's critique of theology that "Once deprived of its ontological support, theodicy falls under the rubric of 'transcendental illusion.' This is not to say that the problem of evil disappears from the philosophical scene, however. Quite the contrary, in fact. But now it refers uniquely to the *practical* sphere, as that which ought not to be and which action must struggle against."[67] Such attempts at redefinition illustrate the powerful sources of the topos of evil in phenomenal experience. If a prevailing mode of symbolization is to be overturned, whatever replaces it has the burden of accounting for those experiential facts that the old symbol system once made sensible. The "rational" or purely practical mode of understanding evil, successful as it was in the late nineteenth and early twentieth centuries, seems to break down when confronted with events of such magnitude as the Holocaust.[68] Hence, in the public discussion of this event, European society is forced to resort to a terminology of collective guilt—an essentially mythic concept.

The next task is to examine the particular forms in which the topos of evil appears when it becomes not only a general problem confronted by all human beings, but a particular problem of Jewish and Christian theology; to discover how, within the framework of monotheistic belief, eschatology offers the perfection (which is to say the annulment) of time as the redemptive solution to the problem of evil. This requires yet another move from a 'phenomenology' to a 'logic' of symbols. Ricoeur again shows the way for this inquiry. "[M]eaning resides in the power of the myth to evoke speculation. . . . Hence, that meaning is to be sought in the relation of the pre-philosophical to the philosophical, according to the maxim: 'The symbol gives rise to thought.' "[69] Ricoeur's maxim is descriptive of the process of rationalization that accompanies any society's attempt to make sense of its own foundational symbols and myths. The symbol, in and of itself, is pre-philosophical; but it develops its meaning in and through the philosophical process of rationalization, which is to say interpretation and the practice of argument.[70] The process of rationalization begins with the philosophical effort to translate mythic narrative into the terms of its propositional logic, which can then be justified on a rational level.

In the preceding pages, this study has attempted to recapitulate this translation from the terms of myth to the terms of practical reason. The analysis will now turn to the next level of justification, on the assumption that the meaning of myth is to be found not only in its internal logic, but in the history of interpretation that both enacts and critiques that logic. The topical logic outlined above in its primary form will be examined as it is developed further in the discourses of theodicy and chronology. Anthropologist Claude Levi-Strauss has argued that "the purpose of myth is to provide a logical model capable of overcoming a contradiction."[71] The next sections of this chapter will provide support for this thesis by showing how eschatological myth functions to resolve the contradiction posed by the problem of evil, and how the consequences of this resolution are developed in a variety of calendrical systems and other symbolic representation of time's passage.

Theodicy and the Topos of Evil

> Every nomos is established . . . against the threat of its destruction by the anomic forces endemic to the human condition. In religious terms, the sacred order of the cosmos is reaffirmed, over and over again, in the face of chaos. It is evident that this fact poses a problem on the level of human activity in society, inasmuch as this activity must be so institutionalized as to continue despite the recurrent intrusion into individual and collective experience of the anomic . . . phenomena of suffering, evil, and above all, death. However, a problem is also posed on the level of legitimation. The anomic phenomena must not only be lived through, they must also be explained. . . . An explanation of these phenomena in terms of religious legitimations, of whatever degree of theoretical sophistication, may be called a theodicy.[72]

As Berger uses the term, a theodicy is any religiously based legitimation of and explanation for the phenomena of suffering, evil, and death. Evil appears as a topos in the symbolism of every human community to the degree that all communities are arranged to shield their members from these phenomena and to soften their pain. As Max Weber notes, however, it is in monotheistic religions that this problem becomes acute.[73] The monotheistic version of the problem of theodicy is succinctly stated in David Hume's *Dialogues Concerning Natural Religions*: "Is [God] willing to prevent evil, but not able? then he is impotent. Is he able, but not willing? then he is malevolent. Is he both able and willing? whence then is evil?"[74] Hume's questions effectively illustrate the inherent tension or contradiction that faces any person who believes in an omnipotent, benevolent creator and at the same time faces evil and suffering as experiential reality. Some explanation for the genesis and purpose of evil must be offered if the tension is not to become unbearable; and many have found it difficult or impossible to reconcile the fact of evil with the belief in God's omnipotence and goodness. My purpose in this section is to demonstrate that mythic and philosophical speculation on the problem of evil within a monotheistic framework follows a pattern of topical elaboration that is usefully described by the classical theory of stasis, and that Christian eschatology functions as a narrative defense of theism that rests on the third stasis, traditionally referred to as the stasis of quality.

The problem faced by all monotheistic cultures is the perceived contradiction between the experiential reality of evil and the belief in an omnipotent and benevolent creator. George Mavrodes's essay, "The Problem of Evil as a Rhetorical Problem," usefully crystallizes the logical structure of this problem as it appears in theological and philosophical arguments into what he terms the "Theistic Set"—five propositions, the apparent incompatibility of which constitutes the problem as it is usually understood. These propositions are: (a) God exists, (b) God is omnipotent, (c) God is omniscient, (d) God is all good, and (e) evil exists. Mavrodes does not try to resolve the contradiction, but only shows that formal logic does not assist us in the effort to find a resolution; for, even if the problem were resolved in formal terms, such a resolution would not necessarily "solve" the problem for a believer experiencing evil. To be effective rhetorically, an explanation for evil must actually succeed in reconciling belief and experience so that individuals find their suffering adequately justified.

To understand how such reconciliation is possible it is necessary to examine the problem of theodicy as an argument, and not simply as a condition of formal contradiction. The odd thing about the traditional version of the problem is that the inherent contradiction among the members of the theistic set is often asserted but rarely argued. McCloskey, for example, boldly asserts that "Evil is a problem for the theist in that a contradiction is involved in the fact of evil on the one hand, and the belief in the omnipotence and perfection of God on the other. God cannot be both all-powerful and perfectly good if evil is real."[75] The problem is constituted here in terms of formal logic, where (a), (b), (c), and (d) are said to imply not-(e). However, an examination of the members of the set reveals no prima facie contradiction among its members; as Alvin Plantinga and Nelson Pike have noted, to get a formally inconsistent set one must add another proposition.[76] To put the problem in the terms of Stephen Toulmin's model of argument,[77] the claim is made that "There is no God," with the evidence offered that "Evil exists." What is missing here is a warrant for the argument. Such a warrant, once formulated, must be added to the theistic set in order to obtain a formal contradiction among its members. Pike has formulated such a warrant, which I will call proposition (f): "An omnipotent, omniscient being would have no morally sufficient reason for allowing instances of suffering."[78] There are other possible versions of this warrant; however, in order to obtain a formal contradiction among the members of the theistic set, that is, to justify the move from data ('evil exists') to claim ('there is no God'), all such warrants must involve a moral (as opposed to an analytic) claim about the nature of deity.[79] Pike's proposition will, therefore, serve as a focus for this analysis.

The addition of proposition (f) to the sequence results in a revised theistic set whose members are clearly contradictory (assuming that the concepts of "suffering" and "evil" are treated as identical). The arguments from evil against the existence of God (or at least of a God with the characteristics defined in the theistic set) are founded on this proposition (though it has not until recently been clearly stated). Yet, unlike the other members of the set, no version of this proposition has ever been a tenet of traditional theism. In terms of the topical logic outlined in the previous section, propositions (a) through (e) represent "truths" of social knowledge affirmed in the literature, art, and ritual of European and American societies for many centuries, while proposition (f) seems to challenge basic social knowledge assumptions. Focusing on this proposition as the point of contention between theistic and atheistic positions adds clarity to the argument. The atheist must either prove (f), or argue that it should be accepted by definition and without proof, in order to demonstrate that the propositions of the revised theistic set are in formal contradiction. The theist, on the other hand, must only attack (f) successfully to demonstrate that the existence of evil does not logically entail the nonexistence of God. Given the crucial role of proposition (f) as the fulcrum of theodicical argument, it is evident that the success or failure of the argument from evil (or of any positive theodicy) may depend on how the terms of this proposition are defined and understood.

It is therefore necessary to discover what is implied in the phrase "morally sufficient reason." The word "sufficient" in this case does not denote logical or natural sufficiency; when considered as part of a rhetorical argument (as opposed to an abstract philosophical one), "morally sufficient" can only mean "sufficient for a given audience." That is, any proposed reason may be judged sufficient by some, and not by others, but its sufficiency can never be determined by logic, empirical evidence, or any empirical standard of judgment. In the courtroom, there are conventional criteria that mandate judgments about an actor's moral culpability for an act committed: homicide may be justified on grounds of self-defense, hospital patients may be allowed to die for reasons of triage, and so forth. If God is to be put on trial for the evils of the world, by what standards can the theodicies or defenses offered by the deity's "attorneys" be accepted or rejected? The phrase *morally sufficient reason* thus indicates that the problem is inherently rhetorical: it involves value judgments that cannot be proved, but can only be argued rhetorically. Mavrodes's advocacy of a rhetorical approach to the problem is thus strengthened by a close examination of the (formerly implicit) warrant now added to the argument. What are the possible forms that a rhetorical solution to this inherently rhetorical problem might take?

The juridical analogy used above may provide a clue. The image of the trial appears throughout popular and philosophical literature on the problem of evil. One book of theological essays, for example, bears the title *God in the Dock*.[80] The prevalence of the analogy suggests that theodicies be examined as a species of forensic rhetoric. The classical theory of forensic stases could thus, if the analogy is extended, be used to illuminate the problem of evil. A 'stasis' is a point of standstill, a place where arguments may clash. In forensic rhetoric, the stases are levels of argument upon which one may attempt a defense. Four stases of forensic rhetoric were identified by classical rhetoricians: factual (or conjectural), definitional, qualitative, and translative (or jurisdictional). Cicero's *De Inventione* explains the stases and their significance:

> Every subject which contains in itself a controversy to be resolved by speech and debate involves a question about a fact, or about a definition, or about the nature of an act, or about legal processes. . . . When the dispute is about a fact, the issue is said to be conjectural (*coniecturalis*), because the plea is supported by conjectures or inferences. When the issue is about a definition, it is called the definitional issue, because the force of the term must be defined in words. When, however, the nature of the act is examined, the issue is said to be qualitative, because the controversy concerns the value of the act and its class or quality. But when the case depends on the circumstance that the right person does not bring the suit, or that he brings it against the wrong person, or before the wrong tribunal, or at a wrong time . . . the issue is called translative because the action seems to require a transfer to another court or alteration in the form of pleading. There will always be one of these issues applicable to every kind of case; for where none applies, there can be no controversy. [81]

Jeanne Fahnestock and Marie Secor's summary of stasis theory distills the lore of the classical rhetoricians into more concise form: "No matter what the particular proposition maintained in an argument, that proposition must be classified as an answer to one of a set of fundamental questions: (1) Does or did a thing exist or occur? (2) How can it be defined? (3) What is its quality? and . . . (4) Whether or where it makes sense to answer or even argue one of these questions."[82]

Immediately obvious, and significant for this analysis, is that these questions are not independent of each other, but develop in a hierarchical sequence. Determination of fact is logically prior to the question of definition, which must in turn be resolved before quality can become an issue; finally, all three questions must be resolved before judgment is rendered or action taken. This hierarchical organization of stasis questions does not, however, mean that an argument will necessarily proceed in a particular temporal sequence; the locus of controversy can move among the stases as specific issues arise and are settled and as forensic defenses are mounted on different levels.[83] Stasis theory is, therefore, not a static conception useful only for the classification of arguments, but a dynamic conception that enables critics to track and predict the evolution of argumentative form as controversy moves from one stage to the next. If one imagines God on trial for the "crime" of creating a universe full of evil and suffering, the dynamics of theological and philosophical arguments about evil can be understood as the movement of argument through the conceptual levels of forensic controversy.

The use of the trial analogy and the application of the forensic topoi to theological discourse must be qualified with one significant reservation, in that debates about the existence and goodness of God do not follow the patterns of legal argument in their apportionment of presumption and the burden of proof. Whereas legal argument in most Western societies begins from the presumption of innocence, this position is not simply conceded to the theologian who would defend divine benevolence. On the contrary, the atheistic position challenges the traditional presumption of innocence by asserting either the culpability or the nonexistence of the defendant! However, the levels of forensic stasis do help to clarify the nature of this debate by providing points around which discussion circles and which form the subjects of recurring controversy. Examination of theological discourse on the problem of evil reveals that defenses have been attempted on each of these levels. To demonstrate properly the applicability of stasis theory to theodicies through the centuries is of course beyond the scope of this essay; a brief sketch should suffice to illustrate the point.

A defense based on the stasis of fact or conjecture argues that the crime did not actually take place. This defense appears in those religions, such as Christian Science, that deny the existence of evil altogether. The founder of Christian Science, Mary Baker Eddy, taught "the nothingness and unreality of evil," declaring that "Evil has no reality. It is neither person, place, nor thing, but is simply a belief, an illusion of material sense." Once evil is defined simply as false belief, the problem is easily "solved" through a shift in perception: "If sin, sickness, and death were understood as nothingness, they would disappear."[84] While it is not my purpose here to accept or reject any particular religious solution to the theodicy problem, it does seem fair to expect that any solution ought to begin by acknowledging the existence of the problem. Although religions such as Christian Science may offer a rhetorically effective consolation to some people, most who have had prolonged experience of gratuitous pain and suffering are unlikely to accept the argument that their experience lacks phenomenal reality.

Arguments based on the stasis of definition admit that an act took place, but claim that it should not be defined as a punishable crime, as when prosecution and defense disagree over whether a killing is to be defined as murder or self-defense. In theological argument, this stasis can be found in the various arguments that hinge on the way that the propositions of the theistic set are defined and understood. Augustine's theodicy of the *privatio boni* is built on the stases of fact and of definition, since it essentially defines evil out of existence: according to Augustine, evil is not "real," since it only "exists" as the negation or privation of the good. Augustine's dialectical skill is evident in *The City of God*, where he argues that evil cannot exist by the very definition of God as the ultimate ground of existence: "Thus to this highest existence, from which all things that are derive their existence, the only contrary nature is the non-existent. Non-existence is obviously contrary to the existent. It follows that no existence is contrary to God, that is to the supreme existence and author of all existence whatsoever." [85] One cannot help but share Kenneth Burke's admiration for Augustine's virtuosic display of the negative,[86] but to admire the thought is not equivalent to accepting the theodicy. Insofar as the theologian's defense depends on the stases of fact and definition, it will appear as sheerly verbal trickery: the experiential problem of the believer faced with suffering and evil will not disappear once the contradiction has been defined away. In similar fashion, the apparent contradiction of the original theistic set can be eliminated by redefining God's benevolence, or omnipotence, or any of the other propositions.

Defenses founded on the stasis of quality may seek to mitigate the supposed crime by explaining the value of the act in terms of an excusing condition or desirable outcome; to this stasis belongs the argument that the victim of the crime deserved his fate. Recognizing that his definition of evil as a privation of the good that lacks phenomenal reality still leaves unsettled the questions of how this privation occurs and why apparently innocent people suffer from it, Augustine turns to another argument that locates the origin of evil in the radical misuse of human freedom and claims that the resulting evils exemplify retributive justice: "[W]e do evil because we choose to do so of our own free will, and suffer it because your justice rightly demands that we do so."[87] Some modern theologians, notably Alvin Plantinga, have developed this notion at greater length in a way that emphasizes the intrinsic value of free will and abandons the idea of evil as retributive justice. Plantinga's "free will defense" places responsibility for the existence of at least some types of evil not on God, but on the freely acting human will, the existence of which itself justifies the moral evils that result:

> A world containing creatures who freely perform both good and evil actions—and do more good than evil—is more valuable than a world containing quasi-automata who always do what is right because they are unable to do otherwise. Now God can create free creatures, but he cannot causally or otherwise determine them to do only what is right; for if he does so they do not do what is right *freely*. To create creatures capable of moral good, therefore, he must create creatures capable of moral evil; but he cannot create the possibility of moral evil and at the same time prohibit its actuality. . . . The fact that free creatures sometimes err, however, in no way tells against God's omnipotence or against his goodness; for he could forestall the occurrence of moral evil only by removing the possibility of moral good.[88]

Plantinga's argument also depends on a clarification of the definition of omnipotence, in that he claims omnipotence does not entail the power to perform acts that are logically impossible or self-contradictory. Just as an omnipotent God cannot create a square circle, so it is impossible for even an omnipotent God to create creatures with free will who always choose the good.[89]

The introduction of free will as a justification and explanation for moral evil represents an attempt to construct a positive theodicy based on some conception of the "morally sufficient reason." An alternative positive defense of theism based on the stasis of quality may be found in John Hick's "soul-building" theodicy. Finding the Augustinian conception of retributive justice inadequate, Hick seeks to explain the human experience of evil not as a punishment of all humanity for a prehistoric Adamic fall, but as necessary to the development of human beings so that they may aid in the realization of a future eschatological harmony:

[T]he end to which God is leading us is a good so great as to justify all the failures and suffering and sorrow that will have been endured on the way to it. The life of the Kingdom of God will be an infinite, because eternal, good, outweighing all temporal and therefore finite evils. . . . This means that if in fact God's purpose of universal good is eventually attained, then in relation to that fulfillment nothing will finally have been sheerly and irredeemably evil. For everything will receive a new meaning in the light of the end to which it leads. What now threatens us as final evil will prove to have been interim evil out of which good will in the end have been brought.[90]

Here, again, is a variation on the "morally sufficient reason," which in effect claims that the end justifies the means. I shall presently return to this eschatological conception, and to the objections raised against it.

The final stasis is that of jurisdiction. A defense based on the jurisdictional stasis may claim that the court lacks authority and/or is unfit to judge the case. This is the argument found in the book of Job, when the Lord appears out of the whirlwind and, in effect, denies the suffering Job the right to argue by posing a stream of rhetorical questions:

Who is this whose ignorant words cloud my counsel in darkness? (38:2)
Where were you when I laid the earth's foundations? (38:4)
Should he that argues with God answer back? (41:2)
Dare you deny that I am just or put me in the wrong that you may be right?
Have you an arm like God's arm, can you thunder with a voice like his? (41: 8–9)

Job, of course, abases himself before God and repents of having dared to question the deity. Similarly, theologians have traditionally argued that the qualities of omnipotence and omniscience place the deity beyond human standards of judgment. Those who have not been granted a vision of the divine presence are likely to find this argument unsatisfying; while one sits upon the ash-heap, one cannot help but demand an explanation for the evils that befall us. Appeals to jurisdictional stasis in theodicy argument do not really provide an answer to the argument from evil; rather, they suspend the argument through refusal to engage in debate. In his essay "On the Failure of All Attempted Philosophical Theodicies," Kant indicts this defense as a retreat from the committment to rationality implied in the very undertaking of theodicy itself: "The author of the theodicy agrees that the case be tried before the tribunal of reason, and agrees to be an attorney who will defend the case of his client under attack by formal refutation of all the complaints of the adversary. Therefore, he may not during the course of the process declare arbitrarily that the tribunal of human reason is incompetent (*exceptionem fori*)."[91] Apologetic arguments that seek to "justify the ways of God to man" by appealing to the poverty of human reason and the inscrutability of the divine will thus appear to be the theologian's defense of last resort. The problem with the Lord's response to Job is that the stream of rhetorical questions does not so much answer the argument as suspend it. To state that we do not have the perspective of eternity that would allow us to pass judgment on the Creator is, in effect, to reiterate Job's complaint: he seeks a good reason for his suffering that only an eternal perspective could provide. The difficulty for theologians who would mount a defense based on the fourth stasis of jurisdiction lies in the fact that the radical inaccessibility of God's purpose to humanity is precisely the problem. An argument based on this stasis alone is, in effect, an admission of defeat in the attempt to find a justification for evil. Hence, theological discourse must perpetually return to the third stasis of quality, to the attempt to imagine the end that will justify the means.

The appeal to an eternal perspective invokes the vocabulary of temporality, prompting a re-examination of the stases for their primary orientation in space and time. Since the stases of fact and definition are concerned with *being as such*, I argue that they are therefore governed by a spatial perspective. The primary concern of theological argument on these levels is to eliminate the contradiction that seems to inhere in the members of the theistic set. From this perspective, it is considered to be inconceivable that God and evil could coexist in the same universe. A solution to the problem of evil based on the first two stases thus must either eliminate evil, or redefine the properties of God. Arguments based on the stases of quality and place, on the other hand, are concerned with *being in time*, and depend on a temporal perspective. To claim that the end justifies the means, that is, that evil will be justified in the ultimate destiny of creation, is to imagine a temporal resolution to the problem, one that will be revealed at some indeterminate future point. In the same fashion, the stasis of jurisdiction depends on a temporal perspective: it is argued that humans are not fit to judge the creator because they lack the viewpoint of eternity. Thus the Lord asks Job, "Where were you when I laid the foundations of the earth?"

The purely spatial formulation of the problem ignores the human experience of time, for people routinely accept the idea that good reasons for things that may seem difficult to accept are not always available at a given moment, but may be revealed with time's passage. Stanley Hauerwas and David Burrell note that it is precisely the apparent absence or inaccessibility of good reasons that constitutes evil as a problem. According to Hauerwas and Burrell, the search for morally sufficient reasons for the existence of evil within a temporal framework leads us inexorably into the realm of story: "Since explanations offer reasons, and evil turns on the lack of reasons, some form other than a causal explanation must be called for. The only form which can exhibit an action without pretending to explain it is . . . narrative."[92] If one is condemned for an action and is unable to deny that he or she committed it, the only defensive strategy available (other than denying one's interlocutor the right to bring a charge or to pass judgment) is to tell a story that justifies or mitigates the action within a temporal framework. The difficulty of constructing such a defense on behalf of the deity is that human beings, lacking the cosmic perspective, can only dimly imagine an ultimate outcome that justifies evil. The search for morally sufficient reasons for the existence of evil thus leads into the realm of mythic narrative. In their attempt to find such reasons, human beings construct stories in which the existence of evil and suffering is no longer senseless, but has a place in the cosmic scheme. Looking to the past, they develop stories of a Fall to explain how evil came into the world; to discover its meaning in the present, Christianity posits the doctrines of incarnation and redemption (for the question of why God allows suffering must necessarily be altered once the existence of a God who takes on human suffering is proposed); looking to the future, an eschatological resolution is imagined in which choirs of cherubim and seraphim chant, "Just and true are thy ways, O King of the ages, . . . for thy judgments have been revealed" (Rev. 15:3–4, RSV). The Christian historical imagination points to a time when the world is made new, when "God shall wipe away all tears from their eyes; and there shall be no more death, neither sorrow, nor crying, neither shall there be any more pain" (Rev. 21:4, KJV). Such narratives are rhetorical in that they persuade believers that their lives do have a meaning and purpose in the face of apparently meaningless suffering and evil.

The experiential reality of suffering must be confronted and justified. Since the beginning of the Christian era, believers have found such a justification in the millennial kingdom of apocalyptic prophecy, which provides a conclusion to the cosmic narrative in which the materiality of evil is counterbalanced by the materiality of redemption. Thus the second-century Christian theologian Irenaeus argued for the necessity of both the millennium and the suffering that precedes it:

> For it is just that in that very creation in which they toiled or were afflicted, being proved in every way by suffering, they should receive the reward of their suffering; and that in that creation in which they were slain because of their love to God, in that they should be revived again; and that in the creation in which they endured servitude, in that they should reign. For God is rich in all things, and all things are His. It is fitting, therefore, that the creation itself, being restored to its primeval condition, should without restraint be under the dominion of the righteous.[93]

Irenaeus' argument on behalf of the millennial kingdom illustrates the theodicical function of Christian eschatology: the narrative of the Apocalypse provides an explanation for evil that is "fitting" and "just." In the terminology of modern rhetorical theory, the millennium lends narrative coherence to the story of evil.[94] The affliction and suffering of the community of believers will be redeemed when the earthly creation comes to its fulfillment. Placing one's faith and hope in this fulfillment not only provides a 'logical' solution to a theological dilemma; it also enables the believer to redefine any *apparent* evil or calamity as a positive good by situating it within the temporal frame of the mythic narrative. Television evangelist Pat Robertson expresses this strategy of redefinition succinctly in an exhortation to his followers: "We are not to weep as the people of the world weep when there are certain tragedies of breakups of the government or the systems of the world. We are not to wring our hands and say, 'Isn't that awful?' That isn't awful at all. It's good. That is a token, an evident token of our salvation, of where God is going to take us."[95] Thus, the mythic narrative of Apocalypse can be used to justify the existence of evil on a cosmic scale by pointing to the promised restoration of an earthly Kingdom of God, while individual experience of evil is itself proof, by an argument from sign, that the cosmic drama of evil is nearing its resolution. Later chapters of this study will analyze the strategy of sign argument more closely; my present purpose is only to note the rhetorical functions of the myth, on the abstract level as a defense against the argument from evil and on the concrete level as a means of reinterpreting one's afflictions in the present.

Defenses of theistic belief against the argument from evil that are based on mythic narrative are, of course, open to attack. From a positivist perspective, eschatological myth is nothing more than a foolish illusion. In Hume's dialogue, for example, Cleanthes scornfully dismisses such a proposed solution when it is offered by Demea, who argues that

> This world is but a point in comparison of the universe; this life but a moment in comparison of eternity. The present evil phenomena, therefore, are rectified in other regions, and in some future period of existence. And the eyes of men, being then opened to larger views of things, see the whole connection of general laws, and trace, with adoration, the benevolence and rectitude of the Deity through all the mazes and intricacies of his providence.
>
> No! replied Cleanthes, no! These arbitrary suppositions can never be admitted, contrary to matter of fact, visible and uncontroverted. Whence can any cause be known but from its known effects? Whence can any hypothesis be proved but from the apparent phenomena? To establish one hypothesis upon another is building entirely in the air; and the utmost we can ever attain by these conjectures and fictions is to ascertain the bare possibility of our opinion, but never can we, upon such terms, establish its reality.[96]

While it does seem that Cleanthes gets the better of Demea in this exchange, the criteria that Hume sets here for evaluating the proposed solution are certainly open to question. Demea has not actually offered a morally sufficient reason for the existence of evil in the universe, but only sets forth the possibility that some reason could exist which will be revealed in a future eschatological denouement. Hume (through Cleanthes) rejects this possibility out of hand as unprovable. That it is unprovable is certainly true, but the same could be said of the counterargument from evil, that there is no God. Demea's "conjectures and fictions" may be unsatisfactory from the positivist perspective, but this perspective is not unassailable; it may be that all humans have to go on are conjectural narratives that can do no more than establish possibility. I am not arguing here for an acceptance of the Christian myths, nor that they are, in fact, adequate solutions to the problem of evil. I merely wish to point out the rhetorical functions that these narratives serve. Evaluated by the rhetorical criterion of psychological effectiveness, they will prove to be adequate solutions for some but not for others. Thus Ivan argues in Dostoevsky's *Brothers Karamazov*:

> I understand, of course, what an upheaval of the universe it will be, when everything in heaven and earth blends in one hymn of praise and everything that lives and has lived cries aloud: "Thou art just, O Lord, for thy ways are revealed." When the mother embraces the fiend who threw her child to the dogs, and all three cry aloud with tears, "Thou art just, O Lord!" then, of course, the crown of knowledge will be reached and all will be made clear. But what pulls me up here is that I can't

accept that harmony. . . . I renounce the higher harmony altogether. It's not worth the tears of that one tortured child. . . . And if the sufferings of children go to swell the sum of sufferings which was necessary to pay for truth, then I protest that the truth is not worth such a price.[97]

A more recent philosophical statement of the same position is offered by Antony Flew:

[L]ogically higher order goods are not necessarily higher order, period. Even if you can show room for saying that all actual evils do in fact serve as the materials for logically higher order goods, you have not thereby shown that everything will be, or could be, for the best. The price could still be too high. When we turn, as one ultimately must, from generalities to particulars it will appear: both that it is, to put it no stronger, extremely implausible to suggest that all the ills we know of are, or could be, thus redeemed; and that we might need a lot of persuading to the conclusion that all is for the best in the end.[98]

Flew is exactly on the mark: we might need a lot of persuading to the conclusion that every evil will be ultimately justified. What he neglects to state are the criteria for evaluating such persuasion, which can only be narrative and rhetorical: for to argue that a proposed future good justifies present suffering is to tell a story containing values that cannot rest on any strictly logical criteria, but can only be evaluated in narrative terms. As Walter Fisher, following Alasdair MacIntyre, has shown, when we search the very ground of our being to discover why things are the way they are, we confront not logic, but stories.[99] And the narratives that are found in this search can give solace to some, but will remain forever unsatisfying to others.

It should be made clear that the preceding analysis does not represent or reproduce a rational process claimed to occur in any premythic culture; no argument has been made that eschatological myth was invented as a forensic defense to a logical argument. I claim, nevertheless, that these narratives were born out of the inherent tensions or contradictions that exist in any belief system even before its tenets have been articulated, rationalized, and justified. As Weber recognized, apocalyptic eschatology is but one of the many creative forms that evolved from human attempts to resolve the paradox of theodicy that appears in every culture.[100] I turn now to the consequences of this solution for the topos of time, as elaborated in the symbolic representations of chronology.

Chronology and the Topos of Time

The human experience of time is not always and everywhere the same, but is subject to discursive manipulation. The rhythms of speech, the evocation of memory and hope through the use of symbols, even the very act of counting time, can affect how people experience its passage. The objective referents by which time is measured (the position of hands on a clock face, a sunset, the phases of the moon) indicate nothing but the individual moment in all its particularity until they are ordered into a symbolic construction by which time's passage is understood. As historian Donald Wilcox argues, time's polysemous nature is evident in the variety of temporal symbolisms produced by different societies.[101] For Wilcox, the transitions from the episodic time of ancient historiography to the absolute time of Newtonian physics and the relative time of the Einsteinian cosmos indicate that time itself is a rhetorical construct that in its myriad forms makes possible a variety of differentiated insights. The "science" of modern history, for example, is founded on the temporal assumptions of Newtonian physics: "The continuous and universal qualities of Newton's time and space have made it possible for historians—as well as the natural scientists— to view the basic components of reality not as processes or organic wholes but as a series of discrete events that can be placed on a single time line and at a single point in space."[102] The power of temporal constructions is evident not only in their ability to foster scientific insight, but in the forms of social control that they make possible. The bell that tolled the hours in the medieval monastery called men to prayer and sent them to the fields as surely as the clock in modern industrial societies dictates the flow of workers through freeways and factories. Not only daily life, but the entire life and organization of a society as expressed in its ritual, is governed by temporal symbolism. In ancient China, the promulgation of calendars and the calculation of astronomical intervals were (like the minting of coins) exclusive prerogatives of the imperial court.[103] During the French revolution, the ideologues who sought to destroy all vestiges of the ancien régime established an entirely new calendar, purging chronology of ecclesiastical associations by dating time not from the birth of Christ but from the declaration of the First Republic (Anno Domini 1792).[104]

The calendars of imperial China and revolutionary France exemplify both the power of temporal symbolism and its precariousness. Throughout history those who have sought to mold human activity to their purposes have recognized that action in the world is constrained and made possible through particular constructions of time, that an age belongs to those who have (or can seize) the power to define it. My purpose in this section is to study the rhetoric of temporality in its widest manifestations by examining the contributions of apocalyptic eschatology to the formation of what John Angus Campbell calls "rhetorical epochs." I shall argue that an understanding of the ambiguous relationship of chronological calculation and apocalyptic expectation in the early Christian church will assist historians and critics in identifying the motives that prompted the development of its unique epochal symbolism.

Campbell defines a rhetorical epoch as "an era so marked by a strategic, stylized symbolism that it divides history into a 'before' and 'after.' . . . Rhetorical epochs and their representative symbols reflect such a major shift in human self-understanding that their advent constitutes a revolution."[105] As Hans Blumenberg has pointed out, the danger of applying the epochal concept to an understanding of history lies in the tendency to interpret past ages in terms of the preoccupations of the present and so impose an artificial unity onto periods of ancient history.[106] To avoid any hint of this "nominalistic" fallacy, let me make clear that I am using the term "epochal symbolism" in its most precise and literal sense, as referring to a society's own epochal understanding, its prevailing mode of symbolizing cosmic and historical time. The epochal understanding of the early Christians was given sequential form in the discourse of chronology; studying the shifts in chronological systems during the first centuries of the Christian era thus provides a clue to the rhetorical motives that led to the creation of its epochal symbolism.

Campbell argues that epochal discourse springs from the "tensional field" of history created by the universal awareness of mortality.[107] The analysis of the preceding section provides support for Campbell's theory by demonstrating the relationship of Christian eschatology, a particular form of temporal symbolism, to the problem of evil. Further evidence of the link between evil and epochal discourse can be found in Eliade's review of temporal mythologies:[108] for it is apparent that in their various doctrines of world ages (whether cyclical or linear in form) all societies agree in situating humanity at the end of a progressive cosmic decline. No symbol system has yet been discovered that posits a progression from an Edenic golden age to a period of catastrophic evils while locating humanity closer to the point of origin than to the point of ending. The religious imagination never fails to to place humankind in the Kali Yuga or the Iron Age; in the mythic awareness of temporality, the present is always the time of greatest evil.[109] The concepts of a cosmic cycle or rhetorical epoch are thus integrally related to the problem of theodicy. This connection is made explicit in Christianity's formulation of its rhetorical epoch.

Given the strictly literal definition proposed above, it may seem misguided to speak of the epochal symbolism of the earliest Christians. For, as Blumenberg notes, "Christianity laid claim only very late to having initiated a new phase of history. Initially this was totally out of the question for it because of its eschatological opposition to history and the unhistorical quality that was (at least) implied by it."[110] According to this interpretation, the earliest Christians proclaimed not a new phase of history, but its absolute End. In what sense, then, can this symbolism be called an epochal formation?

To answer this question, another, more controversial question must be posed: how did the original Christian congregations conceive of time and their place in it? Much recent scholarship has taken for granted the view of Yonina Talmon that "Jesus and his followers expected an imminent inauguration of the Kingdom of God and lived in tense expectation" of its inception.[111] From this perspective, the central problem faced by the earliest Christians was the apparent failure of their original founder's apocalyptic predictions.[112] Opposed to this view is the concept of "realized eschatology," whose proponents argue that the earliest Christian congregations experienced the Kingdom as fully realized in the present, and that emphasis on future expectation was the product of reinterpretation by later generations.[113] Most recently, this thesis has been argued by Bruce J. Malina, who claims that peasant societies of antiquity were oriented not toward the future, but toward the present, and that the received historical interpretation of early Christian consciousness of time is therefore a mistaken application of modern temporal categories.[114] Malina's essay seems to propose an idealized version of the Mediterranean peasant as an ahistorical noble savage, living in a perpetually expanding present uncontaminated by modern notions of time and history, in which "all time worth telling is 'kairotic,' including time for milking the goats."[115] This romanticized notion reaches an extreme with Malina's argument that among the "social inventions and skills that did not exist in the first-century Mediterranean [were] manipulable numerals, arithmetic using a zero, abstract and impersonal chronology, abstract and numerical calendars, *or the abstract categories: past, present, and future.*"[116] One need only point to Aristotle's *Rhetoric* (widely available throughout the Mediterranean three centuries before the era in question) as an example of awareness of abstract temporal categories during this period to render this claim untenable.[117] Finally, Malina's argument that "the only scholarly evidence for the existence of anxiety and concern about a perceived delay of a parousia [return of Christ], for interest in eschatology, or for some future-oriented apocalyptic, was in the eyes of liberal, Enlightenment-oriented, 19th-century northern European biblical interpreters and their 20th-century heirs"[118] can only be maintained through willful ignorance or tortured readings of a number of biblical texts.[119] For example, Jesus' statements that "It is not for you to know times or seasons which the Father has fixed by his own authority" (Acts 1:7) and "of that day or that hour no one knows, not even the angels in heaven, nor the Son, but only the Father" (MK. 13:32) are read by Malina as expressing a normative lack of concern for the future and the relegation of prophetic fulfillment into an "imaginary time" that had no reality for, or influence upon, the original historical audience for these pronouncements.[120] The context of the quotes and the history of their interpretation in the early church,[121] however, clearly indicates that they functioned as injunctions against the very forms of apocalyptic expectation that Malina claims could not have been present in such a "primitive" society.

It is indeed difficult to understand the ideas of temporality present in societies of late antiquity without reference to modern preconceptions. In their effort to avoid the distortions that result from the use of inapplicable categories, however, critics and historians should not be blind to evidence of different temporal orientations and chronological sophistication.[122] The abstract chronology of Newtonian physics and modern historiography did not appear ex nihilo in the seventeenth century, but was developed from the latent assumptions of Christian cosmology. Though this development took place over many centuries, its roots can be found in the earliest documents of Christian history. As the work of historian Richard Landes demonstrates, apocalyptic thought played a central role in the development of chronological skills among the early Christian communities.

According to Landes, the prevailing epochal conception among early Christians was a theory of world ages, often referred to as the World Week, in which the six days of creation in Genesis are understood in terms of the scriptural saying that "with the Lord one day is as a thousand years" (2 Pet. 3:8). The six days of creation thus symbolize the world's duration for six thousand years, while the seventh "day" symbolizes the millennial kingdom. Alhough this notion is derived from Jewish apocalyptic literature,[123] the first Christian formulation of the age of the world in these millennial terms appears in the Epistle to Barnabas (circa 120 CE), a text for catechumens produced within approximately three decades of the book of Revelation and accepted as canonical by the Greek church of Alexandria: "Listen carefully my children to these words: 'God finished his work in six days. . . . ' That means that in 6,000 years God will bring all things to completion, because for Him 'a day of the Lord is as 1,000 years. . . . ' Therefore, my children, in six days, that is in 6,000 years, the universe will be brought to its end. 'And on the seventh day he rested.' "[124] This text does not offer a chronology, but established the temporal foundations upon which later chronological calculations were built. As Landes notes, this text "implies that by dating the Creation of the world, one can know the time of its End."[125]

Christian historians were not slow to pursue this implication. By the early third century (circa 204 CE) Hippolytus of Rome had dated the birth of Christ fairly precisely: "The first Parousia of our Lord took place on a Wednesday, the 8th of the Kalends of January, in the 42 year of the reign of Augustus, 5,500 years after Adam. . . . One must, therefore, get to 6,000 years before the Sabbath, the type and figure of the future kingdom of the Saints who will reign with the Christ after his descent from the heavens, as John tells in the Book of Revelation."[126]

This placement of the life and ministry of Jesus in the exact center of the sixth millennium was quickly adopted as "the cornerstone of Christian chronography"[127] in the works of historians and apologists such as Julius Africanus and Lactantius. In his Divine Institutes (circa 303–313 CE), Lactantius used this calculation as an integral part of his arguments against the epochal conceptions of the pagan philosophers: "Let the philosophers who count thousands of years from the beginning of the world know that the six thousandth year has not been completed. When this number has been reached, a consummation must come and the condition of humanity must be transformed for the better."[128] To those who would ask "when these things we have spoken of will take place," Lactantius offered a hopeful summary of recent chronological calculation: "Those who have written about the ages deduce the number of years from the beginning of the world out of holy scripture and different histories and teach when the whole sum will be completed. Although they vary and disagree a bit about the number, no expectation seems to be more than two hundred years."[129]

Considering the scriptural prohibitions against calculating times of the End, the question that modern critics must ask about such chronological speculations is, why were they accepted as authoritative by patristic authors and their audiences? Landes' explanation is that these calculations served an important polemical purpose: they gave church authorities a useful weapon to counter the unruly tendencies of popular apocalypticism by postponing the millennium to a point beyond the lifetime of the immediate audience. By affirming the validity of scriptural prophecies but delaying their fulfillment by hundreds of years, the authorities of the church attempted to suppress popular excitement that would otherwise have been difficult to control. Such a strategy, however, could only be a temporary means of "buying time" for the church; with the approach of the year 6000 (500 CE), the chronology of Hippolytus and Lactantius was bound to "produce results exactly inverse to its original intent. That is to say that, over the centuries, this chronology would shift from non-apocalyptic to apocalyptic, from delaying technique to countdown."[130]

The response of church authorities to this situation, as Landes shows, was to change their calculations. During the first half of the fifth century CE, Christian historians such as Orosius and Victorious of Aquitane adopted the chronology that soon became the orthodox model for subsequent historiography. These authors placed the birth of Christ at approximately 5200 years after the creation, thereby extending the life of the world by some three hundred years and postponing the millennium yet again, this time until 800 CE. This strategy of redating, of course, had the same result: in the early 700's CE, as the end of the sixth millennium loomed, the chronological system that had once been conservative in its apocalyptic implications began to lend itself to dangerous speculations. It was at this point that the English historian Bede shifted to the chronological system (first proposed in 525 CE by Dionysus Exiguus) that counted time not by Annus Mundi, the World Year, but by Annus Domini, the Year of our Lord. From the perspective of a theory of epochal rhetoric, the implications of this change are momentous. The event that served as the foundation of chronology, marking and defining the beginning of the era, was no longer the Creation, but the Incarnation. Before the shift from Annus Mundi to Annus Domini, the division of history into "a 'before' and an 'after' " that Campbell describes[131] was present in the epochal symbolism of Christianity, but the "after" *had not yet occurred*; dating from the Incarnation meant that the decisive event of salvation history was to be found not in the future, but in the past. An immediate consequence of this shift was that the theory of the World Week no longer had a place in orthodox chronological speculation. Once the Incarnation was defined as Year 1 (a method of calculation that, theoretically at least, was open-ended and without apocalyptic implications[132]), the age of the world was no longer a figure of such symbolic importance. This new epochal symbolism succeeded so completely that it is still in use as the basis of the modern Western calendar.

At this point a summary of these events as presented in Landes' analysis is in order. In the context of a documented, widespread belief that the world would come to its End six thousand years after its Creation, "at least two systems for calculating the age of the world, universally accepted and the object of considerable interest in the period they designate as their own 5700s and 5800s, are overthrown in their 5900s by an alternative set of calculations which rejuvenate the world by some 300 years."[133] Only with the approach of the year 6000, according to Annus Mundi II of Eusebius and Orosius, was the system of dating by reference to the age of the world finally abandoned and the modern system of dating from the Incarnation adopted. The weight of the evidence presented by Landes, the pattern that he traces in the timing of these shifts in calculation, point to an inescapable conclusion: that the development of Western chronometry was intimately linked to the desire of church authorities to count time in a way that would avoid implications of an imminent End.[134]

Landes' study adds a new dimension to Wilcox's analysis of the "rhetoric of relative time" in the works of medieval historians and chronographers. Whereas Wilcox assumes that these writers did not measure time on an absolute scale because they were more concerned to reveal the thematic relations of the episodes of Christian history,[135] Landes' evidence indicates that orthodox historians avoided such measurement not only because of their desire to see events in terms of the thematic unity of narrative, or because they did not know how to calculate in this fashion, but also because such calculations carried subversive apocalyptic implications that they specifically aimed to suppress. Thus, the need to rid chronology of its apocalyptic significance illuminates a hitherto invisible motive for modern historians who seek to understand why their ancient counterparts "might prefer to avoid a single time line."[136] Once historians take seriously the polysemous nature of temporality and cease to assume a lack of sophistication in the temporal thought of the ancient world, linear, sequential time appears not as an invention sui generis of the modern age, but as a mode of temporal understanding that was available to the ancients as well—although its full implications remained to be developed.

It had taken Christian society seven centuries to develop an enduring chronological basis for its epochal self-understanding; prior to the definition of the age in terms of Annus Domini, Christians located themselves not in a new age, but at the waning of the old. In the few decades following Jesus' ministry, the "sense of an ending" had no explicit counterpart in the discourses of chronology and history; such efforts could only have seemed pointless to people who were convinced of the imminent End of creation. When the Apocalypse failed to materialize, however, Christian chronologies were devised that explained the discrepancy between belief and reality by postponing history's End for some centuries, thereby discouraging (for a time) further speculation on the immediate historical relevance of eschatology.

The first conscious formulation of an epochal rhetoric among the early Christians therefore expresses a meaning found in the etymological root of the Greek epoché: literally, a check, a cessation, a suspension of judgment.[137] In this case, the epoch as originally conceived was precisely the suspension of the Last Judgment, a symbolism that explained and justified its postponement. The temporal paradox at the heart of apocalyptic discourse, then, is that the declaration of the End of time is itself constitutive of a community which must then reconceive and redefine its place in universal history in the face of the apparently endless extension of its earthly existence. Once the epochal definitions intended to resolve this problem are codified into chronological form, the human understanding of time may come to be manipulated by its own symbolic constructions: dates take on meanings of their own as significant numbers, and the inexorable logic of numerological calculation comes to the fore as the countdown begins.[138] In the third chapter of this study, I shall examine the theology of Augustine as an alternative strategy of redefining a rhetorical epoch to make room for the apocalyptic community's action in history. To conclude this chapter, however, one final topic must be considered: the problem of authority in eschatology, and the uses of eschatological symbols of authority in political discourse.

Authority as a Topos of Apocalyptic Eschatology

In the preceding examination of eschatology as a response to the universal topoi of evil and time, I have argued (following Ricoeur) that these myths enact in narrative form a speculative logic that follows from certain cosmological assumptions; that the mythic End of history represents the perfection of the cosmos through the purgation of the principle of evil in a final eschatological Judgment through which the divine sufferance of evil will be justified. In following the progress of this speculative logic of myth, however, I have so far ignored the question of how such cosmological speculation comes to be accepted as authoritative or canonical. Until now, the analysis has focused on the topoi of time and evil as they are elaborated in the symbolic discourses of myth and the propositions of cosmological speculation. At this point it is necessary to add a third topos, that of authority, to the analysis. The necessity of this addition can be readily seen from the fact that we do not accept epochal pronouncements from simply anyone who claims to have discovered the cosmic significance of evil or to have calculated the remaining duration of the cosmos. Frequently, new epochs are declared or new ages proclaimed that fail to attain dominance or even acceptance of any sort. Some discussion of why certain prophets and proclamations of a cosmic epoch are accepted as authoritative, while others are not, would therefore seem to be in order. Furthermore, it will be useful to examine the eschatological narratives of Christianity for their characteristic modes of symbolizing power and authority, and to discover how institutional structures of religious and political power have shaped and been shaped by these authoritative symbols.

To introduce the problem of authority is, however, to open up an area of inquiry that could (if pursued to an adequate conclusion) engulf this whole project. For it is evidently the case that all mythic discourse, and not only that of eschatology and apocalypse, must present itself as authoritative, if it is to have any claim at all to our attention (to say nothing of our allegiance and obedience). An examination of the ways in which mythic discourse creates its own authoritative grounds for acceptance, and of the social and contextual factors that lend credence to mythic accounts of the cosmos, would certainly be an exhausting enterprise for the reader as well as this writer, whose concerns lie elsewhere. It is not possible here to do more than acknowledge the importance of authority as a topos of apocalyptic argument, while postponing its full examination to a later date. The problem of canonicity itself, the processes by which the textually embodied myths of early Christianity were produced and adopted by audiences throughout Europe and Asia Minor and ultimately divided by the emerging church hierarchy into scripture and apocrypha, is outside the scope of this study.

This limitation need not be a cause for concern, however, in that the discourse with which this study is chiefly concerned assumes the authority of the Christian revelation as unquestionable. An exception to this rule is the juxtaposition of Augustine's linear conception of cosmic time with the cyclical conceptions that prevailed in the classical cultures of India, Greece, and Rome. This discourse was considered as an example of cosmological argument between competing epochal theories. Since some of Augustine's arguments were directed to those outside the Christian community who endorsed the pagan cosmology, he could not support his cosmological claims by assuming the authority of Christian and Jewish scriptures, but was forced to rely on dialectical skill and appeals to rational conceptions. The argumentative aim of the earliest Christians was to prove to an audience of Jews the authoritative nature of the Christian revelation based on its fulfillment of Jewish prophecy. The attempt to Christianize the Hellenic and Roman cultures was a shift in audiences that mandated a shift in strategy, since skeptical adherents of the pagan cosmology who granted no priviliged authority to Jewish scriptures demanded arguments that were worthy of consideration alongside the cosmological systems of various philosophical schools and cultic mysteries.[139]

It is evident, therefore, that argument conducted across or between cosmological systems must offer good reasons for adherence not grounded in the authority of a canonical or textual tradition. Only in such rare moments, during the collapse of an epochal formulation while other formulations strive for dominance, does authority become an explicit topic of cosmological discourse. This study is not primarily concerned with such exceptional cases, but rather with discourse such as that of the chronologists of the early church, who did not question the sacred authority of Scripture but who merely developed their computational systems to discover its implications. The epochal definition of the cosmos with reference to a time line from the events of Genesis to those of the Apocalypse simply *assumes* the divine origin of these texts.

A useful perspective on the problem of authority can be gained from the theories of its most astute modern scholar, Max Weber. Discussing political power and the authority of the state, Weber asked the question, "When and why do men obey?" and proposed "three basic legitimations of domination," which he characterized as traditional, legal or rational, and charismatic. Traditional authority bases its commands on "the mores sanctified through the unimaginably ancient recognition and habitual orientation to conform." Legal or rational authority derives its force from "belief in the validity of legal statute and . . . rationally created rules." Charismatic authority, in contrast, is based on an "extraordinary and personal *gift of grace*" and appeals to "the absolutely personal devotion and personal confidence in revelation, heroism, or other qualities of individual leadership."[140] Since legitimation can be viewed as a primary function of rhetoric, little imagination is required to consider Weber's typology as a catalogue of argumentative strategies employed by those who seek to achieve or maintain spiritual, as well as political, authority. To conclude this chapter, I shall briefly sketch the development of charisma, tradition, and rationality as forms of legitimation in Western Christianity, with special attention to the impact of shifting concepts of authority on apocalypticism.

The applicability of Weber's concept of legitimation to the problem of the religious canon should be evident. To examine the problem of textual authority in Jewish and Christian prophecy is to confront the nature of charisma: the authority of the prophet comes from a divine gift, a privileged vision of the realm of the sacred. I have no intention here of entering into the debate over what charisma "really" is, or of analyzing at length its various manifestations.[141] In passing over this issue, I will only say that, from a rhetorical perspective, charisma is best conceived as a property *attributed by the audience*.[142] By this definition, a prophet "has" charisma when he or she succeeds in attracting a following, and a textually embodied vision demonstrates charismatic authority when an audience deems it to be authentically divine in origin and accepts it into a canon. The circularity of this definition is perhaps unavoidable.[143] One more point is required, however, to expand the circle to a useful diameter.

From the rhetorical perspective articulated by John Angus Campbell, the audience's act of attributing charismatic authority can be seen as the "human construction of a supreme reality," the "universal audience" that "embodies the basis for authentic human community."[144] Applying this insight to the Judaic and Christian traditions of apocalyptic literature, one may say that the charismatic authority that the historic audiences for the Apocalypse have attributed to their prophets and prophetic texts constitutes an attempt by these audiences to assume the standpoint or perspective of the universal audience. In the act of recognizing itself in the chorus of saints and angels to whom the mysteries of the ages are revealed, in identifying with those who join in the chant, "Just and true are thy judgments, O King of the ages," the historical audience attempts to universalize itself. The promise of the Apocalypse to make known the imminent End of history and the justification of evil in the cosmos is no less than the promise of the human apprehension of the divine or universal perspective, a standpoint for judgment that reveals the narrative unity of all space and all time and forecloses every disagreement. To translate this into more traditional rhetorical terms: recalling Aristotle's dictum that the end of rhetoric is judgment (*Rhetoric* II.18),[145] one could 'logologically' reorder this statement into, (the Last) Judgment is the End of rhetoric—literally and teleologically. The end of the agon of history will remove the possibility of dispute; the devil will no longer have his advocates, since those who survive the final catastrophes will all perceive the Truth directly, rendering disagreement impossible. The existence of this Truth, the perspective of the divine and universal audience, need not (indeed, cannot[146]) be actually revealed in any empirical sense; merely the hypothesis of such a perspective is attractive enough to exert an influence on human communities that sociologists and religious believers alike term "charismatic."

In its initial oracular mode of expression, the authority of the apocalyptic narrative is grounded in the prophet's claim to direct apprehension of the sacred.

Following Weber's typology of legitimation, this type of authority has been termed "charismatic." Once a charismatic vision is textually embodied, the mythic inheritance of the original vision must be revised and applied through the discourse of interpretation. Here the text cannot stand by itself, but is supplanted by the traditional and rational structures of legitimation through which its charismatic authority is mediated for later historical audiences. Christianity's impulse toward traditional authority was manifested in two ways. First, it may be seen in the formation of an authoritative canon of scripture, which stamps prophetic texts as inspired or apocryphal by selecting some, such as the book of Revelation, and rejecting others, such as the *Epistle of Barnabas*.[147] Second, with the formation of the canon came a parallel development, the establishment of a church hierarchy ordained by apostolic succession. These developments are integrally related, since a significant rationale for the development of an institutional hierarchy was the necessity of an authoritative body to determine which texts were to command the allegiance and obedience of believers, and to secure the effective transmission of these texts. Once the structures of traditional authority were formed and invested with the power to define orthodoxy and heterodoxy, they functioned as an interpretive monopoly. Not surprisingly, the monopolization of scriptural interpretation by church authorities had a profoundly negative effect on apocalyptic speculation. Predictions of an imminent overturning of the earthly order are inimical to traditional structures, since the authority of such structures is grounded in and derived from their historical continuity. Hence for centuries apocalypticism was placed on or beyond the fringes of orthodox belief by the church hierarchy, which was anxious to suppress apocalyptic expectations that could and did erupt into challenges to the authority of both church and state.[148]

The interpretive monopoly of the traditional church was reinforced by the fact that the scriptural texts were for many centuries inaccessible to those who did not have access to instruction in the languages of their composition. With the onset of the Protestant Reformation, however, the Bible was translated into many languages, and control over Scripture passed out of the hands of the institutional hierarchy. The Protestant reformers revolutionized interpretation by rejecting the traditional authority of the Catholic church and proclaiming the standard of *sola scriptura*, exemplified in Luther's claim that Scripture itself was "the most certain, most accessible, [and] most comprehensible authority."[149] The reformers believed that this return to Scripture represented a restoration of the original ideals of primitive Christianity; ironically, their actions had the unintended effect of propelling Western Christian audiences into the modern age. The rejection of traditional authority in favor of the authority of Scripture did not bring about the simplification of the problem of authority, but instead resulted in a hitherto unimaginable fragmentation of the sources of authoritative discourse. The focus on *sola scriptura* paradoxically necessitated a new emphasis on interpretation; for the symbolic narrative is inherently ambiguous, its application to current events always a matter for dispute. So long as the ultimate ground of authority was located in the Bible itself, anyone could, in principle, argue for a particular interpretation of Scripture. One effect of the Reformation, then, was the weakening or elimination of traditional and institutional constraints on interpretation, and a recurring tendency toward interpretive subjectivity.[150]

There was less scope for the rhetoric of apocalypse when those determining who should be allowed to speak about the meaning of Scripture were hostile to new interpretations. When the Reformation broke the interpretive monopoly of the Roman church, however, the field was wide open for scores of preachers and writers, who could now attract followings and even start new churches or sects without being branded as schismatic and unorthodox. Often, these groups used typological interpretations of scriptural prophecy[151] to effect a dialectical transformation of the symbols of sacred authority. Thus, the more the Roman Catholic church persisted in its claim that the divine authority of Scripture had to be mediated by traditional authority in the person of the pope, the vicar of Christ on earth, the more reformers such as Luther, Zwingli, and the Puritan divines in New England were prone to view the papacy itself as either a type or the literal fulfillment of the scriptural prophecies of Antichrist. For was it not written that this fearsome figure, the Man of Sin, was to be found in no other place than the church itself, falsely claiming divine authority by taking "his seat in the temple of God claiming to be a god himself"? (2 Th. 2:4).[152] In this way, the originally subversive nature of the Apocalypse was rediscovered by the reformers, who turned against the papacy the symbolic weapons that the earliest Christians had aimed at the hated Roman imperium.[153]

The identification of the papacy with Antichrist was not an invention of the Protestant reformers. The long history of the papal Antichrist legend extends back to the papal-imperial conflicts of the eleventh century CE; it is only one fragment of a complex mosaic of myths and legends whose history reveals significant insights into the use of apocalyptic symbolism for purposes of legitimation and subversion. The period from the tenth to the fifteenth centuries is worthy of an extended study in itself, including as it does many significant transformations in the myths, legends, and interpretations of the apocalyptic tradition—or more precisely, traditions. McGinn's work in particular provides evidence of a fascinating pattern, a kind of evolving dialectic of myth and countermyth that employs both positive and negative symbols of authority. A brief summary of the historical evolution of this dialectic will demonstrate the intertwining of charismatic and traditional authority in the medieval era, and illustrate the variety of rhetorical and political uses for mythic discourse.

The eschatological topoi of time and evil often appear as abstract questions of philosophical speculation; however, when combined with the topos of authority these speculations are given concrete political implications. When a whole world or cosmos is perceived in terms of the ultimate exigence of evil, and the urgency of this exigence is emphasized by an epochal rhetoric that constitutes time through the imminence of its fulfillment, the theme of authority becomes central in Christian eschatology. For, as will be seen in more detail in chapter 3, the Apocalypse is (among other things) a mythic narrative about power and authority, an affirmation of divine and spiritual power over and against the idolatrous claims of state authority. The problem of evil is not only a question of why God allows the innocent to suffer, but also of why the wicked are allowed to rule and how believers may resist their power. Thus, in its original articulation, the Antichrist beast of Revelation 13 was designed as a symbolic subversion of the persecuting power of the Roman empire, which demanded not only political obedience but also formal obeisance to the imperial cult:

> Out of the sea I saw a beast rising. . . . The dragon conferred upon it his power and rule, and great authority. The whole world went after the beast in wondering ad-miration. Men worshipped the dragon because he had conferred his authority upon the beast; they worshipped the beast also. . . . The beast was allowed . . . to wage war on God's people and to defeat them, and was granted authority over every tribe and people, language and nation. All on earth will worship it, except those whose names the Lamb that was slain keeps in the roll of the living, written there since the world was made. [13:1–8]

Earthly political authority is thus clearly depicted in demonic terms, deriving from the dragon, that "serpent of old who led the whole world astray, whose name is Satan, or the Devil" (12:9). However, this authority is allowed to rule only by a mysterious divine permission, and will ultimately be overturned by reassertion of the divine will. The subversive implication of these symbols, for both the ancient Romans and for revolutionaries of later generations, is clear. What has received far less attention from scholars of apocalypticism is that eschatological narrative can be used to legitimate, as well as subvert, political authority.

The conversion of the Roman emperors to Christianity in the third century CE meant that the eschatological scenarios of the earliest Christians had to be radically revised. New and plausible interpretations of the mysterious beast of Revelation, Antichrist, had to be devised; apocalyptic rhetors also faced the problem of finding a place for the Roman imperium, newly endowed with spiritual authority, in their programs for the Last Days. Thus, a legend grew up that validated the institution of the Byzantine Christian empire by fitting it into the popular apocalyptic scenarios of the end: the tradition of the Last World Emperor, a holy Christian "rex Ro-manorum et Grecorum." The late sixth-century *Revelations* of Pseudo-Methodius and the ninth-century *Letter on the Antichrist* by the Frankish monk Adso present this figure as a king of the Last Days who would come at the End of time to defeat the Muslims and lay down his crown in the Holy Land.[154] This legend achieved considerable popularity in the West; it endowed the crusades with an air of apoc-alyptic excitement on occasions when rulers who claimed inheritance of the Roman imperium set off to do battle with the infidel.[155] The legend also provided ideological support to European rulers such as Frederick II of Hohenstaufen, who sought to legitimate his rule by reviving the symbolism of the Roman empire. When popes such as Gregory IX retaliated by reviving the old tradition of the imperial Antichrist, the emperors in turn began to use the Antichrist's traditional associations with Rome and with corrupt spiritual authority against the papacy. Thus, in the twelfth and thirteenth centuries, partisans of both the papal and imperial parties could each appeal to different scenarios for the Apocalypse.[156]

Just as the Christian empire became a historical fact that apocalyptic rhetors sought to account for and legitimate through the dissemination of apocryphal and often pseudonymous prophecies, so the growth of the papacy and its increasing claims to both worldly and spiritual authority had to be accounted for and legitimated. Hence, a new legendary tradition was developed and embroidered, that of the Angelic Pope, a saintlike ruler of the Church who would appear to reform and restore Christianity in the Last Days. This figure is hinted at in the writings of the famous and influential Abbot Joachim of Fiore, regarded by many in his own time as a prophet. As Joachim's followers became marginalized and radicalized, they incorporated new pseudo-prophecies such as the *Angelic Oracle of Cyril* into the Angelic Pope legend. According to McGinn, the *pastor angelicus* legend, like that of the Last Emperor, was "fundamentally an attempt to validate the meaning of the newly potent office in terms of the Christian understanding of history. If the papacy really was the central institution that the Great Reform had made it, it had to have a commensurate role in the final events which gave history its full meaning, even though there was not the slightest hint of such a role in the canonical Scriptures." Unlike the Last Emperor legend, however, the myth of the Pope of the Last Days was never successfully employed by historical popes to legitimate their claims to power. Rather, McGinn notes, it was most often used to attack popes "whose lack of sanctity, opulence of life, or involvement in politics might be an occasion for scandal."[157] Thus, belief in an Angelic Pope to come might coexist side by side with the identification of the current pope as Antichrist, as radical factions within the Roman Catholic church such as the Spiritual Franciscans adopted both legends in their scenarios of history's End.

One can see in this history the growth of parallel and sometimes competing apocalyptic traditions, in which mythic figures of a semimessianic Last Emperor and an Angelic Pope were juxtaposed to legends that personified Antichrist as either an impious king or an evil *pseudopontifex*. Medieval religious authorities were not above appealing to apocalyptic sentiments in their struggles against the power of emperors and kings, but they were distinctly hostile to apocalypticism when it was used to attack their own legitimacy. Those who clung to the hope of an imminent End in spite of the hostility of church authorities had to account for present alignments of earthly power and authority by incorporating them into mythic scenarios of the Last Days. When the canonical apocalyptic texts of the Old and New Testaments did not suffice to explain, justify, or attack the authoritative claims of emperors and popes, apocalyptic rhetors were perfectly capable of concocting new prophecies or "discovering" old ones. Thus, the competing traditions that made up the complex of apocalyptic myth were not founded only on conflicting interpretations of canonical prophecy; these traditions also grew by accretion as apocalyptic audiences demanded new prophetic texts that could represent new political realities.[158]

As these events illustrate, the apocalyptic myth is broad and expansive enough to provide symbolic resources for both the legitimation and the critique of religious and secular power. The medieval contest between popes and emperors, between spiritual and secular authority, seems to have been fueled by the attempts by both sides to encroach on each other's sphere. As the wealth and political power of the papacy grew, its claim to spiritual authority became less plausible; religious authorities were increasingly vulnerable to charges of pride and corruption. At the same time, rulers seeking to legitimate their secular power by grounding this power in sacred myth tended naturally to assume the quasi-religious authority of the Emperor of the Last Days, thereby laying themselves open to charges of impiety and Antichristian messianic pretensions. In this manner, the texts of both canonical prophecies and new apocalyptic texts provided symbolic ammunition for the rhetorical and political struggle between the authoritative institutions of church and state.

The tradition of the Last Emperor continued for centuries in various nationalistic versions, becoming identified in England with Arthur ("the once and future king"), in France with a resurrected Charlemagne, in Germany with Frederick Barbarossa.[159] A contemporary parallel can be found in the veneration of the Ethiopian emperor Haile Selassie by the Caribbean sect of Rastafarians (who are also prone to speculation on the associations of Antichrist with the papacy and with the British royal family!). Though the Angelic Pope story was abandoned by the Protestant churches, a vestige of the tradition survives to this day in the legendary "papal prophecies" attributed to Saint Malachi, which seem to be revived whenever there is a succession in the papacy. The most durable survivor of these multiple apocalyptic legends is that of the papal Antichrist. Originally nurtured by radical factions within the Catholic church, the lineage of this tradition extends through early reformers such as Wyclif and Hus, to Luther and the great Protestant reformers of the sixteenth century, to the Puritans, and from them to generations of American Protestants.

This admittedly sketchy discussion of the evolution of apocalyptic symbolism through the dialectics of sacred and secular authority must suffice for the present. Relying on McGinn's history of the political uses of apocalypticism in the Middle Ages, I have sought to show how Weber's theory of legitimation illuminates certain broad developments in the apocalyptic tradition, and how certain staple themes of American Protestant apocalyptic can be traced back to the church-state conflicts of an earlier era. Having thus briefly examined the charismatic authority claims of the original Christian revelations and prophecies, and the intertwining of charismatic and traditional legitimations in the authoritative rhetoric of popes, emperors, and reformers, I turn now to Weber's third form of legitimation, rationality. To use Weber's famous phrase, I intend to study the "routinization of charisma" as a rhetorical phenomenon. My purpose is not to discover the charismatic ground of the prophetic text's authority, but the authority of statements made about the text, the resources for rational legitimation of interpretive arguments that apply prophecy to contemporary events. In this regard, one final aspect of biblical exegesis in the

Reformation is particularly relevant to the history of apocalyptic interpretation: the privileging of the literal meaning of Scripture.

Medieval theologians had developed elaborate systems of scriptural interpretation that identified at least four senses in which a text could be read: the literal or historical, the allegorical, the moral, and the analogical.[160] The last three of these modes of reading could be used to overcome difficulties presented by texts not easily understood on the literal level; for example, the erotic love poetry of the Song of Solomon was interpreted allegorically as a representation of God's love for the church. The Protestant reformers rejected interpretations based on the mystical senses of scripture, arguing that these could not be used to justify Catholic practices and doctrines that departed from the faith of the earliest Christians. They sought to return to the literal and historical meaning of the Bible as the only certain ground of religious claims. The problem, of course, is that the Bible (and apocalyptic prophecy in particular) very often employs language that is deliberately metaphorical and therefore inaccessible to a purely literal reading. Luther, Calvin, and the other reformers could not simply dispense with figurative readings of the Bible; rather, they could and did employ interpretive devices such as typology to unlock the meaning of scripture, on the assumptions that there was an underlying unity between literal and figurative meaning, and that literal interpretation must always take priority over the figurative.[161]

The Reformation's reassertion of the literal and historical truth of scripture seemed to harmonize nicely with the increasing emphasis on empirical standards in the epistemology of the Enlightenment,[162] and provided a measure of restraint against the more subjective flights of interpretive fancy. By the nineteenth century, many Protestant thinkers took the harmony of religious and scientific truth for granted, and even went so far as to argue for a scientific approach to biblical interpretation. One nineteenth-century theologian, Charles Hodge, argued that the "Bible is to the theologian what nature is to the man of science. It is his storehouse of facts; and his method of ascertaining what the Bible teaches is the same as that which the natural philosopher adopts to ascertain what nature teaches."[163] Even the most arcane figures and symbols in the Bible, Hodge believed, were accessible to scientific interpretation: "[F]igurative language . . . is just as definite in its meaning and just as intelligible as the most literal."[164] As George Marsden and Timothy Weber note, this "scientific" understanding of the Bible was heavily influenced by Baconian science and the Scottish Common Sense philosophers.[165] As this view was applied to apocalyptic texts, interpreters sought concrete historical and scientific fulfillments of prophecy that would provide objective demonstrations of the veracity of Scripture.[166]

The case studies examined in chapters 4 through 7 will illustrate how modern apocalyptic discourse grounds its authoritative claims in part upon the ostensibly scientific rationality of common sense interpretation. Before this is possible, however, it is necessary to examine the Christian Apocalypse more closely, in order to see how the apocalyptic text *as drama* constitutes the world of its audiences. The next chapter will show how modes of apocalyptic interpretation both constitute and are constituted by a dramatistic rhetorical logic, in which history is structured as tragedy or comedy, and how such dramatic constructions may be used to further rhetorical legitimations or subversions of the existing order.

THREE

From Eschatology to Apocalypse:
Dramatic and Argumentative Form in
the Discourse of Prophetic Interpretation

The preceding chapter examined the role of eschatological narratives in human speculation on the problems of evil, time, and authority, and showed that such narratives result from human attempts to explain and justify the phenomenal realities of evil, to locate humanity within a cycle or progression of cosmic time, and to legitimate or subvert the structures of existing power through the resources of sacred myth. The task of this chapter is to show how the narrative theodicies produced in this effort to understand evil and authority in a context of cosmic time are interpreted and applied by audiences to fit their historical situations.

My study of the topical development of the problem of evil focused on eschatology, traditionally identified as the study of the "last things": in the terminology of Christian myth, death, judgment, hell, and heaven. The analysis of the topos of time in early Christian chronology moved from eschatology to apocalypse by focusing on the codification of eschatological narrative into a numerical, sequential form that thereby serves as an impetus to apocalyptic calculation. According to Bernard McGinn, "General eschatology becomes apocalyptic when it announces details of the future course of history and the imminence of its divinely appointed end."[1] In short, some eschatologies offer the doctrine (whether in the form of mythic narrative or theological argument) that history will end at some point in the future, while apocalypticism claims that this End and the manner of its accomplishment are imminent and discernible. The argument developed in this chapter is twofold. First, where the last chapter treated the topical logic of eschatology as narrative in form, this chapter identifies the specific form of Christian eschatological narrative as that of drama. Second, I will argue that *where the question of chronology is moot* (that is, where the system of dating time does not itself indicate the imminence of the End), audiences move from eschatology to apocalypse, from a narrative of the End to an application of this narrative to the present and immediate future, through a discourse of interpretation that exhibits argumentative, as well as narrative and dramatic, form. Interpretive rhetorical argument is needed to build a bridge between eschatological narrative and predictive claims of an imminent End; this argument assumes dramatic form since it is situated by the rhetor within the cosmic drama that the mythic text depicts and the world is seen as enacting. I now propose that the cosmic drama can be "read" as tragedy or comedy, and that Kenneth Burke's tragic and comic "frames of acceptance" therefore offer a useful analytic tool for examining the history of apocalyptic interpretation. I will argue that the topoi of time and evil are elaborated differently in the tragic and comic interpretations of apocalypse, and that Burke's "psychology of form" explains how this topical elaboration is shaped by the interaction of rhetor and audience. Finally, I will examine the nature and function of argument itself within the tragic and comic frames.

The relationship between myth and argumentative rationality is the subject of an ongoing dialogue among rhetorical scholars regarding the criticism of myth and mythic rhetoric[2]— a dialogue that continues and extends the classical debates over the relationship of myth and reason, *mythos* and *logos*.[3] While reason has historically been used to critique and debunk the claims of myth, such an opposition is only one of the possible ways of conceiving the relationship of these two modes of thought. My theoretical approach to myth is grounded in the recent work of Hans Blumenberg, whose monumental study *Work on Myth* argues that "myth itself [is] one of the modes of accomplishment of logos."[4] To clarify this relationship, Blumenberg proposes that the "work of myth" (*arbeit des mythos*) must be distinguished from the "work on myth" (*arbeit am mythos*). As Blumenberg's translator, Robert M. Wallace, explains, "The former refers to the original and essential function and accomplishment of myth as such; the latter to the ongoing reworking of inherited mythical materials, which is the only form and the only way in which we know myth."[5] The "work of myth" describes the process by which a mythic cosmos is constituted through inspired oracular discourse; the "work on myth" describes the process by which this discourse is received and mediated through reinscription, interpretation, and rationalization.[6] The distinction is deceptively simple, for, as Blumenberg notes, "Even the earliest items of myth that are accessible to us are already products of work on myth";[7] that is, any formulation of a myth into an oral or written text has already been shaped by the social forces that call forth a telling or retelling of the narrative.

In the case of the book of Revelation, one may see this process at work in the use of the stock symbols and plots derived from the literature of Judaic apocalypticism and the archaic combat myth of ancient Near Eastern cosmology. The author of Revelation did not invent its symbolic narrative ex nihilo, but employed devices that were already familiar to his audience. The myth itself is thus a product of the "work on myth" that adapts cosmological narratives to the needs of historical audiences, as well as the inspiration and proximate cause of the next succeeding generation of this work. Blumenberg's distinction serves a useful purpose for rhetorical analysis in that it allows critics to separate the original oracular and authoritative functions of myth from its subsequent expressions in interpretive argument and advocacy. This chapter, then, follows the pattern suggested by Blumenberg's dichotomy by first examining the text of Revelation, then proceeding to an analysis of the discourse of its interpretation. The symbolic images of the Christian myth of apocalypse will be analyzed both as potent aesthetic forms that promote certain experiences in readers and hearers, and as inventional resources that enable and constrain the arguments of interpreters applying the text to social and political situations.

It is beyond the scope of this study to attempt a complete symbolic or rhetorical analysis of the book of Revelation itself; my purpose is rather to focus on interpretive argument that invests the mythic narrative with social and political significance. This focus on interpretation nevertheless requires investigation of the structure and symbolism of Revelation, which, as Northrop Frye has said, provides "our grammar of apocalyptic imagery,"[8] defining and naming cultural images of the apocalypse. The drama of the Apocalypse provides a set of symbols that allows the interpreter and his or her audience to view historical events as parts of a cosmic pattern. Understanding the logic of Christian apocalypticism, therefore, requires attention to the elements of the original drama before turning to the discourse of interpretation that imposes a dramatic pattern onto historical time.

Tragedy and Comedy in the Drama of Apocalypse

The Greek word *apocalypse* literally means "revelation" in the sense of unveiling or uncovering. As a message to believers, the Apocalypse of John "unveils" a secret knowledge of the coming of the End; within the dramatic narrative, what is unveiled or revealed is the ultimate truth, *aleitheia*. The plot of Revelation represents the revelation of truth through the defeat of the powers of evil and falsehood; it depicts the plight of the community of believers undergoing suffering and persecution for their defense of the truth, the "companions in tribulation" of its author (1:9, KJV). The ultimate struggle is, of course, between God and "that serpent of old that led the whole world astray, whose name is Satan, or the Devil" (12:9); the vindication of the community of believers takes place in the context of this struggle's resolution. The problem of evil as symbolized by the suffering and persecution of righteous believers thus appears as a central theme of the apocalyptic myth. Hence, the book of Revelation may be characterized as a mythic theodicy, a symbolic legitimation of and explanation for the existence of evil in a divinely created cosmos.

The opening passage features two other prominent themes, which I have designated the topoi of authority and time. The first chapter functions to secure an authoritative foundation for the entire text by presenting a narrative of its origination from a divine source, and to establish a mood of urgent expectation: "This is the revelation given by God to Jesus Christ. It was given to him so that he might show his servants what must shortly happen. He made it known by sending his angel to his servant John. . . . Happy is the man who reads, and happy those who listen to the words of this prophecy and heed what is written in it. For the hour of fulfillment is near" (1:1–2). The prophetic ethos of the author is reinforced through a brief narration of the circumstances of his vision: "I, John, who share with you in the suffering and the sovereignity and the endurance which is ours in Jesus . . . was on the island called Patmos because I had preached God's word and borne my testimony to Jesus. It was on the Lord's day, and I was caught up by the Spirit; and behind me I heard a loud voice, like the sound of a trumpet" (1:9–10). The voice belongs to "one like a son of man [whose] voice was like the sound of rushing waters" (1:13, 15) who declares "I am the first and the last . . . and I hold the keys of Death and Death's domain" (1:17–18). This figure, traditionally identified as Jesus Christ, orders John to "write down . . . what you have seen, what is now, and what will be hereafter" (1:19). The text thus begins by promising its audiences a vision of the future, and assuring them of the divine source of this vision.

What follows is a complex sequence of epistles, visions, hymns, and exhortations that interrupt and recapitulate each other in a fashion that seems to defy coherent analysis but nevertheless forms a powerful artistic whole. Many biblical scholars have attempted to discern a single principle that governs the literary and formal composition of the Apocalypse.[9] Such efforts may well be in vain; for my purposes it can simply be noted that the complexity of Revelation has insured that generations of commentators, exegetes, and would-be prophets would never lack speculative possibilities. Since my concern is with the principal patterns or directions taken by such speculations, I will isolate elements of the text that have figured significantly in its later interpretations.

The theme of temporal urgency is related to another striking feature of Revelation, its radical dualism. The sense of historical crisis is intensified by a binary opposition of good and evil, forming a dialectic with no room for compromise. This is apparent in 3:15–16, where the messianic figure of the initial vision addresses a warning to the proud and boastful church of Laodicea: "I know all your ways; you are neither hot nor cold. How I wish you were either hot or cold! But because you are lukewarm . . . I will spit you out of my mouth." The audience is thus cautioned that there is no middle ground between God and the Devil. This basic polarity is multiplied in a variety of symmetrical plot elements; in the dialectical structure of the myth, each major symbol of good is parodied by a demonic counterpart. The divine figure of the first vision identifies himself as the One who "was dead and now I am alive for evermore" (1:18); he is associated with the redeeming Lamb which has "seven horns and seven eyes . . . [and] was slain" (5:6, 12), while the beast with seven heads and ten horns of chapter 13 "appeared to have received a death-blow; but the mortal wound was healed" (13:3). The followers of the Lamb receive a seal on their foreheads and express their devotion in a hymn (7:2–12). The followers of the great beast, Antichrist, are "branded with a mark on his right hand or forehead" (13:16) as they chant their devotion to his fearsome power. Antichrist's false kingdom is juxtaposed to the true millennial kingdom prophesied in 20:2–6, in which the martyrs who have refused homage to the beast will be restored to life and "shall be priests of God and of Christ, and shall reign with him for the thousand years" (20:6). The Great Whore, "mother of whores and of every obscenity on earth" (17:5) is identified with Babylon, "the great city that holds sway over the kings of the earth" (17:18); the vision of Babylon's fall is paralleled by the establishment of the new Jerusalem, which is seen "coming down out of heaven from God, made ready like a bride adorned for her husband" (21:2).

This basic dualistic pattern is formally reinforced by a second pattern based on the number seven. This number "was sacred among the various Semitic peoples, as well as among many other peoples," and is used in biblical literature to denote "completeness, perfection, consummation."[10] There are seven letters to the seven churches of Asia (chapters 2 and 3); seven seals on the book of the Lamb are opened (5:1–8: 1); seven angels blow seven trumpets (8:7–11, 15); seven angels visit the earth with plagues by pouring out seven vials of wrath (chapter 16). Each opening of a seal, each trumpet, each vial, advances the plot by providing another vision, another stage in the dialectic of good and evil. The seventh trumpet inaugurates a vision in which the demonic beast is depicted as ruling the earth and oppressing the saints by divine permission: "It was . . . allowed to wage war on God's people and to defeat them, and was granted authority over every tribe and people, language and nation" (13:7).

The grand dialectic of God and devil symbols is finally resolved in chapters 19 and 20, when the Lamb appears again in the guise of the rider on the white horse who is "called the Word of God" (19:13). The beast marshals his forces, "the kings of the earth and their armies" (19:19), is defeated by the heavenly army of the Lamb, and "thrown alive into a lake of fire" (19:20). Chapter 20 features the famous vision of the millennial kingdom:

> I saw an angel coming down from heaven. . . . He seized the dragon, that serpent of old, the Devil or Satan, and chained him up for a thousand years. so that he might seduce the nations no more until the thousand years were over. . . . [Then] I could see the souls of those who had been beheaded for the sake of God's word and their testimony in Jesus, those who had not worshipped the beast and its image or received its mark on forehead or hand. These came to life again and reigned with Christ for a thousand years. [20:1–5]

The millennial reign is concluded when Satan is allowed to escape from the abyss and make war upon the saints for the last time. Finally, however, he is defeated and cast into the lake of fire with the beast, "there to be tormented day and night for ever" (20:10). This ultimate defeat of the demonic forces is followed by the Last Judgment, in which the souls of all humanity are judged "upon the record of their deeds." Those "whose names were not to be found in the roll of the living" are cast into the lake of fire (20:12–15), while the elect enjoy eternity in the heavenly city, New Jerusalem. A voice from the the throne of God proclaims the long-awaited End of all suffering and the establishment of the divine order: "Now at last God has his dwelling among men. . . . He will wipe every tear from their eyes; there shall be an end to death, and to mourning and crying and pain; for the old order has passed away" (21:3–4). Finally, as if to caution against interpretations of the prophecy that ignore portions of the text, Revelation concludes with an injunction to all readers and hearers not to add or take away from its words under pain of divine punishment (22:18–19). The author repeats the promise of Jesus ("I am coming soon") and expresses his faith in its fulfillment: "Amen, come, Lord Jesus" (22:20).

This brief rendition of the complex narrative of the Apocalypse will suffice for the purposes of this analysis, since my aim is not to develop a complete understanding of Revelation itself but of the ways that others have understood and applied it. In proposing a dramatistic reading, I begin by noting that many scholars and commentators on this text have found the terminology of drama useful for describing its bipolar symbolism and plot structure, which features no less than God and the Devil, Christ and Antichrist, as its heroes and villains. Others have gone so far as to claim not only that the book has dramatic structure, but that it borrows its narrative devices from the cultic drama of ancient Greece. Thus, according to Elisabeth Schüssler Fiorenza, it possesses *"dramatis personae*, stage props, chorus, a plot, and a tragic-comic ending."[11] Critic John Wick Bowman argues that Revelation is structured as a drama featuring a prologue, seven acts with seven scenes, and an epilogue, and was deliberately patterned after the Greco-Roman theater of its time.[12]

Whether or not the evidence for such a structure is conclusive, textual evidence from the book itself points to the conclusion that Revelation was originally intended to be read aloud in a public, liturgical setting: "Happy is the man who reads, and happy those who listen to the words of this prophecy" (1:3); and biblical scholars are agreed that the customs of early Christian worship involved the reading aloud of sacred texts before a collective audience.[13] Critics are thus justified in viewing the text of Revelation as providing an opportunity for a performative enactment of its cosmic drama. However, few scholars have gone beyond this very basic application of dramatism to the text of Revelation. An exception is Adela Yarbro Collins, who attempts to describe the effect of the text on its audience by applying Aristotle's theory of tragic catharsis:

> There is a certain analogy between Aristotle's explanation of the function of Greek tragedy and the function of Revelation. In each case certain emotions are aroused and then a catharsis of those emotions is achieved. Tragedy manipulates the emotions of fear and pity; Revelation, primarily fear and resentment. [In tragedy] the emotions of the audience are purged in the sense that their feelings of fear and pity are intensified and given objective expression. The feelings are thus brought to consciousness and become less threatening.
>
> Revelation functions in a similar way. Fear of Roman power is evoked or intensified. In various symbolic narratives, conflicts are described, each of which is a paradigm of the hearer's situation. . . . [T]he projection of the conflict onto the cosmic screen . . . is cathartic in the sense that it clarifies and objectifies the conflict. Fearful feelings are vented by the very act of expressing them.[14]

I agree with the substance of this insight, but, following Schüssler Fiorenza's observation that the plot of Revelation borrows from comedy as well as tragedy, I argue that Collins's thesis needs to be expanded to account for the presence of comic elements in the eschatological narrative. Aristotle's prescriptions on tragic and comic emplotment indicates the difficulties that attend any simplistic classification:

> The perfect [tragic] plot . . . must have a single, and not (as some tell us) a double issue; the change in the hero's fortunes must be not from misery to happiness, but on the contrary from happiness to misery. . . . The critics, therefore, are wrong who blame Euripides for taking this line in his tragedies, and giving many of them an unhappy ending. It is, as we have said, the right line to take. The best proof is this: such plays, properly worked out, are seen to be the most truly tragic. . . . After this comes the construction of Plot which some rank first, one with a double story . . . and an opposite issue for the good and the bad personages. It is ranked as first only through the weakness of the audiences; the poets merely follow their public, writing as its wishes dictate. But the pleasure here is not that of Tragedy. It belongs rather to Comedy.[15]

If the book of Revelation is to be interpreted as drama according to Aristotle's poetic theory, it is patently evident that its plot structure must be classified as comic. For Aristotle, the mark of true tragedy is an unhappy ending, a downward movement from happiness to misery. The heroes of the Apocalypse, the martyrs and saints who reign with Christ in the millennial kingdom, are distinctly comic in the sense that their plot motion is upward rather than downward; they are brought from the misery of the beast's persecution to the happiness of the New Jerusalem. Northrop Frye argues that the formulas of classical Roman comedy exhibit "the same *structure* as the central Christian myth itself, with its divine son appeasing the wrath of a father and redeeming what is at once a society and a bride."[16]

However, the happy ending is not the whole story. The narrative of Revelation offers a double plot, with "an opposite issue for the good and the bad personages," in which the virtuous are rewarded and the wicked punished. According to Aristotle, this plot is often misunderstood as tragic, but properly belongs to comedy. The heavenly triumph of the saints is indeed, then, a comic conclusion; but it is perpetually counterbalanced by the tragic fate of the wicked, doomed to a hellish eternal punishment where "the devouring worm never dies and the fire is not quenched" (Mark 9:44). As John Dominic Crossan notes, the fact that the "world of resurrection is itself divided into Hell and Heaven . . . means that tragedy and comedy are simply relocated elsewhere and frozen there into everlasting and unchanging attitudes."[17] From this perspective, the cosmic drama of the Apocalypse is not simply tragic *or* comic; it includes both tragedy and comedy without being bound by the generic demands of either form, depicting a future that is catastrophic for some and blissful for others. If some interpreters have read the drama as primarily tragic, this is because images of the four horsemen, the marauding beast, and the fall of Babylon remain in many reader's minds long after the image of the New Jerusalem has faded away. So also Dante's divine *commedia* is chiefly remembered for its depiction of Hell, while Milton's Satan remains a memorable presence that for many readers overshadows his depiction of Paradise. In this way, the tragic elements of a narrative can eclipse the comic, while both remain as resources for interpretation. Depending on whether an interpreter emphasizes its catastrophic or its triumphalist elements, the drama of Revelation can appear as tragic or comic, but it can never be reduced to either of these.[18]

Burke's conception of the tragic and comic "frames of acceptance," amplified by Susanne Langer's description of the "rhythms" of tragedy and comedy, provide further insights that can clarify understanding of the myriad forms of millennial discourse. In *Attitudes toward History*, Burke observes that frames of acceptance and rejection function as symbolic theodicies. The impulse to express human experience in the form of tragic or comic narratives, he argues, "starts from the problem of evil. In the face of anguish, injustice, disease and death one . . . constructs his notion of the universe or history, and shapes attitudes in keeping."[19] Langer argues that drama exhibits organic form "by creating the semblance of a history, and composing its elements into a rhythmic single structure."[20] The book of Revelation represents the conclusion of human and cosmic history in a mythic drama. If, as Collins, Fiorenza, and others have argued, this drama utilizes elements of tragedy and comedy, one may hypothesize that an audience's view of historical time and human agency will be shaped by these "frames of acceptance" that are found within the dramatic representation of history as myth.

In his essay "Myth, Poetry, and Philosophy" Burke delineates the difference between the tragic and comic frames, arguing that tragedy and comedy differ from each other in their depiction of time, human action, and agency. Burke discusses "two major ways of distinguishing between comedy and tragedy": the test of character, by which "Tragic characters are said to be 'better' than ordinary people, comic characters 'worse' "; and the test of emplotment, by which "Comedy has a plot that builds toward a 'happy' ending, tragedy towards an 'unhappy' ending."[21] The depiction of dramatic character is rhetorical to the extent that the depiction of character offers "equipment for living" to an audience which takes the protagonists of the narrative as models. Burke's discussion of emplotment observes that tragic and comic dramas each resort to differing mechanisms of redemption in their respective narrative constructions. As Hugh Dalziel Duncan puts it, "The difference between tragedy and comedy is not so much in tragedy's 'seriousness' concerning evil, for comedy is equally serious; it is rather in the form of exposure and the principles invoked to resolve incongruities."[22] Tragedy conceives of evil in terms of guilt; its mechanism of redemption is victimage, its plot moves inexorably toward sacrifice and the "cult of the kill." Comedy conceives of evil not as guilt, but as error; its mechanism of redemption is recognition rather than victimage, and its plot moves not toward sacrifice but to the exposure of fallibility. The comic plot, according to Langer, portrays destiny as Fortune, while the tragic plot conceives of destiny as Fate. When destiny is conceived as Fortune, time is open-ended, allowing for the possibility of change, while the tragic conception of Fate promotes a view of time and human action as closed and "predetermined."[23] The story of the tragic drama, ordained by Fate (or, in Burke's terminology, the "Iron Law of History"[24]) is "the restoration of the great moral order through suffering."[25] The story of the comic drama restores the moral order by exposing the foolishness of pretension and vanity. The rhythm of comedy is "episodic"; the crisis of the comic drama is "the upset and recovery of the protagonist's equilibrium."[26] The rhythm of tragedy is progressive and "cadential"; the crisis of the tragic drama "is always the turn toward an absolute close."[27]

I wish to make clear that in applying Langer, Burke, and Duncan's theories of tragedy and comedy to the Christian apocalyptic myth my purpose is not simply to superimpose the forms of Greek drama onto a cultural tradition that operated under a very different set of assumptions (though the argument for the influence of Greco-Roman dramatic forms has been advanced by other scholars[28]). Viewing tragedy and comedy in Burkean terms as "frames of acceptance," I conceive them as ideal types that can be found in dramatic narratives across cultures. In the words of Robert Martin, tragedy and comedy are here considered not as "forms of literature or genres, but [as] formulations of modes of thought, attitudes toward the world, ways of coming to terms with the meaning of its triumphs and vicissitudes."[29]

Here the recent scholarship on the rhetoric of temporality provides an opportunity for critics to move beyond generic classification. Viewing the book of Revelation as an example of epochal rhetoric requires attention to the discursive construction of temporality through the rhythms of drama. The critical questions here are: How does the text *as drama* constitute an epoch for its audiences? What perceptions and experiences of temporality do different readings of the text enable and constrain for different audiences? And how may critics account for the diversity of these perceptions and experiences? I now turn to the history of apocalyptic interpretation to discover how the book of Revelation has shaped its audiences' perceptions of history according to the tragic and comic rhythms. As I shall demonstrate, the interpretative traditions that surround the Apocalypse have tended to emphasize elements of either tragedy or comedy in the eschatological narrative, and thereby to adopt the perspectives of the tragic and comic frames in their constructions of historical time.

The intertwining of the themes of catastrophe and redemption is the principal focus of John Gager's analysis of the function of Revelation in the earliest Christian communities. Finding a binary pattern of alternating symbols of good and evil, hope and despair, he argues that the myth has a therapeutic function akin to that of psychoanalysis: "Just as the therapeutic situation is the machine through which the patient comes to experience the past as present, so the myth is the machine through which the believing community comes to experience the future as present."[30] Symbols of despair alternate with symbols of hope; the vision of the beast raging and making war against the saints is followed by the saints singing praises to the Lamb enthroned on Zion. The text thus oscillates between terror and triumph until the final destruction of Satan and descent of the New Jerusalem collapses the dialectic. Gager's reading of the Apocalypse is essentially identical to Collins' dramatic interpretation; both rely on a medical metaphor (therapy on the one hand, catharsis or purgation on the other). The voices of the great angel announcing "fallen, fallen is Babylon the great" (18:2) and of the "great multitude" that speaks with "mighty thunderings" to announce that "the Lord God omnipotent reigneth" (19:6, KJV), speak in a tense that may be described as the prophetic present; the audience experiences the "not yet" as "now," however fleetingly, in the mimetic process that enacts the vision as it proclaims it. For Gager, the text becomes "a machine for transcending time."[31]

Elisabeth Schüssler Fiorenza dissents strongly from Gager's and Collins's interpretations, arguing that transcending time was not the author's purpose: "The author does not encourage the consistent resistance . . . of Christians by eliminating the difference in time between the present and the eschatological future. Instead, he stresses that Christians do not yet actively exercise their kingship. Eschatological salvation is near but not yet present. . . . He speaks of future salvation for the sake of exhortation."[32] Fiorenza's reading here is not consistent with her earlier insight into the dramatic devices and structures employed in Revelation. Read in this way, the text becomes a message of prediction and exhortation: stand fast, the End is near and your reward will be great. This may or may not be entirely consistent with the author's intention, but a dramatistic analysis must consider not only authorial purpose, but also the audience's aesthetic encounter with the text as performed. The drama of Apocalypse has moved its audiences throughout history to the emotions of hope and despair with vivid imagery and symbols of ultimate good and evil. In its mimetic representation of the reign and defeat of the beast and the establishment of God's kingdom, the text must inevitably enact the Apocalypse it predicts.[33] The reader's fear while marveling at the vivid symbolism of the great beast, the emotions of hope and pride that follow from the hearer's identification with the saints rejoicing in millennial bliss, endow these symbols with an emotional reality that is experienced as present for the audience. The dramatic relief that the audience feels at seeing the worm cast into the everlasting fire can only appear to believers as a foretaste of millennial bliss. To say that time is transcended through this aesthetic experience of the text is not to claim that the distinction between present and future is eliminated permanently; the millennial community's annihilation of time is constantly arrested by contact with what is commonly called the "real world," where hunger, labor, and continued oppression (whether material or rhetorical) serve notice that the millennium has not yet arrived. Consequently, the history of interpretation features a continual dialectic between the Now and the Not-yet, between the text read as prediction and experienced as enactment.

Within the predictive reading of the text, the pattern of sevens readily lends itself to historical periodization in the tragic mode. Just as the seven trumpets, seal openings, and vials of wrath structure the unfolding plot of the drama, these elements provide rich material for predictive calculation by those disposed to read the drama as historical prophecy. The divine number seven represents closure and completion; and from the early church fathers to the Puritans, numerous divines have devoted great argumentative effort to discovering whether or not the seventh vial of wrath had been poured, or what historical events corresponded to the sounding of the seventh trumpet, in order to fix their own position in relation to history's close.[34] The exegetical possibilities are multiplied when another structural feature of the book is taken into account: the visions that make up the Apocalypse are not purely sequential, but seem at times to recapitulate each other, providing different symbolic representations of the same events. Thus the woman clothed with the sun flees from the wrath of the beast into the wilderness for "twelve hundred and sixty days" (12:6), which period is seemingly equivalent to the forty-two months of the beast's reign in the vision that follows (13:5). The calculations grow even more complex when other prophecies of the Old and New Testament are considered: the visions of Daniel and Ezekiel, the "little apocalypse" of Matthew 24, and the Pauline epistles (especially Thessalonians), all provide further prophetic material on the Last Days that must be integrated into the narrative of the End. Taken together, these materials have encouraged successive generations of biblical scholars and would-be prophets to construct historical periodizations that combine, in endlessly inventive ways, the seventy weeks of Daniel, the forty-two months of the beast, the seven vials and trumpets, and other numbers and figures.

The structure of such historical periodization is tragic in that it assumes a predestined sequence of catastrophes announced by cosmic signs, a temporal system that is both linear and closed. The text's radical dualism further underlines its tragic structure: the symbolism of the text admits no ambiguity in its figures of good and evil, the Lamb and the beast, the Great Whore and the Bride of Christ. The dragon and his servants are not redeemed, but are "thrown alive into the lake of fire with its sulphurous flames" (19:20), there "to be tormented day and night for ever" (20:10). Such an absolute separation between good and evil in the cosmic drama directs the plot to the ultimate dialectic of victimage. The sacrifice of the perfect victim, the Lamb, dialectically enables the transformation of victimage into power with the defeat and slaughter of the beast. When such a dramatic pattern is applied to the social world, the consequences can indeed be tragic. Absolute truth inspires absolute commitments; the valorization of martyrdom leads, by the Iron Law of history, toward war and sacrifice. A classic example of such a trajectory can be seen in Julia Ward Howe's famous "Battle Hymn of the Republic," which explicitly invoked the mythic vision of Revelation and offered Americans a tragic frame for understanding the Civil War:

> Mine eyes have seen the glory of the coming of the Lord,
> He is trampling out the vineyard where the grapes of wrath are stored,
> He hath loosed the fateful lightning of His terrible swift sword,
> His truth is marching on.
>
> I have read a fiery gospel writ in burnished rows of steel:
> "As ye deal with My contemners, so with you My grace shall deal";
> Let the Hero, born of woman, crush the serpent with His heel,
> Since God is marching on.

Revelation thus appears to promote an understanding of history as tragic drama.

This understanding is, however, continually balanced by a contrapuntal comic theme that reasserts itself in the aesthetic and hortatory functioning of the text. The dialectic between the interpretation of the text as historical prediction and the aesthetic experience of its resolution of contradictions is integrally related to tragic and comic readings of the mythic drama. When the text is read as predictive, it structures history as a tragic drama and proposes a cathartic ending in the (immediate) future. Insofar as audiences experience catharsis through the mimetic representation of this future, however, the experience of time through the text takes on the episodic structure of comedy; the drama of the end is continually re-enacted and experienced in the present while the End itself is delayed. Revelation also takes on comic aspects when read as an exhortation to the community of saints to stand firm and resist the attacks of the beast; for exhortation implies the possibility of choice and change. Initially, this exhortation may urge the believers to hold on just a little bit longer till the tragic conclusion (which is nevertheless comic in its promise to "wipe every tear from their eyes"—21:4); with the passage of time and ongoing struggles of the millennial community in the world, however, exhortation will take a definite turn to the comic frame by way of allegorical and typological interpretation. The longer the End delays, the more its continual re-enactment will appear as an allegory of the church's struggle against its enemies in all ages.

This allegorical understanding of prophecy developed out of necessity in the centuries after the Apocalypse was produced. To the original audience, the symbols of the beast and the whore of Babylon were clearly identified with the imperial cult and commercial power of the Roman empire: "The seven heads [of the beast] are seven hills, on which the woman sits (17:9). . . . The woman you saw is the great city that holds sway over the kings of the earth" (17:18). As noted in chapter 2, the conversion of Constantine and the adoption of Christianity as the official religion of the empire made this identification untenable; some new understanding of the text was called for that depoliticized the prophecy. The former Antichrist was no longer persecuting Christians; instead, at the behest of bishops, the imperial power was turned toward the enforcement of orthodoxy in the church. In these circumstances, Origen and the patristic authors of the Alexandrian school developed and perfected new allegorical modes of interpretation that gained widespread acceptance.[35] One of the most important influences in the turn away from literal interpretation was Tyconius' influential *Commentary* on Revelation (circa 385). As McGinn notes, Tyconius offered a "moral and typological" interpretation of prophecy in which "apocalyptic symbolism is . . . understood in terms of the constant struggle between the forces of good and evil within the Church in every age," and the Antichrist comes to symbolize "the historical continuum of those who have attacked true religion throughout history."[36]

Whatever one may say about the validity of this interpretation, there is no doubt that it was well suited to the Rome of the Christian emperors. Apart from the shift in political context, the turn toward allegorical and typological interpretation was necessitated by the fact that Christianity's rhetorical epoch as originally constituted was unstable, in that an epoch defined with reference to its imminent End could not be forever sustained in the face of this End's postponement. Christians were forced to reimagine the structure of history in order to include a temporal space for the church's agency. When the tragic drama of history fails to make its turn toward the absolute close, the rhythm of comedy, in which life must go on subject to a divine will experienced as fortune, reasserts itself.

2. Augustine's Anti-apocalyptic Eschatology

The turn toward a comic understanding of prophecy and history is most brilliantly exemplified in Augustine's *The City of God*, which did more than any other single text to articulate a viable historical stance for the Christian church following the apparent failure of its initial understanding of time and history. Augustine here presents what might be called an anti-apocalyptic eschatology. His theological system, which was strongly influenced by Tyconius' moral and typological exegesis, allowed the essentially tragic nature of the Christian view of history by acknowledging that the second coming and Last Judgment would take place according to prophecy at some unspecified time in the future; but he used passages from other books in the New Testament to undercut the predictive use of Revelation and other texts. Augustine's rhetorical training is evident in his masterful use of humor to argue against the tragic exegetes:

> [T]he Scripture says that 'he [Jesus] will kill him [Antichrist] with the breath of his mouth and annihilate him by the splendour of his coming' (2 Thessalonians 2:8). Here the usual question is, 'When will this happen?' But the question is completely ill-timed. For had it been in our interest to know this, who could have been a better informant than the master, God himself, when the disciples asked him? For they did not keep silent about it with him, but put the question to him in person, 'Lord, is this the time when you are going to restore the sovereignty to Israel?' But he replied, 'It is not for you to know the times which the Father has reserved to his own control' (Acts 1:6). Now in fact they had not asked about the hour or the day or the year, but about the time, when they were given this answer. It is in vain, therefore, that we try to reckon and put a limit to the number of years that remain for this world, since we hear from the mouth of the Truth that it is not for us to know this.... [T]o all those who make ... calculations on this subject comes the command, 'Relax your fingers, and give them a rest.' And it comes from him who says, 'It is not for you to know the times, which the Father has under his control.'[37]

Augustine devotes the twentieth book of *The City of God* to a lengthy discussion of the Last Judgment and the millennial prophecy of Revelation. This discussion exhibits a provisionally comic view of destiny as Fortune in chapter 2, entitled "The diversity of human fortunes. God's judgment not absent, but untraceable." The inscrutability of God's purposes will not last forever: on the day of judgment "no room will be left... for the ignorant complaint that asks why this unjust man is happy and that just man unhappy."[38] Until that time, however, we must learn to live with a destiny that appears in the guise of fortune: "In our present situation, however, we are learning to bear with equanimity the ills that even good men suffer."[39] In chapter 9, Augustine interprets the millennial prophecy of Revelation 20 as an allegorical representation of the historical church:

> In the meantime, while the Devil is bound for a thousand years, the saints reign with Christ, also for a thousand years; which are without doubt to be taken in the same sense, and as denoting the same period, that is, the period beginning with Christ's first coming. We can certainly rule out any reference to that kingdom which he is to speak of at the end of the world, in the words, 'Come, you that have my father's blessing, take posesssion of the kingdom prepared for you' (Matthew 25:34); and so, even now, although in some other and far inferior way, his saints must be reigning with him.[40]

The early Christians who awaited the promised second coming while suffering from the persecution of the Roman beast would no doubt have been surprised to find that according to the text's true meaning, they already reigned on earth with Christ. Such an allegorical interpretation must rest on the comic frame since it requires a recognition not only that the saints' reign is not entirely established, but that the church itself contains fallible souls still subject to sin and error:

> So then we must understand the kingdom of heaven in one sense as a kingdom in which both are included, the man who breaks what he teaches, and the man who practices it, though one is the least and the other is great in the kingdom, while in another sense it is a kingdom into which there enters only the man who practices what he teaches. Thus where both are to be found we have the Church as it now is; but where only the one kind will be found, there is the Church as it will be. . . . It follows that the Church even now is the kingdom of Christ and the kingdom of heaven. And so even now his saints reign with him, though not in the same way as they will then reign; and yet the tares do not reign with him, although they are growing in the Church side by side with the wheat.[41]

The radical dualism of the original mythic narrative is thus undercut. Good and evil are no longer so distinct; God's will for the time being is inscrutable, making it difficult to distinguish the good guys from the bad. The conflict between good and evil, in this allegorical mode of interpretation, no longer appears as a predestined final struggle. Rather, in Augustine's eschatology the conflict episodically reappears as ongoing and internal: "It is therefore of this kingdom at war, in which conflict still rages with the enemy, that the Apocalypse is speaking in the passage we are considering. In this kingdom sometimes there is fighting against vices that attack us, though sometimes they submit to being ruled."[42] The Christian's struggle against the beast is thus not solely an external battle against the political agents of Satan, but also an internal battle against vice. Augustine cautions against ignoring the beast in ourselves and projecting absolute evil onto the tragic scapegoat: he uses an argument of authorial intent to this effect when he quotes the first epistle of John (thought by the early Christians to be identical to the author of the Apocalypse): "If we say that we are without sin, we are fooling ourselves and we are remote from the truth" (1 Jn. 1:8).[43]

This interpretation is consistent with what I have defined (following Burke and Langer) as the comic understanding of time, history, and human agency. It is true that Augustine's system retains a tragic view of history in that cosmic redemption still depends on the sacrifice of Christ, who will return in the future to judge the living and the dead; but the definition of this future as part of the absolutely unknowable divine will, and the prohibition against calculating the times of the End, effectively impose a comic substructure onto our experience of history as tragedy. Apocalyptic discourse in the tragic mode purports to reveal the divine plan of history; in Augustine's comic reading, the ultimate features of the divine plan remain inscrutable to believers and nonbelievers alike. The universal human ignorance regarding the time of the End means that disasters and calamities in the natural and social realms take on a different character. If Christians are forbidden to use their collective experiences of evil to indicate a position on the cosmic time line, then these experiences can only be seen as periodic setbacks to the progress of the church. Augustine's interpretation of the conventional signs of imminent Judgment—wars, apostasy, earthquakes, and eclipses—treats these events as recurrent and normative. Replying to an inquiry from a fellow bishop as to the meaning of certain prophecies, Augustine argues in his 199th letter that the traditional signs are unreliable guides because of their omnipresence throughout history:

> Certainly, the Apostle [Paul] said . . . that in the last days shall come on savage times . . . and describes what they will be like, saying: 'Men shall be lovers of themselves, lovers of money, haughty, proud, blasphemous, disobedient to parents, ungrateful, wicked, irreligious, without affection, slanderers, incontinent, unmerciful, without kindness, traitors, stubborn, blind, lovers of pleasures more than of God, having an appearance of godliness but denying the power thereof.' I wonder if such men have ever been lacking. . . . As to wars, when has not the earth been scourged by them at different periods and places?[44]

In the tragic periodization of history, calamities appear as part of a predetermined sequence that will culminate in the reign of Antichrist, whose final defeat will be followed by the millennial kingdom. In Augustine's provisionally comic view of history,[45] calamities become episodes, recurrent events that all human communities must face without recourse to an apocalyptic understanding, while the millennial kingdom becomes an obscure allegory of the church in the present age. Augustine explicitly invokes the comic perspective when he cautions readers to be skeptical in evaluating apocalyptic claims, so that "when we fall into a panic over present happenings as if they were the ultimate and extreme of all things, we may not be laughed at by those who have read of more and worse things in the history of the world."[46] The comic interpretation of the Apocalypse thus neutralizes its predictive function. What remains is the exhortation to the saintly life and the aesthetic functioning of the text experienced as allegory. Augustine's reading of the Apocalypse illustrates the comic possibilities that can be extracted from a narrative that most critics perceive as tragic. This theme will be expanded upon before this study is concluded; my purpose now is to examine the place and structure of apocalyptic argument within the dramatistic frames of tragedy and comedy.

The Topoi of Eschatology and the Psychology of Form

Building on previous scholarship, this chapter has considered the myth of Apocalypse as a dramatic narrative that exhibits features of both tragedy and comedy. The study of the apocalyptic narrative was expanded to include an examination of the discourse of apocalyptic interpretation as enactments of the tragic and comic frames. I argued that interpretations that read the text as literally predictive embody the assumptions of the tragic frame by emphasizing predetermination and catastophe. With the passage of time, however, the aesthetic function of the text undermines its predictive function, and a comic substructure of interpretation springs up that employs allegorical (rather than literal) arguments to make the apocalyptic symbols relevant to the text's historical audience.

Since the structures of tragedy and comedy differ in their temporal rhythms, their depictions of human agency, and their understandings of time, evil, and history, it should be evident that apocalyptic interpretation through the tragic and comic frames of reference will have major consequences for an audience's self-understanding. The structuring of time and history, the definition of evil, and the choice of mechanisms of redemption, according to the tragic and comic modes, in effect sets the stage for the drama that audiences seek to enact in their histories. Subsequent chapters will show how the tragic and comic readings of the Apocalypse have produced differing stances in public controversy and varieties of social and political action. The final task of this chapter is to elaborate an analytic framework for the study of apocalyptic discourse as public argument: to show what claims are made, what questions are asked, and what possible answers can be given, by rhetors and audiences seeking to develop and apply their understanding of the myths of the End, and to examine the dramatic functions of argument itself within the tragic and comic frames.

I have argued that time is the key concept in human efforts to understand and resolve the problem of evil through narrative, and that the eschatological narrative of the Apocalypse represents a particular discursive structuring of temporality intended to solve this problem. To move from the text to the history of its interpretation is to move from narrative to argument, from the telling of a story to arguing about its meaning. My goal here is to show that this argument has been conducted according to certain identifiable forms that can be classified as topical. Up to this point I have considered the topical logic of eschatology and apocalypse as narrative and dramatic in form. Now I wish to extend this notion of topical logic by examining how argument is used to derive apocalypticism from eschatology. This requires that the topoi be considered not only as recurring themes or commonplaces within the mythic narrative, but also as certain lines of argument or characteristic patterns that elaborate upon the original themes or narrative propositions of eschatology. If argument itself is viewed as a kind of performance, the forms of discourse must necessarily be shaped by the interaction of rhetor and audience as well as by the play of symbols within the eschatological narrative itself. Kenneth Burke's essay "Psychology and Form," which has already been invoked to explain the narrative development of eschatology from cosmogony, is equally applicable to the argumentative definition of topical form. Burke defines form as "the creation of an appetite in the mind of the auditor, and the adequate satisfaction of that appetite."[47] Using this audience-centered definition, the topical form of an argument can be understood as developing in the process of interaction between rhetor and audience. A rhetor makes a particular claim (concerning recurring issues or themes) that evokes an audience response. From the claim certain appetites or expectations develop that give rise to questions that are then answered by the rhetor; the audience in turn responds to these responses according to its satisfaction or dissatisfaction with the rhetor's ability to meet the expectations or fulfill the appetites that the discourse has aroused. A more detailed examination of apocalyptic argument will illustrate this functioning of topical argument according to the psychology of form.

This study argues that the essential claim of apocalyptic argument can be reduced to the statement: "The world is coming to an end." Or, as the white-robed and bearded prophet of countless cartoon caricatures has claimed on his picket sign, "The End is near." What are the possible ranges of audience response to this claim? What expectations does it create in the mind of the auditor that the rhetor must satisfy if the discourse is to persuade?

At the skeptical end of the range of audience responses to the claim "The End is near" can be found ridicule; at the credulous or dogmatic end of this range, one can at least imagine an immediate, uncritical acceptance of the claim that would result in experiences of both fear and hope, resulting perhaps in a conversion experience. These responses, however, only define the extremes: located in the middle range are audiences that are willing to entertain the hypothesis but are not yet committed to it. Such an audience will probably respond by posing the questions "How do you know?" and "When?"—if only to test the claim. The speaker must have convincing replies to these questions if he or she is to win the audience's assent.

The first response, the query "How do you know?" was designated in the previous chapter as the topos of authority. The rhetor is making a predictive claim and must establish his or her credentials to do so. The credentials of the prophet are generally established through direct experience of the divine: the one who sees a vision and can persuade others of its authenticity is granted a measure of predictive authority. In the increasingly rational culture of later Protestantism, apocalyptic rhetors who rested their claims on interpretation of canonical prophecy rather than on the charismatic authority of a personal prophetic revelation had an argumentative burden of justifying their exegetical methods. To put it another way, such rhetors had to demonstrate the rationality of their interpretation. A typical strategy for solving this problem may be seen in the cases of William Miller and Hal Lindsey (analyzed in detail in chapters 4 through 8). These authors appeal to "common sense" to support their reading of scripture, on the assumption that the meaning of the sacred text is clearly visible to all who read it by the light of faith. Each offers variations of a strategy that may be termed the "self-effacing interpreter." Miller's innovation resided in his skill in systematically interpreting prophecy by referring to other canonical statements, expressed in the principle that "Scripture is its own expositor." This gave his interpretations an apparently divine sanction: if Scripture was its own expositor, the student of Bible prophecy who was able to discover the correct scriptural exposition of a prophecy could claim that a particular interpretation was not the product of fallible human reasoning but of divine inspiration. In much the same fashion, Lindsey appeals to what he calls "the golden rule of interpretation": "When the plain sense of Scripture makes common sense, seek no other sense; therefore, take every word at its primary, ordinary, usual, literal meaning unless the facts of the immediate context, studied in the light of related passages and axiomatic and fundamental truths, indicate clearly otherwise."[48] Thus, through appeals to the literal meaning of Scripture, and to prior assumptions or "axiomatic" truths that the speaker shares with the audience, the interpreter's role is obscured.

The strategy of the self-effacing interpreter relies upon an assumption that Miller shared with Lindsey, his modern counterpart: that the language of Scripture functions as a coded message to Christians that requires deciphering rather than true interpretation. In cases where the language of Scripture is clearly figurative, and the deciphering of the text could not easily be accomplished through faith and common sense, both Miller and Lindsey tended to bolster their arguments by claiming that they had merely followed interpretive rules laid down by traditional authorities. The case studies examined in the next chapters will illustrate their justifications of interpretive method in more detail. Here I will only note that though such justification does constitute an argumentative burden of proof for the apocalyptic rhetor, the task may be made easier by audiences disposed to suspend disbelief if only to see what exciting predictions or insights into current events might be uncovered through the use of a new method. I recall in particular a lecture at a conference of apocalyptic believers held in Anaheim, California, in December of 1986, in which a certain J. R. Church exposed the "Hidden Prophecies in the Psalms." His interpretive method for making sense of the Psalms—texts not obviously prophetic in nature—was to identify the number of each psalm as indicating a year. Thus, Psalm 86 was said to reveal the secret history of the year 1986, Psalm 87 indicated what was to come in 1987, and so forth. The audience seemed quite willing to allow the method of interpretation, almost as a kind of poetic conceit—notwithstanding the objection raised by one member of the audience that there are 150 psalms, and that a calendrical interpretation of their sequence would have the effect of extending time at least fifty years beyond the End predicted before the year 2000!

If the authority claims of the rhetor are granted by the auditors of the discourse, then a second response to the original claim, the End is near, becomes manifest. This can also take the form of a question: "When?" In making a predictive claim, the prophet or interpreter of prophecy in effect promises a knowledge not hitherto available. This knowledge consists precisely of the proximity of the divine fulfill-ment. If the claim is to be accepted, the audience's natural curiosity will result in a demand for some evidence of this proximity, which can only be furnished by making the date of prophetic fulfillment specific, or at least by specifying a certain temporal latitude in which the prophesied events will take place. It will readily be seen that the proposed date or schedule for the End cannot be too immediate, since this would place the prediction in danger of disconfirmation by external events.[49] On the other hand, if a rhetor predicts an End to occur in centuries or even decades, the predictions will lack saliency for the audience and hence will attract little attention.

The psychology of the apocalyptic audience can be seen in the scriptural account of the disciples who, motivated by fear, fascination, hope, and curiosity, pose the question to Jesus: "Tell us . . . when will this happen? And what will be the signal for . . . the end of the age?" (Mt. 24:3) Jesus' answer to the disciples' question is a curious one. The passage that follows, known as the "little apocalypse," offers a series of cryptic pronouncements and predictions that have spurred generations of readers and interpreters in their attempts to correlate apocalyptic timetables to current events. "For nation will make war upon nation, kingdom upon kingdom; there will be famines and earthquakes in many places. With all these things the birth-pangs of the new age begin" (Mt. 24:7–8). These predictions are rendered immediate to the audience with the controversial statement, "I tell you this: the present generation shall live to see it all" (Mt. 24:34). However, this concrete prediction is immediately qualified by a phrase that presents one of the most significant scriptural limitations on the rhetor's tendency toward date specificity. In Matthew 24:36, Jesus himself claims ignorance of the exact time: "But about that day and hour no one knows, not even the angels in heaven, not even the Son; only the Father." This text functions as an obstacle that all apocalyptic rhetors must overcome when speaking to knowledgeable audiences.

The apocalyptic tradition is full of ingenious solutions to the difficulties pre-sented by this and similar texts. One common strategy can be described as a literal interpretation of the text that qualifies the explicit unknowability of the date. Thus, interpreting literally, the Millerites argued that Jesus' words forbid calculations of the *day* or *hour*, but not the *year*. A modern apocalyptic rhetor, Edgar Whisenant, echoes this argument: "In looking at this statement [Mt. 24:36], you can easily see that it is impossible to know the exact day and hour of the Lord Jesus' return. . . . However, this does not preclude or prevent the faithful from knowing the year, the month, and the week of the Lord's return."[50] Such arguments indicate that the ingenuity of apocalyptic rhetors is sufficient to overcome what would seem to be an explicit scriptural prohibition of calculating the time of the End. Subsequent chapters will show how the Millerites and Hal Lindsey overcame the difficulties presented by this prohibition. Finally, as Lindsey's case will illustrate, the text can be turned to the advantage of the apocalyptic rhetor, in that it provides support for the attempt to resist the pressure of audience expectations and escape the perils of specific prediction.

In *The Late Great Planet Earth*, Lindsey interprets Jesus' statement regarding "the present generation" as referring not to the time of the first Christians, but to "the generation that would see the signs" predicted by Jesus. He therefore anticipates the occurrence of the End within one generation (which he states is approximately forty years) of the founding of the state of Israel, the "sign" that sets his prophetic timetable in motion.[51] A generation would seem to be the widest temporal horizon that a prophet or an interpreter of prophecy can establish for the fulfillment of a prediction while still holding the audience's attention, for the simple reason that people must believe that they will be on hand to see the prediction confirmed or they will lose interest. Even within the temporal framework of a generation, however, the impulse of the audience of believers will always be to try to fill in the blanks, to peer behind the veil. The claim of new or newly available knowledge of the End arouses curiosity about the course of history in the immediate future. If the rhetor predicts a temporal horizon for prophetic fulfillment that is sufficiently wide, disconfirmation may be postponed or made difficult; but, in this case, the discourse (to the degree that it is persuasive) piques the audience's curiosity without satisfying it. If the preacher will not supply dates specific enough to satisfy the audience, the audience will often try to supply them for themselves.

The tendency to set specific dates for the End of the world thus appears not simply as a sensationalist, attention-getting tactic, but as the natural functioning of the psychology of the audience with respect to the topos of time. If the claim that the End is near is accepted (whether absolutely or provisionally), the audience's natural curiosity will cause it to expect a prediction with some degree of specificity and proximity. The rhetor's latitude, or range of inventional choices for meeting audience expectations, is limited on the one hand by the amount of time necessary to gain followers and a public forum for one's message, and on the other hand by the lifespan of the immediate audience. The date proposed can therefore be near or far (though not too far) and more or less specific. If a day, month, or year is not offered, the rhetor must at least propose an allotted time span when the events of the End will take place.

Since a specific claim of a date for the world's End cannot be validated by Scripture, it must be supported through some structure of reasoned discourse that deduces the claim from scriptural premises and figures. Thus, the topos of time gives rise to a discourse of calculation that often reaches a high degree of chronological and mathematical sophistication. The purely formal satisfaction of mathematical proof lends a useful air of deductive certainty to the arguments for an imminent apocalypse. Hence, apocalyptic literature is replete with attempts to coordinate time charts of universal history with biblical periods and contemporary historical events, deducing the age of the world and the date of its End through complex feats of addition, subtraction, and multiplication. Augustine's command that those who calculate dates for the End should "relax their fingers, and give them a rest" was intended to forestall the over-zealous efforts of interpreters given to the pleasures of millennial arithmetic. However, such pleasures are not easily suppressed by the institutional structures of orthodoxy; the history of apocalyptic speculation is littered with reams of feverish calculation aiming to prove the advent of the apocalypse in a particular year: 1260, 1843, 1914, 1988, 2000. . . . The list is seemingly endless.

The apocalyptic rhetor's choices in degrees of proximity and specificity will evoke further variations in audience response, which I will presently explore. At this point I must turn to a brief consideration of the topos of evil. The topos of time is spectacularly evident in the discourse of apocalypse; the history of prophecy and its interpretation is littered with chronological calculations performed with the feverish energy of moths circling a flame, continually tempted and finally burned by predictive overconfidence. As a topos of apocalyptic argument, evil is more ubiquitous but no less central. The function of eschatological narrative as a rhetorical response to the perceived exigency of human and cosmic evil has already been articulated; in the argument of the preceding chapter, Christian eschatology is viewed as a particular kind of response to the question that evil poses for audiences committed to a monotheistic belief system. The link to the conception of topoi as places where rhetors attempt to meet audience expectations should be clear: the problem of evil provides the occasion and context for eschatology, which offers "solutions" to the problem. Once an audience has accepted the eschatological argument that evil will be both eliminated and justified in the Last Judgment, however, their experience of evil will create a hope and expectation for this Judgment that still requires satisfaction. To the degree that an audience faces suffering and persecution, whether such experience be "real" or rhetorically induced, they will not be satisfied with the claim that all will be well in the End, but will desire to know when this fulfillment can be expected. Speculation on the topos of evil may thus turn toward further elaboration on the topos of time with the ancient cry, "How long, O Lord?"

The topos of evil is further manifested in characteristic patterns or lines of argument that seek to comprehend the existence of evil by placing it into a structure of historical meaning. Two primary variations on this topos of apocalyptic argument appear prominently in the literature of the apocalyptic tradition. The first may be termed personification: this strain of apocalyptic argument focuses its speculative efforts on the identity and career of the great beast of Revelation, the mysterious figure that inspired the legend of Antichrist. The second may be termed the apocalyptic jeremiad: this strain finds comfort in the very act of naming and lamenting a list of present-day evils that serves as evidence of history's degeneration into iniquity.

The popularity of the Antichrist legend through the centuries testifies to an enduring human impulse to personify the principle of evil.[52] For many readers, the image of the beast portrayed in chapter 13 of Revelation is the most vivid feature of apocalyptic myth: "It had ten horns and seven heads. On its horns were ten diadems, and on each head a blasphemous name. The beast . . . was like a leopard, but its feet were like a bear's and its mouth like a lion's mouth. The dragon conferred upon it his power and rule, and great authority. . . . The whole world went after the beast in wondering admiration" (13:1–3). I noted in chapter 2 that in its original political context, this mythic depiction was a clear representation of the imperial cult of the Roman emperors, and hence had a clearly subversive implication. Indeed, the story of the beast's defeat has offered hope to generations of believers persecuted by the power of the state. Imperial monarch, false messiah, wonder-worker, son of Satan: throughout the history of Christianity, apocalyptic speculation has continued to focus on the identity of the earthly ruler whose attempt to claim political and spiritual authority signals the advent of the Last Days. Since the time of the Roman empire, the multitude of candidates who have been proposed for the role of Antichrist has included a succession of popes, Napoleon Bonaparte, Adolf Hitler, Henry Kissinger, Ronald Reagan, King Juan Carlos of Spain, and Saddam Hussein.

The venerable legend of the papal Antichrist was briefly discussed in chapter 2. Readers of this book who recall seeing broadsides spread through the airports and thoroughfares of our major cities that identify Pope John Paul II as the Antichrist, occasionally performing numerological calculations on his name to discover its correspondence to the famous "number of the beast," 666, may be interested to know that the history of this type of calculation dates back at least to the mid-twelfth century. McGinn's *Visions of the End* translates a text of the Dominican friar Arnold, a partisan of the Hohenstaufen emperor Frederick II in his struggle with pope Innocent IV during the late 1240s:

> [I]t is necessary that Antichrist appear in the place of the Supreme Pontiff, in which state his avarice and other vices will be most directly opposed to Christ and in which the Church will be most scandalized and corrupted in him. . . . In the thirteenth chapter of Revelation we read: "Let him who has understanding compute the number of the beast," namely what is contained in his mark, "and his number is 666" (Rev. 13:18). This number is found in the new Bull. "Innocencius papa" signifies 666 according to the *Gloss* and to reason. I equals 1, N equals 50 and 50 again, O is 70, C a 100, E 5, N 50, C another 100, I 1, V 5, S 200. . . . P equals 16 because P is the sixteenth letter according to the Greeks and Revelation in which the number of the beast is found was written by John in Greek. A equals 1, another P is 16, and another A 1. When the number is fully added up, the name of the mark of the beast, that is, of the Antichrist who is Pope Innocent, equals 666. . . . There is no doubt he is the true Antichrist."[53]

In Leo Tolstoy's novel *War and Peace* the protagonist, Pierre, is shown busily attempting a similar numerological analysis of the name and imperial title of Napoleon Bonaparte—and shaving letters off the name in order to make the calculation come out properly. So prevalent is the tendency to seek the identity of the beast that one evangelical writer recently found it necessary to warn his fellow believers against their repeated attempts to "Pin the Tail on the Antichrist."[54]

Those who resist the temptation to embody the principle of evil in contemporary world leaders may elaborate on this topos in other ways. The tragic structure of the Christian eschatological narrative ordains that the forces of evil are predestined to reach maximum strength before they can finally be defeated: the dragon must complete the demonic parody of the kingdom of God by establishing the kingdom of the beast, which apes the divine kingdom in its claim to totality ("Who is like the beast? who can fight against it?" [13:4]). The perception that the demonic conspiracy of Antichrist is reaching the apex of its power in the present historical moment must therefore be supported by a calculus of evil that parallels and verifies the chronological calculations evident in the topical elaborations on the question of time. Hence the topos of evil gives rise to efforts to calculate the sum total of human and cosmic evil in the present age, as "proof" that things have never been worse and, therefore, that the promised End is just around the corner. In the persuasive literature of modern apocalyptic, this calculus of evil appears in the form of the litany of the jeremiad: drug abuse and divorce are rampant; homosexuality is shamelessly public, Satanism, occultism, Communism, and a host of other "isms" identified as demonic grow increasingly popular; war and ecological disaster seem inescapable. Although the content of this litany has varied from century to century and from place to place, its form seems to remain fairly constant: the evils of the present day are pyramided into a structure of cosmic significance. The distinctive characteristic of the jeremiad as it appears in the tragic apocalyptic program is that the litany of evils is given a thematic unity through the identification of various ills with the demonic principle and taken as cumulative evidence of an ultimate historical crisis. Rather than being a series of punishments sent by God to encourage repentance and reformation, the list of ills only serves to prove that the end of history is imminent and unavoidable. In addition to functioning as a proof of the proximity of God's judgment, this calculus of evil also provides a short-term theodicy in which each individual evil is justified as a necessary part of the divine plan of history. The apocalyptic jeremiad thus both proves the necessity and proximity of the End (once the temporal structure of history in terms of the progressive increase in demonic power has been accepted), and makes these evils individually and collectively more bearable.

This brief sketch of topical elaborations on the themes of time and evil has so far emphasized the tragic modes of interpretation. A full account of the topical choices embodied in the different rhetorical interpretations of the Apocalypse requires that one seek as well for possible comic realizations of these themes. The tragic reading of Apocalypse naturally places great emphasis on the catastrophic events that usher in the End; but it should also be noted that the prediction of disaster is not exclusively the argumentative property of the tragic exegetes. One can speak of impending catastrophe and yet remain within the assumptions of the comic frame, so long as the catastrophe is depicted as avoidable through human choice, or simply as an episode that, however unfortunate, represents no rupture in the fabric of history. The comic version of the jeremiad might, therefore, exhibit some structural similarities to the tragic jeremiad that appears in apocalyptic argument; it may offer a list of present ills and predict catastrophe if humanity refuses to turn back to the path of righteousness. In the event that the warning is not heeded, the comic jeremiad will seek to interpret the resulting catastrophe in episodic terms, not as a final close but as a moral lesson from which future generations may draw instruction.[55]

With respect to the topos of time, the tragic mode of interpretation in effect utilizes a peculiar variety of the "locus of the irreparable,"[56] positing a date or temporal horizon beyond which human choice is superfluous, a final Judgment that forecloses all individual judgments. Augustine's anti-apocalyptic eschatology shows that, if this moment of Judgment can be relegated to an unknowable future and thereby, in effect, postponed, the comic mode of interpretation will reassert itself in a perception of history as episodic struggles of good and evil that do not necessarily portend the End. Insofar as tragedy and comedy are interpretive poles, then, the tragic mode of interpretation resolves the topical question of time by tending toward greater proximity and specificity in the prediction of dates, while the comic mode tends to both postpone the date and make it indefinite and unknowable.

The fully comic interpretation of the Apocalypse, however, would not merely postpone the End. Rather, it would make the End contingent upon human choice, would assign to humanity the task of ushering in the millennium. To be consistently comic, this interpretation would address the *topos* of evil by defining it in terms of ignorance and foolishness (which can be overcome by exposure, education, and progress) rather than exclusively in terms of sin and guilt that require blood expiation.[57] Such an understanding of apocalyptic fulfillment as a product of human action rather than divine predestination would seem to be difficult to sustain in the face of the apparent historical pessimism of the Apocalypse itself; but it nevertheless appears in American history as the doctrine of "postmillennialism."

The term refers to the place assigned in this interpretation to the second coming of Christ, which was to occur after, and not before, the millennial kingdom foretold in the twentieth chapter of Revelation. The postmillennial scenario presents the transition into the millennial age not as a series of inevitable and catastrophic events, but as a gradual and incremental establishment of God's word on earth. The role of believers in this scenario is to reform society and cleanse the earth in preparation for Christ's return. The emphasis is not on God's omnipotent control over human affairs, but on humanity's free will and ability to bring about progressive change and improvement. The reign of Christ is interpreted not as a personal and literal earthly kingship, but as the general awakening of society to knowledge of the divine. To the extent that the millennial kingdom is understood literally in the postmillennial scheme of history, it is interpreted as a period of peace and tranquillity when the church would succeed in converting unbelievers and reforming society.

Historian James H. Moorhead describes postmillennial eschatology as "a compromise between an apocalyptic and an evolutionary view of time, between a history characterized by dramatic upheavals and supernatural events and one governed by natural laws of organic development."[58] One contemporary adherent of this doctrine describes its characteristic view of history: "The redemption of the world is a long, slow process, extending through the centuries, yet surely approaching an appointed goal. We live in the day of advancing victory although there are many apparent setbacks. Periods of spiritual advance and prosperity alternate with periods of spiritual decline and depression. But as one age succeeds another there is progress."[59]

The progress of this idea of episodic progress has itself been episodic. Postmillennial eschatology enjoyed a long period of ascendancy and even dominance in American Protestant culture. The doctrine was introduced to this country by Daniel Whitby, whose 1727 *Treatise on the True Millennium* influenced Jonathan Edwards and other key religious figures of the colonial and postrevolutionary period.[60] Postmillennialism reached its comic apex in the revivalist efforts of the great nineteenth-century evangelists, whose vision of humanity's capabilities and destiny provided the impetus for the religious reform movements of the Second Great Awakening. In a sermon preached before the General Assembly of the Presbyterian Church in 1806, Union College president Eliphalet Nott asserted that the millennium was near and that it was "to be introduced BY HUMAN EXERTIONS."[61] Another leading preacher of this period, Lyman Beecher, argued against passivity by saying that "if we only pray and wait upon the Lord, He will not come."[62] And Charles Finney, the most famous and successful of the Second Great Awakening preachers, argued that "if . . . [people] were united all over the world the Millennium might be brought about in three months."[63]

With this emphasis on human agency in the divine plan for salvation, the revivalists of the early nineteenth century embarked on a series of reform movements designed to purge society of such evils as slavery and alcohol. Their goal was nothing less than the Christianization of the world and the subsequent inauguration of the millennial kingdom.[64] These reforms ultimately proved unsuccessful. Although postmillennial eschatology suffered many setbacks, it continued its dominance of the mainstream orthodox churches for some time. As late as 1918, theologian Shirley Jackson Case defended postmillennialism against its premillennial opponents: "[S]hall we still look for God to introduce a new order by catastrophic means or shall we assume the responsibility of bringing about our own millennium, believing that God is working in us and in our world to will and to work for his good pleasure?"[65]

The next chapters will tell the story of how the comic understanding of the Apocalypse and of history eventually collapsed and was replaced by the tragic, premillennial vision with which this study is chiefly concerned. For the present, however, this brief account of postmillennial eschatology illustrates the ultimate potential for comic interpretation of the apocalyptic drama. The relationship of the tragic and comic frames to the elaboration of topical form in apocalyptic argument should also be evident. The comic reading of the Apocalypse addresses the topoi of time and evil by either postponing the End, or making its enactment a consequence of human choice and activity in the world, and conceiving of evil (to a limited extent) as something to be overcome by recognition, reform, and education. The tragic reading, in contrast, structures time by placing the End somewhere in the immediate future, and views this End as predestined and catastrophic; evil is depicted in demonic terms, and can only be overcome by divine intervention rather than human action. In the tragic interpretation, the predictive function of the apocalyptic myth is dominant; in the comic interpretation, the hortatory and allegorical functions are emphasized.

The Function of Apocalyptic Argument in the Tragic and Comic Frames

One final issue remains to be addressed before this model of apocalyptic argument can be applied to historical discourse: what is the role of argument itself within the different programs for the Apocalypse? What functions and configurations does rhetorical argument assume in the contexts of the tragic and comic frames for understanding time and history? To answer these questions I return to the topic of temporal prediction, the *locus classicus* of the tragic mode of apocalyptic argument. Consider the effect of this argumentative strategy on the interaction of rhetor and audience. By claiming that "The End is near," the apocalyptic arguer arouses the audience's curiosity about the immediate future. A skillful author or speaker can manage to maintain an audience for the argument by offering a strong case for the imminence of prophetic fulfillment, while claiming uncertainty as to its actual date. Other rhetors may go so far as to give in to the audience's demand for a specific prediction, perhaps because of a cynical desire to manipulate the audience, or perhaps through sincere overconfidence in the predictive force of their own arguments. Once this line has been crossed and a specific date offered for the End, the rhetor has laid the argument open to refutation through the passage of time—and the psychology of the audience at this point assumes a spectatorial quality. The audience becomes not only a collection of rational judges weighing argumentative claims; it also assumes ringside seats at an event that might prove to be either the biggest tragedy in history, or (at the very least) a comedic spectacle of public humiliation.

The prediction of a specific date for the End has the effect of heightening the audience's excitement. As the date approaches, those members of the audience who lean toward accepting the apocalyptic argument will feel compelled to make a decision. Those who have accepted the argument and endorsed the date will look forward with eager anticipation to their ultimate vindication at the Last Judgment. Those inclined to reject and ridicule apocalyptic arguments will look forward to the date as providing an opportunity for public refutation and humiliation of their opponents—an event that is itself a kind of last judgment, in which truth is exposed and falsehood refuted. Such judgments are never absolutely final, however, in the sense that there are a variety of argumentative resources for explaining and rationalizing the failure of the End to materialize. Those in the audience who have committed themselves to apocalyptic beliefs can still withdraw from the public sphere, stubbornly maintaining that the predictions were correct in their essentials and require only some slight chronological recalculation, or even that the predictions were absolutely correct and that the End did in fact come to pass in some fashion that remains mysterious and invisible to nonbelievers. Before the passage of the predicted date for the End, however, the elapsing of time acts as an incentive for people to choose positions. The selection of a specific date thus has the effect in time of dividing the audience into sympathizers or adherents, on the one hand, and skeptics or vilifiers, on the other. Once these lines are drawn and the divisions are clear (however large the number of uncommitted who reserve their own judgment until the end or End), argument itself takes on a different character and function. As time elapses toward the predicted deadline, arguments will assume greater urgency; the specificity of a prediction creates drama and promises narrative resolution (though not necessarily the resolution that tragic interpreters seek), and attracts an audience who may or may not convert but who will listen to the arguments and count the days and years with interest, solely out of the enjoyment of the spectacle.

Apocalyptic argument in the tragic mode seeks to interpret eschatological narrative for predictive purposes. To the extent that it succeeds in convincing its audience, apocalyptic argument cannot avoid enacting the End it predicts by vividly evoking the terror and hope of the last days.[66] Thus, successfully arguing the case for an imminent End is to bring the End closer by performing it rhetorically. Indeed, the end or purpose of argument must reduce to this kind of dramatic enactment if the tragic mode of prediction consistently holds that the End is predetermined and proceeds according to a given schedule; for if the outcome of history (as observed through prophetic interpretation) is predetermined, that is, if the End cannot be postponed by any arguments or actions whatsoever, then argument itself no longer serves the primary purpose of persuasion. Rather than seeking to mold or form the world to one's purpose, all action (including argument) is swallowed up in the divine purpose.

The determination of history according to the divine plan does not render meaningful action impossible. Far from precluding or discouraging action in the world, the historical pessimism of the tragic Apocalypse gives such action a different weight and purpose. The predicted End of the world does not simply reduce people to passive spectators; the tragic drama of Apocalypse offers not only a cathartic conclusion, but also (for those who are persuaded) a role in the cosmic drama. Argument becomes a ritual gesture: an utterance that predicts, embodies, and enacts a revelation of Truth that remains true even if it fails to find or convince its historical audiences. Philosopher Jacques Derrida's cryptic comments upon the Apocalypse reveal, in their apocalyptic obscurity, something of the nature and function of argument in this tragic mode:

> Whoever takes on the apocalyptic tone comes to signify to, if not tell, you something. What? The truth, of course, and to signify to you that it reveals the truth to you; the tone is the revelator of some unveiling in process. Unveiling or truth, apophantics of the imminence of the end, of whatever returns at the limit, at the end of the world. Not only truth as the revealed truth of a secret on the end or of the secret of the end. Truth itself is the end, the destination, and that truth unveils itself is the advent of the end. Truth is the end and the instance of the Last Judgment. . . .
> Then whoever takes on the apocalyptic tone will be asked: with a view to what

and to what ends? In order to lead where, right now or in a few minutes? The end is beginning, signifies the apocalyptic tone. The apocalyptic tone naturally wants to attract, to get to come or arrive at itself, to seduce in order to lead to itself... The end is soon, it is imminent, signifies the tone. I see it, I know it, I tell you it, now you know it, come.[67]

I see it, I know it, I tell you it, now you know it. My telling it is a sign that the End is coming; my telling it helps it to come. Apocalypse is the Truth unveiled; I unveil it with my telling of it. If you believe me, that is a sign of the End. If you do not believe me, that too is a sign of the End. The telling of it and the reception of it (whether positive or negative) are proof of it: "And this gospel of the Kingdom will be proclaimed throughout the earth as a testimony to all nations; and then the end will come" (Mt. 24:14). How is this powerful notion of Truth embodied in argument? or, what does argument become when contingency, traditionally held to be a necessary feature of rhetorical argument,[68] is eliminated? If the preaching of apocalyptic Truth is itself a feature of the mythic narrative of Truth's unveiling, then argument partakes of the unveiling of Truth in a different fashion than is usually assumed. The function of argument in the tragic mode is not to convince, but to retrace the pattern of the divine revelation. Argument becomes only secondarily an instrument for achieving conviction and belief; it is primarily ritual, a fulfillment of prophecy, a symbolic enactment that constitutes its own proof even (and perhaps especially) when it fails to convince.[69] Tragic apocalyptic argument does not gain its urgency from any attempt to influence the outcome of events; rather, it seeks to orient its hearers into proper alignment toward cosmic forces locked in a titanic struggle with a predetermined outcome. Since the mythic narrative itself predicts that the majority of humankind will be deceived and worship the demonic beast, the true believer will not be surprised if the audience for the apocalyptic message rejects the doctrine. The characterization of one's interlocutors as servants of the devil (wittingly or unwittingly) is a useful device for those who seek an explanation of their own persuasive failure, one with obviously chilling effects on the practice of argument. An apocalyptic evangelist who sincerely wishes for the conversion of his or her opponents may still choose to see their obstinate refusal to agree as foreordained; when the situation is defined in this fashion, the function of evangelical argument may well be to tell the Truth in order to provide one's opponents with a chance to reject the Truth—and so to seal their damnation.

Thus far I have described apocalyptic argument as it appears to those who have accepted the tragic frame for their understanding of history. To those who do not accept the arguments of the tragic apocalypticists, however, these predictive claims can only appear as comedy: as humorous examples of human fallibility and overconfidence. The division of the audience for apocalyptic argument into adherents and skeptics that results with the approach of the predicted date can be identified as a choice between tragic and comic frames: there will be those who believe that, in warning the world of its impending doom, they are actors in a tragic drama, and those who gleefully sit as spectators or participate as actors in a comic drama of humiliation as the date proposed for the End passes without incident, thereby exposing ignorance and false confidence to public ridicule. The social spectacle presented in the drama of apocalyptic argument promises to conclude on the cosmic plane of tragedy, but ultimately must settle for an ending on the human plane of comedy.

Having surveyed the place of argument within the tragic program for Apocalypse, and the comedic function of tragic argument as viewed from a comic perspective, the only topic that remains is the comic view of argument, or the conduct of argument within the comic Apocalypse. I will address this issue at greater length in the final chapter of this study; for now, I will round out this portion of my argument by referring the reader to A. Cheree Carlson's excellent study of Gandhi's use of the comic frame.[70] Carlson observes that the difference between argument conducted through the tragic and comic frames is that "Whereas a 'tragedy' will emphasize scapegoating and violent confrontation, a 'comedy' will recognize the 'evil' that exists in all humankind, and thus have charity for the enemy."[71] With Carlson, I believe that argument as conducted through the comic frame is more humane, in that it offers an open temporal horizon that emphasizes contingency in history and recognizes a significant role for human choice. Rhetorical scholars will not fail to note that these assumptions regarding contingency and choice form a significant part of the foundation of our tradition of deliberative rhetoric.

A Comic View of Tragic Apocalypse: Some Conclusions

In this chapter, I have tried to demonstrate that the history of apocalyptic interpretation itself takes on comedic dimensions, and that the text of the Apocalypse may appear as comic when read through the history of its interpretation. Throughout the history of the apocalyptic tradition, in learned textual commentaries and in popular movements from the third to the twentieth centuries, scholars can see repeated over and over again a similar pattern. A tragic interpreter of prophecy offers a date for the End, arousing a spectrum of reported reactions from scorn to curiosity to hysteria; the date approaches, interest is roused; with the passage of time the prediction is disproved and the prophet or prophetic interpreter sinks back into obscurity, losing public credibility but perhaps retaining a loyal following who may eventually form into a church or congregation. Such repetition becomes ever more hilarious each time an interpreter duplicates the mistake of preceding generations and confidently predicts a schedule for the End.

Those who read the histories of these failed predictions and ask why anyone would venture to predict the conclusion of history underestimate the motivational force of the apocalyptic promise, the ultimate carrot-and-stick tactic. The apocalyptic tradition dangles the messianic kingdom—the end of war and poverty, the attainment of earthly bliss, the certainty of divine Truth, the vindication of the righteous, and the punishment of the unjust—as a sort of millennial carrot before humanity; the history of interpretation is a series of attempts to declare, with tragic finality, that the millennial carrot is within our grasp. Over and over again across time, the passage of time transforms these tragic declarations into comic exposures of the absurdity of human claims to absolute knowledge. The comic interpretation of the Apocalypse, on the other hand, places the carrot of the millennial kingdom perpetually just beyond human reach. In Augustine's allegorical understanding, apocalyptic perfection is never absolutely achievable within history, and can at best be approximated through the humility that follows from measuring one's fallible self against an absolute divine standard. In the comic vision of nineteenth-century American postmillennialism, perfection seems to be achievable if only people would try just a little bit harder and have just enough faith. Thus is the "pursuit of the millennium" (to use Norman Cohn's famous phrase) domesticated by the comic frame. While the tragic Apocalypse claims possession of the object of pursuit, the comic Apocalypse offers a goal that recedes even as it is pursued—and harnesses this pursuit as an engine of social change.

The study of apocalypse, a tragic discourse that announces radical discontinuity, paradoxically leads to a comic reaffirmation of continuity: for critics may discover in this tradition a continuous history, always recapitulating itself, of human attempts to break the continuity of history. The succeeding chapters of this study seek to evoke such a comic reaffirmation through an examination of two key moments in the history of American apocalyptic interpretation, and to demonstrate the utility of the topical and dramatistic theory of apocalyptic rhetoric by applying it to two case studies of discourse that announced the End and argued strenuously for its imminence. Chapters 4 and 5 will examine the nineteenth-century Millerites, who predicted the End with predictably comedic results: all know now that the world did not end in 1843. In chapters 6 and 7, I will examine predictions that have not yet been falsified, and attempt to place Hal Lindsey's arguments into a perspective that cannot be fully assumed until humanity's safe passage into the twenty-first century.

Since these chapters will require a lengthy excursus into historical narrative, it is appropriate at this point to distill the argument of the preceding chapters into categories through which the analysis and criticism will be conducted. I have argued that the propositions of cosmological speculation contribute topoi (considered as themes or commonplaces) to the social knowledge base of a given culture. The key topoi of eschatology, a particular variety or form of cosmology, are authority, time, and evil. This is to say that time and evil are the perceived exigencies that give rise to eschatological narratives and appear as themes within such narratives. Once a particular narrative achieves canonical or authoritative status within a given culture, it must then be freshly applied or reinterpreted in each historical situation, a process that involves argument, in that interpretations must be justified and supported with reasons. Time and evil are thus transformed from commonplaces or themes within eschatological narrative to subjects for interpretive argument that follow characteristic and identifiable patterns. Considering these patterns or lines of argument, it is evident that there are various possible resolutions to the questions posed by eschatological discourse. For purposes of this analysis, these are the pertinent questions: How does an arguer support his or her authority to make predictive claims? Is the proposed End near or distant? How wide or narrow is the temporal latitude proposed for prophetic fulfillment? How is the present order defined, and in what manner and by what means will the world be brought to its End and this present order overturned? Is the course of time predetermined or subject to alteration by human actions? Are people free actors within the drama of history, or (to rephrase the question) to what extent may human beings exercise authentic choice between good and evil?

Answers to these questions do not fall neatly into simple categories. They are distributed along a continuum of choices that individual interpreters and whole communities can opt for and organize their lives around. Predictions may be validated by direct revelations from God, by appeals to the authority of tradition, or by more or less "rational" interpretations of scripture. The time of the End may be tomorrow or it may be a thousand years hence; it may be predicted down to the year, day, and hour, or it may remain vague or ambiguous, specifying only a time span that can vary greatly in length. In the discourse of Christian eschatology, the present world order is seen as dominated by evil, whether such evil is understood as ignorance and error or as demonic, malicious, and conspiratorial forces or beings. The choice of one or another symbolism of evil will in turn condition one's expectations of the manner and means by which the End will be accomplished: a supernatural source of evil will require divine intervention, while ignorance and error can be rectified through human action. The End itself may, therefore, be brought about through divine agency, human agency, or some combination of these. The End may be described as sudden and catastrophic, as a gradual, incremental, and peaceful transformation, or as an allegory that is continually re-enacted in humanity's struggle to achieve its ideal forms of order and virtue. Finally, human actions, indeed the whole course of history, may be defined as free and open to a wide horizon of possibility, as predetermined by divine decree and utterly immutable, or as fixed and predetermined in some respects and allowing for free choice in others.

These eschatological choices are evident in the various interpretations of the Christian Apocalypse that have appeared throughout history. From Irenaeus in the third century to Hal Lindsey in the twentieth, those who interpret the mythic narrative of Revelation as a prediction of catastrophic events occurring in the near future have opted for an eschatology that scholars term apocalyptic. In Augustine's anti-apocalyptic eschatology, the End is both postponed by hundreds of years and relegated to an unknowable future. At the same time, the resources of allegory are employed to apply prophecies of the End to the present in a way that threatens no disruption of the episodic pattern of historical time. Without claiming to account for the entire spectrum of choices throughout all eschatological and apocalyptic discourse, this study proposes that the present examples can usefully be viewed as enactments of the tragic and comic frames. Tragic interpretations offer an End by divine fiat that is both immediate and catastrophic; comic interpretations variously postpone the End to a distant or unknowable future, make the End contingent on human choice and action, or propose an End that is re-enacted (allegorically and/ or historically) in every age without ever bringing history to a close.

Tragedy and comedy are differentiated not only by the substantive elements that each proposes for the dramatic emplotment of history, but also as strategies for living and coming to terms with the world. Here, I argue, the rhetorical understanding augments the theories of tragedy and comedy offered by literary scholars, theologians, and philosophers. The tragic and comic frames are interpretative devices for lending meaning to personal and collective human experience by arranging events into a coherent system of signs. As such, they serve as resources for the invention of arguments that enable people to explain otherwise terrifying or anomalous events and incorporate them into a structure of meaning. The comic assumption that human beings are free actors and the tragic assumption of divinely ordained fate do not only determine the shape of historical narratives; they also serve as elements of self-definition that constrain and enable arguments for different audiences.[72] Likewise, conceiving of evil as a demonic and malevolent cosmic force, or as the natural functioning of human limitations and fallibility, will have significant consequences for discursive practice in that such conceptions provide the rhetor with models for understanding both one's audience and the rhetorical exigence. Thus, when considered not only as narrative patterns, but also as interpretative devices, the tragic and comic frames offer a working logic, that is, a configuration of motives, which both governs an individual's participation in an apocalyptic movement and enables scholars to make sense of the movement's formal developments as it conceives of and strives to achieve its own modes of perfection.

Burke's notion of the tragic and comic frames provides a thread that can guide the critic through the labyrinthine history of the apocalyptic tradition and the movements it has spawned. I hope to demonstrate that the topical resolution of the essential eschatological questions chosen by each interpreter of the Apocalypse determines (or, to make the minimal claim, provides an important clue that enables the critic to determine) the political, social, and ethical stance of the individuals and groups who make up the apocalyptic movement. Taking particular note of the temporal predictions or equivocations of apocalyptic rhetoric, and of its peculiar definitions of the evil of the present order, will enable critics to see such rhetoric as an alignment with the symbolism of the tragic and comic frames. Identifying apocalyptic argument as tragic or comic in its orientation may in turn help to provide an explanation for a phenomenon that has baffled more than one historian and critic, the political activism of conservative American premillennialists in the 1980s.[73] In order to better understand the rhetorical situation of apocalyptic arguers in the 1980s and the 1990s, however, I now turn to the story of their predecessors in the early nineteenth century.

FOUR

Millerism as a Rhetorical Movement

In the decades following the War of 1812, the American Zeitgeist seemed to be borne upon a wave of optimism. These were years that saw the Jacksonian revolution, the so-called "Era of Good Feeling," the revivals of the Second Great Awakening, and a host of reform movements that sought a variety of social, political, and religious ends. During this period, many revivalist preachers departed radically from the bleak Puritan vision of humanity's innate sinfulness and inability to work toward its own salvation, and adopted a conception of human progress that was both rationalist and perfectionist. In his classic study *The Kingdom of God in America*, theologian H. Richard Niebuhr associates the preaching of the first and second Great Awakenings with the prevailing Enlightenment conceptions of rationality, and argues that the dominant theme among these evangelists was "the insistence that the reign of Christ was above all a rule of knowledge in the minds of men."[1]

In the previous chapter, I followed the conventional historian's typology and classified this interpretation of the messianic kingdom as "postmillennialist." I argued that the premises of this system of prophetic interpretation are rooted in the comic frame. My purpose now is to demonstrate that the comic assumptions of postmillennial reform set the stage for the enactment of the tragicomic drama of the Millerite apocalyptic movement. In essence, my argument here is that internal tensions in the discourse and external social pressures combined to make the comic optimism of postmillennialism unsustainable. With the collapse of the comic frame of acceptance, Millerism offered a tragic interpretation of history as predestined and moving toward its catastrophic close, an interpretation that was distinctly pessimistic about the utility of political and social reform. From a study of Millerism's roots in revivalism and the reform movements of abolitionism and temperance, this chapter moves to a critical account of the movement itself, to illustrate how the expectations fostered through Millerism's discursive construction of temporality created internal and external tensions that were reflected and enacted in the movement's history.

Revivalism and Reform in the Early Nineteenth Century

Historian Ruth Doan relates that in the early 1830s, "a herd of itinerants . . . carried messages of salvation through temperance, education, nonresistance, and abolition, as well as through conversion."[2] When William Miller set out on the path of the itinerant evangelist, he followed in the footsteps of this herd, competing with a host of preachers and advocates of an astonishing variety of religious and social causes. My purpose in this section is to demonstrate that the evangelical reform movements led by preachers such as Lyman Beecher and Charles G. Finney developed and perfected the rhetorical forms employed by the Millerites, and to account for the fact that many of the most noted advocates and followers of Miller's doctrines were active in the movements for abolition and temperance before they converted to faith in the imminent Second Coming.

I begin by noting the comic assumptions shared by evangelical reformers during this period. In general, the revivalists of the Second Great Awakening believed in the ability of human agency to convert sinners and combat evil through reasoned persuasion. They interpreted the Bible as indicating the gradual and incremental nature of temporal sequence in prophetic fulfillment. These assumptions differ significantly from those that supported the revivals of the First Great Awakening a century earlier. From the early 1820s to the late 1830s, Finney, Beecher, and others helped to move the mainstream of American religious thought increasingly toward the Arminianism that, a century earlier, Jonathan Edwards had preached so strenuously against. Humanity's free will was increasingly emphasized; conversion and sanctification came to be seen as a matter of individual choice, no longer dependent on the mysterious action of a sovereign and unknowable God. The Protestant churches that encouraged conversion on the basis of this theology of human potential followed their revivals with an emphasis on social reform that was entirely in keeping with this optimism. If individual men and women could choose their own salvation and approach perfection, so also could they reform society in order to realize God's plan. In fact, such reform was not only possible, it was a moral imperative, a logical consequence of the individual's conversion choice. According to P. Gerard Damsteegt,

> the remaking of society in the light of the establishment of the kingdom of God was considered as important as converting people and building churches. . . . As the century progressed, the interest of Protestantism in temperance, peace, prison reform, poor relief, proper Sunday observance, education, abolition of slavery, and many other moral and social problems grew steadily until social reform became the absorbing passion of many Christians who embraced revivalism.[3]

In addition to these mainstream reform movements, a host of others sprang up, ranging from societies for the propagation of often bizarre cures to utopian experimental communes meant to serve as the seed of the new divine order on earth.[4] Though these movements usually found their niches outside, or on the fringes of, mainstream Protestantism, they were based on the same faith in the perfectibility of man and society. The millennial kingdom was the most vivid and tangible symbol of this faith, one which functioned as the ultimate incentive in the argument for reform. Charles Finney's claim that "if [people] were united all over the world the Millennium might be brought about in three months" thus expressed a prevailing spirit of optimistic apocalypticism and offered his audience a powerful motivation for action.[5] As Damsteegt notes, "The prospect of a millennial perfection to be established through the Christianization of society by voluntary human endeavor reinforced and sustained evangelical revivals."[6]

Thus the revival meetings of the Second Great Awakening had as their goal not only the conversion of individuals and the strengthening of their religious conviction, but also the actual Christianization of the world. Evangelists used every means at their disposal to produce the desired effects of conversion and activism; their faith in human rationality did not prevent them from skillfully playing upon emotions to achieve their ends. During this period, Charles Finney and others perfected the techniques used by subsequent generations of itinerant preachers, including the "anxious bench," all-night prayer meetings, and direct exhortation of sinners by name. Finney's first use of these techniques in the revivals of the 1820s produced remarkable effects in his audiences. Many of those who heard these sermons "became so thoroughly wrought up that they literally fell off their seats in a state of shock and ecstasy."[7] Finney was in this respect conservative, compared to some of his fellow evangelists: he later argued against the notion "that all religion consists in highly excited emotions or feelings."[8] The fact that Finney saw the necessity of arguing against this notion attests to its prevalence in the revival movement. Finney himself contributed to this development with the 1835 publication of his *Lectures on Revivals of Religion*, a compendium of evangelistic strategies and tactics for the rational and methodical manipulation of human emotions.[9]

Having discovered a set of "new methods," the revivalists were not slow to use them, and their rhetorical artistry electrified audiences in community after community. Finney's visit to Rochester, New York, in the winter of 1830–1831 produced a revival with consequences that may be seen as typical. After hearing Finney preach, the members of the Brick Presbyterian Church in that city rewrote their church covenant. The document that they produced as a result of Finney's revival, which was signed by all church members, included these words: "We promise to renounce all the ways of sin, and to make it the business of our life to do good and promote the declarative glory of our heavenly Father. . . . We promise to make it the great business of our life to glorify God and build up the Redeemer's Kingdom in this fallen world.[10] The individual's renunciation of sin was thus tied directly to social reform based on postmillennial premises. Preaching that deliberately sought to engender powerful emotions in audiences, and that employed social and family pressures by publicly naming and praying over unconverted sinners, had as its ultimate end not only individual conversion but social activism leading to the establishment of the millennial kingdom.

The link between revival and reform in Rochester and elsewhere is dramatically illustrated in the consequences of a temperance sermon preached by Finney's associate Theodore Weld on New Year's Eve of 1830. Weld demanded of his audience that they not only stop drinking but that they also unite to stamp out the pernicious habit in their city: they were not to drink or sell liquor, to rent property to sellers, to sell grain to distillers, or to patronize merchants who traded in spirits. After the sermon, many vendors in the audience vowed to stop their selling immediately. The next day Albert and Elijah Smith, owners of Rochester's largest grocery and provisions retail business, rolled their entire stock of whiskey onto the street in front of their store and smashed the barrels as cheering crowds looked on. Such performances were repeated throughout the city in the following weeks.[11]

The antislavery movement could claim no such easy successes. Slavery was not practiced in New England and upstate New York, where the revival fires burned strongest; reformist evangelists in the Southern states produced few, if any, scenes of tearful plantation owners setting their slaves free and renouncing participation in the slave trade. Abolitionist reformers in the North were reduced to preaching against an evil that was geographically removed and could only be opposed through political mobilization in the legislatures and governing bodies of various church denominations. The temperance cause, too, after its initial successes, found that it would take more than revivals and conversions to remove such a deeply ingrained habit as alcohol use. The next step for revivalists who entered into reform efforts was thus to move beyond the simple task of moral persuasion toward the more complex task of legal and political transformation. As their movements progressed, advocates of temperance and abolition relied less and less on revivals as a means of bringing about their aims, and entered the political arena in efforts to pass laws that would abolish the evils of alcohol and slavery. While Charles Finney continued to devote his efforts to revivals that emphasized personal conversion, some of his ablest associates and successors, such as Weld and Elon Galusha, traveled the country mobilizing the churches in support of abolition. Galusha helped to found the American Baptist Antislavery Society and became its first president; Weld formed a political alliance with New York philanthropists of the Finney circle and William Lloyd Garrison's *Liberator*, and participated in the formation of the nondenominational American Anti-Slavery Society.[12]

The newly formed political movement for abolition was quickly beset by internal disputes over strategy and tactics. Antislavery evangelists caused schisms in a number of denominations by declaring the sinfulness of slavery and the immorality of allowing slave owners to participate in worship; and on other issues also, dissension between absolutists and moderates was expressed in bitter conflicts that diminished the successes of revivalism.[13] The radical reform movement, according to historian Whitney Cross,

> carried the seed of its own destruction in abolition as in temperance. The height of fervor, whenever the various segments of the movement attained it, could never last more than a year or two. After 1837 the disintegration of this phase of antislavery agitation proceeded rapidly. What more could be done, after all, by religious enthusiasm than to record a mass conviction of the sinfulness of slavery and urge its remedy at the earliest moment? One could, and many did, renounce the United States government, criticize its constitution, or break its laws by stealing and transporting slaves to freedom. But such methods raised resentments in North and South alike and only made emancipation more difficult, while few in any case had a taste for radicalism as extreme in action as so many admired in words. One could, and many did, denounce affiliation in any form with the evil institution, to save himself from collusion in sin. But such a course would hew great clefts in religious organizations and disrupt the revivalism which foretold millennial glory. ... [E]vangelicals who had first seen the [abolitionist] cause as one step toward the millennium and had gathered their intensity from revivalism, evolved toward direct action on the one issue alone, by whatever political methods were required to achieve it.[14]

Cross identifies a historical cycle of revivalism, defined by phases of enthusiasm and reaction, in which the adherents of controversial doctrines moved increasingly toward the fringes of society as people reacted negatively to both their novel methods of evangelism and their attempts at political reform.[15] The reaction against revivalist reform movements took place on at least two levels, which may be characterized as the psychological and the political-economic. First, as Cross notes, "[E]nthusiasm could not be perpetually sustained, and the increasingly sensational efforts to defy this religious law of gravity only generated reaction."[16] A preacher's histrionics might produce a strong response in an audience new to these tactics, but after such an audience had sat through a number of all-night meetings and had been exhorted and cajoled by a variety of logical and emotional appeals, enthusiasm became more and more difficult to produce. Overwrought emotional appeals could produce bursts of short-term activity but were not suitable for a political movement with long-term goals. Second, the political activism of both temperance advocates and abolitionists was in direct opposition to deeply entrenched economic interests in both North and South, and these interests were not slow to counterattack with vigorous defenses of the morality of their positions. In particular, the vehemence of the Southern reaction over the slavery issue made an optimistic faith in the progress of future reforms seem untenable. A letter from Charles Finney to Theodore Weld in the late thirties reveals the displacement of millennial optimism by a tragic sense of foreboding:

> [I]s it not true ... that we are in our present course going fast into a civil war? Will not our present movements in abolition result in that? ... The church and the world, ecclesiastical and state leaders, will become embroiled in one common infernal

squabble that will roll a wave of blood over the land. The causes now operating are
in my view as certain to lead to this result as cause is to produce its effect, unless
the publick mind can be engrossed with the subject of salvation.[17]

As the idealistic rhetoric of the reformers degenerated into "infernal squabbling,"
the evangelists' moral authority only diminished. In the words of historian Bernard
Weisberger, "the revival impulse was dissipated in the political excitements to which
it gave birth."[18]

One other significant factor in the decline of revivalism and reform that should
be noted was the financial panic and severe depression of 1837. As Cross notes,
"The optimistic mood had overextended itself in politics, economics, and religion
alike when the panic of 1837 pricked the bubble."[19] Not until 1844 did the national
economy began to recover. Severe economic hardship may be a fertile ground for
some types of religious activity, but the postmillennial optimism of the 1820s and
early 1830s had a weaker foothold in this environment. The benevolence societies
had great difficulty raising money for their tasks; they had in large part depended
for funds on wealthy benefactors who were hard hit by the depression.[20] A sermon
preached by the Reverend N. T. Bent to the congregation of Saint Paul's church
in Philadelphia indicates the impact of the financial crisis of the late 1830s on
prophetic interpretation. The publication of this sermon in pamphlet form, with
the title *The Signs of the Times, or the Moral Meaning of Our Present Commercial
Difficulties,* is evidence that some segments of the American audience were disposed
to view current events in light of a pessimistic reading of biblical prophecy. Es-
chewing optimistic progressivism, Brent's sermon interpreted the depression as a
sign of the impending Apocalypse: "This deep meaning will the Christian see in
what is passing; the sin of the nation—the first fruits of that sin—the displeasure
of God, and solemn omens of a coming judgment."[21]

Evidence, then, indicates that the crisis of the late 1830s was not simply economic or political. In the terminology of this study, it can be described as a
breakdown of the comic frame, the revelation of the apparent inadequacy of the
optimistic view of history that inspired reform efforts. The labors of the revivalists
to reform American society had not achieved the desired effects: the millennium
was not visibly any closer than it had been at the beginning of the movement.
Reformers were forced to confront the enormity of the tasks that they had set for
themselves and the vehemence of the reaction against them, particularly in the
antislavery cause. Political and religious divisions in the nation were not being
healed by the revival efforts; on the contrary, they were worsening. The depression
of 1837 and its aftermath, accompanied by the growing awareness that it would
take more than revivals to abolish slavery, drink, and other evils, made the optimism
of the earlier reform movements seem hollow. And the emotional fervor generated
by the first wave of revivals naturally subsided in the face of the increasingly
sensationalistic efforts of the later evangelists. It was against this backdrop that
William Miller appeared on the national scene in the late 1830s with a radically
different message, one which accepted the rationalism of the earlier reformers but
rejected their perfectionism.

The Midnight Cry: Miller and His Followers

Then shall the kingdom of heaven be likened unto the ten virgins, which took their lamps, and went forward to meet the bridegroom. And five of them were wise, and five *were* foolish. They that were foolish took their lamps, and took no oil with them: But the wise took oil in their vessels with their lamps. While the bridegroom tarried, they all slumbered and slept. And at midnight, there was a cry made, Behold, the bridegroom cometh; go ye out to meet him. Then all those virgins arose, and trimmed their lamps. And the foolish said unto the wise, Give us of your oil; for our lamps are gone out. But the wise answered, saying, *Not so*; lest there not be enough for us and you; but go ye rather to them that sell, and buy for yourselves. And while they went to buy, the bridegroom came; and they that were ready went in with him to the marriage; and the door was shut. Afterward came also the other virgins, saying, Lord, Lord, open up to us. But he answered and said, Verily I say unto you, I know you not. Watch therefore, for ye know neither the day nor the hour wherein the Son of Man cometh. (Mt. 25:1–13, KJV)

This favorite parable of the Millerite movement provided a scriptural model for many who saw their persuasive efforts as the true "midnight cry" that might awaken a slumbering world. Millerism, which began with one man's solitary attempt to decipher scriptural prophecy, grew to become "as popular a millenarian movement as America has seen."[22] What follows is a history of this movement that differs from those offered by previous scholars in one respect. The focus of this account is rhetorical and argumentative; I intend to study the movement's persuasive strategies and tactics, to view it, in fact, as an expanding system of argument. Such a perspective is entirely appropriate for a movement that defined its own success solely in regard to the achievement of argumentative adherence, rather than in regard to the adoption of a policy or the establishment or reform of social institutions.[23] As Millerism gained adherents and grew to become the most notorious religious phenomenon of its day, it provoked public responses and controversy that in turn contributed both to the movement's self-definition and to social knowledge on the End of time. Ruth Alden Doan's study of Millerism and its opponents provides an excellent introduction to a rhetorical history of this movement:

The development of a general critique of Millerism took place through a process of statement, attack, defense, reconsideration, and regrouping. Both those things that Millerites actually said and did and those things that opponents thought Millerites said or did, or meant to say or do, or would have said or done, entered into the emerging public perception of Millerism. . . . [A]s they squared off against Millerites and Millerism, critics refined their own position and even shifted their ground to distinguish their stance from that of the Millerites. The study of Millerism, then, can also be a study of a process of change within American religious culture— indeed, within American culture as a whole.[24]

The history of Miller and his followers is thus best understood dialectically, as the articulation of arguments that produced conviction in some, provoked counterarguments from others, and ultimately resulted in a reformulation of the contours of public controversy over the nature and destiny of humanity. My purpose in this section is to sketch the historical outlines of this dialectic, reserving close textual analysis of the systematic characteristics of Millerite argument for the next chapter.

William Miller was a farmer from upstate New York who had begun his adult life as a deist. He eventually came to accept Christianity and turned to close study of the Bible in an effort to prove its divine origin. He grew increasingly preoccupied with the apocalyptic texts of Daniel and Revelation, and began to develop an interpretive method for the study of these texts that would enable him to predict when the events of the End would occur. According to Miller's memoirs, he first began to reach his conclusions about the impending Apocalypse in the years 1816–1818, after his service in the war of 1812. The essence of his premillennialist doctrine was that Jesus was to return not at the end of the millennial period but before it, and that the millennium would not be preceded by a gradual reform of the world's institutions but by catastrophic destruction of all earthly kingdoms. Of the manner in which he arrived at these conclusions, Miller wrote:

> I found, on a close and careful reading of the Scriptures, that God had explained all the figures and metaphors in the Bible, or had given us rules for their explanation. . . . And I discovered that God had in his word revealed 'times and seasons,' and in every case where time had been revealed, every event was accomplished as predicted . . . in the time and manner; therefore I believed all would be accomplished.
>
> I found, in going through with the Bible, the end of all things was clearly and emphatically predicted, both as to time and manner. I believed; and immediately the duty to publish this doctrine, that the world might believe and get ready to meet the Judge and Bridegroom at his coming, was impressed upon my mind.[25]

In spite of this conviction, it was thirteen years before Miller began to preach his views to the general public. He relates that during this period, he tried to interest neighbors, friends, and family members in his interpretation of scriptural prophecies. But the postmillennial doctrine was in its greatest ascendancy, and few people listened to his message. Miller became a respected man in his community, of sufficient stature that he was invited to attend an honorary dinner for Lafayette when the revolutionary hero toured America in 1825.[26]

As early as 1822, Miller had fixed on the year 1843 for the fulfillment of the prophecies. As time passed and that date grew closer, interest in his ideas grew. In 1831, he was invited to speak before a Baptist revival in Dresden, New York. Previously he had avoided airing his views on the Apocalypse except to acquaintances; but he now felt that he could no longer escape the call from God to warn the people. His first lecture was received enthusiastically; he was invited to continue with further expositions of the prophecies, and afterwards he went on to speak before other meetings in New York and Vermont.[27] Although his message did not spread rapidly at first, Miller continued to speak publicly on his views, and in 1832 published a series of eight lectures on the Second Coming in a Vermont Baptist newspaper. The publication of these lectures resulted in more speaking invitations;

enough interest was aroused to allow for their reprint in pamphlet form with the title *Evidences from Scripture and History of the Second Coming of Christ about the Year A.D. 1843*. This publication made Miller's apocalyptic arguments available to a wider audience than any he could address in a church or at a revival meeting. Many of the ministers who later become strong advocates of Miller's cause were initially persuaded by this dense and carefully reasoned exposition of prophecy, which concluded with an invitation "for any person to show me failure of proof on this point, or where possibly according to scripture there may be a failure in the calculation I have made."[28] Among the many who were persuaded by this work was Methodist minister Josiah Litch, who took up Miller's invitation with the intention of refuting his arguments, but ended by concluding that Miller's arguments were "so clear, so simple, and withal so scriptural, that it was impossible to disprove the position which Mr. Miller had endeavored to establish."[29]

In 1833, Miller was granted a license to preach by the Baptist church in his home town of Low Hampton, New York. He began to acquire followers; by late 1833, he had five cohorts to help him spread his message of repentance and impending doom. In November of 1833 an event occurred that seemed to lend credence to his predictions: an unusually spectacular meteor shower, described by many as a "rain of fire from the heavens" that seemed to portend the catastrophic events foretold in Revelation.[30] Miller used this as evidence, and public interest in his message increased. In March of 1835 forty-three Baptist ministers who had heard Miller lecture signed a statement to the effect that Miller's views were "worthy to be read and known of all men."[31] His audiences grew ever larger. As the wave of revivals in the early 1830s died down, other preachers turned to Miller to keep the revival fires burning, viewing his apocalyptic message as a useful means to bring out the crowds. One such preacher wrote to Miller that, though he disagreed with his views on prophecy, he was of the opinion that "more Souls [will be] converted to God in six months under the influence of your sentiments, than would be under those I embrace in six years, even if these were so extensively circulated as yours. My heart Rejoices to know that Souls are converted to God, I care not by what means, if true penitence, producing true piety is clearly manifested in their fruits.[32]

Until 1839, Miller's preaching had been confined to rural New York, Vermont, and Ontario. He had been invited to address an evangelical conference in New York City in 1838 but had declined; though he had overcome his original fear of speaking in public, he was reluctant to bring his message before the more sophis- ticated audiences of the large cities. In the autumn of 1839, however, while at- tending a Christian conference in New Hampshire, he met a Boston minister who was active in the abolition and temperance movements, Joshua V. Himes. An able speaker and publicist, Himes was captivated by Miller's ideas, and persuaded him to give a series of lectures at his church in Boston. With the collaboration of these two men, the Millerite (also called the Adventist) movement began its period of rapid expansion. Himes quickly threw all the energy that he had formerly devoted to the antislavery cause into spreading Miller's doctrines. He began the first Adventist newspaper, the *Signs of the Times*, in 1840. This was followed, before long, by many other periodicals with titles such as *Advent Witness, Voice of Warning, Trumpet of Alarm,* and *Midnight Cry.*[33] Himes had a hand in the establishment of many of these papers. He arranged for the publication and distribution of a new edition of Miller's *Lectures;* he printed Adventist charts, pamphlets, hymnbooks, broadsides; he arranged a series of Adventist "General Conferences," where preachers and interested believers of many denominations met to examine the evidence for the impending millennium and to discuss how to further the spread of the Adventist message. Twenty-six of these conferences were held during the years 1840–1844, in Massachusetts, Vermont, New York, Rhode Island, Connecticut, New Hampshire, and Pennsylvania.[34] Many of these conferences produced reports and proceedings that in turn were printed and distributed.

The first General Conference, held in Boston in October 1840, featured addresses by such men as Henry Dana Ward, a prominent Episcopal clergyman who had been educated at Harvard (and who had played a prominent role in the anti-Masonic movement of the late 1820s), Josiah Litch, who had been converted by Miller's arguments in spite of his initial hostility, Henry Jones, a Congregationalist minister who had been a militant abolitionist, Charles Fitch, a Presbyterian minister and antislavery activist associated with Finney's Oberlin group, and a number of others. Miller himself was unable to attend due to illness; but by this time the movement that bore his name had acquired an impetus of its own. The report of this conference, a document of nearly two hundred pages, was printed in an edition of ten thousand copies.[35] Of particular interest is the address by Henry Dana Ward, titled "History and Doctrine of the Millennium." Ward traced the history of the millennial doctrine, marshaling evidence from church history and the Bible in an attempt to demonstrate that the postmillennial doctrine was a modern invention without basis in Scripture. Bemoaning the prevalence of postmillennial interpretations of prophecy, Ward spoke for many in the growing Adventist movement: "My heart is sick of the new gospel, which is not the gospel our Lord preached, or that his ministers preached, until within about a century and a half past; and already it has so fastened upon the public mind, that it is exceedingly dangerous to attempt to remove it, lest we pluck up the wheat with the tares."[36]

Although an early advocate of the cause of Adventism, Ward was later to break with others in the movement because of his unwillingness to commit to a date for the Second Coming. The Millerites were thus not unanimous on this point, as is evident from the proclamation produced by this conference, addressed to "all that in every place call upon the name of Jesus Christ our Lord":

> Our object in assembling at this time, our object in addressing you, and our object in other efforts, separate and combined, on the subject of "the kingdom of heaven at hand," is to revive and restore this ancient [premillennialist] faith, to renew ancient landmarks. . . . We have no purpose to distract the churches with any new inventions, or to get ourselves a name by starting another sect among the followers of the Lamb. We neither condemn, nor rudely assail, others of a faith different from our own, . . . nor seek to demolish their organizations, nor build new ones of our own; but simply to express our convictions like Christians, with the reasons for entertaining

them which have persuaded us to understand the word and promises, the prophecies and the Gospel, of our Lord, . . . in the faith and hope that [he] will "come quickly," "in his glory," to fulfill all his promises in the resurrection of the dead. . . .

Though in some of the less important views of this momentous subject we are not ourselves agreed, particularly in regard to fixing the year of Christ's second advent, yet we are unanimously agreed and established in this all-absorbing point, that the coming of the Lord to judge the world is now specially "nigh at hand."[37]

Having established a unanimous acceptance of premillennialism, though disagreement existed over the question of the date, the members of the conference dispersed to their communities to further the apocalyptic message.

As its ministry expanded, the Millerite movement gained a substantial number of converts from the ranks of abolitionist and temperance advocates. Joshua Himes had preached temperance in the early 1830s; he served on the board of the Massachusetts Anti-Slavery Society and was elected president of the Young Men's Anti-Slavery Society. He played an active role in the Friends of Universal Reform even after he began his involvement with Millerism. Among those who attended conventions of this society at Himes' Chardon Street Chapel in Boston were William Lloyd Garrison, Bronson Alcott, Theodore Parker, James Russell Lowell, and Ralph Waldo Emerson.[38] While these individuals did not support the Adventist movement, Himes' association with them is indicative of the affinity of Millerism and reform. Miller's antislavery sentiments were well known; Himes, Fitch, and Jones were only a few of those abolitionists who endorsed and actively sought to convert others to Miller's views. Other prominent reformers who crossed over to the Adventist cause included Elon Galusha, George Storrs, Luther Boutelle, Joseph Bates, and Angelina Grimké Weld.[39] It seems, then, that many, if not most, of the prominent leaders of the Millerite movement were associated with reform causes.

The second session of the General Conference, held in Lowell, Massachusetts in June 1841, was primarily concerned with the development of persuasive strategies for the movement. The declaration produced by this session emphasized the responsibility of believers in the advent message to convert others to their faith. Nine specific tactics were advocated for this purpose. Among them were personal conversation, the formation of Bible classes based on Miller's principles of exegesis, "social meetings for prayer and exhortation . . . where there are a sufficient number of believers to sustain them," the circulation of books, and the establishment of "Second Advent Libraries."[40] Shortly after this conference Himes wrote to Miller (who was still incapacitated by illness) to inform him of its success. In this letter Himes writes that "the brethren in this vicinity are firm and much engaged. One thing is manifest in regard to the time: they are *more confirmed* as the time draws *near.*"[41] The conviction of believers thus seemed to be strengthened as Miller's date approached. The increasing importance of the time element as the year 1843 approached is apparent in the records of the General Conference held in Boston in May 1842. For the first time the conference passed resolutions aimed at promoting Miller's prophetic chronology:

Resolved, that in the opinion of this conference, there are most serious and important reasons for believing that God has revealed the time of the end of the world and that that time is 1843. . . .

Resolved, that the time has fully come for those, who believe in the Second Advent of our Lord Jesus Christ in 1843, to show their faith by their works.

Resolved, that we cannot discharge our duty to God and the souls of our fellow men, without doing our utmost to lay before the world as extensively as possible the truth of God on this subject as we find it in the Holy Scriptures.[42]

The selection of the date was justified not only by "serious and important reasons" deriving from a supposedly rational interpretation of Scripture, but also on the grounds that it produced results: more interest was aroused, and more conversions achieved, when a specific date was advocated.[43]

At the same conference it was resolved that, as "our time for giving the *Midnight Cry* is short," a series of camp meetings should be held. These meetings were the largest events that the movement had organized up to that point. More than 124 such meetings were held in the years 1842 and 1843; some of them attracted thousands of people, and they were counted a huge success by Miller and his followers.[44] With the camp meetings the Millerite movement snowballed to the point where it could no longer be controlled by any group of leaders, let alone Miller himself. There were probably well over fifty thousand dedicated Millerites by this time, and as many as a million who, though they might not count themselves as full believers, were expecting or at least watching for *something* to occur on the predicted date.[45] Hundreds of itinerant preachers had carried the advent message all over the northern United States; most of these were beyond the control of the General Conference leaders.

That Millerism had acquired a momentum of its own, apart from the efforts of its founder, is evident from the controversies over date setting that began to occur at this point in the movement's development. Miller had always invited anyone who took issue with his calculations to propose alternate chronologies for the fulfillment of prophecies.[46] Many of his followers took this invitation seriously and began to set more specific dates than he was willing to commit to, basing these dates on a variety of interpretations. Miller felt bound to repudiate these attempts. An editorial in the *Signs of the Times* of November 9, 1842 argued against too much specificity in date setting:

The editors . . . solemnly PROTEST against the setting of the hour, day, or month, of the end of the world. There are various events, the anniversaries of which, within the year, may be the end of all things, but we have never fixed on any particular day. Different individuals have fixed upon several different days, and it has gone forth to the world that we have fixed the day. This has only been done by individuals upon their own responsibility, and contrary to our knowledge. Neither does Mr. Miller or the principal lecturers look to any particular time in 1843. That, we are willing to leave in the hands of God, and will endeavor to be ready whenever he may come.[47]

It is apparent from this account that the pressure to set a specific date must have been intense, so much so that "different individuals" took the matter into their own hands. Miller himself, though he had fixed on the year 1843, indicated that the calculation was approximate. He expressed his belief that "the periods would terminate in 1843, *if* there were no mistake in my calculation; but that I could not say the end might not come even before that time. . . . In 1842, some of my brethren preached with great positiveness the exact year, and censured me for putting in an IF."[48] The founder of the movement was being criticized by some of his followers for lack of certainty. While Miller and the other leaders of the movement, such as Himes and Litch, equivocated, those who sought more precise definition in the prophetic chronology set dates of their own. A group of New Hampshire Adventists predicted that "all things here below, or the end of the world, will happen on the 3d day of April 1843," while others predicted dates in February, March, and September of that year.[49] The secular press seized on these predictions as a means of discrediting the movement, and mistakenly reported that Miller himself had authorized these predictions. Miller eventually published a denial that he had ever predicted any time more specific than 1843, or had ever "fixed on any month, day, or hour."[50]

In January 1843 Miller published a synopsis of his system of prophetic calculation, in which he specified that by "1843" he meant not the year of the Gregorian calendar, but the year "according to Jewish mode of computation." This he reckoned as running from one vernal equinox to another, which placed the last possible date for the End in March, 1844: "I am fully convinced that sometime between March 21st, 1843, and March 21st, 1844 . . . Christ will come and bring all his saints with him."[51] This seemed to allow a fair amount of latitude, but had the effect, as the year progressed, of focusing attention on March of 1844.

As the great date approached, the Millerites' missionary zeal increased. At the same time, antagonism toward the movement grew. Ministers who had previously welcomed Adventist preachers into their churches, whether as a stimulus toward revival or out of interest in the apocalyptic message, closed their doors to the movement's spokesmen. Churches began to take action against members who espoused Miller's views; many were expelled or "disfellowshipped." The Millerites were in a situation of great difficulty: to remain true to their convictions, they had to preach their urgent message, yet to do so could result in the severance of their ties to the community. The official position of the movement's leaders until this time had been that Adventist believers should stay within their churches in order to warn their fellow Christians. The preaching of the Adventist message had aroused such controversy, however, that remaining within the churches was for many no longer an option. The Millerite leader Charles Fitch finally addressed this situation in September 1843, in a sermon titled *Come Out of Her, My People!* Here he redefined the enemies of the movement in terms of biblical prophecy. Whereas the Millerite prophetic exegesis had previously identified the pope as the Antichrist and the Roman Catholic Church with "Babylon the great, the mother of harlots and abominations of the earth" (Rev. 17:5), Fitch now said that anyone "whoever is opposed to the PERSONAL REIGN of Jesus Christ over this world on David's throne, is ANTICHRIST."[52] This meant that the Protestant churches who rejected Miller's

message and held to the postmillennial view were nothing less than agents of the
devil. They had, preached Fitch, "turned away their ears to the groundless fable
of a spiritual reign of Christ, during what is called a temporal millennium when
they expect all the world will be converted; and each sect is expecting at that time
to have the predominant influence. . . . The professed Christian world, Catholic
and Protestant, are Antichrist."[53] Fitch went on to quote Revelation 18: "Come
out of her, my people, that ye be not partakers of her sins, and that ye receive not
of her plagues." To many Adventists, Fitch's exposition was a persuasive explanation
for the hostility they were facing, which seemed to increase as the date predicted
for the End drew closer. The sermon was reprinted and widely discussed within
the movement, and many members did indeed leave their home churches.[54] Although the Millerites had begun as an interconfessional movement disavowing any
intention of starting a new church or sect, they had inadvertently brought about
more schism. Fitch's sermon may be seen as the beginning of what was to become
the Seventh-Day Adventist Church.

When the End failed to materialize by March 22, the movement's first crisis of
confidence occurred. Various attempts to recalculate the chronology were made.
The puzzling failure of the Lord to return was interpreted as the "tarrying time" of
the biblical parable of the wise and foolish virgins (Mt. 25:1–12), a key text for the
Millerites. Attempts were also made to justify the failure of prophecy on the grounds
that the Lord was testing the believers' faith.[55] During this time missionary activity
continued, but at a more subdued pace. Miller, Himes, and the other leaders failed
to come up with any statement that amounted to more than "Any minute now; keep
waiting." Meanwhile unbelievers ridiculed the Millerites unmercifully. During this
period, from March to August of 1844, many dedicated followers of the movement
searched the Scriptures for evidence that would lead toward a new date and explain
their previous miscalculation. Finally, at a camp meeting in New Hampshire on
August 12, a certain Samuel Snow offered an interpretation that restored vigor to
the movement. The prophetic chronology, according to Snow, pointed toward "the
tenth day of the seventh month of the Jewish sacred year, as the day of the Lord's
Advent."[56] This date was identified with October 22 of the Gregorian calendar. The
believers at the camp meeting, who until Snow spoke had been hearing a series of
sermons exhorting them to stand fast and not abandon their faith, were electrified.
Joseph Bates, a prominent Adventist preacher who presided over the meeting, described the reaction a few years later:

> There was light given and received there, sure enough; and when the meeting closed,
> the granite hills of New Hampshire rang with the mighty cry, Behold the Bridegroom
> cometh, go ye out to meet him! As the stages and railroad cars rolled away through
> the different states . . . the rumbling of the cry was still distinctively heard. Behold
> the Bridegroom cometh! Christ is coming on the tenth day of the seventh month!
> Time is short, get ready! get ready![57]

The new date spread rapidly throughout the movement. Followers who had
previously endured the ridicule of their neighbors seized on Snow's calculations

and redoubled their efforts to spread the message of warning. What is interesting about these new efforts, which quickly came to be called the "seventh-month" movement, is that they were initially opposed by the prominent Adventist leaders. Miller and Himes resisted Snow's arguments as long as they could; their followers were less scrupulous and eventually convinced the leadership not by rational persuasion but by the force of a massive bandwagon effect. The following account from the *Advent Herald* illustrates the manner in which the prediction took hold:

> At first the definite time was generally opposed; but there seemed to be an irresistible power attending its proclamation, which prostrated all before it. It swept over the land with the velocity of a tornado, and it reached hearts in different and distant places almost simultaneously, and in a manner which can be accounted for only on the supposition that God was in it. . . . The lecturers among the Adventists were the last to embrace the views of the time, and the more prominent ones came into it last of all. It seemed not to be the work of men, but to be brought about in spite of men. The several advent papers came into the view only at a late hour; and this paper was the last to raise its voice in the spread of the cry. . . . For a long time we were determined to take no part in the movement, either in opposition, or in the advocacy of it. . . . It was not until within about two weeks of the commencement of the seventh month [about the first of October] that we were particularly impressed with the progress of the movement, when we had such a view of it, that to oppose it, or even to remain silent any longer, seemed to us to be opposing the work of the Holy Spirit. [58]

In this late stage of the movement's development, the leaders clutched at arguments that depended not on rational calculation but on God's influence and inspiration within the movement itself. These arguments are quite evidently appeals of last resort; they may be characterized as arguments *ad populum*, as the movement leaders seem to have taken the maxim *vox populi, vox dei* quite literally. Under the pressure of elapsing time and the failure of their previous predictions, Himes, Miller, and their cohorts had altered their standards for the evaluation and acceptance of arguments. Whereas the leading Adventist preachers had at one time claimed to rely exclusively on logical arguments to prove the date for the End, their reluctant acceptance of Samuel Snow's interpretation rested not on a rational examination of his chronological calculations, but on the rapid and seemingly miraculous spread of the new date, which appeared to indicate that it did indeed have divine sanction. "The Advent bands," one author wrote, "have been every where electrified by the proclamation of a definite time—viz. the tenth day of the seventh month of the present Jewish sacred year. This cry has gone on the wings of the wind. . . . It has . . . been so like a fulfillment of the parable of THE TEN VIRGINS, in the 25th of Matthew, that we see not how it can be disproved, that this is the 'Cry,' which was to be made at midnight,—'Behold, the Bridegroom cometh, go ye out to meet him!' " Casting themselves as the wise virgins of the parable, the Millerites proclaimed the midnight cry, now identified with Snow's October 22 prediction. The delay of the Lord's return, which appeared to disconfirm earlier

Adventist predictions, was reinterpreted, according to the parable, as a fulfillment of prophecy. "The Bridegroom was to tarry; and while he tarried, all would slumber and sleep. . . . And thus has the coming of our Bridegroom been delayed beyond the Jewish year in which we looked for his return."[59]

Miller was one of the last to embrace the October 22 date. Not until October 6 did he send an endorsement of Snow's calculations to the *Advent Herald*:

> I see a glory in the seventh month which I never saw before. . . . I see a beauty, a harmony, and an agreement in the scriptures, for which I have long prayed, but did not see until to-day. Thank the Lord, O my soul. Let Bro. Snow, Bro. Storrs, and others, be blessed for their instrumentality in opening my eyes. I am almost home, Glory! Glory!! Glory!! . . . I now do not know of a single text, which disproves Christ's coming, this 7th month; and I have no drawback in my mind. If he does not come within 20 or 25 days, I shall feel twice the disappointment I did this spring.[60]

Miller's anticipation of disappointment was both prophetic and conservative. Many believers expressed their faith in the "seventh-month" calculation by taking radical steps: crops were left unharvested, debts were paid and forgiven, fortunes were disbursed to unbelieving heirs.[61] When October 22 passed without incident, the material and spiritual deprivation felt by those who had placed their faith in Snow's prediction was more severe than anyone could have foreseen. The cold winter of 1844–1845 lay ahead, and many had failed to provide for their needs; but the experience of hunger and cold was trivial, compared to the desolation of the spirit that overcame those who had staked all their personal faith and public credibility upon the Lord's return by the predicted date. Of this ordeal, which came to be called the "Great Disappointment," one of Miller's followers later wrote: "Our fondest hopes and expectations were blasted, and such a spirit of weeping came over us as I never experienced before. It seemed that the loss of all earthly friends could have been no comparison. We wept and wept until the day dawn."[62]

The words are those of Hiram Edson, who later became a leader of the Seventh-Day Adventist Church, formed out of the splinters of the Millerite movement. As the above accounts indicate, the Millerites saw the hand of God in the "seventh-month" movement even after suffering such severe disappointment; and this perception of divine influence helped them to regroup and form a church that still exists today. The movement thus endures, in institutionalized form; and its endurance testifies to the resilience of religious communities in formulating an effective response to the apparent disconfirmation of their most deeply held beliefs.[63]

Divine inspiration is certainly one possible hypothesis for the origin and progress of Millerism; rhetorical critics and historians of apocalypticism may be able to offer an alternative explanation. The story of the Millerite movement offers the critical historian a paradigmatic case of the formation of apocalyptic communities through a hypertrophy of the tragic sense of life. The omnipresence of evil in the world, and the apparent futility of reform, prompts a search for an ultimate solution to the world's ills. The announcement of this solution in the form of an imminent

End of time attracts believers who seek a wider audience for their urgent message; their preaching produces public reactions that range from ridicule to excommunication; the experience of rejection produces a counterreaction that takes form in the creation of a new community. With the passage of time and the apparent disconfirmation of the predictions that provided its raison d'être, the community must then seek a more enduring mode of temporal understanding, a new definition of its rhetorical epoch. By interpreting the apparently failed prediction as itself a point of divine intervention in history, the apocalyptic community may validate its own origin and discover a rationale for its existence while the End tarries.

From William Miller's first attempts to calculate the time of the End, to the gathering of his first converts from the ranks of disappointed reformers, to the convening of the first Adventist conference in 1840, Millerism contained no explicitly separatist communal impulse. As time grew short before the predicted date, movement rhetors grew increasingly zealous in arguing their case, a development that gained converts for the cause but simultaneously intensified the negative reaction from the public. Charles Fitch's exhortation to "Come out of Babylon" marked a shift toward separatism that brought Millerites toward a newly defined understanding of themselves as a community of the last days. The shared experience of the Great Disappointment was the crucible that inaugurated the transformation of the remnants of this community from a loose-knit group of individuals whose avowed aim was to persuade others of the accuracy of their prophetic exposition to a denominational body defined by a set of doctrines that bore little relation to its original message or purpose.[64]

The events of 1843 and 1844 provide support for the theory offered in the previous chapter regarding the functioning of the topos of time according to the psychology of the audience. Even before the time span allotted by Miller for the fulfillment of his predictions had expired, his followers displayed such a restive eagerness to set dates that he was forced to discourage them. In the period after the March 1844 date had passed but before the "tenth day of the seventh month" interpretation had been offered, Millerites were at a loss. Without a specific date to look forward to, while they could only preach that believers should "watch and wait," their movement faltered. The speed with which the new date was accepted and the increased missionary zeal of the Millerites after its adoption indicate that the prediction of an imminent End does foster audience demands for specificity. Miller had previously rejected the selection of any one day for the fulfillment of prophecy, giving a time span of a full year; but once this year had passed, it became necessary to restore the movement's credibility by selecting a date that was more precise than any that had previously been authorized by the leaders of the movement. With the passage of this date, it was no longer possible to credibly recalculate and postpone the time of the End: after the Great Disappointment of October 22, 1844, those who clung to the Adventist teachings had to devise an interpretation that showed that the prophecy had, in fact, been fulfilled, though in an unexpected fashion that was not obvious to nonbelievers.[65] It was at this point that Millerism lost its status as a mass movement that could attract the attention of the million or so people who were willing to entertain apocalyptic arguments without commiting themselves to the Adventist belief. Such a drastic reduction in both public credibility and membership left Millerites with few options: they could disband and face the taunts of their fellow citizens, or they could form a church that would insulate them from public humiliation by reassuring them of the divine origin of their movement. Those who chose to remain committed to Millerism were therefore forced to repudiate their original intention not to form just another sect within American Protestantism. The selection of a date had enabled the Millerites to grow at such a rapid pace that they became the most controversial religious movement of their day. The approach and uneventful passage of this date forced members of the movement to struggle for an institutional identity in isolation from the main-stream of American churches whom they had sought to convert. The next chapter will offer an analysis of the topoi of apocalyptic argument in Millerite discourse, in order to see how the movement built upon accepted premises to reach its radically unorthodox conclusions.

FIVE

Millerite Argumentation

This chapter is devoted to a close textual analysis of Millerite arguments. Building upon the insights derived from the previous chapter's rhetorical history of the movement, I will seek to demonstrate the manner in which Millerism both built upon and contributed to the reformulation of the topoi of American social knowledge. As a case study in the application of a theory of apocalypticism, the chapter as a whole seeks to account for the social and political stances assumed by Millerite rhetors and followers (before and after their involvement in the movement), and for the changes in the substantive and stylistic features of the movement's discourse as Millerism attempted to move into the American mainstream.

Many preachers involved in the Millerite movement employed a wide variety of persuasive tactics, some of which were widely disputed. It is thus necessary to specify that an analysis of the arguments employed by Miller or any other figure in the movement is not necesarily generalizable to the movement as a whole. Nevertheless, some generalizations about the discourse of Millerism are possible. A theory of rhetoric as symbolic interaction allows the critic to draw conclusions about persuasion in Millerite speeches and pamphlets as a process in which rhetor and audiences play active roles in the creation of meaning. My purpose now is to demonstrate that the rhetoric of Millerism, considered as a social process, can be usefully illuminated by employing Max Weber's typology of legitimation to make sense of the changes in both style and substance that characterize movement discourse from its inception through the Great Disappointment. After considering rational, traditional, and charismatic legitimations as strategies of argumentative proof, I will examine the Millerites' use of these strategies as they elaborated the topoi of apocalyptic argument—authority, time, and evil—into a systematic logic that both drew upon and contributed to the premises of American social knowledge.

Weber's division of the legitimations of authority into rational, traditional, and charismatic can be seen as an imperfect analogue of Aristotle's division of "artistic" proofs into the canons of logos (logic or reason), ethos (character), and pathos (emotion). Logos is easily identified as rational legitimation; ethos and pathos are somewhat less obviously linked to tradition and charisma as modes of justification. Considering Aristotelian ethos in Weber's terms, it is evident that the argument from authority can be used to support the claims of both "charismatic" leaders and traditional leaders; that is, "ethos" can refer to the authority of persons or institutions. When the argument from authority is personal and self-referential, the rhetor may be said to be assuming a charismatic ethos. The office of the traditional leader, in contrast, is legitimated not by character so much as by the force of time and history: ethos in this case is institutionally derived, embodied in succession, hence equivalent to tradition. Pathos, or emotional proof, is clearly associated with the qualities of Weberian charisma: rhetors dubbed "charismatic" by their audiences are those whose power is based on an emotional identification with the audience and who are noted for producing powerful emotional effects.

This tentative identification between the canons of Aristotelian proof and Weber's legitimations of authority is not intended as an academic exercise, but as a heuristic tool. Examination of Millerite discourse reveals that charisma and emotion, the role of rational argument, and the nature and significance of spiritual authority as manifested in individuals and institutions were themselves topics of debate and controversy in the movement and in society at large, and that each of these forms of rhetorical legitimation played a different role at different points in the movement's development. For example, Himes' and Miller's endorsement of the October 22 date was supported not by a rational examination of Snow's argument but with reference to the "irresistible power" that attended the proclamation of the "true Midnight Cry," a power that "reached hearts in different and distant places almost simultaneously," and which was identified with the Holy Spirit, the bringer of charismatic gifts. Weber's perspective on the processes of symbolic interaction allows us to describe this as an abandonment of rational demonstration in favor of charismatic proof, an acceptance of emotion itself as a legitimating factor. This marked a stark contrast with the rhetorical practices of Millerism in its early and formative years.

Their emphasis on rational proof was in fact a principal factor that distinguished Miller and his early associates from other revivalists. Contemporary accounts of the preaching that took place at Millerite meetings indicate that emotional appeals were used much less frequently than was common at the time. The Reverend L. D. Fleming, pastor of a church in Portland, Maine, wrote in 1842 that "the interest awakened by [Miller's] lectures is of the most deliberate and dispassionate kind, and though it is the greatest revival I ever saw, yet there is the least passionate excitement."[1] Another witness to Miller's preaching described him as "a serious, earnest man with a wonderful power of holding the attention of his audience and of bringing them round to his belief. He did not shout or rant the way so many revivalists do; he made his impression by his earnest manner and his serious way of addressing his listeners."[2] Miller's revivals were restrained compared to those of the older evangelists. He rejected such techniques as the "anxious bench"[3] and relied heavily on the logic of his scriptural exposition. The extent to which other preachers in the movement practiced such restraint is impossible to determine; but that it was to some degree characteristic of the movement as a whole is evident from another contemporary account: "[T]he present season of religious excitement has been, to a great degree, free from what, I confess, has always made me dread such times,—I mean those excesses and extravagances which wound religion in the house of its friends, and cause its enemies to blaspheme."[4] Miller's memoirs recount that when he first began to express his ideas he was regarded as a fanatic or madman; he probably went to great lengths to appear reasonable. This may account for the plodding logic and carefully reasoned argument of his initial lectures as published in pamphlet form, lectures originally addressed to audiences accustomed to the exhortations of the evangelists of the Second Great Awakening.

Miller was often accused of claiming personal authority for his predictions, of offering dreams, new revelations, or other spiritual gifts.[5] However, he explicitly denied any such claims to charismatic authority: "We have sought to spread the truth, not by fanatical prophecies arising out of our own hearts, but by the light of the scriptures, history, and by sober argument. We appeal only to the Bible, and give you our rules of interpretation."[6] Largely by the force of "sober argument," Millerism succeeded in attracting a large following. But having gained thousands of adherents to their arguments, Miller, Himes, and their cohorts were powerless to satisfy them; they could only await divine intervention. As opposition to Millerism intensified with the approach of the predicted date, movement periodicals devoted less space and effort to the attempt to convince unbelievers, while more discourse was devoted to encouraging and strengthening those who held fast and waited for the Second Advent faith to be fulfilled. The discourse during this period of waiting was marked by oscillation between two contradictory courses. Once the goal of argumentative adherence had been achieved for a sufficiently large audience, adherents could argue among themselves about the meaning of certain obscure prophetic passages, about harmonizing differences among various historians and chronologists, or about the mathemetical complexities of the argumentative system itself.[7] Such arguments tend toward the fanatical intricacy and obscurity of true believers differing over the implications of an idea. When not tangled in the knots of a complex logic woven over a period of years and through the pages of countless pamphlets and newspapers, the discourse could veer from extreme rationality toward a picaresque drama full of emotive force. The front page of *Signs of the Times* for May 24, 1843 offers colorful scenes from the drama of the Last Days:

> With what horror and consternation will many of the living be struck by the awful cry "there shall be time no longer!" The hero will pause in the midst of his half

fought field, to listen to that sound which drowns the loud roar of the cannon forever. The tongue of the orator will cleave to the roof of his mouth in utter astonishment; while the lips of scandal will cease to move, and ashy paleness gather upon the brow; the reeking dagger will drop from the hand of the midnight assassin, and he who has just breathed out his last expiring groan beneath his hand, will again start into life to meet his murderer at the bar of God.

Such purple prose conjures up a vivid picture to satisfy the impatient believer; until the End materializes, its realization in discourse must suffice. William Miller's own recreation of the End completes the scene:

See, see!—the angel with his sharp sickle is about to take the field! See yonder trembling victim fall before his pestilential breath! High and low, rich and poor, trembling and falling before the appalling grave. . . . See crowns, and kings, and kingdoms tumbling to the dust! See lords and nobles, captains and mighty men, all arming for the bloody, demon fight! See the carnivorous fowls fly screaming through the air. . . . Behold, the heavens grow black with clouds; . . . the seven thunders utter loud their voices; the lightnings send their vivid gleams of sulphurous flame abroad; and the great city of the nations falls to rise no more forever and forever! At this dread moment, look! look!—O, look and see! What means that ray of light? The clouds have burst asunder; the heavens appear; the great white throne is in sight! Amazement fills the universe with awe! He comes!—he comes! Behold, the Saviour comes! Lift up your heads, ye saints,—he comes! he comes!— he comes![8]

This passage recreates the vision of the End with an intensity that verges on the orgasmic. If Miller himself, with his reputation for "sober argument," was prone to such outbursts of excitement, it is little wonder that his followers were often unable to contain their anticipation, and that as the time of the predicted End approached and passed this anticipation found expression in "charismatic" behavior that the movement's opponents attacked as unhealthy fanaticism. *Signs of the Times* of September 20, 1843 laments the fact that a camp meeting near Bridgeport, Connecticut "exhibited some scenes of fanaticism, at which most of the brethren present were much pained. A few young men, professing to have the gift of the discerning of spirits, were hurried into extravagances which they themselves since regret." Millerite advocate Josiah Litch condemned these manifestations in un-ambiguous terms:

The origin of it, is, the idea that the individuals thus exercised are entirely under the influence of the Spirit of God, are his children, and that he will not deceive them or lead them astray; hence every impulse which comes upon them is yielded to as coming from God, and following it there is no length of fanaticism to which they will not go.

That good men, yea, the best of men, have fallen into the error, and have been ruined for life, so far as their Christian influence is concerned, is a lamentable fact. They begin well, but are pushed beyond the mark, become captivated by a delusion of the devil that they are divinely inspired to perform certain acts, and are infallible, until they are beyond the reach of advice or admonition.

The only way to deal with it, is to nip it in the bud, and stop it at once. They may be hurt; but depend upon it, one had better suffer than many. . . . May the Lord save us from all such fanaticism the few days which yet remain, until he comes.[9]

Six weeks after Litch's letter, Miller himself weighed in against charismatic manifestations of the Spirit and noted their appearance as a disturbing tendency in the Adventist movement:

It does seem that something ought to be done, if possible, to save from distraction and fanaticism, our dear brethren who are "looking for the blessed hope and glorious appearing of the Great God and our Savior Jesus Christ." I know that our enemies will exult over us in part, if he [sic] can draw us into any improprieties of faith or practice. My heart was deeply pained during my tour east, to see in some few of my former friends, a proneness to the wild and foolish extremes of some vain delusions, such as working miracles, discerning of spirits, vague and loose views on sanctification, &c. As it respects the working of miracles, I have no faith in those who pretend before hand that they can work miracles. . . . You may depend upon it, whosoever claims this power has the spirit of anti-christ. . . . The discerning of spirits is, I fear, another fanatical movement, to draw off the adventists from the truth, and to lead men to depend on the feeling, exercise, and conceit of their own mind, more than on the word of God.[10]

The "wild and foolish extremes" to which those who held the "blessed hope" were prone can clearly be described in Weberian terms as an outburst of charismatic excitement. The rhetorical scholar can go further, and view the appearance of charisma as a product of a rhetorical construction of temporality. A rational, logical discourse had fostered an intense expectation and anticipation that, according to the psychology of form, required some satisfaction. In the early stages of the movement, the formal satisfaction afforded by the deductive completion of argument, the feeling of certainty that followed an apparently successful refutation of opponents and critics, was sufficient to keep the audience's "wild and foolish extremes" in check; when meditation on the topos of time caused anticipation to so dominate the minds of the audience that mere formal satisfaction no longer sufficed, some tangible and visible sign of the proximity of the End was required, and it appeared in the form of "spiritual gifts." The critic may conclude, then, that with the passage of time, charismatic manifestations are a predictable outcome of arguments that predict the End of time with a high degree of specificity. Millerite leaders viewed such manifestations, with reason, as a considerable threat to their own authority and credibility. Claims to charismatic authority are therefore both in contradiction to, and an outgrowth of, the purely "rational" claims of apocalyptic argument.

Authority, Time, and Evil in the
Millerite Argumentative System

As the preceding account demonstrates, apocalyptic argument, however rational and logical it may be, tends ultimately toward charisma and "fanaticism." It is important to remember, however, that this tendency was considered an aberration by Millerite leaders, and that their discourse exhibited an intense concern for rationality and logical argument. One of the more active preachers of Miller's doctrines, Josiah Litch, published an essay in *Signs of the Times* in 1842 in which he wrote:

> For two years this has been the subject of my study, and the result is, that every successive step brings out new truths in favor of the system, and increases my conviction of its immutability, when taken as a whole. That this work, or indeed any other on this subject, is free from error or imperfection, it is not pretended. . . . But that every point, materially and vitally affecting the system, is founded on the rock of truth, I firmly believe.[11]

Here is a testament to the systematic nature of the Millerite complex of arguments from a man who labored to develop arguments within the movement. What are the characteristics of this system of argument and how can its components be described? What follows is an attempt to answer this question through a close examination of the logic of Millerite discourse, an examination that aims to illustrate and validate the topical theory of apocalyptic argument developed in the second and third chapters. I will argue that the Millerite argumentative system was constructed through elaboration upon the apocalyptic topoi of authority, time, and evil, and that this elaboration was rational in one specific and restricted sense: it sought to prove the case for the imminent End deductively, from accepted premises of American social knowledge embedded in Scripture and in currently authoritative Scriptural interpretation.[12] Building on the topos of authority as represented in canonical prophecy and interpretive tradition, the Millerites elaborated the topoi of time and evil into an epochal rhetoric, a chronology of universal history that was soon to culminate in a final Judgment that would forever banish the apparently intractable evils that disappointed reformers had struggled so hard to remove.

Authority and Interpretation

I have previously argued that apocalyptic rhetors who rest their claims on interpretation of prophecy rather than on the charismatic authority of direct revelation have an argumentative burden of justifying their exegetical methods; or, to put it another way, such rhetors must demonstrate the rationality of their interpretation. William Miller's "Rules of Interpretation," as reprinted in the 1842 tract *Views of the Prophecies and Prophetic Chronology*, indicate the way in which the claim to interpretive authority is supported by the appearance of rationality. These rules are a key to understanding Miller's logic; they functioned as premises from which he could develop his arguments syllogistically. There are thirteen rules for biblical exegesis laid out here. The following are relevant to this analysis:

I. Every word must have its proper bearing on the subject presented in the Bible. *Proof*, Matt. 5:18.

II. All scripture is necessary, and may be understood by a diligent application and study. *Proof*, 2 Tim. 3:15–17.

III. Nothing revealed in the scripture can or will be hid from those who ask in faith, not wavering. *Proof*, Deut. 29:29. Matt. 10:26, 27. . . .

IV. To understand doctrine, bring all the scriptures together on the subject you wish to know; then let every word have its proper influence, and if you can form your theory without a contradiction, you cannot be in error. *Proof*, Isa. 28:7–29; 35:8. Prov. 19:27. Luke 24:27, 44, 45. . . .

V. Scripture must be its own expositor, since it is a rule of itself. If I depend on a teacher to expound it to me, and he should guess at its meaning, or desire to have it so on account of his sectarian creed, or to be thought wise, then his guessing, desire, creed or wisdom, is my rule, and not the Bible. *Proof*, Ps. 19:7–11; . . . Mat. 23:8–10. 1 Cor. 2:12–16. . . .

VI. God has revealed things to come, by visions, in figures and parables, and in this way the same things are oftentime revealed again and again, by different visions, or in different figures, and parables. If you wish to understand them, you must combine them all in one. . . . *Proof*, Ps. 89:19. . . . Acts 2:17. 1 Cor. 10:6. . . .

VIII. Figures always have a figurative meaning, and are used much in prophecy, to represent future things, times and events; such as mountains, meaning governments, Dan. 2:35, 44; beasts, meaning kingdoms, Dan. 7:8, 17; waters, meaning people, Rev. 17:1, 15; day, meaning year, &c. Ezk. 4:6. . . .

XII. To learn the meaning of a figure, trace the word through your Bible, and when you find it explained, substitute the explanation for the word used; and, if it make good sense, you need not look further; if not, look again. . . .

XIV. The most important rule of all is, that you must have *faith*. . . . We must believe that God will never forfeit his word; and we can have confidence that He who takes notice of the sparrow's fall, and numbers the hairs of our head, will guard the translation of his own word, and throw a barrier around it, and prevent those who sincerely trust in God, and put implicit confidence in his word, from erring far from the truth.[13]

Rule XIV, which Miller styled as the most important of all, indicates the root assumption of his system: that faith in the Scriptures as the revealed word of God must precede any attempt at interpretation. Another assumption not specified but clearly implied here is that the divine truth must be one and therefore cannot contradict itself. The interpreter who locates concordances between different scriptural passages and discovers the biblical rule for interpreting each prophetic figure could be sure of the truth of an interpretation by testing it for consistency: "if you

can form your theory without a contradiction, you cannot be in error." The inerrancy of Scripture and the impossibility of divine self-contradiction meant that any
interpretation based solely on Scripture that met the test of consistency must be
the truth. When combined with the fifth rule, "Scripture must be its own expositor,"
these apparently innocent propositions had revolutionary implications. Crucial to
Miller's method, this premise allowed, and even required, the commentator to
interpret prophecy with reference to other canonical statements. This gave the
interpretation an apparently divine sanction: if Scripture was its own expositor, the
student of Bible prophecy who was able to discover the correct scriptural exposition
of a prophecy could claim that a particular interpretation was not the product of
fallible human reasoning but of divine inspiration.

What was unusual about Miller's system was not the claim that Scripture was
the ultimate source of divine truth, but the hermeneutic claim that Scripture itself
provided the key to human interpretations of the divine message. Miller attempted
to "prove" the validity of these interpretive rules by citing scriptural passages that,
he claimed, supported their adoption as hermeneutic guidelines. The student of
Millerism who diligently tracks down each of the biblical references offered as
"*proof*" of these rules may well be puzzled by their seeming irrelevance to the
principle as expounded. While the identifications of the prophetic figures are often
supported by Miller's references, none of the scriptural proofs offered in support of
rule IV (to choose but one example) affords the kind of certainty against error that
Miller here claims for his own method. Isaiah 35:8, for example, speaks of a
"highway," which "shall be called The way of holiness: the unclean shall not pass
over it; but it shall be for those: the wayfaring men, though fools, shall not err
therein." No support is offered for the identification of the "way of holiness" with
Miller's rules of interpretation. Likewise, Proverbs 19:20 is an innocuous injunction
that bears no obvious relation to biblical interpretation: "Hear counsel, and receive
instruction, that thou mayest be wise in thy latter end." These discrepancies between
the substance of texts and the probative burden that Miller assigns to such passages
appear not to have disturbed his followers. What is important about these "proofs,"
in spite of their flaws and fallacies, is that Miller's justification of his interpretive
system is grounded in the uncontested assumptions of the divine origin and authority
of Scripture. By making Scripture "its own expositor," the human expositor effaced
himself and gave his interpretations divine authority.

An illustration of a deductive argument that combines these premises and
derives from them the "logical" conclusion that God himself had predicted the
End of time can be found in an Adventist biography published many years after
the Great Disappointment. This presumably historical account represents Miller
expounding his views in a conversation with a fellow minister before a group of
skeptics:

> The minister said that he did not believe that God had revealed the time. Mr. M.
> replied that he could prove by the Bible that God had revealed it; and that, if he
> were an honest man, he would make him acknowledge it, by asking him a few
> questions in reference to the Bible. . . .

Mr. M. Asked the man to read the first three verses of Dan. 12. . . . Mr. Miller then asked if the resurrection was brought to view in those verses. . . . [Upon receiving an affirmative,] Mr. M. asked him to read the 6th verse—How long shall it be to the end of these wonders?'—and say what wonders were referred to. . . . The elderly minister . . . replied, that the 'wonders' referred to must mean the resurrection, &c. . . . "Well," said Mr. M., "is the reply of the one clothed in linen, who sware 'that it should be for a time, times, and an half,' given in answer to the question, how long shall it be to the resurrection?". . . .

The elderly minister replied that he thought it must be given in answer to that question. . . . Mr. M. asked who it was that gave this answer. The other readily replied that he was undoubtedly the Lord Jesus Christ.

"Well, then," said Mr. M., "if the Lord Jesus Christ, in answer to the question, How long should it be to the resurrection, has sworn with an oath that it shall be for a time, times, and an half, is not the time revealed?" . . .

"Why," said the minister, "I never saw this in this light before. Can you tell what is meant by time, times, and an half?"

Mr. M. "I will try. Read, if you please, the 6th verse of Rev. 12."

Min: " 'And the woman fled into the wilderness, where she hath a place prepared of God, that they should feed her there a thousand two hundred and three-score days.' "

Mr. M. "Now read the 14th verse."

Min. " 'And to the woman were given two wings of a great eagle, that she might fly into the wilderness, into her place, where she is nourished for a time, and times, and half a time.' "

Mr. M. "Do not these two denote the same period of time?"

Min. "Yes."

Mr. M. "Then must not the time given in answer to the question be the same as the 1260 days?"

The minister acknowledged it must be so.[14]

Whether or not this account is a verbatim transcript of an actual rhetorical transaction, it seems to be a paradigmatic case of Millerite argument. The literature of the movement is full of cases of men who came to meetings and lectures with the determined intention of proving Miller false, and came away convinced against their will through the force of logic.[15] The critic who seeks an explanation of this argumentative force can find it in the dialectical skill with which Miller applied his principle that "Scripture must be its own expositor." This sample of argument depicts Miller skillfully using Socratic cross-examination to derive his conclusions on the topos of time from the authoritative premises contained in his rules of interpretation. "God has revealed things to come, by visions. . . . The same things are oftentime revealed again and again, by different visions. If you wish to understand them, you must combine them all in one." In this case, the correspondence between the prophecies of Daniel and Revelation in effect allows Miller to claim that God, in the person of "the Lord Jesus Christ," has granted knowledge of the End time to the believing interpreter through the direct revelation of scripture. Thus, the divine authority of Scripture, a nearly uncontested social knowledge assumption of nineteenth-century America, was employed in support of a contested temporal conclusion. I will return to the topic of authority presently with a discussion of Millerite arguments from tradition. However, since the calculation of the "definite time" was the most striking feature of the Millerite argumentative system, it is necessary to confront the question of time itself.

Time and Chronology

Particularly crucial to Miller's system of chronological calculation was the equation between the biblical "day" and a year of ordinary time. Using this equation as a premise, Miller could derive the date for the End from numerous scriptural passages, notably the following from the book of Daniel: "Unto two thousand and three hundred days; then shall the sanctuary be cleansed." In a manuscript from 1831 he interprets this passage as follows: "[B]y days we are to understand years, sanctuary we understand the church; cleansed we may reasonably suppose means that compleat redemption from sin, both soul and body, after the resurrection, when Christ comes the second time. . . ."[16] For those who accepted these equations, it only remained to find the date from which to begin the 2,300-year cycle of events. This date Miller fixed at 457 BCE, "in the reign of Artaxerxes, when the Decree went out to restore & build Jerusalem in troublous times. See Danl. 9:25";[17] 2,300 minus 457 led to the date 1843; and *if* the reader or hearer had accepted the premises that day equals year and sanctuary cleansing equals second coming, and accepted the beginning of the cycle in the year specified, he was led to Miller's apocalyptic conclusion by an act of mathematical deduction that represents the topos of time in its purest form. In this discourse, just as in the writings of the early Christian fathers Hippolytus and Lactantius, apocalyptic chronology becomes a calculative logic in which numbers carry a symbolic force. Many rejected the premises, of course, and those who accepted them might well reject his choice of 457 BC to begin the cycle. But Miller had arguments ready for most objections. He did not depend solely on the 2,300 calculation; there are a wealth of numbers to make use of in the apocalyptic prophecies of the Bible, and Miller worked out systems of concordance among these numbers (such as the 1,260 days of Revelation 12) and events such as the French Revolution, the crucifixion, and the history of the papacy.[18]

The theory of the "millennial week," which, as noted earlier in this study, originated with the apocryphal second-century *Epistle of Barnabas*, also played a prominent role in Millerite chronology. Based on a correspondence between the famous dictum of 2 Peter that "the day of the Lord is as a thousand years" and the seven days of creation in Genesis, the "millennial week" theory posited that the created world would last six thousand years, a period stretching from the events told in Genesis to the events foretold in Revelation. The seventh "day" would inaugurate a newly created world that would last a thousand years, corresponding to both the millennial kingdom and the Sabbath day of rest. This ancient notion had survived into the nineteenth century through the calculations of Bishop Usher, who had fixed the creation of the world at 4,004 years before the birth of Christ, and whose chronological tabulations had long been printed in the margins of the Authorized Version of the King James Bible used by almost all American churches.[19] Adventists coupled Usher's widely accepted chronology with the "general tradition . . . which supposes that the present order of things is to be changed at the end of six thousand years."[20] Acknowledging errors in the calculations of Usher and other historians and chronologists, Miller claimed to have repaired their errors while preserving their accepted epochal divisions. In a lecture entitled "The Great Sabbath," Miller argued that his chronology derived from the best evidence available to respected historians of the day, and that no one had offered a plausible alternative calculation of the age of the world. His chronological proofs, he said, were based on

> very clear evidence of every period of time given from the creation to Christ, which makes our present year, from the creation of Adam, 5997. If this should be the true era of the world, then we live within three or four years of the great sabbath of rest. You are under obligation to examine for yourselves. Whether any one of the above calculations concerning the age of the world is right, no man can . . . possibly determine with entire certainty. But I have never seen any chronology with so few difficulties to my mind as the one here presented.[21]

However, since they wished to prove that the End would occur in 1843, while Usher's chronology placed the End of the 6,000-year period in 1996, Millerites were forced to revise Usher's calculations.

> Archbishop Usher, whose chronology is generally followed by historians, and which has been adopted in the margins of most Bibles, falls short 152 years of making this earth 6,000 years old with the termination of this present year. He however gives but 17 years for the length of Joshua's reign, but for which Josephus gives 25, and he gives but 318 years from the death of Joshua to Samuel, when Josephus gives 18 years for the elders and anarchy, and the Hebrew text gives 430 years for the Judges and captivities—making 448 years for that period. . . . He also takes no notice of an interregnum of 11 years, which we find, according to 2 Kings, xiv and xv., existed between the reigns of Amariah and Azariah. These three errors in Usher's chronology make 149 years; and he falls short on other points some 3 or 4 years, from other and more accurate chronologers, all of which, added to his chronology of the world's age, give us about 6,000 years for the duration of the curse to the present time; and we have reason to believe that it may be consummated with the present Autumn, and we should therefore live in continual expectation of the times of the restitution of all things.[22]

This attempt to predict the End by revising Usher's widely accepted chronology may be described as a chronological argument from authority. Usher's prestige helped to establish the orthodoxy of attempts to calculate the age of the world and linked such calculations to the ancient "Great Sabbath." After correction by the best technical knowledge available from contemporary historical and chronological authorities, kindly supplied by Miller and his cohorts, Usher's system appeared to imply an immediate and inexorable countdown toward apocalyptic fulfillment.

Arguments from tradition and authority did not always coincide so well with the attempt to calculate the concords between the chronologies of Scripture and history; in fact, these lines of argument could appear to contradict each other. In an address entitled "History and Doctrine of the Millennium," delivered to the first Adventist General Conference, Henry Dana Ward tried to prove the validity of the premillennial apocalyptic doctrine by citing theologians from Justin Martyr in the second century to Martin Luther in the sixteenth, all of whom taught the doctrine of the impending End. His list of authorities is well researched, and he generally does not misrepresent their views; yet there is an inherent tension in the attempt to base the argument for a proximate end of the world on the views of the ancient authorities. The Millerites were quick to realize this: in the pamphlet version of the conference proceedings, the editors introduce the address with the words:

> A plausible objection has been made to the antiquity of the doctrine of the near coming of the Lord, which deceives some, to wit, That a hope cherished by the apostles, and by them soon expected to be realized, is not a proper hope for us to cherish, and to expect soon to realize; because the experience of eighteen hundred years is enough to prove it a false hope . . . which no man in his senses can cherish and pursue. This objection lurks in the bosom of men, who are restrained from uttering it by its manifest impiety. . . . For them we observe: . . . Eternity admits of points of time two thousand years in duration, scarcely visible to faith. . . . O fool to think, and mad to say, that with Him whose works are so extended, eternity is limited; and two thousand years of experience is enough to prove the delusion of his promise; and the ages of the church are sufficient to convict His holy apostles of mistaking the times; and also to warrant the wise at this day in departing from His counsel, and from the example of the primitive church![23]

The editors continue in this fashion for some three pages, trying to reconcile the apparent inconsistency. Arguing against the objection that "If the event *was* at hand in the apostles' days, reason, manhood and philosophy cry out upon him who thinks it has not already come to pass," they reply that "Reason, manhood, and philosophy do no such thing. They admit and approve of paradoxes in the visible world greater than this."[24] What they identify and accept as a paradox is in fact a conflict between the two lines of argument they have developed, the chronological calculation and the argument from authority. As their argumentative system expanded over time, such "paradoxes" became increasingly common. More and more effort was devoted to the attempts to iron out the wrinkles in the fabric of their arguments; but, as one wrinkle was flattened, another one would pop up in a different place. All of these efforts may be characterized as "systems maintenance": once the argumentative system had been fully developed and extended, the bulk of the Millerites' arguments were devoted to the explanation of various anomalies. Whether these anomalies were problems that appeared within the system itself, or events in the world that seemed to disprove their arguments (the most notable of these events being, of course, a nonevent, when Jesus failed to materialize for the last time), the Millerites showed great resourcefulness in maintaining the system they had developed.

An example of such resourcefulness was their response to an opposing argument from authority used by the movement's opponents. Simply put, the argument was that if Miller's doctrine were correct, surely there would be more contemporary religious authorities, that is, more ministers of the church, who adhered to it. The response of an editorial writer in *Signs of the Times* illuminates the system's self-sealing nature:

> We are . . . assured [in prophecy] that the world will be as it was before the flood; that the day will come as a thief in the night, it will come as a snare upon the earth, the foolish virgins will not expect his appearing till he comes. . . . Now it is very evident that if our ministers were all awake to this question, it would arouse the church and startle the world; so that it would not be in the condition predicted respecting it at that day. It therefore follows that the coldness of the clergy and church is one of the signs of that day. We also learn that all the signs which were to mark the approach of that day, the fulfillment of prophecies and the termination of prophetic periods, will be so little different from those which have been in days previous, that they will not catch the attention of any but those who are with humble prayer looking for the approach of that day. . . . If then the church and world were all expecting the second advent of Christ immediately, we should know that that event would not now come, because the world would not be in the condition that we are assured it will be when Christ comes. The fact, then, that the church and ministers are still sleeping over this thrilling truth, instead of being an argument against the truth of our theory, is one of the strongest arguments that can be advanced in its favor.[25]

Here is an elegant and seemingly rational proof that illustrates the perfectly self-sealing nature of Millerite argument. The negative argument from authority is transformed into an affirmative argument from sign; the very failure of the argumentative system to persuade its opponents becomes a sign of its correctness. There seems to be an inherent circularity in the Millerites' interpretation of signs to support their case: as the writer of this editorial admits, scriptural prophecy indicates that "the signs . . . will be so little different from those which have been in days previous," that they will not be noticable by "any but those who are with humble prayer looking for the approach of that day." In other words, the signs of the impending End will not be visible except to those who have already accepted the conclusion that the world is about to end! The Millerite arguments from sign thus depended on the hearer's acceptance of the *claim* as a *premise*. For argumentation theorists, this raises the question whether any argument from sign can escape such circularity; for signs do not exist in a vacuum, but can only be interpreted according to a given belief system. Those Millerites who eagerly read the "signs of the times" in *Signs of the Times* did not seek for proof, but for confirmation; they knew, with a certainty that not even the Great Disappointment could shake, that they lived in the last days of the last age of the world's history.

Nearly three months after the Great Disappointment, the *Advent Herald* published a front-page editorial that, while admitting certain errors in previous Adventist arguments, defended the movement as a product of divine inspiration. Retreating to what he calls "The Safe Position," the author conceded that a key premise of Miller's argument had been false, but defended the system as nevertheless valid:

> We are . . . bound, in all deference to the Word of God, to abandon our ground of definite time. . . . Our conviction is, that for wise reasons, the divine mind has forever concealed the precise rise of those periods, at the end of which his Son shall be revealed from heaven. So that we believe it above the power of man, to demonstrate either the year, the month, or the day, of their consummation.
>
> In making the above concession, we have no intentions of throwing ourselves back on the old ground of entire ignorance in relation to the chronological prophecies; the real truth in the case may be approximated; and our past labors have tended to this result. The system, therefore, as it has been styled, is as good now as ever, since it is not dependant for its existence on the expiration of one or more points of time.[26]

This position obviously seems safer with the benefit of hindsight. Had Miller and his followers adopted this position in 1840, however, there would probably have been no movement and no controversy. Since the Adventists had by this time lost all credibility with the general public, this attempt to repair Miller's argumentative system was an exercise in self-persuasive rationalization. Noting that the preaching of "definite time" had converted many souls to God, the author went on to argue that spiritual benefits accrue to those who focused with intense concentration on the imminence of the End:

> It is said again, that *time* wrought a great work in our own sanctification and consecration to God. . . . [A] period of time was encompassed within our feeble comprehension, and its tendency was to humble, abase, and purify us, just as sudden premonitions of approaching death affect every pious heart. But because death does not consummate its work at the period apprehended, we are not to conclude that all our reasonings in relation to it have been incorrect. Our apprehensions have only been premature. . . . Let a trial be made of looking for the Lord *to-day*, TO-DAY, TO-DAY: let every morning and every evening be occupied in this service: let the conviction everywhere follow us, that the Lord may come the present moment. Such a position will not only be followed by a highly blessed effect, as our own experience can testify, but it is a practical position . . . [that] will impart constant fervor to our prayers, induce a spirit of abiding watchfulness over our thoughts and words, regulate our plans, and give nerve and activity to our religious actions.[27]

The injunction to look for the return of the Lord "TO-DAY" and every day illustrates the perfection of the tragic frame for understanding the Apocalypse. Thus perfected, the tragic expectation of the End turns the believer ever and again to the dramatic re-enactment of the vision in the mind's eye, seeking the "internal" purification provided by contemplation of the cathartic drama while the "external" purification of history is delayed. The purifying tendency of a specific resolution to the topos of time is evident throughout the history of Millerism. From this author's account, which provides first-hand evidence of the effects of such temporal constructions on the psychology of the audience, the critic may infer that the preaching and contemplation of "definite time," like the awareness of impending death, engendered a feeling of guilt that required a mechanism of redemption. The purification and sanctification that followed from the attempt to prepare one's self for the final Judgment was its own reward, one that did not depend for its value on the fulfillment of prophecy. Charles Fitch's call to "Come out of Babylon" was only one expression of this urge to disassociate from the forces of evil, a moment of public self-definition in which the critic may locate the inception of Adventism as a sect apart from other churches. The common experience of the Great Disappointment, a ritual of mortification and public humiliation, completed the process of sanctification and marked those who remained as a new community of saints.

The Millerite movement thus retraced the ancient pattern defined by the enactment of the topos of time in the tragic mode: the declaration of the End of time calls into existence a community that then struggles to make sense of its unexpected historical continuance. The early Christians who first endured this struggle turned, with the passage of time, to a provisionally comic interpretation of the Apocalypse that identified the church itself as the realization of the millennial promise; but the earlier, tragic expectation of history's imminent turn to an absolute close remained, embedded like smoldering coals in Scripture and in prayer: "Thy kingdom come, thy will be done, on earth as it is in heaven." Adventists could truly say that "THE FAITH ONCE DELIVERED TO THE SAINTS . . . was in accordance with our own"; and that in their movement, as "in the first age of the church, the literal interpretation of the scriptures prevailed."[28] Christianity's initial epochal insight, its self-perception as a community uniquely situated at the End of the age, endured through the ages and through all the reformulations of the Christian epoch to remain a potent force capable of generating new communities that recapitulated the temporal definitions and redefinitions of their forebears. The example of Adventism shows how, through the rhetorical construction and reconstruction of time itself, apocalyptic communities continually renew and regenerate themselves.

Evil and Reform

As I have shown, the Millerite preaching of "definite time" was the constitutive feature that established the group's identity and literally set it apart from other religious sects. The analysis of the topos of time as a mechanism of purification and redemption suggests that the critic must also account for the role played by the topos of evil in the discourse of the movement. To illustrate the Millerite use of this topos of apocalyptic argument, I return to the subject with which I began the last chapter, the relationship between Millerism and another, competing rhetorical form that sought a different kind of purification. I have already noted the extent to which many of the leaders of the Millerite movement had been involved with the causes of temperance and abolition. The affinity of Millerism with abolition and other reform movements was noticed (and bemoaned) by William Lloyd Garrison, who was forced to admit that "a considerable number of worthy abolitionists" had joined "multitudes who were formerly engaged in the various moral enterprises of the age" in the Adventist movement.[29] The critic who seeks to account for this affinity between Adventism and reform cannot rest with the simplistic assertion that conversion to the Second Advent doctrine represented a contradiction or reversal of a stance previously held by the reformers. It is true that Millerites did not advocate any reforms in society. They viewed the incremental purifications achievable by social movements as wasted effort since the nations of the earth could never reach millennial perfection without divine intervention; their efforts were concentrated on the spreading of the warning message so as to effect individual conversions. Yet as Whitney Cross notes, the Millerite flurry can also be seen as "the summation of all the reforms of the age":

> An immediate judgment day was the shortest possible cut to millennial perfection, the boldest panacea of the era. Such a simple solution to all earthly problems could have appeared only among a people bred to a buoyant optimism. But that is not the whole story. The movement developed in a specific atmosphere of deep pessimism. While it aimed at the final accomplishment of all reform in a single stroke, it was actually the compensatory dream of persons who had abandoned lesser reforms in despair. . . . Basically founded upon similar premises and objectives, it yet ran counter to the other campaigns of its era.[30]

Cross's comments on Millerism anticipate the insights that I have argued are available through an application of Burke's tragic and comic frames. The cosmic optimism of Miller's ultimate solution to the world's ills was born out of social pessimism: in this case, the realizations that a purely rational (that is to say, comic) understanding of evil was insufficient, that evil was more than ignorance, that people sometimes willfully prefer to choose evil even when much labor is expended to set the good before them. If evil prevails in the world not through human ignorance of the good, but through a demonic power that is ordained to rule until its abolition at the End of time, then no human agents, however numerous and well meaning, will suffice to rid the world of its ills.

A 1844 poem from a Millerite periodical, entitled "A Voice from Slave Land," exemplifies this tragic view of evil. The Adventist's sympathy with the plight of slaves is revealed in the first stanza:

> Three millions! yet in servitude, a captive host we lie,
> Oh, is there none of all the earth, to rescue ere we die?
> Must we be slaves when Freedom reigns in all the northern land?
> Must we be slaves, deep ground in dust—nor freemen ever stand? . . .

To this plaintive cry comes a "Response from the North":

> Forth to the rescue! on we come! ye crushed and sorrowing,
> Sad are our hearts, that long ere this we could not freedom bring;
> Toil on a little longer, slave, and we will set thee free!
> And then o'er gloated [sic] Slavery's grave we'll have a Jubilee.

This response, however, is finally corrected and reproved by the "Voice of Truth":

The Lord from Heaven alone can break, the bondman's clanking chain,
And in his Holy Word we read that he will come again
To free the oppressor's galling yoke, and burst his prison door,
To wipe the tear from sorrow's eye; that grief may be no more.[31]

The "Voice of Truth" exposes the vanity of abolitionism, and ultimately of all human efforts to rid the world of evil. The best intentions and efforts of the abolitionists could never bring about the end of slavery, since this could only be accomplished by "The Lord from Heaven alone." Just as in the tragic drama of ancient Greece, a deus ex machina is required to bring the plot to a redemptive conclusion. In spite of its dependence on divine intervention, however, the Millerite interpretation of history did not entirely reject reforms or dismiss them as useless. Rather, the efforts of the reformers were fitted into the prophetic program of history in a way that both justified them and explained their failure. In this way Miller explained the significance of the temperance movement with reference to the parable of the wise and foolish virgins:

> Therefore, in order that men might be in a suitable frame of mind to receive instruction at the close of this dispensation, and be in a situation to listen to the midnight cry, God ordered the virgins, and they arose and trimmed their lamps, and in all human probability thousands who would have met a drunkard's grave if this society had not arose [sic], are now watching, with their lamps trimmed and burning, ready to meet the bridegroom at his coming.[32]

The temperance movement had failed in its stated objective, to end the consumption of alcohol; but its significance to the Millerites lay in the fact that it had prepared the way for Miller's message of warning, allowing thousands to be saved. In fact, the parable not only gave the temperance movement a new significance as a harbinger of Miller's "midnight cry"; it also explained the failure of both movements to succeed in convincing the whole society in which they lived. For was it not written that half the virgins had had the door shut before them, so that the Lord said to them, "Verily, I say unto you, I know you not"? (25:12)

In their earlier efforts, the reformers had sought to convert and purify the world; as Millerites, they had neither obligation nor impetus actually to convert everyone, but simply to lay the message before them so they could choose for themselves. It was ordained by the prophecy that many would reject the message, and be separated from the believers at the coming of the Lord as the sheep were separated from the goats, as the wheat is separated from the tares at harvest time. Charles Fitch's call to "Come Out of Babylon" in effect sought to anticipate this division of the final harvest. Believers were to separate themselves from all association with sin and impurity, wherever it might be found, remembering that "not only the churches, but governments too constituted Babylon."[33] The Adventist attitude toward purely secular politics is indicated by the warning of one writer in *Midnight Cry* on the national elections of 1844. Believers were to avoid "being connected with the human governments of this world" by voting or holding office; rather, they should "be united to a man in our glorious candidate, the son of God, the true heir to David's throne."[34] The Millerites thus withdrew from political activism as such, but not from the public sphere; they were obliged to continue their "midnight cry" until the Lord returned.

The shift from social reform to Millerism resulted from a growing perception that the evils of American society were systemic, rooted not only in ignorance and apathy but also (and most important) in the nature of the cosmos. Using Burke's psychology of form to develop a rhetorical theory of apocalyptic discourse, I argued earlier in this study that this perception of systemic evil inspires attempts to calculate the sum total of human and cosmic ills as "proof" that things have never been worse and that the promised End is therefore imminent. The topical elaboration of evil is thus expressed in a calculus that parallels and verifies the chronological calculations evident in the topical elaboration of time. This topos of apocalyptic argument can be found in its purest form in an Adventist pamphlet entitled *The Groaning Creation*. The author of this remarkable essay announces at the outset his intention to search "the whole creation, animate and inanimate" for "continual evidence of disorder and suffering."[35] Surveying the entire planet, from the noble palaces of Europe to the slave plantations of America, the author quotes from Scripture, history, and the popular press to prove his point that

> The whole creation groaneth, and travaileth in pain together. . . . Every thing you see or hear, or can contemplate, sympathises in this groaning,—yea, all nature is restless and uneasy. . . . Misfortune greatly augments the sum of human wo [sic]. Pass round the world, visit the hospitals and prisons and every other place that justice or mercy have provided for the punishment of the guilty and for the relief of the afflicted, in town and country, the world over, and you will see the same forms and grades of vice and suffering.[36]

Ranging around the globe, the author considers the multitudinous forms of exploitation and degradation, piling evil upon evil in an overwhelming calculation: "Still you can add to the frightful aggregate already swelled enormously." The sum of all present-day evils is multiplied by considering the problem of evil diachronically, for "From time immemorial this has been the way of mankind almost all over the earth." Pausing to consider the objection that this picture "is overdrawn" since "the people are for the most part happy," the author dismisses the argument as based on an invalid statistical sample: "From . . . exhibitions of enterprise and gaiety you cannot infer how it is with the rest of your neighbors. When the truth is known, every second house contains an invalid, and possibly every hundredth person you meet is a fresh mourner."[37] Slaves and kings alike suffer under the divinely instituted curse: "The Judge of all the earth has subjected us to pine away with old age, or be wasted with consumptions, burned with fevers, scalded with hot humors, eaten with cancers, putrified with mortifications, suffocated by asthmas, strangled by quinsies, poisoned by the cup of excess, stabbed with the knife of luxury, or racked to death by disorders as loathesome, and accidents as various as our sins."[38] Here the topos of evil is elaborated almost as a musician improvises upon a theme: the rhetor lists the varieties of disease and sin with a repetitive form that seeks to overwhelm the reader's consciousness with an awareness of the extent of cosmic pollution. The repetitive form of this restatement of the themes of disease, pollution, and death eventually, however, gives way to progressive form[39] as the sheer number and magnitude of evils calls forth considerations of the various mechanisms of redemption:

> [T]here is a great positive evil in existence. It is seen everywhere and felt every moment. The devil roams, death devastates, man oppresses, and diseases and a thousand evils afflict. Now how shall these evils be removed? Is there indeed a remedy? Everyone feels as if something must be done, and every expedient is proposed by the suffering inhabitants. Casuists are writing and preaching ethics; divines are imposing their dogmas, and drawing out their hair-spun theories, or forming cast-iron creeds. Reformers of every kind are in the field. Lecturers and professors of every science are laboring to leaven the whole lump with philosophy. Statesmen, politicians, and socialists are all pressing their claims upon the attention of a distracted, distressed, unsettled world. Revivalists, Evangelists, and pastors, are trying to convert the world in their peculiar ways, to their faith, notions, and measures— and especially to an awful distrust of Millerism, or of the kingdom of God on earth, which is the same thing. But alas! the best of these measure are only conservative— can save some, cannot reform all.[40]

One after another, the author considers the various remedies offered by the reformers, lecturers, statesmen, and revivalists, only to reject them all. *"Can civilization and refinement of nations, with the arts and sciences,* REMEDY *the evils?* No. What says all history? Does it not say NO? In proportion as nations go up in the scale of power, civilization, and popularity, they degenerate in morals. . . . Prosperity at the last has never failed to be a calamity." With prosperity defined as an evil, the tangible signs of improvement in the world only serve as further confirmation of the author's thesis. The advancements of science, industry, commerce, are dismissed as causes of further suffering: railroads and steamboats "make large annual contributions upon human life," while "canals also, both in their construction and operation, do much evil."[41]

Turning from secular to spiritual solutions for the world's problems, the author asks *"Can the Christian religion or the Gospel furnish a remedy?"* Organized religion is rejected: the churches he finds to be in complicity with the forces of evil in the slave trade. Revivals offer no solution since "the theology of the day is spurious, the piety of the age is stinted and weak, and infidelity is ripening into a rank harvest." The gospel itself can "hand us over the rough places in our path," but "Nothing short of the [general] resurrection will meet the necessities in the case. Every other imaginary cure or preventive must fall short of the remedy."[42] The author concludes with an eloquent apostrophe addressed to the very forces of nature:

> *It will not be deferred!* The event will soon come—and hasten it thou groaning creation! Earthquakes, repeat your terrible shocks, and prolong your mighty agony,

and bellow out your frightful groans! Floods and storms, devastate, and fire, devour
the foundations of the earth. Ye beasts that prowl the forests, and roam in fields,
or toil in harness, join in the cry for a new creation. Ye birds that tremble on the
wing, or warble your feeble notes, sing on for the woods of Eden. And you that
have the first fruits of the Spirit, "groan within yourselves," and languish for . . . *the
redemption of the body.* . . . The Lord hasten it in his time. Amen.[43]

Published four years after the Great Disappointment, this essay implicitly defends Miller's doctrine, and in so doing reveals the essence of early Adventism as
a religion of the tragic frame. Contemplating the creation, the writer finds it marred
by a cosmic evil that touches every human soul but that no purely human redemption can alleviate; the "frightful groans" of the quaking earth echo the interior
groaning of his soul, sick with the ills of the whole universe. The terrible shocks
of the earthquake, the devastating floods, and the devouring fire hold no terror for
someone whose hope rests in the fulfillment of the millennial promise; such calamities are in fact to be welcomed, they hasten the Lord's work of destruction.
The author obviously feels the sufferings of the earth deeply; his vision is expressed
with power and eloquence. Yet when confronted with the desire for destruction of
the old creation to make room for the new, the reader and critic may well recoil
at the inhumanity of this tragic vision. The framework for understanding the problem of evil offered here provides no encouragement for the admittedly imperfect
and incomplete efforts that must suffice to alleviate suffering until the fulfillment
of the divine promise—an ethical failure that is not unique to Millerite apocalypticism.

In spite of this failing, however, the author does capture brilliantly a sense of
despair that must have been felt by many reformers who did not become Adventists.
It is little wonder that, confronted with the intractable problem of slavery, the
author should reject the reform movement as a rhetorical form inadequate for
addressing injustice: "Reforms cannot go on slowly and surely at the same time.
The devil likes slow reforms."[44] The impatient desire for a sudden and total change,
the premonition of great and terrible events in the offing, were not peculiar to
Millerites. Others who meditated deeply on the problems of the nation also give
evidence of a widespread sense of foreboding of an imminent historical rupture.[45]
Millerite rhetoric incorporated such premonitions as premises of an apocalyptic
argument:

[I]s there not at this moment a vague consciousness of great changes coming upon
society? Does it not pervade all orders? The statesman expects a political regeneration,
the philosopher a mental one, and the religionist a moral one, after his own creed
or party idiosyncracy. Each individual looks for his own kind of change, yet he looks
for a *change.* . . . [A] silent rapid, irresistible preparation has been making—making,
perhaps, for a sudden, subversive, and universal change,—What will it be? The
battle of Armageddon? The Millennium? The new Heavens and Earth? Perhaps all
of these, preceded by the coming of the Son of Man in clouds of heaven. . . . I
expect no reign of peace, till human passions and human interests shall once more
have expended themselves in a grand convulsion—until the nations who have given

their power to the Beast, shall have made a battle field of the globe, and the earth be once more drenched in the blood of her presumptuous and haughty sons.[46]

In a sense, one may say that the Millerites were correct in predicting an apocalyptic rupture of history; their prophecy proved to be off by only a generation. America was preparing to play out its own grand apocalyptic drama: the Civil War appeared on the horizon to discerning viewers, and Julia Ward Howe's apocalyptic hymn captured the sense that many Americans had of impending doom. In this context, the popularity of William Miller's message may seem less than strange. He was but one of many men in that time whose eyes had "seen the glory of the coming of the Lord"; and it would not be long before the troubled nation began to trample the grapes of wrath.

Conclusions

In his final judgment of Millerism, Whitney Cross argues that the Millerite doctrine was "nearest to strict orthodoxy of all the creations of the period." In a passage that may be read as an implicit rebuke to those scholars who have sought simplistic explanations for millennial movements, Cross argues that the distinguishing feature of Millerism "lay not in radical change from traditional notions but in intensified adherence to them. The Millerites cannot be dismissed as ignorant farmers, libertarian frontiersmen, impoverished victims of economic change, or hypnotized followers of a maniac, thrown into prominence merely by freak coincidences, when the whole of American Protestantism came so very close to the same beliefs. Their doctrine was the logical absolute of fundamentalist orthodoxy."[47] Miller and his followers only extended basic fundamentalist beliefs in the literal truth of Scripture, as history and as prophecy, to a conclusion that was at once radical and rational—given their prior faith commitment. The appeal to "literal" interpretation is always a powerful resource for apocalyptic argument, since apocalyptic expectation is expressed throughout the canon of Scripture. What moved the Millerites from orthodoxy into heterodoxy was their insistence that God intended, and even commanded, the church to employ Scripture to discern the shape of future events. Interpreting the figures of apocalyptic prophecy as literal predictions of discrete and identifiable events and time periods, they simply deduced, as rigorously and logically as they could, their conclusions about the impending End from scriptural premises.

To their reading of the Bible Millerites brought the common experience of a generation of failed reformers who were acutely aware that they lived in the shadow of war. The normative propositions of social knowledge that the Millerites distilled from their attempts at reform can be characterized as follows: those who undertake to rid the world of injustice and imperfection will only provoke anger and further injustice; human nature is hopelessly corrupt, and human evil is stronger than any human attempt to overcome evil; the structure of history is therefore not progressive, but degenerative, and the removal of evil is subject to a divine destiny that allows no significant role for human agency. These propositions found their full expression in the tragic, premillennial scheme of history, but seemed to contradict a basic comic optimism that underlies American political life. The Adventist shift from postmillennialism to premillennialism was a direct attempt to reformulate the social knowledge base of American culture. Miller's followers rejected postmillennialism, one of the prevailing "conceptions of symbolic relationships among problems, persons, interests, and actions," and sought to substitute for it a conception that was far from new, but that implied very different "notions of preferable public behavior."[48] Their tragic understanding of history called believers to condemn, not reform, human sinfulness; the "midnight cry"was a warning intended not to change society but to alert some individuals to the impending Judgment.

The Millerite prediction of a date for the End was thus a radical conclusion drawn from basic truths affirmed by Scripture, by interpretive authorities, and by social knowledge based in shared experience. That few other movements went so far as to predict the End so specifically, or rather that none attained the popularity of Millerism, is evidence of the movement's influence as well as of its oddity. Indeed, the very rarity of this phenomenon is a testament to the movement's enduring impact and to its contributions to American social knowledge, for the failure of Miller's predictions served as a cautionary example to all the preachers that followed him. As historian Ernest R. Sandeen notes in his study of *The Roots of Fundamentalism*,

> [T]he Millerite movement appears to have virtually destroyed premillennialism in America for a generation. In the wake of the tragedy of 1844, who could lift up his head and proclaim the message of an imminent advent? Miller's success before 1844 is matched only by the difficulties he created for anyone brave enough to attempt to preach a millenarian message after 1844. It took a long time for Americans to forget William Miller.[49]

In fact, Miller has not been forgotten, and his story is still cited in some circles as a cautionary example of the dangers of predictive overconfidence. A recent article in *Christianity Today* cites Miller in an effort to remind that magazine's evangelical readers not to repeat his mistake: "It would be well for those in our age who predict details and dates for the End to remember how many before them have misread the signs of the times."[50] There is ample evidence to indicate that the desire to establish dates for apocalyptic events remains a temptation for preachers of the doctrine; modern exponents of apocalypticism tend, however, to be much more cautious than Miller and his followers. Miller's unfulfilled predictions established a precedent by which later declarations of specific dates for the End of the world would be judged; the preaching of "definite time," a novelty to Miller's contemporaries, was after his failure considered an eccentricity.[51] While many preachers have continued to predict the End on specific dates, their willingness to commit to such predictions is now in itself a mark of marginality, a step beyond the boundaries of acceptable public discourse. No one who has specifically predicted the time of the End has come close to duplicating Miller's success in convincing eminent divines and prominent public figures, or even in having such claims taken seriously by the American public. The contours of apocalyptic argument from the 1840s to the present have thus, to some degree, been affected by William Miller's famous failure. In the next chapter, I will examine Hal Lindsey's apocalyptic arguments as symptomatic of another moment in the history of American prophetic interpretation, in order to determine what modern preachers have and have not learned from the tragicomic example of Millerism.

SIX

Hal Lindsey and the Apocalypse of
the Twentieth Century

From the 1840s to the 1990s is a very long leap. The period of time marked on one side by the disconfirmation of William Miller's predictions, and on the other by the long-awaited close of the second millennium of Christian history, spans only four "biblical generations" of forty years; yet this period took the American public through three cataclysmic wars and a series of scientific discoveries that created the conditions for unprecedented technological and social change. Through all this, apocalyptic interpreters continued to search for the "signs of the times." Although the disconfirmation of Miller's predictions turned the Adventist movement into the laughingstock of the evangelical world, effectively discrediting the premillennial school of interpretation for many years, American premillennialism survived the catastrophic nonappearance of its catastrophe despite rejection by the religious establishment and by the public. The story of the men whose doctrinal innovations made this survival possible has been well told by historians and need not be recounted here.[1] My concern in this chapter is to examine the topical logic of modern apocalypticism as it appears in the writing of its pre-eminent popular expositor, an author more successful than anyone since William Miller at making apocalyptic arguments credible to a mass audience. Hal Lindsey's best-selling presentations of the Apocalypse will be studied as an example of the reformulation of the apocalyptic topoi into cultural commonplaces of continuing relevance.

The chapter will proceed as follows. First, I shall show how the essential elements of premillennialist belief were reconstituted following the public demise of Millerism, and how these new (or newly revised) apocalyptic doctrines combined with certain momentous historical events—the invention and use of nuclear weapons, and the tragedy and triumph of the Jewish people in the 1940s—to create the context for a contemporary resurgence of apocalyptic argument. Understandably, the frame for this argument was tragic. Second, I shall argue that, since the modern audience for apocalyptic is not differentiated by any measurable activity or group affiliation, as was the Millerite audience, the surest way to detect the audience for whom this discourse was persuasive is to examine relevant texts to discover their implied audience.[2] The text I have chosen is Hal Lindsey's *The Late Great Planet Earth*, the most popular text in twentieth-century apocalyptic literature and perhaps in all of history. I shall examine Lindsey's argument to determine how he elaborates the topoi of authority, time, and evil into a tragic frame for understanding world events.

Premillennialism in the Twentieth Century

The last chapter concluded the story of the Millerite movement by quoting Ernest Sandeen's claim that it "virtually destroyed premillennialism in America for a generation." Considering premillennial apocalypticism solely in regard to its public credibility, this judgment is certainly true; but the resilience of the apocalyptic mentality is such that the destruction wrought by the failure of Millerism was both incomplete and temporary. Premillennialists did survive the disconfirmation of the well-publicized predictions of 1844, but major shifts in interpretation and in strategies of public advocacy were required for them to again become a credible public force. Reconstitution of American premillennialism took place gradually, from the mid-1800s through the 1920s. Inspired largely by the teachings of John Nelson Darby, perhaps the most influential of the new generation of prophetic interpreters, such men as James H. Brookes, C. I. Scofield, Dwight L. Moody, and Arno Gaebelein organized a series of prophecy conferences that rallied the premillennialist cause and provided a forum for the systematic development of new theories of biblical interpretation.[3] The associations formed at these conferences eventually bore fruit in the form of journals devoted to interpreting biblical prophecy and theological seminaries established to train missionaries who would disseminate the new interpretations. In the pages of journals, with titles like *Our Hope* and *Truth*, and in the halls of the new Bible institutes, premillennialists could debate among themselves about the fine points of doctrine while honing their scholarly arguments for confrontations with a largely hostile church establishment and public. The history of these men and the conferences, journals, and seminaries with which they accomplished the rehabilitation of premillennialism is beyond the scope of this study; my intention is only to summarize the basic features of their doctrines in order to establish the parameters of the rhetorical situation for apocalyptic argument in the late twentieth century.

Timothy Weber has told the story of how premillennialism's survival and ultimate prosperity came about through renunciation of Miller's "historicist" interpretation in favor of a novel theory of prophecy:

> [B]y 1875 a new kind of premillennialism, called "dispensationalism," began gaining wide acceptance among the same evangelicals who had considered the earlier Ad-

ventists fools and heretics. . . . In order to succeed where their predecessors had failed, the new premillennialists fought to establish two related truths: that they had nothing essentially in common with the discredited Millerites and that they were just as evangelical and orthodox as the rest of the Protestant mainstream. . . . Dispensationalists used a "futurist" interpretation of prophecy which held that no "last days" prophecy will be fulfilled until just before Christ's return. . . . Since they denied that prophecies were intended for the church age as a whole, they were for the most part relieved of the dangerous and often embarrassing task of matching biblical predictions with current events, and the task of setting dates for the second coming.[4]

Responding to the need to disassociate themselves from Miller's disgraced followers, the new generation of premillennialists produced a theory of prophetic interpretation that excluded any attempts at falsifiable prediction. Advocates of dispensational theology sought to maintain an intense expectation of Jesus' imminent return without resorting to date setting; they were careful to qualify their claims. As one preacher argued in 1915:

The Lord Jesus is coming back! He may be here at any moment! He may come today! . . . Now this is not a foolish assertion that He will come today. Nor is it the setting of a specific time for Him to come, which would be equally foolish and wrong. . . . It is the sober statement of a fact, to arouse souls from their carelessness and indifference, and point them to the clear testimony of God's only Word that the Lord Jesus *is* coming again, and *may* be here today.[5]

The new premillennialists were on solid scriptural ground in claiming that the Lord "*is* coming again," so long as they laid emphasis on the qualification, saying only that he "*may* be here today." Should anyone attack dispensationalist doctrine by associating it with the "foolish assertions" of those who had expressed their predictions with more certainty, its proponents only needed to stress the centrality of the "*may*" in order to disavow any predictive intent. Thus purged of its most dangerous error, premillennialism became, as it had for the Adventists after their retreat to the "safe position," a mechanism of ethical purification. One premillennial author clearly expresses the way in which belief in an imminent second coming could be used as an incentive to personal holiness:

I want to speak a word to the man who would be free from unclean personal sin: the next time the temptation comes, fix your mind on the hope of His coming. No man can easily do an unclean and unholy thing expecting at that moment that Jesus Christ might come. Can I cross the threshold of the questionable place? Can I read the questionable book? Can I be found with that questionable story on my lips? Can I be caught on the verge of that sin, if I am expecting that at that very moment Jesus Christ may come?[6]

The lack of a specifically anticipated date for the Lord's return strengthened the "purifying" motive of apocalypticism by keeping the believer in a perpetual state of excitement that required a constant awareness of guilt and repentance. The new premillennialism placed heavy psychological demands upon believers: enjoined to practice self-purification in anticipation of the final Judgment, they had to consistently hold their intense anticipation in check and turn their attention to organizing their everyday lives by planning for a future that most believed was unlikely at best. As Weber puts it,

> Dispensationalists were in an irresolvable bind: they had to live as though Christ might return at any time, but also as though he might delay his coming for years. The Millerites had the luxury of "millennial arithmetic." The dispensationalists, on the other hand, were forced to live with "maybes" and theoretical possibilities. Under such circumstances the new premillennialists did not dare sell their homes, quit their jobs, or break off all earthly ties. Their eschatology demanded that they live both in the present and the future, and most premillennialists recognized the danger of putting too much emphasis on either extreme. . . . Their hermeneutic forced them to live in the tension of now / not-yet.[7]

The danger of emphasizing the "now" in the anticipation of the Lord's return was that taking radical steps based on this belief might expose the premillennial believer to the type of public ridicule directed at those Millerites who had closed their businesses and let their crops rot in the ground unharvested. The danger of emphasizing the "not-yet" was that the believer might grow complacent, falling into worldly cares and temptations as consciousness of the imminent End receded and was replaced by anticipation of further delays. The new form of apocalyptic belief, then, required one to maintain a precarious balance that accorded proper weight to present and future considerations, simultaneously taking into account the imminence of the Lord's return and its possible postponement. To lose this balance was to risk material ruin and public derision, on the one hand, and the loss of one's eternal soul, on the other.

Earlier chapters of this study have established a framework that enables the critic to view this solution to the apocalyptic riddle as a discursive construction of temporality. The viability and durability of this construction can be understood once it is seen as another example of an epochal rhetoric, a systematic symbolic division of historical time that accords certain weight to actions and events in history and mediates the relationship of past, present, and future. The epochal theory of the new premillennialism divided history into biblical eras known as "dispensations." C. I. Scofield, whose influential Scofield Reference Bible popularized the new eschatology by presenting it in the margins of the King James version, defined premillennialism's divisions of epochal history as follows:

> The Scriptures divide time, by which is meant the entire period from the creation of Adam to the "new heaven and a new earth" of Revelation 21:1, into seven unequal periods, called . . . "Dispensations" (Eph. 3:2), although these periods are also called "ages" (Eph. 2:7). . . . Five of these dispensations, or periods of time, have been fulfilled; we are living in the sixth, probably toward its close, and have before us the seventh, and last—the Millennium.[8]

Just as did the prophetic interpreters that had preceded them, dispensationalists identified the present age as the penultimate historical era that would usher in the millennium. What distinguished their epochal rhetoric from earlier interpretations was its strict literalism in interpreting the dispensations as separate covenants that God had made with both Israel and the church. Whereas millenarians and non-millenarians alike, from Augustine to the Millerites, had assumed that the church had inherited the covenant from the Jewish people and was therefore the inheritor of God's promises to Israel, dispensationalists held that God's promises, once made, could never be revoked, and that the divine plan for history therefore involved the future fulfillment of prophetic promises to the Jews as well as to the church. The first coming of Jesus was intended to fulfill the dispensational promise of the Abrahamic covenant. However, the failure of the Jews to recognize their Messiah meant a disruption of the divine plan. After the rejection of Jesus by the Jews, "God had broken the continuity of history, stopped the prophetic clock, and instituted the church."[9] The epoch of the church was a new dispensation of grace, which occupied a "mysterious, prophetic time warp, a 'great parenthesis,' which had no place in God's original plans."[10] When the age of the church on earth ended, God would resume the Israelite dispensation and bring it to its conclusion. The apocalyptic prophecies in the Scriptures thus did not apply to the church at all, but only to that period of time when, it was anticipated, God would restore the Jewish dispensation. It is in this sense that the new premillennialists adhered to a "futurist" intepretation of prophecy, as distinct from the "historicist" interpretation of the discredited Millerites. Their strictly literal understanding of the relationship of Israel and the church as two distinct peoples of God required dispensationalists to disavow almost all attempts to read apocalyptic meanings into current events.

An obvious problem with this doctrine, given the necessity of maintaining a balance between present and future consciousness, is that it seems to lose sight of the imminence of the Lord's return. How could the believer anticipate the apocalypse at any moment, while at the same time reject any application of scriptural prophecy to current history? The answer lay in what was perhaps the most distinctive doctrine of the new premillennialism, that of the "secret rapture." This doctrine was based on a literal interpretation of certain scriptural passages, in particular 1 Thessalonians 4:16–17: "[A]t the sound of the archangel's voice and God's trumpet-call, the Lord himself will descend from heaven; first the Christian dead will rise, then we who are left alive shall join them, caught up in clouds to meet the Lord in the air. Thus we shall always be with the Lord." Adherents of this doctrine held, and still hold, that Jesus would actually have two Second Comings. The first Second Coming would be a secret one, in which Jesus' return would be visible only to his saints, who would be "caught up in clouds" and taken off the earth. This event would signal the end of the church's dispensation and the resumption of the dispensation of Israel; with the "great parenthesis" in history brought to a close in the rapture, God's prophetic countdown would resume with the final years of the Jewish era. The second Second Coming would be visible to the rest of humanity including the Jews, and would inaugurate a literal millennial reign of Christ on earth. The exact timing of the first Second Coming, the rapture, was a matter of some dispute among premillennialists. Most believed that the interval between the rapture and

Christ's visible return to inaugurate the millennium would comprise a seven-year period called the Great Tribulation, during which the demonic ruler of the Last Days, the Antichrist, would rule over a revived Roman Empire until his final defeat by Jesus in the catastrophic battle of Armageddon. Others believed that the rapture would occur in the middle or at the end of this seven-year period.[11] In spite of their differing views on the timing of the rapture, virtually all premillennialists believed that the return of Jesus was closely linked to the fate of the Jewish people, whose prophetically foretold restoration to the land of Israel in the last days was an article of faith.

The doctrine of the rapture, also known as the "any-moment coming," provided at least three observable rhetorical advantages. First, by positing what was in effect a floating "locus of the irreparable," a temporal threshold that would cut the audience off from the chance to avoid the persecutions of the Tribulation, it functioned as a strong incentive for the conversion of unbelievers. Second, as I have already shown, the thought of Christ's imminent return for his saints in the rapture functioned as a mechanism of ethical purification by helping believers to maintain their faith and resist temptation. Third, it gave believers hope that they might avoid not only the catastrophic events of the last days, but also their own personal deaths. The violent wars, earthquakes, persecutions, and plagues of the last days held no terror for those who were convinced that they would be literally snatched away into the air before any of these events occurred; and for at least some of the new premillennialists, the fear of dying was a significant motive in their personal commitment to the rapture as an article of faith.[12]

The epochal rhetoric of the new premillennialists, then, constructed time by balancing dispensationalism against the doctrine of the rapture. Dispensationalist theory discouraged historicist interpretations of prophecy and encouraged believers to look for prophetic fulfillment in a future division of time on the other side of the "great parenthesis" occupied by the church. Belief in the imminent Rapture offered an incentive for believers to organize their personal lives around the thought that Christ could return at any moment, without committing them to a falsifiable scenario of last-day events. Their prophetic scenario could not be falsified, since they had not committed themselves to any predictions of historical events that would occur before their own departure from the earthly scene. Those who believed in the rapture expected to view the catastrophic end of all earthly kingdoms from a vantage point in heaven, where they would be safe from the taunts and persecutions of an unbelieving world. The temporal insight that had provided the impetus for the formation of apocalyptic sects through the ages, the sense of a community uniquely situated at the edge of historical time, could thus be maintained in a more stable form, since the new premillennialists did not predict an immediate End of the world as such but only of the era of the church.

With the doctrines of the rapture and the dispensational division of history as the two pillars of their faith, supported on a foundation of "biblical inerrancy," premillennialists enforced a rigid orthodoxy in their prophetic journals, and established seminaries and Bible institutes to train ministers for the task of disseminating dispensationalist doctrines. Among the most prominent of these schools was Dallas Theological Seminary, where Hal Lindsey received his theological training, and which one scholar has termed the "center of institutional dispensationalism . . . the academic and ideological 'Vatican' of the [premillennialist] movement."[13] The Bible institutes and seminaries were fonts of much missionary activity, and eventually came to have influence and prestige that extended far beyond denominational boundaries.

Dispensationalists did make one significant exception to the rule that prohibited believers from reading apocalyptic meanings into current history: their emphasis on the literal fulfillment of God's prophetic promises to Israel resulted not only in increased attention to events involving the Jews, but also in efforts to convert American Jewry and in active relationships with the political cause of Zionism. While the legend of the final restoration and ultimate conversion of the Jewish people had been a minor topos of prophetic interpretation since at least as early as the twelfth century,[14] political conditions in the centuries after the diaspora and Jewish resistance to evangelization had combined to render this legend an unlikely fantasy. For this reason, those who hoped for an imminent End of history (such as the Millerites) were generally unwilling to accept any scheme of prophetic events that made apocalyptic fulfillment contingent upon the Jewish people's return to Palestine or upon an inexplicably sudden positive response to Christian conversion efforts.[15] With the growth and development of a viable Zionist movement agitating for a Jewish return to Palestine, however, this situation changed dramatically. Although their evangelizing efforts were never successful, American premillennialists followed the news of Zionist agitation for a Jewish state with eager fascination and even gave the movement significant political support.[16]

The Jewish return to Palestine was evidently a topic of portentous significance for American premillennialists. They believed that these events heralded God's preparation of the world for the close of the church era; with the restoration of the Jewish state, the stage would be set for the conclusion of the Israelite dispensation. When, in 1917, the Turks surrendered the city of Jerusalem to British forces under General Allenby, and His Majesty's Government promulgated the Balfour Declaration, which expressed the official support of the world's major colonial power for the idea of a Jewish state in Palestine, premillennialists in Britain and the United States were ecstatic. Conferences were organized to assess the significance of these events in light of scriptural prophecy; most premillennialists were predisposed to see the latest events as the fruition of the prophecy of Luke 21:24: "And Jerusalem shall be trodden down by the Gentiles, until the times of the Gentiles are fulfilled" (RSV). With the establishment of the state of Israel in 1948, premillennialists went into a veritable paroxysm of apocalyptic frenzy. The new state seemed miraculous enough even from a purely secular standpoint; apocalyptic interpreters regarded it as divinely instituted, the clearest proof God had yet offered that the age was drawing to a close. While premillennialists needed no such proof to convince themselves, the fact that they had been anticipating the restoration of the Jewish state since the late 1800s bolstered their credibility and supplied them with arguments that could be used to convince people who did not share their dispensationalist presuppositions, but who were impressed with the apparent religious and spiritual significance of the new nation.

No summary of the historical background of modern apocalypticism would be complete without referring to one other event that also seemed to offer proof of an imminent apocalypse to a wider audience than premillennialists. I refer, of course, to the discovery and use of atomic weapons in 1945. The epochal significance of this event was apparent to the entire world from the moment the bombing of Hiroshima was publicly announced. With the detonation of the first atomic bomb, the catastrophic vision of the Christian Apocalypse seemed to take on a whole new meaning. One need not, after all, be a believer to shudder at the words of the second epistle of Peter: "But the day of the Lord will come as a thief in the night ... the heavens shall pass away with a great noise, and the elements shall melt with fervent heat, the earth also and the works that are therein shall be burned up" (2 Pet. 3:10 KJV).[17] Historian Ray Petry noted in 1956 that the apparent similarity of this ancient catastrophic vision to modern technological realities had forced fundamentalists and nonfundamentalists alike into a sobering confrontation with the apocalyptic tradition. In light of the increasing proliferation of nuclear weapons, his assessment is even more relevant today than when it was first written: "[A] number of religious enthusiasts now find sudden and unprecedented support for their most frenzied contentions. More than one person not of their persuasion asks whether these wildest predictions may not shortly be translated from the realm of shadowy aberration into the blaze of stark actuality."[18] The triumphant rebirth of Israel had been anticipated since the late nineteenth century; in contrast, the invention and use of nuclear weapons was beyond anyone's power to foresee. Yet both of these events provided powerful new grounds for apocalyptic claims.

While historians of religion have duly noted the effects of these events on American apocalypticism, rhetorical scholars can offer a fresh perspective by viewing them as transformations in both the evidentiary base for persuasive argument that seeks to prove the imminence of the world's End, and the dramatistic frame through which public discourse is conducted. Claims that had seemed clearly incredible after the failure of Millerism in 1844 were suddenly entertained again by millions of Americans who were forced to ponder anew the ultimate destiny of humanity and the very real possibility of its extinction in a ghastly day of judgment. Contemplation of this fate naturally tended to increase the plausibility of the tragic view of history. As the world's superpowers competed in a deadly race for nuclear superiority, a race that seemed as inevitable as it was horrifying, the world audience froze into the passive role of spectators transfixed by a historical drama engendering "pity and terror" on a scale that Aristotle could never have imagined. Thus, in the terms of both argumentation and dramatism, modern audiences have been prepared by the nuclear realities of the world since Hiroshima for a resurgence of apocalyptic discourse in the tragic mode. I turn now to an analysis of the works of Hal Lindsey, whose effort to make sense of the nuclear age by interpreting it as the literal fulfillment of the ancient epochal rhetoric of the Christian Apocalypse achieved unprecedented success in the 1970s and 1980s.

Hal Lindsey and the Modern Apocalypse

There are significant differences between the previous chapter's criticism of Millerite rhetoric and the criticism of Hal Lindsey's discourse attempted in the pages that follow. Before Lindsey's works can be assessed, something must be said about the methodological issues raised by these differences. The study of the Millerites examined millennialism both as a social movement and as a complex system of argument, and sought to discover a pattern or progression of arguments from the earliest days of the movement to the period of time immediately following the Great Disappointment. This necessitated a dual methodology: a chronological account of the movement's history and a close textual analysis of Millerite arguments. This procedure is inappropriate to the study of modern apocalypticism. Although many contemporary preachers and authors have offered apocalyptic doctrines to the public, with varying degrees of success, no discernible social movement has coalesced around these doctrines. In spite of the phenomenal commercial success of Hal Lindsey's publications, they have not been taken as the basis for any concerted effort at mass persuasion such as that attempted by William Miller's followers, and it is difficult (if not impossible) to imagine them serving as an impetus to the creation of a new church or sect. The history of apocalyptic belief in the latter half of the twentieth century problematizes any attempt at establishing direct correlations between religious arguments and the behavior of audiences for such arguments. Thus, while the last chapter viewed apocalypticism in the nineteenth century as movement and as text, the study of recent apocalypticism does not permit a parallel analysis. The twentieth-century audience for apocalyptic discourse is considerably more difficult to delineate than its nineteenth-century counterpart.

A composite picture of the Millerite audience can be reconstructed from the records of the public controversy that surrounded the movement, from available attendance figures at public lectures and camp meetings, from information about the circulation of newspapers and pamphlets, and from the textual evidence of their own arguments. It is more difficult to reach firm conclusions about the audience for Lindsey's discourse. The only measure of audience response available to scholars at this time are imprecise sales and distribution figures for his numerous books and films. Many who heard William Miller's message felt compelled to convert others in their home churches, or at least to take some public stand in defense of their new beliefs (though one may infer from the circulation figures of Adventist newspapers that there were many more who followed the message with interest but without further commitment). The purchase of a mass-market paperback at a supermarket checkout counter, the watching of a television evangelist or a rented film in one's living room, do not require a person to commit publicly to a church or sect; the increasing pluralization and secularization of American civic life have made such commitment largely irrelevant.[19] This privatization of religion has made it increasingly difficult to devise meaningful measures of degrees of belief or commitment arising from an audience's contact with a particular text. The use of information such as sales and distribution figures to reconstruct audience characteristics prompts scholars to view Lindsey's readers as *consumers* of the discourse, rather than as argumentative interlocutors. This difference is to some extent a necessary consequence of the privatization of modern life that accompanies the mass-market distribution of media products.

Critics can, however, find in the text itself an argumentative structure that projects an "implied auditor" for the author's persuasive attempt at conversion. This method of rhetorical criticism, according to Edwin Black, "does not focus on a relationship between a discourse and an actual auditor. It focuses instead on the discourse alone, and extracts from it the audience it implies. . . . [In applying this method,] we would be claiming nothing about those who actually attended the discourse. . . . But we are able nonetheless to observe the sort of audience that would be appropriate to it."[20] Black's method necessitates a primary focus on textual criticism, but I do not intend the analysis to stop with the study of the text. The chapter that follows will link Lindsey's implied audience with the historical audience by focusing on public controversies over apocalyptic beliefs in the 1980s. The following analysis therefore seeks to reconstruct the appropriate audience implied by Lindsey's arguments, without losing sight of the historical audience that must ultimately be defined by an analysis that goes beyond patterns of consumption.

Authority and the Implied Audience

When William Miller set out to prove that the world's End was imminent, he could confidently assume that his audiences had already accepted a fundamental premise of his argument: that the Bible was the divinely inspired word of God. Hal Lindsey, in contrast, ostensibly seeks to convince a secularized audience that does not necessarily accept the Bible as authoritative. Consequently, he devotes the first three chapters of his initial best-seller, *The Late Great Planet Earth*, to establishing the accuracy and reliability of the Bible, as history and as prophecy.

Lindsey's arguments on the topic of authority are principally devoted to overcoming the skepticism of his primarily youthful audience. He was well prepared for this task by his years of experience as a missionary and preacher for Campus Crusade for Christ in the late 1960s. When Lindsey left the preaching circuit in 1969 and sat down to condense his sermons into a book, he used his experiences on college campuses as a guide to the construction of arguments that would prove appealing to the most skeptical of readers. In a published interview, Lindsey himself provides a description of the auditor he had in mind when he composed *The Late Great Planet Earth*: "As I wrote, I'd imagine that I was sitting across the table from a young person—a cynical, irreligious person—and I'd try to convince him that the Bible prophecies were true. If you can make a young person understand, then the others will understand too. A young person isn't hesitant to call you on something, and it forces you to come to grips with people who aren't in the religious 'club.' "[21]

Lindsey's attempt to address the implied audience of cynical, irreligious youth is evident in his introduction, which functions as a prelude to his demonstration of the authoritative nature of the biblical revelation. It is clearly aimed at the youthful reader who is reluctant to accept the traditional answers to life's questions provided by both religion and secular society. As Lindsey addresses and identifies with this reader, the implied audience for his argument is revealed. It consists of those who are curious about the future and whose quest for personal meaning is motivated both by dissatisfaction with the solutions of the older generation and by a yearning for absolute certainty: "We have been described as the 'searching generation.' We need so many answers—answers to the larger problems of the world, answers to the conditions of our nation, and most of all, answers for ourselves. How do we know in what direction we should go? How can we separate truth from opinion? In whom can we trust?"[22] A synopsis of possible answers to these questions follows. Just as the author of the Adventist pamphlet "The Groaning Creation" did more than a century before, Lindsey rejects in turn the various secular solutions proposed to the world's problems:

> On one side we hear that the answer to our dilemma is education. . . . Has the academic community found the answers? There are many students who are dissatisfied with being told that the sole purpose of education is to develop inquiring minds. They want to find some of the answers to their questions—solid answers, a certain direction.
>
> What do the politicians say? "We have the solutions to the problems. Elect us and we'll prove it to you." . . . And yet governments change, men falter and fall, great ideas are sometimes rejected by the shortsightedness of other men. Are we able to say that the answer is in the realm of political action?
>
> There are other places men search for answers: philosophy, meditation, changing environment, science. Please don't misunderstand me, all these are good if used properly. However, if we are absolutely honest, if we are to use our intellectual integrity, let's give God a chance to present His views.
>
> In this book I am attempting to step aside and let the prophets speak. If my readers care to listen, they are given the freedom to accept or reject the conclusions.[23]

Lindsey's rejection of secular answers to life's questions reveals his perception of the generation that constitutes his target audience. The "many students" who he claims are not satisfied with simply developing an inquiring mind are searching for deeper answers than can be provided by a purely skeptical intelligence: their willingness to experiment with philosophy and meditation is part of a larger phenomenon of cultural experimentation with religious alternatives. A 1977 article in *Publisher's Weekly* reveals that Lindsey's success was due in part to the marketing of his books to those with a general interest in the supernatural: "[B]ookstores shelve Lindsey's titles next to books about the I Ching and Transcendental Meditation;

[the Bantam edition] uses cover art that mimics *Chariots of the Gods*. As a result, Lindsey has gained a following among the same readers who made pop psychology, pseudo-science and futurism into the trendy topics of the 70s."[24]

The fascination of Lindsey's readers with the supernatural does not, however, extend to the most traditional source of supernatural guidance—the Bible. In his effort to overcome the selective skepticism of his audience, Lindsey appeals to honesty and "intellectual integrity," promising that his book will "give God a chance to present His views." The conclusions that his readers are given "the freedom to accept or reject" are portrayed not as interpretations that can be contested on the level of hermeneutic analysis, but as divine decrees. This appeal, the familiar argumentative strategy of the self-effacing interpreter, in effect identifies Lindsey's claims with the Word of God. Lindsey never betrays any hint of awareness that the meaning of the prophecies has ever been a subject of controversy. To admit otherwise would perhaps cast doubt on the certainty of the "solid answers" and "certain direction" that Lindsey seeks to provide for his searching readers.

Lindsey's conversational style makes his imaginary auditor a palpable presence throughout the book. This presence is particularly evident in the first three chapters, since before Lindsey can prove his case to the "cynical, irreligious" audience, he must first attract and hold its attention and overcome the inbred cynicism that prevents readers from attending to his argument. Chapter 1, "Future Tense," appeals to the reader by providing an overview of humanity's fascination with foretelling the future. Lindsey discusses some of the common methods of divination, noting that "Astrology is having the greatest boom in its history,"[25] while psychics and "prophets" such as Edgar Cayce and Jean Dixon have excited much interest. According to Lindsey, these various manifestations of spiritualism and mysticism are symptoms of a general fear of what the future will bring and a desire for certain knowledge. He provides a portrait of his reader's concerns: "In talking with thousands of persons, particularly college students, from every background and religious or irreligious upbringing, this writer found that most people want reassurance about the future. For many of them their hopes, ambitions, and plans are permeated with the subconscious fear that perhaps there will be no future at all for mankind."[26]

The portrait of the audience functions as a statement of intentions: Lindsey promises to reassure his readers and alleviate their subconscious fears. While the popular seers and clairvoyants also make such promises, Lindsey holds that they are unreliable guides because they have frequently been mistaken. In contrast, the Bible provides the clearest and most accurate knowledge of what is to come: "The Bible makes fantastic claims; but these claims are no more startling than those of present day astrologers, prophets and seers. Furthermore, the claims of the Bible have a greater basis in historical evidence and fact. Bible prophecy can become a sure foundation upon which your faith can grow—and there is no need to shelve your intellect while finding this faith."[27] Here Lindsey betrays his underlying purpose with disarming frankness. His book is a conversion appeal directed to those who have previously found the claims of Christianity unbelievable. He will seek to demonstrate the accuracy of biblical predictions in order to bring his audience into the Christian faith. Lindsey argues that those willing to grant credence to the claims of psychics and astrologers must, for the sake of fairness and consistency, be willing at least to investigate the predictions offered in the Bible. If they are willing to make "an honest investigation of the tested truths of Bible prophecy," then they are offered "hope for the future, in spite of the way the world looks today."[28]

Chapter 2, "When is a Prophet a Prophet?", is devoted to establishing the ethos of biblical prophets. Unlike the modern psychics and astrologers, these men were "willing to stake their lives on the absolute truth of their claims," and did "not allow themselves errors in judgment or mistakes in the smallest detail." The Old Testament prophets did not confine their predictions to events in their own time: "They not only made short-range predictions which would be fulfilled during their lifetimes, but also projected long-range predictions about events far in the future. . . . [M]any of these prophecies are predictions of exact historical happenings which will lead to the end of history as we know it." Lindsey demonstrates the accuracy of biblical prophecy by examining the predictive track records of Jeremiah, Micah, and Isaiah. Each took unpopular positions in the Israel of their day, predicting that their country would be defeated in battle and that the Jewish kingdom would be destroyed. In each case, he claims, their ability to foretell the future was confirmed by historical events: "They passed the test—summa cum laude."[29]

Lindsey's examination of fulfilled predictions of ancient events is brought to a climax in chapter 3 with a discussion of the messianic prophecies. The Jewish prophets predicted a messiah who would come to redeem his people but would be rejected by them. Two portraits of this individual emerge from the prophetic literature, indicating that He would have two comings: the first as a "humble servant who would suffer for others and be rejected by His own countrymen," the second as a "conquering king with unlimited power, who comes suddenly to earth at the height of a global war and saves men from self-destruction."[30] Lindsey asks, "Why did the majority of the Jewish people, who knew the teachings of their prophets, reject Jesus of Nazareth as their Messiah when he came?" He provides two answers to this question. First, he says, "the Jews didn't take their prophets literally," seeing only the prophecies of the conquering messiah but failing to note the predictions of his first appearance as a humble servant. This cardinal error, from the point of view of a biblical literalist, was compounded by another: "The second reason why the Jewish people rejected the Messiah was one of indifference. . . . They couldn't be bothered. They were too busy. They had a chariot race or a party to attend." Lindsey thus indicts the Jews of ancient Israel in terms designed to be clearly understood by modern readers, and urges his audience not to repeat their mistakes:

> Will we repeat history? Will we fail to take the prophets literally and seriously? . . .
> There are many more predictions about the reigning Messiah who is *yet to come* than there were about the suffering Messiah. Will we fail to weigh these prophecies for ourselves, in spite of what others may say?
>   The remainder of this book will present the prophecies which are related to the specific pattern of world events which are precisely predicted as coming together

shortly before the coming of the Messiah the second time—coming in power to rule the earth. . . . Do we dare allegorize away the meaning of these?

Will these predictions be fulfilled just as certainly and as graphically as those of the first coming?

This writer says positively, "Yes."[31]

Lindsey's warning against allegorical readings of scriptural prophecy is followed by his appeal to what he calls "the golden rule of interpretation": "When the plain sense of Scripture makes common sense, seek no other sense; therefore, take every word at its primary, ordinary, usual, literal meaning unless the facts of the immediate context, studied in the light of related passages and axiomatic and fundamental truths, indicate clearly otherwise."[32] This is as close as Lindsey ever comes to a defense of his own hermeneutic method. As I noted in chapter 3, Lindsey's appeal to the principles of "common sense" and literal, factual interpretation gives his argument a patina of scientific rationality, while eliding the role of the interpreter. Although he appears to acknowledge that the symbolic language of some prophecies cannot be taken literally, he fails to articulate the "axiomatic and fundamental truths" that allow interpreters to move beyond the literal, common-sense meaning. This topic will be taken up again later in this chapter. For now, I will follow Lindsey as he moves from the topos of authority into the real heart of his argument. The topos of time now comes to the fore as he begins to set forth his own program of end-time events.

Lindsey's Prophetic Timetable

As I have shown, the opening chapters of *The Late Great Planet Earth* laid the foundation for Lindsey's own predictions by identifying and addressing his target audience and constructing the authoritative grounds for this audience to accept the claims of biblical revelation. In developing his argument on the topos of authority, Lindsey utilizes a form that can be summarized as follows: "The biblical prophets predicted X; X came true. They predicted Y; Y came true. Since their predictions of past events have been proven accurate, the biblical prophets are an authoritative source of accurate predictions about the future." The concluding assertion functions as a warrant that, if accepted, effectively prepares the reader for the crucial deductive argument of the fourth chapter, which completes the pattern: "The biblical prophets predicted Z; since their predictions of past events have been proven accurate, and *since* part of Z has come true, the rest will be fulfilled within our lifetime." The demonstration of the historical accuracy of past predictions functions as a powerful argument in support of the authority of the Bible as divinely revealed truth. With his authoritative foundation secured, Lindsey can safely turn to those predictions that he claims directly concern present historical events. In the terminology of this study, his argument must now address the topoi of time and evil by showing when and how the demonic forces of the last days will coalesce to produce the climax of world history.

Chapter 4, entitled, "Israel, O Israel," opens with a reference to a "seven-year countdown," a "period climaxed by the visible return of Jesus Christ." Lindsey announces his intention to continue with the investigation of the "tested truths" of Bible prophecy: "Most prophecies which have not yet been fulfilled concern events which will develop shortly before the beginning of and during this seven-year countdown. The general time of this seven-year period couldn't begin until the Jewish people re-established their nation in their ancient homeland of Palestine."[33] Thus in the first paragraphs of the chapter the reader is given a hint of the chronology of last-day events and of their immediate relevance to our own historical era. My purpose in this section is to demonstrate that Lindsey's arguments achieved credibility in the American mainstream through an artful use of strategic ambiguity in his discussion of the timetable of prophetic fulfillment.

Lindsey's discussion of Israel and Middle East politics in this chapter provides evidence of the approach of this seven-year countdown to the return of Christ. The "Keys to the Prophetic Puzzle" are to be found in biblical predictions of Israel's restoration. The return of the Jews to the land of Palestine was the "paramount prophetic sign: Israel had to be a nation again in the land of its forefathers." The prophesied events of the end time could not take place until this condition had been fulfilled. Previous interpreters discredited prophecy by failing to recognize this fact: "The people who have fled to the mountains to await the end of the world haven't had the faintest idea about the truths in Bible prophecy. It is because of these unscriptural attempts at calculating dates that some eyebrows rise when we speak of Bible prophecy today."[34] Lindsey thus employs dispensationalist teaching on Israel to defend prophetic interpretation from the attacks of skeptics who point to its previous failures, and to dissociate his own interpretations from the failed predictions of the past. He argues that misguided attempts of previous interpreters to predict the End without taking seriously the prophecies of Jewish restoration have blinded contemporary readers: "The same prophets who predicted the world-wide exile and persecution of the Jews also predicted their restoration as a nation. It is surprising that many could not see the obvious: since the first part of these prophecies came true we should have anticipated that the second part would come true, also."[35]

Having demonstrated the veracity of biblical prophecies relating to the past, Lindsey now focuses his attention on the present. The "second part" of the prophecy to which he refers predicts not only the creation of the state of Israel, but also the subsequent catastrophic destruction of earthly kingdoms and the establishment of the messianic reign. Lindsey gives three direct scriptural references to support the purported link between the modern restoration of Israel and these catastrophic end-time events: Zechariah 12–14, Ezekiel 37–39, and Matthew 24.

In the prophecies of both Ezekiel and Zechariah, the restoration of the nation of Israel is a prelude to a final catastrophic battle that culminates in the establishment of the divine kingdom. Zechariah's prophecy, as interpreted by Lindsey, emphasizes the spiritual conversion of the Jewish people in the last days. The text of Ezekiel 38–39 offers another side of the apocalyptic vision with its bloodcurdling description of the destruction of Gog, "the prince of Rosh, Mesech, and Tubal, in the land of Magog" (38:2), whose military expedition against the people of Israel is destroyed by an eruption of divine fury:

> On that day, when at length Gog comes against the land of Israel, says the Lord GOD, my wrath will boil over. . . . I will summon up universal terror against Gog, says the Lord GOD, and his men shall turn their swords against one another. I will bring him to judgment with pestilence and bloodshed; I will pour down teeming rain, hailstones hard as rock, and fire and brimstone, upon him, upon his squadrons, upon the whole concourse of peoples with him. Thus will I prove myself great and holy and make myself known to many nations; they shall know that I am the LORD. (38:18–23, NEB)

Lindsey interprets Ezekiel's prophecy of the restoration of Israel and the destruction of the hosts of Gog as follows:

> [T]his physical restoration to the land is directly associated with triggering the hostility which brings about a great judgment upon all nations and the Messiah's return to set up God's kingdom. In other words, it is the presence of this reborn nation of Israel, flourishing in prosperity, that excites a great enemy from the uttermost north of Palestine to launch an attack upon them which sets off the last war of the world.[36]

The identity of the "great enemy" is revealed in the chapter that follows, entitled "Russia is a Gog." I will presently return to this politically loaded interpretation. However, a pivotal interpretive move in chapter 4 remains to be examined: the discussion of time. For, although both Ezekiel and Zechariah associate the re-establishment of Israel with a catastrophic battle depicted in apocalyptic terms, neither text contains any hint of chronology or any statement about when these events would take place. Lindsey must therefore offer interpretations of other prophetic texts that make these prophesied events directly salient to his audience and establish beyond any doubt the temporal link between the restoration of Israel and the final battle that marks the conclusion of the age.

The text of Matthew 24 provides Lindsey with the link that he requires. This famous prophecy, often called the "little apocalypse," depicts Jesus answering an inquiry from the disciples: "Tell us, . . . when will this happen? and what will be the signal for your coming and the end of the age?" His reply to this paradigmatic apocalyptic question contains many of the traditional signs: wars and rumors of wars, earthquakes and famine. There is also an obscure reference to a mysterious prophecy of Daniel:

> So when you see the "abomination of desolation," of which the prophet Daniel spoke, standing in the holy place (let the reader understand), then those who are in Judaea must take to the hills. If a man is on the roof, he must not come down to fetch his goods from the house; if in the field, he must not turn back for his coat. Alas for women with child in those days, and for those who have children at the breast! Pray that it may not be winter when you have to make your escape, or Sabbath. It will be a time of great distress; there has never been such a time from the beginning of the world, . . . and will never be again. (Matthew 24:15–21, NEB)

Lindsey interprets this passage in a way that supports his argumentative claim of a link between the restoration of Israel and the final battle of Armageddon: "[Jesus] speaks of the Jewish people being in the land of Palestine as a nation at the time of His return." A careful reading of the passage turns up no such direct statement: Lindsey's argument here rests on his interpretation of a geographic identification in political terms. "He speaks of 'those who are in Judea' [sic] fleeing to the mountains to escape the great battles that immediately precede His return." Lindsey also offers the injunction to pray for a favorable time of escape as evidence for the restoration of Israel as a sign of the End: "Another statement of Jesus demands a national existence with even their ancient worship restored. 'Pray that your flight may not be . . . on a Sabbath' (Matthew 24:20). This indicates that the ancient traditions regarding travel on the Sabbath would be in force again, thus hindering a rapid escape from the predicted invasion." Finally, "the 'abomination of desolation' has a technical Jewish meaning, which is to desecrate the Temple by bringing a Gentile or an unholy thing into the holy place. . . . The point is this, in order for there to be a Temple, there would have to be a repossession of the Temple site in ancient Jerusalem." Lindsey argues that this condition was fulfilled with the recapture of Jerusalem in the six-day war of 1967, which "set the stage for the other predicted signs to develop in history. It is like the key piece of a jigsaw puzzle being found and then having the many adjacent pieces rapidly fall into place."[37]

Lindsey's puzzle is not yet complete, however. Even if the reader grants that crucial conditions of the prophesied climax of history have been fulfilled with the existence of a Jewish state in Palestine and the repossession of Jerusalem, Lindsey has offered no direct evidence that establishes a timetable for the apocalypse; the End might still be centuries away even though the necessary conditions for the End are present today. In other words, Lindsey's argument must do more than establish that the Jewish restoration is a necessary condition of the apocalypse; it must establish the salience of these events for his contemporary readers by addressing the topos of time and resolving this topos into a direct temporal claim. Lindsey bases his temporal claim on a passage from the text of Jesus' prophecy in Matthew, the parable of the fig tree, which he claims "predicts an extremely important time clue": "Now learn the parable from the fig tree: when its branch has already become tender, and puts forth its leaves, you know that summer is near; even so you too, when you see all these things, recognize that He is near, right at the door. Truly I say to you, *this generation* will not pass away until all these things take place" (Mt. 24:32–34 NASB).[38] Like other passages in the "little apocalypse," this parable seems to have been deliberately obscure; the fig tree as a figure of the End times leaves considerable room for temporal ambiguity. Lindsey blithely ignores a multitude of possible interpretations of this passage and argues that the metaphor's true meaning is to be found in the tenor he selects in accordance with his interpretive bias:

> When the signs just given begin to multiply and increase in scope it's similar to the
> certainty of leaves coming on the fig tree. But the most important sign in Matthew

has to be the restoration of the Jews to the land in the rebirth of Israel. Even the figure of speech "fig tree" has been a historic symbol of national Israel. When the Jewish people, after nearly 2000 years of exile, under relentless persecution, became a nation again on 14 May 1948 the "fig tree" put forth its first leaves.

Again, it must be stressed that although Lindsey identifies the political rebirth of the Jewish nation as "the most important sign" of the impending End, the prophecy in question contains no direct reference to this event. Lindsey's argument rests on his inferences of a Jewish presence in Palestine and of the ongoing practice of temple worship, and on his interpretation of the parable of the fig tree. If the identification of the fig tree with the nation of Israel is accepted, the parable implies a temporal link between the Jewish restoration and the end-times. This link is strengthened by Lindsey's artful interpretation of the phrase *"this generation shall not pass away until all these things take place."* Other prophetic interpreters through the centuries, including the Millerites, have interpreted "generation" as a synonym for a race or people. Lindsey's argument rests on his reading of this word as a unit of temporal measure: "What generation? Obviously, in context, the generation that would see the signs—chief among them the rebirth of Israel. A generation in the Bible is something like forty years. If this is a correct deduction, then within forty years or so of 1948, all these things could take place. Many scholars who have studied Bible prophecy all their lives believe that this is so."[39]

Other translations render this crucial prophecy somewhat differently. The New English Bible renders the final sentence as "I tell you this: the present generation will live to see it all," a reading which seems to rule out Lindsey's interpretation and which apparently places Jesus among the ranks of failed prophets. As might be expected, Lindsey tends to select whatever translation provides the best evidence to support his apocalyptic claims. In view of the fact that Lindsey's argument depends almost entirely upon a disputed translation, it is interesting that he never acknowledges the controversy over the significance of the word "generation." Interpreted as a temporal measure, the word suits his predictive purpose admirably: it connotes a definite span of time that nevertheless allows a degree of flexibility and thus makes disconfirmation difficult. Linking a biblical generation to a period of "something like forty years" is as specific as Lindsey's predictions ever get.

Note here the strategy of using an argumentative form that implies deductive certainty without completing the syllogism to arrive at a falsifiable date. Note also Lindsey's skillful use of qualifiers: phrases such as *"something like* forty years," "within forty years *or so,*" and "all these things *could* take place," allow him to reap the benefits of predictive certainty without committing him to any claim that can be disproved with the passage of time. Finally, the appeal to the authority of biblical scholars has the effect of bolstering Lindsey's case even though not a single scholar is cited by name, and even though he fails to specify whether these anonymous scholars have endorsed all, or merely some, of the links in his elaborate chain of argument. The careful reader is left wondering whether the expert scholars of Bible prophecy are in agreement with Lindsey's contextual identification of "this generation" as those who are alive when the signs of the End first appear, or with his interpretation of the rebirth of Israel as the chief prophetic sign, or with his counting of a "generation" as forty years, or with the implied conclusion that the End will occur sometime around the year 1988, or with all of the above.

As I argued in chapter 3, apocalyptic speculation on the topos of time must resolve into a specific temporal claim if it is to capture the attention and command the adherence of its immediate historical audience. Millerite speculation solved this problem by predicting the End of time in a specific year, 1843, and gradually modified the argument into an even more specific prediction of a particular date, October 22, 1844. The flaws in this argumentative strategy have already been noted: although the prediction of a specific date for the End may well attract and convince an audience, the argumentative stance necessarily dissolves with the passage of the date in question. Since this resolution of the topos of time had been discredited by the disastrous failure of Millerism and other apocalyptic sects, the prediction of a specific date was not an available option for Hal Lindsey. In order to gain a hearing for his argument, Lindsey had to discover other avenues for rhetorical invention. The issue that he faced in his best-selling books *The Late Great Planet Earth* and *The 1980's: Countdown to Armageddon* was, therefore, how to predict the End of the world without predicting it. How could he promise and deliver to his readers a program of events for the future that satisfied present needs for understanding, without committing either author or reader to a specific date for fulfillment that would necessitate troubling attempts at justification after the predicted fact failed to materialize?

Given these problems, Lindsey's ability to establish a rhetorical stance that does not dissolve itself with the passage of time appears as a masterful use of strategic ambiguity. His reliance on the term "generation" provides a temporal measure specific enough to satisfy the audience's desire for certainty but vague enough to fend off attacks from those who seek to render his arguments outdated by the mere fact of history's continuance beyond his carefully unspecified target date of 1988. The multiple associations of the term, which denotes not only "the average period . . . between the birth of one generation and that of the next" but also "all the people born and living at about the same time" and "a group of such people with some experience, belief, attitude, etc. in common,"[40] are also significant. These associations help to promote a powerful identification with Lindsey's target audience, described as the "searching generation" in his introduction. Lindsey's use of this term fits the pattern of what G. Thomas Goodnight has termed "generational argument," discourse that represents and builds upon "each generation's unique encounter with human culture" and that is especially evident as it emerges at perceived "turning points of history."[41] The universal recognition of the nuclear age as a turning point that possibly represents the conclusion of world history provides a foundation for Lindsey's generational argument. His identification with the preoccupations of the postnuclear generation—which, as I have shown, he defines in terms of a search for personal meaning overshadowed by fear of planetary destruction—is certainly sincere, yet there is no doubt that he exploits these preoccupations adroitly and effectively.

In his later book, *The 1980's: Countdown to Armageddon*, Lindsey is considerably more vague about the question of dates, but leans even more heavily on his generational argument. He quotes the same scriptural passage that refers to "this generation" (Mt. 24:34), while eliminating his earlier equation of this time period with an approximate span of forty years. Although this text carefully excises the specific temporal references of his earlier best-seller, Lindsey still argues that the present era is destined to see the fulfillment of scriptural prophecy:

> But what generation was Jesus talking about? . . . He could only have meant the generation that would see all the prophetic predictions come together. The generation that witnesses that coming together will not pass away until all things predicted come to pass.
>
> WE ARE THE GENERATION HE WAS TALKING ABOUT! I say that because, unmistakably, for the first time in history, all the signs are coming together at an accelerating rate.[42]

A complete and thorough falsification of this predictive identification would require the death of every member of Lindsey's historical audience. By being no more specific than this, Lindsey manages to stir up apocalyptic excitement without ever facing the argumentative predicament faced by apocalyptic preachers through the centuries who failed to restrain their predictive overconfidence. Acknowledging the importance of caution, Lindsey justifies his own vagueness by referring to the favorite scripture of those who would suppress apocalyptic expectation: "Jesus went on to say, 'No one knows the day or the hour' of his return. But he tells us how to 'recognize' the generation during which he would come. We won't know the exact day or hour, He said, but we can know the general time."[43] Upon consideration of the history of apocalyptic argument, as documented by scholars from Festinger to McGinn, it can be said that this "general time," the span of prophetic fulfillment, will (or at least can in principle) remain infinitely extensive. Given the argumentative agility exhibited by Lindsey and his prophetic predecessors, one can safely predict that if he and the rest of humanity manage to successfully pass into the next millennium, updated editions of his books will appear with revised timetables that fit current events as neatly as they ever did.

Though Lindsey is careful not to predict an exact date or year for the End of the world, he does not shy away from predictive certainty on other matters. Reasoning from the prophecy's single, cryptic reference to the "abomination of desolation," *The Late Great Planet Earth* deductively argues that "first, there will be a reinstitution of Jewish worship according to the law of Moses with sacrifices and oblations in the general time of Christ's return; secondly, there is to be a desecration of the Jewish Temple in the time immediately preceding Christ's return. We must conclude that a third Temple will be rebuilt upon its ancient site in old Jerusalem."[44] The certainty of this argument derives from its enthymematic form; but critics may legitimately question whether Lindsey's unspoken premise—that the "abomination of desolation" can only refer to the desecration of a rebuilt Jewish temple—is strong enough to support the weight of his conclusion that the rebuilding of the temple *in the twentieth century* was foretold in prophecy. This topic is especially troubling in view of the fact that one of the holiest Muslim shrines, the Dome of the Rock, currently occupies the Temple Mount site in Jerusalem, and would presumably have to be removed or destroyed if the Jewish temple is to be reconstructed. Such an action would most likely have the effect of provoking just such a murderous war as Lindsey predicts for the final battle of Armageddon.[45] It is to the characteristics of this final cataclysm, and the confluence of political and religious forces that Lindsey predicts for the last days, that this analysis now turns in order to determine how he addresses the apocalyptic topos of evil.

Apocalyptic Demonology in the Nuclear Age

Chapters 5–9 of *The Late Great Planet Earth* are devoted to Lindsey's discussion of the geopolitical alliances that he claims will clash in the final battle of Armageddon. Chapters 5, 6, and 7 establish the identities of the nations that prophecy depicts as joining in a demonically inspired alliance that will invade Israel and be destroyed through divine intervention; the eighth and ninth chapters are concerned with the disintegration of the Western alliance into a revived Roman empire to be headed by the legendary Antichrist. My purpose in this section is to show how Lindsey's anticommunism leads him to predict a satanic role in the drama of the End for the United States' opponents in the cold war, the Soviet Union and China. Further, I will show how Lindsey's interpretation of the Apocalypse reconciles him to a pessimistic view of the fate of Western society, including the United States. Thus, I argue, Lindsey explains both foreign adversaries and domestic ills as rooted in their nature and origin in the cosmic evil that will be justified by the impending conclusion of history.

I have already mentioned Ezekiel's prophecy of the invasion of Israel by Gog, the king of the north, and Lindsey's identification of this tribe with the Soviet Union. The fifth chapter of *The Late Great Planet Earth* seeks to substantiate this claim and to identify by name the nations and peoples that will be allied with the Soviets in the final conflict. Lindsey justifies this approach by announcing his fundamental assumption about the prophet's intention:

> Ezekiel describes this northern commander as "Gog, of the land of Magog, the prince of Rosh, of Mesech and Tubal" (Ezekiel 38:2, Amplified). This gives the ethnic background of this commander and his people.
>
> In other words, the prophet gives the family tree of this northern commander so that we can trace the migrations of these tribes to the modern nation that we know.[46]

The basic premise that underlies Lindsey's interpretive method is, as Adela Yarbro Collins puts it, that biblical images "are simple code-words for historical entities . . . [and] were created primarily to convey historical information."[47] Given the assumption that the prophecy was intentionally constructed to provide clues to audiences far distant in time, it is only natural that a reader would use whatever tools are at hand to crack the code. Since the turn of the century, dispensationalist readers of the Scofield Reference Bible have found their key to the interpretation of Ezekiel's prophecy in the margins of that edition, where Scofield claims, "That the primary reference is to the northern (European) powers, headed up by Russia, all agree. . . . The reference to Meshech and Tubal (Moscow and Tobolsk) is a clear mark of identification."[48] Although Lindsey does not cite Scofield in support of his interpretations, he follows him on almost every point. Using etymological identifications derived from nineteenth-century biblical scholarship, and citing sources from the Roman historian Pliny to the *Bulletin of the Atomic Scientists*, Lindsey develops a picture of the military and political alliance that is destined to be destroyed after the attack on Israel in the final days.

"Meshech" is claimed to be equivalent to Moscow, according to Wilhelm Gesenius, who is introduced by Lindsey as the "great Hebrew scholar of the early nineteenth century." Tubal is identified with "the Tiberini, a people dwelling on the Black Sea to the west of the Moschi." Lindsey cites the authority of Josephus, the first-century Jewish historian, and Pliny, the historian of early imperial Rome, for his identification of Magog with the Scythians, the tribal ancestors of the modern Russian people.[49] A reader who is impressed with his scholarly research might do well to check his footnotes for these identifications: both citations are traced not to the original classical sources but to two modern biblical interpreters of the dispensationalist school. Finally, the word "Rosh" is interpreted by Lindsey as "a designation for the tribes . . . dwelling in the neighborhood of the Volga." Following Gesenius, he concludes that "in this name and tribe we have the first historical trace of the Russ or Russian nation."[50]

The evidence that Lindsey regards as conclusive proof of the identity of Gog is the statement in Ezekiel's prophecy that the Lord "will bring you [Gog] up from the uttermost parts of the north and lead you against the mountains of Israel" (39:2, RSV). Lindsey adds: "You need only to take a globe to verify this exact geographical fix. There is only one nation to the 'uttermost north' of Israel—the U.S.S.R." For those not persuaded by his etymological and geographical proofs of the identity of the leader of the military alliance—proofs founded on scriptural authority—Lindsey adds a quotation from a secular source, Israeli general Moshe Dayan: "The next war will not be with the Arabs but with the Russians."[51] (Although Lindsey does not give a source for this quote, he does date it to 1968, five years before the Yom Kippur War of 1973—in which, of course, the Russians were not combatants.)

Other members of the alliance that the prince from the north will lead against Israel, according to Ezekiel, are: Persia, Cush, Put, "Gomer and all his hordes," and "Beth-togarmah from the uttermost part of the north with all his hordes" (Ezek. 38: 5–6, RSV). Persia is identified with little difficulty as modern Iran; Lindsey counsels his readers to "Watch the actions of Iran in relation to Russia," since "significant things will soon be happening there," which will presumably have the effect of moving Iran into a military alliance with the Soviet power. Cush and Put have traditionally been identified with Ethiopia and Libya (and are translated as such in the King James Version), but Lindsey expands these designations to include

"Black African Nations" and "Arabic African Nations," and notes that "One of the most active areas of evangelism for the Communist 'gospel' is in Africa. As we see further developments in this area in the future, we realize that it will become converted to communism." Again following the lead of Gesenius and other authorities, Lindsey concludes that "Gomer and its hordes are part of the vast area of modern Eastern Europe which is totally behind the Iron Curtain. This includes East Germany and the Slovak countries." Finally, Beth-togarmah, or Togarmah, is identified with the Cossacks of Southern Russia. Lindsey views this as significant since the Cossacks have historically been noted for their horsemanship, and Ezekiel refers specifically to the destruction of the horses of the invading army of the northern kingdom. "Today they [the Cossacks] are reported to have several divisions of cavalry. It is believed by some military men that cavalry will actually be used in the invasion of the Middle East just as Ezekiel and other prophets literally predicted."[52]

Critical readers whose credulity has not yet been strained by Lindsey's propensity to twist historical details to fit his prophetic interpretations will surely pause in wonder at the picture he paints of an immense force of cavalry traveling over the vast mountain ranges and deserts that separate the Soviet Union from Israel. Lindsey's "literal" reading of the prophecy does not lead him to what might be considered the next logical step, arguing that "some military men believe" the hosts of Gog will attempt their invasion carrying the weapons enumerated in the prophecy: "I will lead you out, you and your whole army, horses and horsemen, all fully equipped, a great host with shield and buckler, every man wielding a sword, . . . all with shield and helmet," "bow and arrows, throwing-stick and lance" (Ezek. 38:4, 39:9, NEB). This indicates that Lindsey's biblical literalism finds its limits when it no longer suits his argumentative purpose. However, this distortion of history to fit the prophetic text is by no means the most egregious fallacy committed here. Where history cannot be twisted to fit the prophecy, Lindsey is quite capable of twisting the prophecy to fit history.

The dispute over the word "Rosh" will serve as an example. Lindsey admits that this term "literally means in Hebrew the 'top' or 'head' of something." For this reason the King James and other translations, such as the New International, render the passage in question as "*chief* prince of Mesech and Tubal." These alternative translations indicate that biblical critics are divided as to whether the passage should be read as "prince of Rosh" or "chief prince"; yet Lindsey glosses over the evidence of uncertainty even among evangelical scholars, saying only: "According to most scholars, this word is used in the sense of a proper name, not as a descriptive noun qualifying the word 'prince.' "[53] Perhaps by "most scholars" Lindsey means his teachers at the Dallas Theological Seminary, whose interpretations may provide support for Lindsey's dogmatically anti-Communist reading of the Bible, but are clearly contradicted by a wealth of modern scholarship even from within the evangelical camp. Some examples of such scholarship will serve to clarify this point. On the general issue of translating proper names, Larry Walker, one of the translators of the NIV and a professor at Mid-America Baptist Theological Seminary, says that "Many place names are so uncertain that translators must make a judgment with little evidence at hand. Whether in the mind of the ancient Hebrews the reference to a place in the Bible should be understood as a common noun or a proper noun may be uncertain."[54] With regard to the particular passage in question, premillennialist Ralph Alexander comments: "Some understand *rosh* to mean modern Russia, but this identity has no basis. Those holding such a view appeal to etymology based on similar sounds . . . but such etymological procedure is not linguistically sound at all. The term Russia is a late eleventh century A.D. term."[55] The conservative *Encyclopedia of Biblical Prophecy* presents G. R. Beasley-Murray's assertion that the "equation [of Meshech and Tubal] with Moscow and Tobolsk, and Rosh with Russia, is unsupportable."[56] Finally, evangelical scholar John B. Taylor comments on the various efforts by Scofield and other dispensationalists to read this passage as a reference to Russia by pointedly observing that such "attempts to read too much into the incidentals of the prophecy betray the ingenuity of the speculator rather than the sobriety of the exegete."[57] To this I need only add that Lindsey's ingenuity at prophetic speculation is compounded by a considerable measure of cold war ideological bias.

The chapters that follow provide further evidence of this bias. In the interest of brevity, I will not attempt a detailed critique of their arguments. However, chapter 7, notable for its explicitly racist title, "The Yellow Peril," is also distinguished by a lengthy anti-Communist polemic, and is worth pausing over in view of its unambiguous prediction of a nuclear conflict. Lindsey here turns from Ezekiel to the Apocalypse. Revelation 9:13–18 depicts another massive army, this time led not by the Russians but by demonic angels:

> The sixth angel then blew his trumpet; and I heard a voice [saying]: 'Release the four angels held bound at the great river Euphrates!' So the four angels were let loose, to kill a third of mankind. . . . And their squadrons of cavalry, whose count I heard, numbered two hundred million. . . . [T]he horses had heads like lion's heads, and out of their mouths came fire, smoke, and sulphur. By these three plagues, that is, by the fire, the smoke, and the sulphur that came from their mouths, a third of mankind was killed.

Lindsey couples this account with the portrayal in 16:12–16 of the "kings from the east" who assemble to take part in the final battle on the plain of Armageddon: "The original Greek words translated 'east' (Revelation 16:12) are literally *anatoles heliou*, which mean, 'the rising of the sun.' This was the ancient designation of the Oriental races and nations. John describes this vast horde of soldiers assembled at the Euphrates River as 'the kings of the sun rising' and thus definitely predicts the movement of a vast Oriental army into a war in the Middle East."[58]

Since the fall of Rome to the forces of Attila, and the Mongol and Tatar invasions of Eastern Europe, prophetic commentators have fantasized on the theme of barbarian armies overrunning the citadels of civilization.[59] The invading "hordes" of the Orient were at one time a real threat to Western society; today the invocation of this threat seems clearly xenophobic, as the title of this chapter clearly indicates.

Consulting a standard dictionary for a definition of the phrase "yellow peril," I found the following: "the alleged danger to the world supremacy of the white, or Caucasoid, peoples created by the vast numbers and potential political power of the yellow, or Mongoloid, peoples."[60] This hardly requires comment; however, it is worth specifying that I do not claim that Lindsey *deliberately* invokes such racist fears, only that they are called forth by his use of these terms whether he intends such connotations or not. (One would not refer to even the most massive of European or American armies as a "horde.") With regard to the size of this army, Lindsey notes: "We live at a time in history when it is no longer incredible to think of the Orient with an army of 200 million soldiers. In fact, a recent television documentary on Red China . . . quoted the boast of the Chinese themselves that they could field a 'people's army' of 200 million militiamen. In their own boast they named the same number as the Biblical prediction. Coincidence?"[61]

Coincidence? Of course not. The rhetorical question scornfully dismisses the possibility. Lindsey's eagerness to find meaning in such details recalls Aristotle's prescription for the construction of tragic plots: "Even chance events arouse most wonder when they have the appearance of purpose."[62] In Lindsey's tragic world, there are no coincidences, and there is certainly no consideration of the probability that, like the hypochondriac poring over a medical textbook who constantly finds his own ailments mirrored in the symptoms of every rare disease, an interpreter of prophecy who searches the world around him for apocalyptic signs of the times is likely to find that for which he seeks. In just such fashion Lindsey reads the prophecy of Revelation as a perfect description of atomic warfare. The fire, smoke, and sulphur ("brimstone" in many translations) that cause the death of a third of mankind are read by Lindsey as signifying a vast nuclear holocaust: "The thought may have occurred to you that this is strikingly similar to the phenomena associated with nuclear warfare. In fact, many Bible expositors [note again the appeal to anonymous experts] believe that this is an accurate first-century description of a twentieth-century thermonuclear war."[63] In another book, he goes even further with his "literal" reading of this prophecy, arguing that the horses with lion's heads actually describe "some kind of mobilized ballistic missile launcher," and that "smoke represents the immense clouds of radioactive fallout and debris, while brimstone is simply melted earth and building materials."[64]

An adversary that would resort to nuclear weapons for conquest must certainly be unredeemably evil; and Lindsey now elaborates on this theme with a polemic on the Communist doctrine of world domination. Lindsey details the emergence of China as a world power, and in particular the Chinese development of nuclear ballistic missiles, with an eye to demonstrating that China intends to use its nuclear capability to conquer the world. He quotes Lenin and Mao to prove that a Communist takeover of the free world is the ultimate goal of both the Soviets and the Red Chinese, and documents the Chinese progress in nuclear technology with copious quotations from the *Bulletin of Atomic Scientists*. Disputes within the Communist bloc are dismissed as a minor quibble over the means by which communism will conquer the West: "The Chinese insist that the world can be captured only by force of arms and violence: the Russians now believe that the free world can be captured by the relatively limited violence of internal subversion . . . masquerading under the guise of 'peaceful coexistence.' It should be marked well, however, that neither have [sic] disembarked from their goal of total world conquest for Communism."[65]

If this statement of Communist intentions is taken for granted, it is not difficult to believe that the Chinese might well invade the Middle East and employ nuclear weapons in their effort to achieve world domination. The unredeemed evil represented by the two major Communist powers is not, however, the only threat that faces Western civilization. The external threat of Communist subversion and invasion is compounded by the internal threat posed by domestic crises in Europe and America, crises that will result in the ascent of the fabled world dictator, the Antichrist. In chapters 8 and 9, titled "Rome on the Revival Road" and "The Future Fuehrer," Lindsey predicts the revival of the Roman Empire as the final geopolitical power that will set the stage for the climactic battle of Armageddon, and details the conditions that will pave the way for the Antichrist's rise to the head of this empire. Lindsay illuminates the career of the beast with seven heads and ten horns (Rev. 13) by returning to the original source of this striking image, the prophecy of the seventh chapter of Daniel. According to this scripture, the beast signifies a "kingdom which shall appear upon earth . . . [which] shall devour the whole earth, tread it down and crush it," while "the ten horns signify the appearance of ten kings in this kingdom, after whom another king shall arise, differing from his predecessors. . . . He shall hurl defiance at the Most High and shall wear down the saints of the Most High" (Dan. 7:23–25, NEB). The ten kings, according to Lindsey, symbolize the ten nations of the European Common Market: "We believe that the Common Market and the trend toward the unification of Europe may well be the beginning of the ten-nation confederacy predicted by Daniel and the Book of Revelation."

Lindsey cites various factors that he believes will impel the nations of Europe to revive the Roman Empire as a modern economic and political entity. Prominent among these factors is the fear of the Soviet threat. In view of the "basic weakness of the United States in its will to resist Communism," Lindsey claims that "Europe does not feel that it can count on us in a real showdown." The decline of American power is thus an irreversible consequence of history's acceleration toward its catastrophic conclusion: "[A]ccording to the prophetic outlook the United States will cease being the leader of the West and will probably become in some way a part of the new European sphere of power. . . . We realize that the United States is not mentioned in the Bible. However, it is certain that the leadership of the West must shift to Rome, in its revived form, and if the U.S. is still around at that time, it will not be the power it now is." Those who fret over the loss of America's preeminent status can rest assured that its decline is part of the divine plan of history. Replacing America as the leader of the Western alliance "will be a man of such

magnetism, such power, and such influence, that he will for a time be the greatest
dictator the world has ever known. He will be the completely godless, diabolically
evil 'future fuehrer.' "[66]

Developing this theme further in chapter 10, Lindsey turns to the ills of modern
society, which provide fertile ground for the growth of Antichrist's diabolical dictatorship. The topos of evil, which until this point has been elaborated in terms of
the foreign threat represented by communism, now reaches its full summation with
an apocalyptic jeremiad on the decadence of America and the entire modern world.
"[A]narchy, lawlessness, moral decadence, human desperation, and false hero worship" are only some of the conditions that "fertilize the fields that produce despots."
One after another, Lindsey cites statistics that show a numerical increase in the
evils of our society and places these evils into a grand prophetic calculus that
incorporates every dire prediction of the secular doomsayers. "While the number
of crimes in America was increasing 122 per cent, the population rose only 11 per
cent"; a United Nations report projects that "world population will reach 7.5 billion
by the year 2000," a development that will bring the world to an imminent crisis
by causing "pollution, congestion, . . . widespread famine, increased illiteracy, un-
employment, squalor, and unrest threatening the very foundations of public order
in developing countries"; emotional disturbance is on the rise, and "Youngsters are
being admitted to mental hospitals in numbers seven times their share of the total
population." Wars and guerilla conflicts increase in both numbers and ferocity;
revolutions and revolutionary movements "are becoming a way of life." The rise
in these various manifestations of evil is (it would seem) indirectly proportional to
the decline in traditional morality; together these conditions prepare the world for
the great tyranny of the End-time. "It doesn't take a 'religious' person to discern
the fact that what is happening is setting the world in the proper frame for a dictator.
We see anarchy growing in every country. We see established standards of morality
thrown aside for a hedonistic brand which is attractively labeled the 'New Morality.' " Demonstrating his claim that one need not be religious to discern the apocalyptic signs of the times, Lindsey cites more respected secular authorities who have
contributed to the doomsaying trend. Stanford professor Paul Erlich is cited as
saying, "Mankind may be facing its final crisis." Historian Arnold Toynbee is
brought onstage to declaim, "[T]echnology has brought mankind to such a degree
of distress that we are ripe for the deifying of any new Caesar who might succeed
in giving the world unity and peace."[67]

The statistics and expert testimony Lindsey cites are enough to alarm even the
most level-headed atheist; there is no denying the reality of the problems he enum-
erates. What can be contested is the apocalyptic framework through which he
chooses to understand these problems. In spite of the element of novelty introduced
by technological threats, the critic can discern in Lindsey's list of evils echoes of
an ancient lament, with antecedents going back to Plato and farther. The paradox
of scientific advancement coupled with moral degeneration, in the face of threats
posed by foreign aggressors, is by no means unique to our era.

Lindsey concludes his elaboration of the topos of evil in chapter 11, "Revival of Mystery Babylon." The previous chapters are concerned with the military and political roles to be played by the various apocalyptic figures of evil: Gog and his allies, the kings of the east, the Antichrist beast. One more role remains to be cast in Lindsey's drama of the world's End, that of the Great Whore depicted in the seventeenth chapter of Revelation as allied with the beast: "Babylon the great, the mother of whores and of every obscenity on earth" (Rev. 17:3–5, NEB). Lindsey interprets this as a figure of the apostate church that will lead humanity astray in the last days, "an all-powerful religious system which will aid the Antichrist in subjecting the world to his absolute authority." Though this church will profess to be Christian, in actuality its religious practice will be centered in the occult. The target of Lindsey's attack in this chapter is thus twofold: he condemns both the practitioners of the occult arts and the established churches that, in their zeal for ecumenical unity, are opening themselves up to "destructive heresy."[68]

Although the opening pages of The Late Great Planet Earth deliberately appealed to those interested in astrology and other methods of divination, Lindsey now attacks these practices as demonically inspired. The resurgence of interest in occult practices is part of a trend that will culminate in the apostate church of the last days, Mystery Babylon. Also contributing to this trend is the ecumenical movement in the Christian denominations, which has substituted "political pronouncements and ecclesiastical shenanigans" for the "doctrinal truths of the true church." Under the guise of true Christianity, the religion of Mystery Babylon prepares the way for the international dictatorship of Antichrist by establishing "a one-world religious system which will bring all false religions together in one unit."[69]

To those who argue that Christianity has always had its share of false preachers (and therefore that the turning away of today's church is not a reliable sign of apocalypse), Lindsey replies that the present apostasy is worse than ever before: "Some of you may be thinking that every generation has seen this apostasy in the church. This is true, but the Bible says that as the countdown before Christ's return comes closer, the teachings of the false leaders of the church will depart farther and farther from God's Word." While cautioning his readers to be on the alert for such false teachings in churches that appear orthodox, Lindsey manages to defend his own apocalyptic argument against attacks by other religious leaders. He implicitly characterizes those who disagree with him as participants in the false church of Antichrist:

> How can we recognize the apostasy in the church today? What are the characteristics of this harlot?
> Peter writes that in the "last days" there would be "mockers" who would say: "Where is the promise of his coming?" (II Peter 3:4 NASB)
> John, the apostle of love, spoke strongly about false teachers who deny the fact that Christ will return bodily to earth the second time. He wrote: "For many deceivers have gone out into the world, those who do not acknowledge Jesus Christ as coming in the flesh. This is the deceiver and the antichrist" (II John 7 NASB).
> We need to be alert. When we hear church leaders, teachers, or preachers questioning the visible return of Christ, this is a doctrine of apostasy.[70]

In the context of the mood of apocalyptic urgency that Lindsey has established, it would be difficult to argue against his position without falling under this condemnation. One can hardly imagine a better strategy for inoculating an audience against counterarguments than to dub one's opponents as "deceivers and antichrists." Lindsey's warning echoes the Millerite preacher Charles Fitch's claim that "whoever is opposed to the PERSONAL REIGN of Jesus Christ over this world on David's throne, is ANTICHRIST"; just as Fitch did, albeit in a slightly more understated fashion, Lindsey urges his readers to "come out of Babylon" and dissociate from the forces of evil in their apostate churches.[71]

Lindsey has now addressed all of the apocalyptic topoi : authority, time, and evil have each been elaborated into arguments that demonstrate the veracity of biblical prophecies, predict their imminent fulfillment within the lifetime of the reader, and detail the various political and religious manifestations of evil that will occupy center stage in the last act of the drama of history. Lindsey now moves to draw together the threads of his argument and summarize its import. Chapter 11, "The Ultimate Trip," is concerned with the rapture, the final event that will close the age of the church and inaugurate the "seven-year countdown before the return of Jesus Christ to earth." Lindsey urges his unconverted readers to accept the Christian message and be raptured with all other true believers. Appealing primarily to fear, Lindsey promises his readers that by exercising personal choice they may avoid their own deaths as well as the calamities to come:

> The big question is, will you be here during this seven-year countdown? . . . Will you be here when the world is plagued by mankind's darkest days?
>
> It may come as a surprise to you, but the decision concerning your presence during this last seven-year period in history is entirely up to you.
>
> God's word tells us that there will be one generation of believers who will never know death. These believers will be removed from the earth before the Great Tribulation—before that period of the most ghastly pestilence, bloodshed, and starvation the world has ever known. . . . This is the reason we are optimistic about the future. This is the reason that in spite of the headlines, in spite of crisis after crisis in America and throughout the world, in spite of the dark days which will strike terror into the hearts of many, every Christian has the right to be optimistic![72]

There is no mistaking the nature of this appeal in the context of Lindsey's generational argument; if the reader has accepted Lindsey's earlier claims, then it follows logically that he must be part of the "one generation of believers who will never know death." Lindsey has constructed the various evils of the world into a historical structure of inevitability: the only avenue of escape from the catastrophes of the Last Days is personal conversion. By deciding *now* for Christ, the individual can miraculously evade the terrors of history and even death itself. The prospect of avoiding death is a powerful incentive to conversion, and this incentive is strengthened by Lindsey's graphic depiction of the *manner* of death that believers will avoid. Who would not grasp at any chance of salvation from the events of the Tribulation, events that Lindsey tells the reader will include not only "ghastly pestilence, bloodshed, and starvation," but also the gruesome destruction of thermonuclear war?

Lest the reader miss this point, the chapters that follow continue the argument with a display of "apocalyptic pornography"[73] that is calculated to turn the reader's stomach, in which the Lord is depicted as employing nuclear arms to punish the troops marshalled against Israel:

> The nature of the forces which the Lord will unleash on that day . . . is described in Zechariah 14:12: "And this shall be the plague wherewith the LORD will smite all the people that have fought against Jerusalem; Their flesh shall consume away while they stand upon their feet, and their eyes shall consume away in their holes, and their tongue shall consume away in their mouth" (KJV).
>
> A frightening picture, isn't it? Has it occurred to you that this is exactly what happens to those who are in a thermonuclear blast? It appears that this will be the case at the return of Christ.[74]

The vengeful nature of Zechariah's prophecy is indisputable, but it is surely blasphemy of the highest order to interpret this text as a prediction that God will resort to nuclear weapons to punish opponents. In Lindsey's mind, there is no question here of the innocent victims of such weapons; for, if the argument for the rapture is accepted, there will be no people left on earth who can claim innocence at the time of this nuclear battle. The victims of the nuclear blast, those whose flesh is consumed by the divine firestorm, will have deserved this gruesome fate through their refusal to accept the divinely revealed truth. Thus the rapture doctrine allows Lindsey and his audience to contemplate with equanimity the most horrific fate imaginable, for the nuclear war to come will represent the judgment of a wrathful God against the sinful remnants of humanity.

A final significant feature of the rapture doctrine is its ambiguity with regard to temporal prediction. Lindsey is forced to admit that no one can know when it will happen, even though the prophetic signs indicate its proximity: "When will the Rapture occur? We don't know. No one knows. But God knows. However, we believe that according to all the signs, we are in the general time of His coming. . . . If you know what the prophets have said, and if the spirit of God has spoken to you, then you should be alert. There's nothing that remains to be fulfilled before Christ could catch up [sic; us?] to be with Him."[75] As I have argued above, it is precisely the indeterminacy of the timing of the rapture that explains its psychological effectiveness. Believers are kept on their toes, in a perpetually excited state of watchful waiting that keeps them from falling into sin and worldly cares. However, this indeterminacy also has a disadvantage, that becomes apparent upon consideration of the argument of chapter 3 of this study, which traced the operation of Burke's psychology of form in apocalyptic argument. There I argued that the preacher who claims that the End is imminent arouses audience expectations and stimulates a desire for predictions with a certain degree of specificity. The example of the Millerites shows that if a prophetic interpreter has left too much temporal latitude in his predictions, an audience will not hesitate to fill in the blanks with more specific dates. Lindsey's generational argument, which offers the widest timespan for the fulfillment of prophecy that will still hold the reader's attention, provides something of the specificity required in a prediction, but leaves much to the audience's imagination. According to the psychology of form, one might predict that such a wide temporal horizon would result in audience demands for further predictions.

In this regard, the doctrine of the rapture plays a significant role: it allows Lindsey to satisfy audience demands by being very specific about the timing and the nature of events that he predicts will take place *after* the believing Christians have been rescued from the Tribulation. In this way Lindsey is able to offer in chapters 12 and 13 (entitled "World War III" and "The Main Event," referring to the return of Jesus) a chronology of the seven-year Tribulation period that satisfies the audience's demand for specific predictions and for details of end-time events but does not expose the author's arguments to any risk of falsification. The Tribulation period is to last exactly seven years, from the treaty between Antichrist and the Jews until the battle of Armageddon; Antichrist will enter the Temple and declare his own divinity exactly three and a half years after the treaty is signed; the messianic kingdom that follows the Tribulation will last exactly a thousand years. With these specific predictions, audiences that have accepted the indeterminacy of the date of the rapture are provided with a kind of temporal precision that is virtually risk-free. Lindsey's calculations may be subdued, compared to those of the Millerites, but overindulgence in the pleasures of millennial arithmetic is a gamble that he can ill afford.

Lindsey's history of the future begins with a series of quotations that illustrate the gravity of humanity's peril in the nuclear age. The words of Albert Einstein ("There is no defense in science against the weapons which can now destroy civilization"), J. Robert Oppenheimer ("In the next war, none of us can count on having enough living to bury our dead"), John Kennedy ("Mankind must put an end to war—or war will put an end to mankind"), and Pope Paul VI ("A war would be an irreversible and fatal occurrence. It would not be the end of difficulties but the end of civilization") are juxtaposed to the now-familiar words of Jesus in Matthew's "little apocalypse": "You will be hearing of wars and rumors of wars—then there will be a great tribulation, such as has not occurred since the beginning of the world until now, nor ever shall." These modern scientific, political, and religious authorities drew conclusions very different from Lindsey's: they emphasized the catastrophic nature of war in the nuclear age in order to avert the possibility. Lindsey, in contrast, assumes that the final conflict that will end civilization is inevitable, and that humanity's fear of war and desire to avoid its terrors will ultimately help to bring it about: "Fear of war will grow until it prepares man to accept the Antichrist's solution for preventing war."[76] Thus, the very desire for peace will propel humanity, willy-nilly, into the trap set by the demonic forces of the last days. Only the return of Jesus will save the earth from total destruction.

Having "shown [in earlier chapters] the predicted powers that would arise shortly before the return of Jesus Christ and how these powers are simultaneously developing in world history," and how "world conditions in this generation are launched into a countdown that will end in the final collapse," Lindsey now proposes to "trace consecutively the predicted events that lead to the Armageddon campaign: the various sequence [sic] of battles, the particular powers who fight each other, and how in turn each is destroyed."[77] What follows is an extended discussion of military strategy in the battle of Armageddon, complete with maps of the Middle East showing the movement of the different national armies. There is no need (and certainly not enough space) to detail all of this strategic discussion here; it will be enough for my purposes to provide a synopsis of Lindsey's chronological account and show how it satisfies his audience's demands for specificity while preparing the way for his closing conversion argument.

According to Lindsey, "the Middle East crisis will continue to escalate until it threatens the peace of the whole world." Fearing for its safety, the nation of Israel will sign a treaty with the Antichrist in his role as leader of the revived Roman Empire (the ten-nation European Common Market), who will promise to defend the Jewish state from the attacks of its hostile neighbors. As soon as this treaty is signed, "God starts his great timepiece which has seven allotted years left on it"; this begins the Tribulation period, in which mankind will be deluded by the Antichrist's false promises. Under the protection of Antichrist, the Jews will rebuild the Temple of Solomon and reintroduce the tradition of animal sacrifice. At the midpoint of his reign, after "three and a half years of remarkable progress," Antichrist will enter the Temple sanctuary and declare himself to be God incarnate (the "abomination of desolation"). The rebuilding of the Temple will trigger an attack upon Israel by an Arab-African confederacy (the "king of the south"), joined by Soviet forces ("Gog") and armies from Eastern Europe ("Gomer"). After overrunning the Middle East with "amphibious and mechanized land forces"[78] (presumably including the Cossack cavalry), the Russians will betray their Egyptian allies and sweep southward into Egypt to destroy that country's army. They will then turn back to do battle with the forces of the Common Market nations led by Antichrist. The Red Army of Gog will be destroyed by a hail of "fire and brimstone," which Lindsey interprets as a tactical nuclear strike. Whether by divine command or permission,[79] there will be an exchange of nuclear ballistic missiles in which not only the Soviets, but other nations including the United States, will be severely damaged.

This nuclear strike is not yet the End, however. Somehow (Lindsey is not very clear on this point), "two great spheres of power [will be] left to fight the final climactic battle of Armageddon: the combined forces of the Western civilization united under the leadership of the Roman Dictator [Antichrist] and the vast hordes of the Orient probably united under the Red Chinese War machine." The Chinese will mobilize their armies, 200 million strong, and send them on foot across the Asian continent to the land of Israel, there to do battle with the forces of Antichrist in the valley of Armageddon or Megiddo. The battle line will extend throughout Israel; the resulting carnage will be so great that "blood will stand to the horses' bridles for a total distance of 200 miles northward and southward of Jerusalem." This battle will escalate into "an all-out attack of ballistic missiles upon the great metropolitan areas of the world," in which "All the cities of the nations will be destroyed."[80] But, just as hope for humanity's survival appears utterly lost, Christ will return.

> As the battle of Armageddon reaches its awful climax and it appears that all life will be destroyed on earth—in this very moment Jesus Christ will return and save man from self-extinction.
>
> As history races toward this moment, are you afraid or looking with hope for deliverance? The answer should reveal to you your spiritual condition.
>
> One way or another history continues in a certain acceleration toward the return of Christ. Are you ready?[81]

The test of a true believer, according to Lindsey, is whether he or she can contemplate this terrifying scenario without fear, and even anticipate it with hope. This can be explained by the belief that (as has already been mentioned) those who have converted and become Christians before the Tribulation will not have to endure these events. Yet, however "rational" (on its own terms) this solution may be, many who consider themselves Christian will find Lindsey's hopeful anticipation of such an orgy of destruction an appalling departure from the message of Jesus. Lindsey considers the rapture, and the millennial kingdom that will follow the catastrophic nuclear Armageddon in a newly restored earth cleansed of radioactive fallout, to be the essence of the Christian hope; but any understanding of Christianity that turns this tale of horror into "a consummation devoutly to be wished" (to quote Shakespeare's Hamlet somewhat out of context) has, I submit, lost something of its founder's original spirit.

Lindsey skillfully incorporates into his account a wealth of specific details from secular sources that function both to satisfy curiosity and to enhance the credibility of his fantastic scenario. For example, he discusses at length the wealth and natural resources of the land of Israel, which will tempt the Russian forces into their mission of plunder, in order to render the prospect of this invasion more plausible: "One of the chief minerals in the Dead Sea is potash, which is a potent fertilizer. When the population explosion begins to bring famine, potash will become extremely valuable for food production. It is strategic wealth of this sort that will cause the Russian bloc to look for an opportunity to invade and conquer Israel, according to Ezekiel."[82] Perhaps the most striking example of Lindsey's attempts to support his prophetic predictions with precise evidence from secular sources is the claim that geological surveys confirm his account of the physical return of Christ:

> Jesus' feet will first touch the earth where they left the earth, on the Mount of Olives. The mountain will split in two with a great earthquake the instant that Jesus' foot touches it. The giant crevice that results will run east and west through the center of the mountain. . . .
>
> It was reported to me that an oil company doing seismic studies of this area in quest of oil discovered a gigantic fault running east and west precisely through the center of the Mount of Olives. The fault is so severe that it could split at any time. It is awaiting "the foot."[83]

As these examples illustrate, Lindsey often attempts to validate his interpretations of biblical prophecy with copious references to secular news reports and technical evidence derived from often anonymous but supposedly authoritative sources ("some military men," "many Bible scholars") as well as personal testimony ("It was reported to me that . . . "). These supporting arguments are weakened by their lack of documentation and, from a skeptical perspective, appear inadvertently comical in their literalism. Yet their effectiveness, such as it is, does not lie in their argumentative validity, but in their ability to subsume evidence and authoritative testimony from secular sources into a religious perspective.

Chapters 11, 12, and 13 deal in sequence with the events of the last seven years of history: the Rapture, World War III, and the Second Coming. In chapter 14, "Polishing the Crystal Ball," Lindsey concludes his argument by moving from the grand scenario of the seven years that follow the rapture to the years that lie immediately ahead for his readers. Here he predicts a series of developments which will move history further on the road toward prophetic fulfillment. These include: apostasy and departure from sound biblical teaching in the ministry; a decline in the political and economic strength of the United States, which will force the nations of Western Europe "to unite and become the standard-bearer of the Western world" in the face of continued efforts of Communist military expansion; and a marked worsening of social evils such as "crime, riots, lack of employment, poverty, illiteracy, mental illness, illegitimacy, etc.," all of which are bound to "increase as the population explosion begins to multiply geometrically in the late '70's." As for international politics, Lindsey advises the reader to "Keep your eyes on the Middle East. If this is the time that we believe it is, this area will become a constant source of tension for all the world."[84] This last directive seems to be a clear invitation to commit the fallacy of "affirming the consequent" warned against in every basic text of logic and argument: "If A then B; B, therefore A." Since B (the Middle East remains "a constant source of tension") can be easily affirmed with a glance at a daily newspaper, the reader is led through enthymematic logic to the conclusion A ("this is the time we believe it is," that is, the time of the End).

To charge Lindsey with promoting fallacious reasoning here may, however, be beside the point. There is nothing in these predictions that Lindsey has not presented, or at least hinted at, in earlier pages; his aim in this chapter is not to prove his argument that the world's End is imminent, but to restate his earlier themes in a final summation, a last dire warning that vividly recreates the sense of history hurtling toward its ordained catastrophic conclusion for the benefit of the skeptical inquirer addressed in the opening pages. In his final paragraphs, Lindsey asks his readers, "After considering the incredible things in this book, what should our attitude and purpose be?" Not surprisingly, this question is a prelude to an appeal for Christian conversion:

First, if you are not sure that you have personally accepted the gift of God's forgiveness which Jesus Christ purchased by bearing the judgment of a holy God that was due your sins, then you should do so right now wherever you are. It may be that you are bothered because you can't understand it all, or you feel that you don't have enough faith. Don't let either of these things bother you. . . . Right at this moment, in your own way, thank Jesus for dying for your sins and invite Him to come into your heart.[85]

The appeal to accept Lindsey's version of the Christian message as the authoritative plan for salvation is followed by advice on how to live one's life (as Weber puts it) "in the shadow of the Second Coming." Lindsey counsels his readers to avoid despair; the horrifying scenarios of nuclear war presented earlier are outweighed by the more hopeful expectations of Christ's imminent return. Here his advice reflects a concern that those who have accepted his message might be prone to the extreme manifestations of End-time excitement that have discredited apocalyptic believers of the past:

> [F]ar from being pessimistic and dropping out of life, we should be rejoicing in the knowledge that Christ may return any moment for us. This should spur us on to share the good news of salvation in Christ with as many as possible. . . . [W]e should plan our lives as though we will be here our full life expectancy, but live as though Christ may come today. We shouldn't drop out of school or worthwhile community activities, or stop working, or rush marriage, or any such thing unless Christ clearly leads us to do so. However, we should make the most of our time that is not taken up with the essentials.[86]

Lindsey's historical pessimism is counterbalanced by a cosmic optimism, which offers Christ's imminent return as an inspiration to missionary activity. As Lindsey well knows, however, finding the proper balance between historical pessimism and cosmic optimism, between the "now" and the "not-yet," is no easy task. The temptation to drop out not only of political life, but of one's daily responsibilities, remains ever present for those believers whose anticipation can barely be contained. In his conclusion, Lindsey urges his readers to stand fast in the premillennial faith and reiterates the need to continue working right up to the time of the End.

> As we see the world becoming more chaotic, we can be "steadfast" and "immovable," because we know where it's going and where we are going. We know that Christ will protect us until His purpose is finished and then He will take us to be with himself. . . .
>
> So let us seek to reach our family, our friends, and our acquaintances with the Gospel with all the strength that He gives us. The time is short.
>
> In the early centuries the Christians had a word for greeting and departing; it was the word, "maranatha," which means, "the Lord is coming soon." We can think of no better way with which to say good-by—
>
> MARANATHA![87]

From the opening pages, which evoked the fears and uncertainties of a generation reaching an uneasy maturity in the shadow of the Bomb, to the certainty of the farewell, which evokes the apocalyptic hope of the ages, Lindsey has come full circle. The world's descent into chaos no longer threatens the reader; rather, it provides a foundation for security. History's progress toward a final massive (and quite literal) bloodbath is itself evidence of the sure word of divine prophecy, and with the knowledge of this word, the reader is rescued from chaos and uncertainty. The cry of "maranatha," which is a greeting as well as a good-bye, welcomes the new world as it bids farewell to the old. With the knowledge of our destiny comes the awareness of our missionary task; time is short, and there is the Lord's work to do. This work is not to be understood as a misguided attempt to reform society; in view of the prophesied slide into world anarchy and dictatorship, there is clearly no point in entering and reforming public life. Rather, our efforts should be directed to reaching those in a private sphere composed of "our family, our friends, and our acquaintances."

Lindsey's reformulation of the apocalyptic topoi certainly achieved a degree of success; but any critical evaluation of the significance of his work must depend on how this success is measured and defined. Rhetorical success is clearly best understood as the ability to reach and persuade an audience; however, the meaning of success will differ as we turn from considering the text's implied audience to the actual audience of those who came into contact with its message. Although Lindsey's achievement in reaching the historical audience can be measured in millions of books sold, it is impossible to determine how many people actually read these books, let alone the number that were persuaded by them. Still, the critic may point to certain signs indicating that a considerable portion of the American public have accepted key portions of Lindsey's arguments. For example, a 1984 Yankelovich survey on American attitudes toward nuclear war confirms the widespread perception of a connection between biblical prophecy and the nuclear threat. Thirty-nine percent of those surveyed in this study expressed agreement with the statement, "When the Bible predicts that the earth will be destroyed by fire, it's telling us about nuclear war."[88] While the prevalence of this belief cannot be attributed directly to Lindsey, it is logical to conclude that the millions of copies of his books that were sold in the fourteen years before the survey was taken played a significant role in its widespread acceptance.

Lindsey's success in convincing those represented by his implied audience of "cynical, irreligious" skeptics is another matter. Here the critic can expand upon Edwin Black's notion of the implied auditor. Whereas Black treated the "audience that would be appropriate" to the discourse as virtually identical to the "model of what the rhetor would have his real auditor become," Lindsey's text appears to imply two audiences, or rather a transformation from an appropriate audience to an ideal one. At the outset, the appropriate audience is composed of cynics and skeptics; by the time he reaches his conclusion, the audience addressed is an ideal audience, secure in the Christian faith (as Lindsey has defined it). In this regard, the critic may define rhetorical success as the author's inducement of the reader to traverse the path from doubt to faith. It is worth pausing to dwell on the means by which this transformation is effected. Lindsey's argument on the topos of authority ostensibly proves the accuracy and reliability of biblical prophecy as a prelude to his supposedly literal interpretation of the apocalyptic signs of the impending

End. His claim that the culmination of history must be expected within the lifetime of his audience rests on sign arguments, which depend in turn on the argument from authority. Yet the argument from authority is flawed by Lindsey's failure to acknowledge the interpreter's role. Although William Miller assumed the divine authority of the Bible, he at least spent considerable effort in defending his exegetical and interpretive principles, and was willing to engage others in debate over the meaning of a prophetic text. Lindsey, on the other hand, never admits that the meaning of any prophecy is a disputable issue. Furthermore, as I have shown, he shifts between literal and figurative interpretations as it suits his purpose to do so, and fails to justify these shifts. Thus, he violates a major premise of his authoritative argument, the "golden rule of interpretation" that enjoins readers to "take every word at its . . . literal meaning unless the facts of the immediate context, studied in the light of related passages and axiomatic and fundamental truths, indicate clearly otherwise."[89] He inaccurately depicts unanimity among biblical scholars, and condemns all those who do not subscribe to this supposed unanimity as the "false teachers" whose apostasy was foretold in scripture.

Lindsey's strategy thus, in effect, duplicates the circularity of the Millerite argument from sign: he denies the credentials of all authorities who disagree with his central apocalyptic claim, and transforms their disagreement into further support for the claim by interpreting it as itself a sign of the End. This sign argument, of course, will only make sense to someone who has already accepted Lindsey's interpretation of the Bible as authoritative. Readers who share the cynicism and skepticism of Lindsey's implied audience might well refuse to allow this move. Thus, it may be that many of Lindsey's proofs, like those of the Millerites, are exercises in self-persuasion; that the actual audiences that Lindsey's book targets are those who have already accepted many of the tenets of premillennialism, and for whom the authoritative arguments are largely superfluous.

On the other hand, the critic might look to the text again to discover other, more subtle strategies for convincing the skeptical reader. "Rational" arguments from authority and sign are not the only tactics Lindsey uses to propel his audience from doubt to faith; his underlying strategy is best characterized as an appeal to fear. Lindsey seeks to bring about conversion by heightening the reader's anxiety about the future while removing all purely secular solutions to this anxiety. Thus motivated by fear and anxiety, and with secular avenues of escape blocked on all sides, the audience is meant to stampede into the corral of apocalyptic dogmatism. The causes of this fear, the prospects of nuclear war, societal breakdown, and ecological catastrophe, appear to indicate the limits of a purely secular frame of acceptance. The comic view of history as infinite episodic progress breaks down before the Bomb, which appears as a rent in the fabric of history; the frame of the tragic apocalypse explains the feared nuclear catastrophe not as historical rupture, but as the culmination of the Christian rhetorical epoch. Fear is thus overcome through a narrative frame that endows catastrophe with a transcendent teleological meaning. To the extent that actual readers of Lindsey's book are motivated to convert by the experience of fear and anxiety that he evokes, these readers follow the path Lindsey has marked off for his implied audience.

I have already made note of the fact that Lindsey's appeal to the postnuclear generation was crafted and polished from the sermons that he preached on college campuses in the late 1960s. There is surely enough significance in this fact, and in the book's publication date of 1970, to permit a brief comparison with the rhetoric of the Millerites. At least one scholar has claimed that the decade of the 1960s marked a "Fourth Great Awakening" that paralleled the religious revivals of the 1830s in spirit if not in content.[90] Both historical eras were characterized by a myriad of reform movements seeking changes in American spiritual, political, and economic life. Both sustained for a time a mood of giddy optimism about the future that foundered in increased social conflict and the failure of political reform. In each era, various members of the generation of discouraged reformers challenged the legitimacy of contemporary religious and political authority by experimenting with new forms of communal living and exhibiting fascination with a variety of occult and spiritual manifestations. It would be a mistake to push this comparison too far; there are significant points of contrast as well as of similarity between the 1830s and the 1960s. Yet in spite of the many diverging forms that the pursuit of piety can assume, from a temperance movement to a quest for mystical experience through drugs, it is surely reasonable to view the religious and political upheavals of the early nineteenth and mid-twentieth centuries as essentially similar struggles to define and achieve new ideals of the good life. If such struggles are periodic and cyclical, as some historians of American revivalism and reform maintain, then it should come as no surprise that the apocalypticism of each postawakening period reflects the difficulty of implementing these ideals. Comparing the modern "awakening" of the 1960s to its counterpart in the 1830s, William McLoughlin finds evidence in our era of a "shift from postmillennial optimism to premillennial pessimism among major segments of the population."[91] If this perception is accurate, then the rhetorics of William Miller and Hal Lindsey appear to have served identical functions in their respective eras, as a restatement of the tragic view of history and a rejection of the comic. Just as Miller did for his generation, Lindsey presented in *The Late Great Planet Earth* a message of social pessimism that saw reform as contrary to the tide of history. As time passed, however, this rhetorical stance proved mutable. In my next chapter, I will show how Lindsey adroitly revised his apocalyptic message to provide an ideological basis for the conservative political activism of the 1980s.

SEVEN

Apocalyptic Politics in
the New Christian Right

The last chapter concluded with a comparison of William Miller's apocalyptic rhetoric to that of Hal Lindsey. This comparison seems to break down rapidly when one contrasts the movements associated with each. Millerite apocalypticism was utterly apolitical; the movement's single focus was to spread the doctrine of the approaching End. Yet it must not be forgotten that, for many Millerites, the "Great Disappointment" was the culmination of a lifetime of lesser disappointments in the reform causes of abolition and temperance. Lindsay's writings provoked rhetorical effects that were subtler than Miller's but no less dramatic; ultimately, his audience's apocalyptic beliefs led them not away from, but into, public life. Although *The Late Great Planet Earth* had adopted an apolitical stance, it did not actively discourage believers from entering the public realm. What no one, certainly not Lindsey himself, had foreseen in the early 1970s was the surging strength of American evangelicals and fundamentalists on the American political scene. Although it was Jimmy Carter who brought the "born-again" constituency to national attention, it was not until the presidential candidacy of Ronald Reagan, who had maintained ties to the fundamentalist community throughout his political career, that this constituency gained a measure of real power. The unexpected prominence of what came to be called the New Christian Right in American political life in the late seventies and early eighties provided conservative premillennialists like Lindsey and Jerry Falwell with an irresistible opportunity to help elect one of the Elect to the White House—an opportunity that had no place in the prophetic scenarios of *The Late Great Planet Earth*.

The increasing political activism of fundamentalists in the 1980s has proved puzzling to some scholars. Timothy Weber, for example, argues that Jerry Falwell and Hal Lindsey's advocacy of conservative military and economic policies simply contradicts their pessimistic interpretation of prophecy.[1] An essay by three rhetorical critics poses the problem as follows: "How can the [fundamentalist] movement embrace a pessimistic doctrine of God-willed world decline while optimistically advocating political action?"[2] While acknowledging the apparent inconsistency, I argue that a dramatistic theory of apocalypse can account for this peculiar blend of optimism and pessimism, and that the supposed inconsistency between belief and practice only presents a problem to those outside the belief system. To simply assume a contradiction leads critics to view these belief systems as rationalizations that hastily patch together positions that ultimately are irreconcilable. The critic's task, in my view, is rather to study political action not as a contradiction, but a fulfillment, of religious doctrine, not assuming the irrationality of any reconciliation between the two, but studying the rationality of religious activism on its own (narrative and dramatic) terms.

The phenomenon of activist fundamentalism cannot be explained solely in terms of premillennial apocalypticism; the dispensationalist theory of history was only one of the symbolic resources upon which the movement drew. Numerous social, economic, and technological factors combined in the late seventies and early eighties to create an opportune political moment for the fundamentalist movement. The growth of Christian broadcasting helped to shape a vast audience for religious rhetoric, while giving some religious entrepreneurs an economic base that enabled forays into hitherto untouched secular realms. Local opposition to abortion, gay rights, the Equal Rights Amendment, and "secular humanism" in school textbooks was welded into a national coalition through the efforts of conservative activists such as Richard Viguerie and Paul Weyrich, who pioneered the use of computer technology for direct mail campaigns. Joining forces with groups such as Christian Voice and the National Christian Action Coalition, Jerry Falwell's Moral Majority coordinated legislative battles and became a lightning rod of public controversy as it led what seemed to be a national attack on liberalism and the welfare state.

The politics of the early 1980s can be described as apocalyptic in a particular and restricted sense: arguments on both the left and right seemed to appeal to ultimates. On the right, politicians and preachers invoked the spectre of a world Communist dictatorship that would threaten America with either enslavement or apocalyptic destruction if we did not invest in new weapons systems. On the left, the nuclear freeze movement blanketed the cultural landscape with images of the nuclear devastation that would result if such purchases were not halted. Given the polarization of these rhetorical visions, it is not surprising that their proponents tended to demonize each other. For many Americans, the fundamentalists' entry into politics appeared to threaten not only the hard-fought victories of the New Deal and the Great Society, but also the ideal of separation between church and state. Liberal commentators decried the efforts of Falwell, Lindsey, and their cohorts to base foreign and domestic policy on their reading of the Bible; and for a time, considerable ink was shed in the pages of both popular magazines and scholarly journals by those seeking to interpret and explain the strident new voice of religious conservatives.[3] A few years have passed, and although this voice has not departed, it has died down somewhat. The secular republic no longer seems threatened by fundamentalist Christians. The collapse of the Moral Majority, the financial and sexual scandals that brought down the powerful ministries of televangelists Jim Bakker and Jimmy Swaggart, and the failure of Pat Robertson's presidential bid are symptomatic of a changing religious and political climate that should allow a more sober and less alarmist assessment of the contributions of American premillenni- alists.

My purpose here is to make an introductory contribution to this assessment by examining apocalyptic dimensions in the rhetoric of the New Christian Right. While fundamentalism cannot be called an apocalyptic movement in the narrow sense of the term, the spokesmen for this movement did employ significant apoc- alyptic themes. Furthermore, their religious and political efforts sparked a public controversy over apocalyptic doctrines that flared intermittently through the 1980s. In order to gain perspective on Hal Lindsey's apocalypticism, I will compare Lind- sey's political rhetoric to that of two prominent spokesmen for the New Christian Right, Ronald Reagan and Pat Robertson. Examining these three rhetors as ex- emplary spokesmen for the fundamentalist movement, I will argue that the discourse of the New Christian Right enacts a pattern of "diffused expectation" that is char- acteristic of modern apocalypticism. The examination will illustrate how tragic expectations were diffused as each of these rhetors adopted elements of the comic perspective in their rhetorical constructions of public time.

Hal Lindsey's *Countdown*

Lindsey's historical pessimism proved to be tempered by his commitment to the ideology of American conservatism. At the very beginning of the Reagan years, Lindsey published *The 1980's: Countdown to Armageddon*, a prophetic update to his earlier best-seller. In this work, which remained on the New York Times best- seller list through much of 1981, Lindsey explicitly endorsed the conservative Republican program and sought to find a place for the political reforms of the Reagan administration within his prophetic scheme of history. I do not intend to offer a complete analysis of this text. My concern here is only to examine Lindsey's shifting political stance in the context of the fundamentalist movement of the 1980s, and to illustrate how a dramatistic theory of apocalyptic discourse can account for this shift.

In the context of Lindsey's earlier work, his subtitle, *Countdown to Armageddon*, appeared to imply a specific prediction: he had, after all, written that the End would come "within forty years or so of 1948." The image of the countdown, associated as it is with missile launches, connotes a sense of tragic inevitability; and yet this sense is modified within the book itself, which studiously neglects the subject of chronology. Lindsey begins with a surprisingly upbeat account of the reception accorded to his message in some surprising places. He writes:

Shortly after *The Late Great Planet Earth* was published I began to see a most unusual phenomenon taking place. People from all walks of life were becoming captivated by an intense interest in the relevancy of the predictions made by the Hebrew prophets thousands of years ago.

This interest wasn't confined to religious people, either. It extended all the way from college students to government officials both here and abroad.

Lindsey then tells of invitations to deliver lectures to a conference of Jamaican officials, to groups of high-ranking officers at the American Air War College and the Pentagon, and to a top-secret "elite group" of military intelligence experts. According to his account, at each of these places he received an enthusiastic reception from crowds eager to hear the message of prophetic fulfillment. Some members of these audiences, according to Lindsey, reported a striking concordance between contemporary military strategy and the fundamentalist interpretation of biblical prophecy: "After my talk, one officer told me that various Pentagon officials had independently come to the same conclusions I had reached regarding the future of the Middle East . . . with virtually no knowledge of what the Hebrew prophets had predicted 2,000 to 3,000 years earlier." Likewise, the anonymous military intelligence experts revealed that "A few days before our meeting, their computer had predicted the same events and outcomes that had been forecast by Daniel."[4]

Even allowing for a considerable degree of hyperbole, if these accounts have any factual basis at all they are deeply disturbing to those who do not share Lindsey's convictions. If those entrusted with our country's nuclear defense are finding a concordance between their own strategic projections and Lindsey's scenario of a divinely ordained nuclear catastrophe, it would seem that this scenario has moved a few steps closer from speculation to enactment. As one might expect, however, this prospect presents no threat to Lindsey himself. The obvious pleasure Lindsey exhibits over his contacts with military and government officials indicates that since the publication of his earlier book he has grown more confident. By choosing to open his book with these anecdotes, Lindsey hints at his new political agenda: as the audience for his interpretation of biblical prophecy had expanded to include the powerful, so too the public space seemed to have expanded, allowing room for the entrance of fundamentalists into political life.

Most of *The 1980's: Countdown to Armageddon* is devoted to the events of the decade since the first book's publication. The power and flexibility of the apocalyptic myth as an explanatory frame for viewing current events is demonstrated in the ease with which Lindsey incorporates events in the secular realm into his tragic scheme. Not surprisingly, there are no surprises in Lindsey's updated application of prophecy to history; he finds confirmation of his earlier predictions at every turn. The entry of Greece into the European Economic Community in 1979 brought that union to its full complement of ten nations to match the ten horns of Daniel's beast, while the formation of a European parliament was the first step toward the government of Antichrist, who, Lindsey believes, "is alive somewhere in Europe; perhaps he is already a member of the EEC parliament." The Iranian revolution and the fall of the Shah's pro-American government removed a major impediment to the prophesied Soviet invasion of the Middle East. The Soviet invasion of Afghanistan proved the expansionist intentions of that nation and gained it a "spring-board to overthrow Iran and gain control of the Persian Gulf Area."[5] Lindsey's account of these events includes plenty of new evidence, including pages of graphs that purport to show vast expansions in Soviet military capabilities as compared to the United States. However, these chapters contain no obvious departure from the positions taken in *The Late Great Planet Earth*. Only in chapter 10, called "What About the U.S.?", does Lindsey give full expression to his new political agenda.

While acknowledging that "there are no specific or even indirect references to America in Bible prophecy," Lindsey argues that "there are things we do know from which we can make some deductions." Reiterating his pessimistic predictions from 1970, Lindsey affirms that "from the standpoint of Biblical prophecy, the U.S. *must* fade from its place of leadership for the west and its former supreme superpower status." He then presents a list of four "possible fates for the U.S." These include:

- A takeover by the communists.
- Destruction by a surprise Soviet nuclear attack (I don't even like to *think* about this possibility).
- Becoming a dependent of the 10-nation European confederacy.
- A far more hopeful fate than any of the above. Let's explore this final possibility.

In this manner, Lindsey introduces what is boldly characterized as "A RAY OF HOPE." Although the Antichrist's world dictatorship cannot be prevented, there is nevertheless an opportunity to stave off total subjection to his demonic rule. Lindsey offers Americans a choice that he had not previously hinted at: "If some critical and difficult choices are made by the American people *right now*, it is possible to see the U.S. remain a world power. We could become an equal ally of the European confederation. . . . In that way, America could keep much of its sovereignty and freedom."[6]

Lindsey proceeds to set forth a program for preserving American power in the face of what he terms the "crisis of leadership," the "crisis of internal decay," and the "crisis of military weakness." This program includes an attack on the welfare state and government bureaucracy, and a rejection of the SALT treaty process in favor of a dramatic military buildup of strategic and conventional forces. "SALT is finished. There's no more basis for negotiation. It is time to use our vast and superior technology to create the world's strongest military power. Only this will stop the Soviet's insane rush toward nuclear war."[7] Lindsey's political positions are undergirded with appeals to the Bible, which he claims supports an antiwelfare social policy and a strong military. As he continues his argument, Lindsey reveals his new conception of the relationship of fundamentalist belief and political practice:

[W]e must actively take on the responsibility of being a citizen and a member of God's family.
    We need to get active electing officials who will not only reflect the Bible's

morality in government but will shape domestic and foreign policies to protect our country and our way of life.

We need to elect men and women who will have the courage to make the tough decisions needed to insure our nation's survival. They must be willing to clamp down on big government, cut exploitation of the welfare system, keep our strong commitments to our allies and stand up to communist expansion.

We need people who see how important a strong military is to keeping peace for us and what remains of the free world.[8]

Though he is never mentioned by name, Ronald Reagan looms large in this scenario. Every one of Lindsey's proposals for domestic and foreign policy was part of Reagan's campaign platform. In the political climate of 1981 no one could have missed the fact that Lindsey's political program was virtually identical with that of the newly elected president. The parallels between Reagan's favorite themes and Lindsey's rhetoric are at times almost eerie, as when, in order to reinforce the gravity of the Soviet nuclear threat, Lindsey portrays an imaginary conversation between the leaders of the superpowers:

If something isn't done quickly, the Soviet Premier may soon telephone the American President. The Premier will say: "We can destroy your missile silos.

"We can intercept and destroy all incoming submarine launched missiles with our laser beams.

"We can destroy your obsolete bombers with our MIG-25 fighters and SS-5 ground-to-air missiles.

"So, Mr. President, will you surrender? Or shall we destroy your country? You have 20 seconds to decide."

What would you advise the President to do at that moment? Let's get tough and not let that moment happen.[9]

Compare candidate Reagan's oft-quoted assertion about the so-called "window of vulnerability," a purported disparity between the strategic forces of the United States and the Soviet Union so massive that "the Russians could just take us with a phone call."[10] Lindsey simply added dramatic color to Reagan's hypothetical scenario of bloodless surrender. In the political context of 1980–1981, Lindsey's dramatic scenario amounted to an unmistakable partisan polemic.

It is evident that Lindsey's language of temporality has shifted from that used in his earlier writing. Note in particular the introduction of the conditional tense: "If some critical and difficult choices are made by the American people *right now*" and if we "use our vast and superior technology to create the world's strongest military power," we can "stop the Soviet's insane rush toward nuclear war." Readers of *The Late Great Planet Earth* had reason to be puzzled; Lindsey's earlier books contained no hint that the catastrophic war foretold in prophecy could be avoided, nor indeed of any significant contingency that could affect the pattern of prophetic fulfillment. Lindsey's original apocalyptic message did not appear to impose any specific political obligations on his readers. Why, then, did he change his mind? What did Lindsey (and other fundamentalist preachers) hope to achieve by their entry into politics, and how did their ambitions square with their dispensational eschatology? What logic governs this strange reconciliation of belief and practice, so opaque and mysterious to liberal critics?

I argued in chapter 3 of this study that, from the dramatistic perspective, the predetermination of history according to the divine plan does not render meaningful action impossible. The historical pessimism of the tragic apocalypse does not necessarily preclude or discourage the believer from acting in the world; rather, it gives such action a different weight and purpose. Although some react to the tragedy of apocalypse by becoming passive spectators, others may find that the prediction of the world's End offers not only a cathartic conclusion, but also a role for the believer to play in the cosmic drama. The strategic ambiguity of Lindsey's temporal predictions plays a crucial role in this solution. If, as I have claimed, the tragic apocalypse tends toward greater specificity in predicting dates for the End, while the comic apocalypse tends to postpone the End and make its date more mysterious, then the transition from Lindsey's original argument that the End will come "within forty years or so of 1948," to the more ambiguous argument that "this generation is the one that will see the end of the present world,"[11] can be described as a shift from tragic specificity (albeit qualified) toward comic indeterminacy. Though this shift is ever so slight, it has crucial consequences for the practice of politics. For if, as was the case with the Millerites, the effect of setting a specific date for the End is to turn the audience for apocalyptic rhetoric into passive spectators awaiting the fall of the final curtain on history's drama, then it can readily be seen that proposing a fluid generational timetable, rather than a specific date, opens up a temporal space that may allow the audience to participate as actors in the dramatic finale. A declaration of the End of time in 1843 makes the purely political endeavors of 1842 seem superfluous; an announcement of the End of time "during this generation" diffuses audience expectations by denying them a temporal focus, thereby allowing considerably more latitude for movement, while at the same time forging a generational identity that may endow political acts with sacred significance. When a specific deadline for the apocalypse is proposed, the audience's excitement and anticipation will tend to focus on the date to the exclusion of every other consideration. If no specific date is offered, audiences accepting apocalyptic claims will nevertheless experience excitement that can, under some circumstances, be channeled into political action as a way of preparing for the impending End.

From the dramatistic perspective, then, Lindsey's solution to the dilemma of apocalyptic politics is a revision, but hardly a reversal, of his previous stance. After eliminating any hint of a specific date by excising his earlier reference to the forty-year length of the prophetically foretold generation, Lindsey lacked a specific temporal focus for anticipation and turned his attention to the topos of evil in the realm of politics, where, he claimed, Christians may do some good while they await the Lord's return. The role that he proposes that Christians should enact as the cosmic drama draws to its close can be described as a Last Stand of the Elect in the Last Days. As demonic forces rage outside the gates, believers are urged to hold the fort, staving off catastrophe until rescue arrives for the chosen few. The military metaphor is entirely apt. Describing the fundamentalist approach to politics during the 1980 presidential campaign, Jerry Falwell said "We are fighting a holy war . . . and this time we are going to win." In a phrase that gained much currency among prem-illennialists in the 1980s, Falwell defined the nature of the expected fundamentalist victory: Christians were "called to occupy until He comes."[12] Falwell's position is essentially identical to Lindsey's. In the prophetic scheme espoused by both men, the tide of history cannot be reversed, but if Christians enter political life and bring our foreign and domestic policies into line with the truths of the Bible, "America will survive this perilous situation and endure until the Lord comes to evacuate His people."[13] The promise held out by Lindsey in *The 1980's: Countdown to Armageddon* is therefore nothing more than the preservation of the American way of life for a few more years until the rapture; and presumably, after believers are evacuated in the divine airlift, Fortress America will crumble and the catastrophic conclusion of history will proceed as predicted. This is surely only a minor qual-ification of Lindsey's original historical pessimism, but it is enough to make a crucial difference in his political philosophy.

To liberal interpreters, the prospect of a temporary "victory" for Christians during the short space of time before the rapture is hardly sufficient to account for the fervor with which fundamentalist believers entered politics in the 1980s. To the fundamentalists, however, this prospect was enough to revitalize a religious ap-proach to politics and the public sphere; for even if their victory was destined to be short-lived in the face of the catastrophe that would soon engulf the world, their struggle embodied the tragic virtues in a grand gesture that simultaneously accepts and denies fate. Tragic resignation does not abandon the struggle, but finds nobility in its continuation in the face of impossible odds. The political stance of modern fundamentalists makes narrative and emotional sense once it is seen as an enactment of the martial virtues of the tragic hero, which include "courage, loyalty, duty, honor, pride, indomitable will, unquestioning obedience, [and] uncompromising dedication."[14] A dramatistic theory of apocalypse thus enables critics to view the synthesis of American premillennialism and political activism as both made possible by the barest nod toward comic indeterminacy on the question of the date, and entirely consistent with the "tragic sense of life" that dominates the fundamentalist interpretation of the apocalyptic drama.

With the publication of *The Late Great Planet Earth* in 1970 and *The 1980's: Countdown to Armageddon* in 1981, Hal Lindsey's apocalyptic predictions found an audience of millions. As I have tried to show in the preceding pages, Lindsey's adroit manipulation of the public's fear of nuclear war and other potential modern catastrophes, coupled with his skillful management of his audience's temporal expectations, provides a partial explanation of his success. Indeed, it does not seem farfetched to credit Lindsey with helping to inspire the political triumphs of Amer-ican fundamentalism in the early 1980s. To illustrate further how the diffusion of apocalyptic expectation served as a resource for the rhetoric of the New Christian Right, I turn now to the man who became the movement's most eloquent spokes-man, Ronald Reagan.

Ronald Reagan and
"The Last Best Hope of Man on Earth"

An examination of Ronald Reagan's political discourse will show that Hal Lindsey's blend of political advocacy with the language of apocalypse is hardly unique. From the very beginning of his oratorical career, Reagan's rhetoric was characterized by appeals to eschatological ultimates. In his televised appeal at the close of the 1964 Goldwater campaign, the speech that launched his entry into national politics, Reagan spoke of the redemptive struggle against the evils of totalitarianism in terms that clearly conveyed its apocalyptic finality:

> If nothing in life is worth dying for, when did this begin— just in the face of this enemy?—or should Moses have told the children of Israel to live in slavery under the pharaohs? Should Christ have refused the cross? Should the patriots at Concord Bridge have thrown down their guns and refused to fire the shot heard round the world? The martyrs of history were not fools, and our honored dead who gave up their lives to stop the advance of the Nazis didn't die in vain!...
>
> Winston Churchill said that "the destiny of man is not measured by material computation. When great forces are on the move in the world, we learn we are spirits—not animals." And he said, "There is something going on in time and space, and beyond time and space, which, whether we like it or not, spells duty." You and I have a rendezvous with destiny. We will preserve for our children this, the last best hope of man on earth, or we will sentence them to take the last step into a thousand years of darkness.[15]

As Kurt Ritter notes, this speech seems to be a peculiar blend of optimism and pessimism: "Even in his darkest passages of apocalyptic language, Reagan held out hope that Americans could alter history, that they could turn back the tide of liberalism."[16] Yet the essentially tragic nature of Reagan's apocalyptic vision is clear. Though he appeared to confront his audience with a choice, to empower them to make history, the choice is that of the tragic hero: to accept or reject one's divinely ordained fate. "Freedom" is the freedom to choose one's destiny; recognition of the ultimate reference point beyond time and space transmutes choice into duty, and duty compels us to accept sacrifice and perhaps death. In his stump speech from the 1964 campaign, Reagan often added a peroration to this vision, one that emphasized the redemptive nature of a losing struggle: "If we fail, at least let our children and our children's children say of us we justified our brief moment here. We did all that could be done."[17]

Yet Reagan's appeal to the eschatological topoi of time and evil not only threatens an imminent historical rupture; it also establishes a rhetorical continuity with the past. The description of America as "the last best hope of man on earth," an echo of Lincoln's second inaugural address that was a staple of Reagan's speeches throughout his presidency, recalls the Civil War, America's national tragedy and a struggle that was regarded in its time as apocalyptic. It is easy to pass over such a familiar phrase as a mere rhetorical embellishment; yet it is nevertheless worth asking, what is the nature of the hope that America represented for Reagan and his followers?

And are there eschatological implications in the reference to the United States as humanity's *last* hope?

In 1964, American conservatives were an embattled minority; their political prospects seemed to have foundered in Barry Goldwater's failed candidacy, and it should come as no surprise that their rhetoric glorified the nobility of a losing struggle. Twenty years later, the tide had changed, and religious and political conservatives could celebrate victory rather than console themselves in defeat. In his 1983 speech to the National Association of Evangelicals, Reagan argued that the movements to ban abortion and restore prayer to public schools were evidence that America was "in the midst of a spiritual awakening and a moral renewal." However, Reagan went on to describe this renewal in terms that reveal the limits of the New Right's political optimism:

> Now, obviously, much of this new political and social consensus I've talked about is based on a positive view of American history, one that takes pride in our country's accomplishments and record. But we must never forget that no government schemes are going to perfect man. We know that living in this world means dealing with what philosophers would call the phenomenology of evil or, as theologians would put it, the doctrine of sin.

Reagan thus rejected any political program founded in the sort of perfectionism that inspired some postmillennial movements of the nineteenth century. In his tragic world view, the power of evil was such that it could never be overcome by governmental efforts. Believers were still commanded to struggle against sin, but Reagan left no doubt about the focus of that struggle and the identity of the true enemy:

> There is sin and evil in the world, and we're enjoined by Scripture and the Lord Jesus to oppose it with all our might. . . . [L]et us pray for the salvation of all those who live in . . . totalitarian darkness—pray they will discover the joy of knowing God. But until they do, let us be aware that while they preach the supremacy of the state, declare its omnipotence over individual man, and predict its eventual domination of all the peoples on the Earth, they are the focus of evil in the modern world.[18]

In this speech, which came to be known as the "Evil Empire" address, the rhetoric of the tragic apocalypse is muted but unmistakable: temporal expectation is diffused, and emphasis is placed on the struggle against a demonic enemy. An eschatological vision of absolute evil is thus made to serve as an ideological grounding for the Reagan administration's foreign policy and arms buildup. Delivered at the peak of the antinuclear movement, on the same day that the House Foreign Affairs Committee had endorsed the nuclear freeze, the speech ignited controversy among administration critics disturbed by the use of biblical imagery to demonize the Soviets.[19]

On occasion, apocalyptic elements in the ideology of the New Christian Right became more explicit. When those who expressed such thoughts were holders of high office, the political implications of religious belief became an issue of public concern. Secretary of the Interior James Watt was held up for public ridicule when he justified the Reagan administration's policy of exploiting natural resources before a congressional committee with the words, "I don't know how many future generations we can count on until the Lord returns."[20] Some critics wondered uneasily about Secretary of Defense Casper Weinberger's expression of fascination with the book of Revelation.[21] By the end of 1983, Reagan's flirtation with apocalyptic symbolism had begun to attract considerable attention and alarm from liberal critics, and speculations and rumors circulated about the president's commitment to apocalyptic beliefs. The *Jerusalem Post* published an account, widely reprinted in the American press, of a 1983 conversation between Reagan and Thomas Dine, a lobbyist for the American-Israel Public Affairs Committee, in which he was reported to have said: "You know, I turn back to your ancient prophets in the Old Testament and the signs foretelling Armageddon, and I find myself wondering if—if we're the generation that's going to see that come about. I don't know if you've read any of those prophecies lately, but believe me, they certainly describe the times we're going through."[22] Other, similar accounts appeared and were eagerly seized upon by those seeking an issue to use against the popular president.[23]

As the election season of 1984 came to its climax, Armageddon became a full-blown political controversy. Liberals were uneasy when Dallas fundamentalist James Robison, known for his fiery sermons on premillennial eschatology, was chosen to deliver a benediction at the Republican National Convention.[24] In October, liberal clergy from a number of denominations held press conferences to draw attention to Ronald Reagan's interest in apocalyptic prophecy, and the theme was echoed by a chorus of newspaper articles and editorials.[25] Much of the news coverage was generated by an hour-long radio documentary called "Ronald Reagan and the Prophecy of Armageddon," which was broadcast throughout the nation on National Public Radio in September–October, 1984. This program patched together some of the president's words with samples of fire-and-brimstone preaching from some of the more colorful figures in the evangelical world, and contained (among other allegations) a statement by Reagan's legal secretary, Herb Ellingwood, that, while governor of California, the president had read and "repeatedly discussed" *The Late Great Planet Earth* with friends and acquaintances such as evangelists Pat Boone and George Otis.[26]

On at least two occasions, Reagan was given the opportunity to respond to the controversy that had ignited over his religious beliefs. Each time, he attempted to allay the concerns of critics in terms that left no doubt about his fascination with apocalyptic ideas, but that studiously avoided the step from speculation to prediction. In a December 1983 interview with *People* magazine, Reagan referred to conversations with unnamed "theologians" who, he said, "have been studying the ancient prophecies—What would portend the coming of Armageddon?—and have said that never, in the time between the prophecies up till now has there ever been a time in which so many of the prophecies are coming together. There have been times in the past when people thought the end of the world was coming, and so forth, but never anything like this." However, Reagan went on to say, "I think whichever generation and at whatever time, when the time comes, the generation that is there, I think will have to go on doing what they believe is right."[27]

Finally, when President Reagan was questioned about his apocalyptic beliefs during the second televised debate with Walter Mondale, the disturbing possibility that the premillennial prediction of an all-out nuclear conflict involving the Soviet Union might become a self-fulfilling prophecy was raised before a nationwide audience. In response to reporter Marvin Kalb's query as to whether "we are heading for some kind of biblical Armageddon," Reagan characterized his statements on the subject as "just some philosophical discussions with people who are interested in the same things." Arguing that "a number of theologians for the last decade or more have believed that this was true, that the prophecies are coming together that portends that," the president nevertheless denied that his beliefs on this subject had ever influenced his policies: "But no one knows whether Armageddon, those prophecies mean that Armageddon is a thousand years away or day after tomorrow. So, I have never seriously warned and said we must plan according to Armageddon."[28]

One must surmise that the president's answer to Kalb's question had been carefully prepared. Reagan, after all, had undergone extensive coaching to prepare him for any questions that might be raised at the debate, and the Armageddon issue had caused a considerable stir. In any event, the reply indicates both the depth of the president's interest in apocalypticism and his linguistic skill in satisfying his fundamentalist constituency while allaying the fears of critics. Reagan could neither accept apocalyptic doctrines nor reject them outright; he had to find a public language for the expression of his religion that would avoid giving offense to true believers as well as skeptical adversaries. In this language, critics may find evidence of the rehabilitation of apocalypticism and of its movement from the fringes of our culture into the very center. In typical premillennial fashion, Reagan pointed to unnamed theological "experts" who would confirm the prophetic significance of current events, while relying on his profession of ignorance regarding the date to keep him within the bounds of orthodoxy. The president's public expressions of fascination with prophecy, and his expressions of agnosticism with regard to the date of its fulfillment, may be said to define a middle-of-the-road position. From this evidence, it seems legitimate to conclude that a vast portion of the American audience seems willing to engage in (or at least tolerate) apocalyptic speculations on the eschatological significance of contemporary history, but is uncomfortable when conjecture turns into prognostication. It may be that, for Ronald Reagan as for millions of Hal Lindsey's readers, apocalyptic prophecies are lumped with astrology as simply one more source of entertaining insights into the occult meaning of current events, no more or less significant than the daily horoscope in helping one to navigate one's life.[29] Whatever the epistemic status of Reagan's meditations on Armageddon, the critical alarm over his public and private statements was apparently not shared by the voters who re-elected him. It seems reasonable to conclude that, in this area as in so many others, Reagan gave voice to thoughts that, though unpalatable to liberal pundits, are shared by millions of Americans.

Pat Robertson's Millennium

President Reagan managed to fend off the concerns of liberal critics fearful of a nuclear Armageddon, but troubling questions remained. Two years after the election of 1984, the editors of *Policy Review*, the journal of the conservative Heritage Foundation, regarded the Armageddon controversy as serious enough to merit the publication of a defense of premillennialism by two associates of Jerry Falwell, Ed Dobson and Ed Hindson. These authors attempted to refute the notion that "because we evangelicals look forward to the second coming of Christ, we will try to hasten that event." Insisting there was no contradiction between premillennial eschatology and political activism, they sarcastically argued: "[I]f we really wanted to accelerate the end, we would surely support the nuclear agenda of the American left and the Communist Party, because we firmly believe that unilateral disarmament is a sure way to send this country into the arms of its Maker."[30]

The specter of a nuclear catastrophe engendered through misguided religious conviction was evoked again in 1987 by born-again Christian and former Nixon associate Charles Colson. In his book *Kingdoms in Conflict*, a meditation on the proper relationship of Christianity and politics, Colson presented a fictive scenario of an evangelical president who, following the advice of premillennial Bible scholars, brings the world to the brink of nuclear war by allowing Israeli soldiers to destroy the Dome of the Rock in Jerusalem. Into the mouth of his fictional "President Hopkins," Colson placed a published quotation from the real President Reagan:

> "Ezekiel tells us that Gog, the nation that will lead all the other powers of darkness against Israel, will come out of the north. Biblical scholars have been saying for generations that Gog must be Russia. What other powerful nation is to the north of Israel? None. But it didn't seem to make sense before the Russian revolution, when Russia was a Christian country. Now that Russia has become communistic and atheistic, it does. Now that Russia has set itself against God, it fits the description of Gog perfectly."
>
> President Hopkins put down the Bible, removed his glasses, and ran a hand through his hair. . . . "I ran my campaign on the Bible," Hopkins said, "and I intend to run this nation on the Bible. Let's keep in mind while we make our plans that God has already made his."[31]

Published as evangelist Pat Robertson prepared his presidential candidacy, Colson's disturbing tale offered an implicit criticism of fundamentalist politics and cautioned against fanaticism. The fact that this criticism appeared from a spokesman whose religious convictions made him a natural ally of the fundamentalists lent credence to the claim that the controversy over "Armageddon theology" was not a desperate attempt by liberal critics to locate a campaign issue that could be used against a popular president, but rather reflected an authentic concern over the implications of apocalyptic beliefs in the nuclear age. The point was reinforced in 1988 during Robertson's unsuccessful presidential campaign, in which Armageddon repeatedly surfaced as a political issue—much to the dismay of the candidate.

Since I have elsewhere subjected Pat Robertson's apocalyptic beliefs and political ideology to a detailed analysis, there is no need to perform this task here. A brief outline of some the main points from that analysis will suffice for a comparison of Robertson's political theology to Hal Lindsey's. The essay traced a gradual transformation in Robertson's apocalyptic interpretation from 1980 through 1988 and characterized this transformation as a rhetorical trajectory from premillennialism toward a nebulous postmillennialism. At the beginning of the decade, Robertson espoused a premillennial theology virtually indistinguishable from that presented in *The Late Great Planet Earth*. A 1980 edition of Robertson's newsletter offered "Prophetic Insights for the Decade of Destiny" which included, in addition to the standard predictions of economic crisis and a Soviet invasion of Israel, the startlingly specific claim that *"there is a man alive today, approximately 27 years old, who is now being groomed to be the Satanic messiah."*[32] With the reign of Antichrist imminent, readers were told only that "Christians are now in the middle of a brief period of grace when conditions are at an absolutely optimum point for world evangelism"; no mention was made of any concerted political effort.[33] It is impossible to ascertain exactly when Robertson began to develop political ambitions; what is clearly evident, however, is that his interpretation of biblical prophecy began to change as he considered a political career.

In a series of books and speeches from 1983 to 1987, Robertson gradually moved away from the pessimistic scenarios of Antichrist, Soviet invasions, and socioeconomic catastrophe, and began to offer visions of the future that resembled the postmillennial apocalypse of the Second Great Awakening revivalists. Robertson's new spirit of optimism was apparent in a televised speech broadcast in December 1984. Here he recklessly proposed something that premillennialists had always rejected as heresy, that Christians could enjoy the benefits of the millennium before the return of Jesus:

> What's coming next? . . . I want you to think of a world . . . where humanism isn't taught any more and people sincerely believe in the living God . . . a world in which there are no more abortions . . . juvenile delinquency is virtually unknown . . . the prisons are virtually empty.
>
> And I want you to imagine a society where the church members have taken dominion over the forces of the world, where Satan's power is bound by the people of God, and where there is no more disease and where there's no more demon possession. . . .
>
> We're going to see a society where the people are living Godly, moral lives, and where the people of God . . . will have so much they will lend to others but they will not have to borrow . . . and the people of God are going to be the most honored people in society. . . . There's a spirit-filled President in the White House, the men in the Senate and the House of Representatives are Spirit-filled and worship Jesus, and the judges do the same. . . . You say, that's a description of the Millennium when Jesus comes back . . . but these things can take place now in this time . . . and they are going to because I am persuaded that we are standing on the brink of the greatest spiritual revival the world has ever known! . . . God is going to put us in positions of leadership and responsibility and we've got to think that way. . . . You

mark my words, in the next year, two years, the next three or four, we're going to see things happen that will absolutely boggle our minds! Praise God![34]

This prophetic vision seems closer to that of Charles Finney than Hal Lindsey. Its presentation of the future contains not the slightest hint of terror or foreboding; in fact, no hint is given that the future is anything but bright. The prediction that "Satan's power [will be] bound by the people of God" is a clear reference to the millennial kingdom of Revelation 20:2–3, where an angel "seized the great dragon, that serpent of old, the Devil or Satan, and chained him up for a thousand years . . . so that he might seduce the nations no more until the thousand years were over" (NEB). With Satan bound, the way is clear for the theocratic rule of the "spirit-filled" president and Congress. Robertson's rhetorical vision of a spirit-filled president is comparable to an earlier mythic legend, discussed briefly in chapter 2, that of the Last Roman Emperor. Just as Christians of the late Roman empire and the medieval period sought to legitimate their monarchs through an imperial apocalyptic myth, so Robertson seems to draw upon apocalyptic fervor as he proposes to Christianize the American presidency. What emerges from this fusion of familiar millennial imagery to the political symbols of the United States government is not, perhaps, a full-blown eschatological legend of the "President of the Last Days," but a synthetic apocalyptic vision that incorporates key features of American "civil religion."[35]

Robertson's trajectory was completed in the 1987 address that formally announced his presidential candidacy, "A New Vision for America." Here Robertson listed the present-day evils of American society in a jeremiad that paralleled the classic diatribe of the tragic Apocalypse—but with a crucial difference. Whereas the Millerites, and Hal Lindsey in *The Late Great Planet Earth*, had listed the symptoms of moral decay and impending disaster in order to establish the tragic inevitability of the world's decline, Robertson's jeremiad adopts the assumptions of the comic frame by proposing a political solution that appears to reverse, and not merely arrest, the decline of our civilization. Invoking the Puritan sense of America's covenantal destiny, Robertson claimed that the answer to the nation's troubles lay

in a new rise of faith and freedom that will give to every American a vision of hope— a vision of opportunity—a vision that will take us past these troubled days and show us the promise that lies ahead for each of us. . . . A new vision for America. A vision of a great nation. A shining city on a hill. The undisputed leader of the free world. And together as we join our hands, our hearts, and our voices as one—we will once again see this great land truly one nation under God![36]

These texts indicate that Robertson's solution to the problem of apocalyptic politics is considerably more optimistic than Lindsey's. In his scenario, Christians were not destined merely to hold the fort until the divine cavalry arrived, but to move "past these troubled days" and become again "the undisputed leader of the free world." Both Lindsey and Robertson sought to justify a religiously based political activism, but their symbolic solutions were different. Lindsey's advocacy remained within the assumptions of the tragic frame, while Robertson adopted substantial elements of the comic vision of postmillennialism—presumably out of rhetorical necessity. Ronald Reagan had been compelled to remain ambiguous on the subject of eschatology: as president, he had derived considerable support from those who embraced the tragic apocalypse, but his rhetorical efforts to satisfy this constituency (such as the speech to the National Association of Evangelicals) involved him in controversy, and he employed more optimistic language when he spoke to and for the entire nation. But Reagan had the legitimacy of an incumbent to fall back upon; the rhetorical demands facing a candidate are different. Robertson's quest for legitimacy in the political context of the debate over "Armageddon theology" made it necessary for him both to resign his ministry and to renounce the tragic vision in such explicit terms that he lost a good measure of fundamentalist support. It is impossible to know whether the transformation in Robertson's apocalyptic vision was a deliberate effort to compromise his theology in order to broaden the base of his political appeal, or whether it resulted from an unconscious effort at self-justification. What can be determined is that his synthesis ultimately failed to convince two crucial audiences: the fundamentalists, who might have been expected to be his natural allies, and the representatives of the secular media.

Premillennialists denounced Robertson's eschatological shift as a heretical embrace of secular humanism and postmillennialism. In September 1986, two years before the sexual scandal that destroyed his ministry, Jimmy Swaggart pointedly attacked Robertson in the pages of his magazine, *The Evangelist:*

As much as we would all like to believe what Pat had to say . . . what are we to do with Bible prophecies concerning the Great Tribulation, the antichrist, and Armageddon?

Tragically, this idea that we Christians can overwhelm the world and transform it into a community of peace and prosperity is remarkably similar to the secular humanist philosophy. Basically, both paint the false picture of a utopia . . . constructed by *human hands* and *human minds*. . . .

To be brutally frank (but scriptural), *dark days are coming.* Instead of the scenario being painted by the Kingdom-Agers, the Bible tells us the very opposite. It speaks of millions dying of hunger. It speaks of unimaginable conflicts and excruciating suffering.

Is this doom and gloom? I'm sure it is, *but it is the truth.* [37]

At the same time, evangelist Charles Pack alerted readers of his *Prophecy* newsletter that Robertson was espousing "what we call POST-millennial teaching," and warned against "the false teaching of the Kingdom Age that is to come. We will *not* bring it in; the King (Jesus) will set up His Kingdom, and only *after* the Tribulation is over." [38] At a "prophecy conference" attended by this author in December 1986, where Pack was a speaker, seven out of eleven premillennial preachers denounced Robertson's political efforts as unscriptural, while one, Constance Cumby, even hinted darkly at Robertson's connections to the international Antichrist conspiracy. [39] At the same time, however, these preachers, and the assembled audience of approximately 250, vigorously expressed support for President Reagan, who was regarded with near reverence as one of their own, and in particular of Reagan's

Strategic Defense Initiative.[40] These premillennialists obviously distinguished between Robertson's comic apocalypticism and the tragic apocalypticism endorsed by
both Reagan and Hal Lindsey.

Such distinctions were too fine, however, for members of the press in the 1988
campaign. Unable to perceive that Robertson's interpretation of the apocalypse had
changed, they persisted in questioning Robertson about statements he had made
eight and ten years previous to the campaign that expressed the classic fatalism of
the tragic Apocalypse.[41] In so doing they linked him uncritically to the popular
conceptions of "Armageddon theology" and thereby contributed to his marginalization and ultimate defeat in the primaries. The extensive publicity given during
the election year to the apocalyptic predictions of Edgar Whisenant, a retired NASA
engineer, served as an ironic counterpoint to Robertson's attempt to repudiate his
earlier views. Whisenant's pamphlet, *88 Reasons Why the Rapture Will Be in 1988*,
compiled a variety of ludicrous computations and "proofs" in support of his contention that the rapture would occur on September 11, 12, or 13 of that year, and
predicted a nuclear war resulting in "destruction . . . so complete that you can walk
from Little Rock to Dallas over ashes only."[42] Whisenant's predictions caused a
considerable stir in evangelical circles until they were finally proved false with the
passage of his dates—months after Robertson's candidacy had foundered. Though
no one explicitly linked Robertson to Whisenant, the comic drama provided by his
tragic predictions kept the topic of the Apocalypse in the public eye at a crucial
time and may have hindered Robertson's efforts to put the Armageddon controversy
behind him.

Two conclusions can be drawn from Robertson's failure to convince the fundamentalists, the media, and the general public, and from the fact that both Reagan
and Robertson were forced to disavow the tragic scenario of a nuclear battle of
Armageddon. First, as I argued in my earlier essay, while the flexibility of the
mythic forms of apocalypse "may allow the creation of a synthetic vision persuasive
enough to support some political and social efforts . . . it does not guarantee acceptance of the synthesis by audiences who reject the myth entirely," or who are
reluctant to allow its interpretation to be monopolized.[43] Second, while a significant
proportion of the American people may have eagerly devoured Hal Lindsey's books
and accepted the connection between nuclear war and biblical prophecy, the evident
concern among certain segments of the public over the religious beliefs of politicians
indicates that while citizens may at times be attracted to tragic visions of impending
catastrophe, they are not necessarily willing to tolerate the expression of these visions
in propositional form by their elected officials. Images of Apocalypse and the
millennium are potent and volatile; they are capable of arousing disparate emotions,
including terror and fear as well as hope and patriotism, and rhetors who employ
these images have often found that audience reactions are difficult to control. Even
the most familiar millennial symbols have unexpected connotations that may cause
the politician who uses them to be accused of violating what Roderick P. Hart has
called the unwritten "contract" that governs expressions of American civic piety.[44]

Nevertheless, the evidence examined here provides ample support for the claim that the tradition of "civil millennialism" (to use Nathan O. Hatch's apt phrase) remains today as a strong and vital source of rhetorical appeals. Hatch argues that civil millennialism originated in an "amalgam of traditional Puritan apocalyptic rhetoric and eighteenth-century political discourse." The pietistic strand of the American apocalyptic tradition, inherited from the Puritans and New Lights preachers such as Jonathan Edwards, placed its faith in revivalism; the nationalistic strand, in contrast, looked to the establishment of a civil society that would realize the millennial hope. Hatch notes that the politicizing of millennial appeals in the rhetoric of the American Revolution resulted in a transformation of the apocalyptic tradition:

> In a subtle but profound shift in emphasis the religious value that traditionally defined the ultimate goal of apocalyptic hope—the conversion of all nations to Christianity—became diluted with, and often subordinate to, the commitment to America as a new seat of liberty. . . . The New Light confidence in the progressive force of history was based on the spread of vital piety; Christ's kingdom advanced toward its completion by the effusion of God's spirit in widespread revivals. The Revolutionary millennialist, on the other hand, based his apocalyptic hopes on the civil and religious liberty that American victory over Britain would insure . . . [and] interpret[ed] existing American society as the model upon which the millennial kingdom would be based.[45]

The pietistic strand seems rooted in the perspective of tragedy: inspired by the central myth of Christ's sacrifice, adherents of this vision often saw themselves as "praying bands of pious saints . . . who would drive back the forces of darkness."[46] The nationalistic strand, by contrast, seems rooted in the comic frame; its adherents tended to eschew catastrophic scenarios in favor of a rationalist view of human progress. As the rhetoric of Hal Lindsey, Ronald Reagan, and Pat Robertson shows, the disparate strands of the apocalyptic tradition endure to this day. Though pietism and nationalism have often been opposed to one another, they have just as often been combined in uneasy tension. Pat Robertson's example in particular seems to indicate that American civil millennialism is ultimately grounded in the comic frame; we require our politician-priests to express faith in the gradual improvement, if not perfectibility, of humanity and society. In spite of the occasional popularity of tragic visions of catastrophe, it is the comic vision that sustains our culture with the notion of an open temporal horizon of possibility in which America appears, however hazily, as the "shining city on a hill" that points the way into a new age.

Conclusions: Prophetic Interpretation in the Wake of the Soviet Collapse

The millennial ideal of America as a "redeemer nation," which, as Ernest Tuveson has shown,[47] powerfully informs this nation's historical self-understanding, is founded in the premises of the comic frame. Yet there is a tragic underside to the American version of the comic Apocalypse. Belief in the United States as a "righteous empire," the community of the elect chosen to embody God's will in the world, can lead all too easily to a literal demonization of one's opponents. Thus the comic faith in America's divinely ordained role has a tragic dualism as its natural corollary. The division of humanity into forces of light and darkness, historical embodiments of absolute good and absolute evil, that is so characteristic of the tragic Apocalypse, perfectly mirrored the cold war ideology of the post–World War II years. Hal Lindsey's dubious etymologies linking the Soviet Union and China to the demonically inspired kings of the north and the east in the prophecies of Ezekiel and Revelation thus translate the secular cosmology of the cold war into religious terms. The *reductio ad absurdum* was completed by the exegetical efforts of Charles Taylor, author of *World War III and the Destiny of America*, who in 1985 informed readers of his *Bible Prophecy News* that the initials of three prominent Soviet leaders bore apocalyptic significance and combined to fulfill Ezekiel's prophecy: "For the first time in history, GOG has a meaning: qualifying the chief leaders of the Soviet Union, the land of Mesech and Tubal as GOG: GROMYKO, OGARKOV & GORBACHEV."[48] Such extensions of tragic assumptions into comical absurdity are both ludicrous and deeply disturbing. They are easily laughed away as the ravings of a few religious crackpots; however, the fact that similar speculations have been entertained by the man recently entrusted by American voters with nominal control of our vast nuclear arsenal is enough to leave critics with a disquieting sense that such dismissive laughter has a hollow ring.

In spite of such lingering fears, current prospects for the comic vision appear considerably brighter in light of recent hopeful trends. The astonishing political developments in the Soviet Union and Eastern Europe in the late 1980s and early 1990s have effectively ended the cold war; the tragic bipolar division of humanity into forces of absolute good and evil has dissolved into a multipolar world, where good and evil are not so distinct and things are, quite apparently, not what they seem. While the prophetic scenario endorsed by Lindsey (and by virtually every other modern exponent of premillennialism) would seem to have been rendered obsolete by the dissolution of the Soviet Union into the Commonwealth of Independent States, the collapse of communism in Czechoslovakia, Poland, Hungary, and East Germany, and by the turn of almost the entire Soviet bloc toward a market economy, one may surmise that the exponents of these scenarios will admit their errors reluctantly— if at all. While it may be too soon to tell what effect these events will have on apocalyptic schemes of history, it is instructive to see how prophecy interpreters have reacted to them.

Over the past few years, Lindsey and his cohorts have displayed great ingenuity in explaining away past predictions and producing new scenarios that make a tragically determined catastrophic war appear inevitable. As long as the final outcome of the Soviet reforms remained in doubt, most preachers of the apocalypse simply refused to acknowledge that any real change was taking place. Evangelist Zola Levitt argued in his January 1990 letter to contributors that "Old hard-line Communists have a way of digging in their heels at the last moment. . . . Having insight to the prophecy, we should still keep our eyes on Russia as an expansionist nation and not as any sort of peacemaker."[49] Similarly, Hal Lindsey continued to insist that the Soviet reforms were a sham. In a 1990 issue of *Countdown*, his monthly journal of prophecy and current events, he argued: "The reality is that the 'collapse' of Communism is part of a masterful game of deceit engineered by Mikhail Gorbachev and the Soviet KGB. It is part of an elaborate strategy to secure Western aid and technology, buy time, persuade the West to unilaterally disarm and, at the same time, continue a covert but nevertheless dramatic military buildup of its own.[50]

When the idea that the transformations in the Soviet Union were a deliberate deception intended to lower the guard of the West was utterly disproved by the final collapse of Gorbachev's government and the creation of the Commonwealth of Independent States, Lindsey and others who had predicted a Soviet invasion of Israel shifted their stance without ever acknowledging their mistake. Tim LaHaye, whose 1972 book *The Beginning of the End* presented a prophetic scenario nearly identical to that of *The Late Great Planet Earth*, now claims that the country that will invade Israel "is not the Soviet Union; it has never been. . . . It has always been the Republic of Russia itself."[51] In his most recent work, *The Magog Factor*, Lindsey argues that "The world has not been stabilized by the elimination of the Soviet military power; quite the opposite." The first two chapters of this text trace the history of Magog, the invader prophesied in the the thirty-eight chapter of Ezekiel, repeating Lindsey's earlier identification of this power with the Scythian ancestors of modern Russia. However, his revised scenario for the End times now focuses on "the allies of Magog," the Islamic nations who, he claims, will join with the five Central Asian republics of the former Soviet Union: "Kazakhstan, Turkmenistan, Uzbekistan, Tadzhikistan, and Kyrgystan . . . will intrigue with their Islamic brethren in Iran, Syria, Iraq, Pakistan, and Libya . . . to destroy Israel" with what remains of the Soviet nuclear arsenal. Invoking fears of a fanatical Islamic *jihad* armed with nuclear weapons, Lindsey continues: "The world is more at risk of a global holocaust than ever before in history. The weapons are being distributed, arming irrational leaders. The tensions increase. Ezekiel 38 is more imminent than ever before. It is ever more evident that the climax is nearing."[52]

It appears, then, that Lindsey's solution to the dilemma created by the disconfirmation of his earlier predictions is to recast the villains of his apocalyptic drama: since atheistic Russian Communists are no longer available, he relies on "fanatical" Muslim fundamentalists to play the role of the prophesied invaders. The revised scenario remains incoherent, however, in that Lindsey's prediction still depends upon the claim that "Magog"—that is, the Russians—will play a key role in these events. Though he eagerly searches for evidence of increased anti-Semitism in the Russian republic, he fails to provide a plausible motive for why the *Russians* would join their Islamic neighbors in the predicted invasion.

Readers of this book should not be surprised that Lindsey, his fellow evangelists, and their audiences are able to revise their scenarios while remaining unfazed by direct refutation of previous predictions. For, as we have seen, prophetic interpreters have displayed such ingenuity before and explained away greater anomalies. The history of apocalyptic interpretation gives us no reason to suppose that modern apocalypticists will cease to predict a tragic conclusion for history's drama. Whatever the fate of the former Soviet Union and its allies, we certainly have not seen the end of "wars and rumors of wars"; as new conflicts flare up around the globe, we may be sure that interpreters of the Apocalypse will be quick to fit them into their scenarios of the End. For example, the recent war in the Persian Gulf came at an opportune time for apocalyptic rhetors. Just as the Soviet threat was receding, Iraq's invasion of Kuwait and subsequent missile attacks upon Israel sparked a remarkable increase of interest in biblical prophecy. A revised edition of John F. Walvoord's *Armageddon, Oil and the Middle East Crisis* was rushed into print, and booksellers reported vast increases in sales of this and other books of prophecy.[53] When the Iraqi conflict concluded with a decisive victory for U.S. forces (thus failing to escalate into the global conflict that some apocalyptic interpreters had anticipated), Lindsey and others seized upon President George Bush's call for a "New World Order" as evidence that the world government of Antichrist was just around the corner.[54]

For the foreseeable future, political instability in the Islamic world and in countries recently freed from Communist rule will probably encourage the preachers of apocalypse to continue speculating that an invasion of Israel by Russia and her former Soviet-bloc allies is imminent. Even if the situation in the Middle East were to stablilize, however, prophetic interpreters have an "ace in the hole" in certain scriptural texts that provide an apparently airtight argument to defend catastrophic scenarios against the threat of peace. As advanced by an editorial in Lindsey's *Countdown* newsletter, the argument demonstrates the difficulty and even impossibility of disproving the tragic vision: "It's interesting that in I Thessalonians, Chapter 5:1–3, it talks about a time 'When people say "There is peace and security," then sudden destruction will come upon them . . . and there will be no escape.' The Bible is very clear that there will be a period of time in the last days when the whole world lets down its guard. It will be a time of great hope, but it will be a false peace."[55] By invoking the scriptural doctrine of the "false peace" that precedes sudden destruction, preachers of doom can effectively insulate themselves from the dangers of disconfirmation presented by apparent improvements in the world situation. In this manner, any evidence that the world's conflicts are heading toward peaceful resolution rather than a nuclear catastrophe serves to confirm rather than refute the main claims of contemporary apocalyptic argument.

In the preceding pages, I have attempted to show how the topoi of evil and time reappear and are refashioned into topics of continuing relevance in the arguments of modern apocalyptic preachers. As they argued for the relevance of the ancient apocalyptic topoi, these preachers appealed to the dramatic sensibility of tragedy, a sensibility evident in the words of Hal Lindsey's mentor John F. Walvoord, former president of Dallas Theological Seminary:

> The world today is like a stage being set for a great drama. The major actors are already in the wings waiting for their moment in history. The main stage props are

already in place. The prophetic play is about to begin. . . . Our present world is well prepared for the beginning of the prophetic drama that will lead to Armageddon. Since the stage is set for this dramatic climax of the age, it must mean that Christ's coming for his own is very near.[56]

Walvoord's choice of metaphors is entirely apt; it indicates that the logic of apocalypse is indeed a dramatistic logic. As this logic is played out upon the historical stage, it is evident that the argumentative topoi of the apocalyptic tradition are continually resolved into dramatic conclusions by overeager audiences anticipating the tragic End. Within the past ten years, avid followers of the drama of the Last Days have cast various historical figures into the apocalyptic role of Antichrist, including Anwar Sadat, Moammar Qadhafi, Mikhail Gorbachev, Ronald Reagan, Henry Kissinger, King Juan Carlos of Spain and (most recently) Saddam Hussein, and have proposed a number of dates for the grand finale, including 1982, 1986, 1987, 1988, and 1994.[57] Can there be any doubt that with the approach of the millennial year 2000 there will be no shortage of actors to play the Antichrist role, or that there will be a dramatic increase in temporal predictions focusing on the epochal deadline?

The tragic apocalyptic vision remains a constant presence at the fringes of our culture, and sometimes succeeds in moving closer to its center. The temptation to predict dates for the End continues to lure apocalyptic preachers into comical excesses of predictive specificity that relegate them to the cultural margins. The effect of specific resolutions to the *topos* of time is to limit both the length of time for which apocalyptic arguments can remain relevant and the number of people to whom they may appeal. Advocates skillful in the uses of ambiguity, such as Hal Lindsey and Ronald Reagan, can overcome this marginalization and move into the cultural mainstream by avoiding temporal specificity while interpreting the symbols of the tragic apocalypse concretely enough to make them relevant to their audiences. The continued presence of the threat of nuclear destruction, the approach of the millennial year, and the massive changes in the world's military and political alliances, will provide ample grist for the prophetic interpreter's mill for years to come. As a consequence, speculation on the tragic apocalypse may occupy a position close to the center of culture until well after the millennial deadline is passed. In my concluding chapter, I will attempt to distill some insights from this detailed study of the dramatistic logic of apocalyptic advocacy, in the hope of shedding further light on humanity's eschatological dilemma in the nuclear age.

EIGHT

The Apocalypse of Apocalypses

The end approaches, but the apocalypse is long lived. The question remains and comes back: what can be the limits of demystification? No doubt one can think— I think this—that this demystification must be led as far as possible, and the task is not modest. It is interminable, because no one can exhaust the overdeterminations and indeterminations of the apocalyptic stratagems. [1]

This investigation has attempted to untangle the thickets of apocalyptic argument in the discourse of nineteenth-century Millerites and twentieth-century fundamentalists. The exploration appears to confirm Derrida's assessment that apocalyptic stratagems are endless. The task of demystifying these stratagems by tracing their logic through discourse that spans centuries and diverse genres does, indeed, seem interminable. Yet, in spite of the fact that this task can never be completed, the close analysis of the literature of apocalyptic advocacy has not been a wasted effort. Some recurrent rhetorical patterns and structures are clearly discernible; their discovery is illuminating and perhaps useful, to the extent that they contribute to critical understanding of apocalypse and of rhetoric. This study has attempted to sketch the outlines of a general theory of apocalyptic discourse. Although many more apocalyptic sects and arguments could be studied to make the case for this theory more conclusive, sufficient evidence has been compiled to enable an evaluation of its utility. This chapter recapitulates the rationale of the study, the conceptual and critical processes by which its discoveries were generated, and the insights that emerged from the investigation. Implications of these insights for future studies in apocalypticism and in rhetoric will be adduced. Finally, the chapter concludes with an ethical judgment of apocalyptic argument in regard to its two fundamental patterns—the tragic and the comic—as representations of history, as frames for discursive practice, and as proposed solutions to the problem of evil.

The Topical and Dramatistic Theory of
Apocalyptic Rhetoric

The first chapter of this book argued that much of the previous scholarship on apocalypse fails to account for the persuasive force of this discourse, that such scholarship has relied on simplistic explanations that classify texts according to rigid generic criteria, or reduce the apocalyptic mentality to economic, socio-logical, and psychological causes. In place of such explanations, I offered a rhetorical study that examined the rationality of this discourse as it is advanced in argumentation, and thereby promised to shed new light on the attraction of the apocalyptic vision. The utility of the rhetorical methodology has been amply demonstrated by its ability to explain the substantive and stylistic features of apocalyptic discourse. However, the rhetorical method encompasses more than the study of texts. By employing Kenneth Burke's psychology of form, which explains the response of audiences as a function of expectations created by and embodied in discourse, this analysis uncovered not only regularities of style and substance in this discourse, but also its characteristic modes of audience in-ducement. In short, the study considered apocalyptic argument as a social process, a cooperative interaction between rhetor and audience, who jointly participate in the creation and revision of meaning through the arousal and fulfillment (or disappointment) of expectations. Rhetoric, conceived in this broad fashion, oc-cupies a unique position with regard to other disciplines or fields of inquiry. Since it is explicitly concerned with the relationship of texts and audiences, rhetoric enables the critic to view apocalypse as both literary text and social movement, and to incorporate insights from sociology, psychology, history, the-ology, and literary criticism without being bound by the limitations of these fields.

Apocalyptic is a particular form of *eschatology*, a term that refers to the logos of the farthest or last things. In explaining this discourse, I began with the hypothesis that apocalyptic rhetoric is a symbolic theodicy, a rhetorical solution to the problem of evil that operates on both a rational and a mythic level. Further, I claimed that apocalypse achieves its solution to the problem of evil by its discursive construction of temporality. The project of explicating the rationality of this solution began by setting aside Kant's dismissal of eschatology and all other forms of the "transcen-dental dialectic." Kant rejected all questions concerned with humanity's ultimate destiny as illusory, or lacking objective referent; this study countered Kant's dismissal of these questions, and human attempts to answer them, by employing Burke's "logological" perspective, which "involves only *empirical* considerations about our nature as the symbol-using animal."[2] From this perspective, discourse on escha-tological questions is itself an empirical fact that must be accounted for, and the attempt to discover the principles that govern such discourse implies no endorsement of a particular solution to the cosmological questions. The major contribution of this study lies in its illumination of the logic of apocalyptic eschatology through an application of two bodies of theory from the rhetorical tradition: Aristotle's theory of topical argument and Burke's dramatism. I will summarize the insights derived from each of these applications in turn.

The Topoi of Eschatology

Chapter 2 reviewed various conceptions of the topoi in the history of rhetorical theory and distilled them into a form useful for analyzing eschatological discourse. Following Aristotle and modern rhetorical theorists such as Michael Leff, the topoi were considered as recurring themes or subjects of rhetorical argument, as "places" or *loci* of controversy, as inventional resources for the discovery of arguments, and as the patterns, forms, or analytic categories by which argument is conducted. The common or universal topoi were described as basic categories of human practical reasoning, applying to all fields of human inquiry; they relate decisions in the present to questions of "past fact," "future fact," "the more and the less," and "the possible and the impossible." Special topoi are "based on such propositions as apply only to particular groups or classes of things," and are thus rooted in knowledge produced by specific fields; they appear as warrants in rhetorical arguments, and when verbalized can take the form of proverbial knowledge. When cosmological speculations about time are brought to bear upon present choices, the universal topoi of temporality increase in significance, as the scope of temporal considerations is widened to include that which is at the limits of human understanding. Eschatology, as a species of cosmology, also contains its own special topoi, or propositional truths that express the social knowledge of a given culture. The special topoi of eschatology concern questions of ultimate significance: the nature of time, the destiny of humanity and the cosmos, the sources of spiritual authority, and the meaning and significance of human suffering and evil.

These issues appear and reappear in apocalyptic discourse through the ages. An understanding of their significance requires critics to view apocalypticism not simply as a collection of revelatory and interpretative texts, or as a series of discrete and identifiable social movements with economic, sociological, or psychological causes. Rather, the discourse of apocalypse constitutes a rhetorical tradition in the fullest sense of that word, as defined by Alasdair MacIntyre:

> A tradition is an argument extended through time in which certain fundamental agreements are defined and redefined in terms of two kinds of conflict: those with critics and enemies external to the tradition who reject all or at least key parts of its fundamental agreements, and those internal, interpretative debates through which the meaning and rationale of the fundamental agreements come to be expressed and by whose progress a tradition is constituted.[3]

In proposing a rhetorical theory of apocalypse, this study viewed this discourse as "an argument extended through time," and sought to examine the logic of this argument on two levels: the internal logic of eschatological speculation and the external, public logic of apocalyptic advocacy. The fundamental agreements, or topoi, that form the basis of this tradition constitute the contributions of eschatology to what modern rhetorical theorists term social knowledge.[4]

Considering apocalypse as tradition, the relationship between apocalyptic texts and apocalyptic movements can be defined more precisely. From the evidence examined, I conclude that the apocalyptic tradition, founded in mythic narratives and canonical scriptures and augmented by debates about the meaning of these texts, provides the social knowledge base that enables apocalyptic movements to appeal occasionally to a wider audience than the tradition's devotees and caretakers. Such an expansion beyond the base of the tradition is possible when the conventionally accepted understanding of a culture's destiny seems unable to account for social ills that challenge and threaten normal mechanisms for dealing with life's "ultimate exigence" of time and evil. At such times, eschatology becomes an essentially contested issue. Fresh confrontations with the ultimate exigence, as embodied in the prospect of individual and cultural death, prompt a re-examination of eschatology and a redefinition of the meaning and rationale of the fundamental agreements of the apocalyptic tradition. To the extent that apocalyptic topoi are successfully revised in interpretive debates, that is, to the extent that interpreters can coherently employ these topoi to account for the particularities of experience, apocalyptic rhetors may succeed or fail in gaining the adherence of audiences outside the tradition. Alternatively, as the case of Pat Robertson's shifting theology illustrated, the need to gain the adherence of external audiences may itself serve as an incentive to reinterpretation of fundamental assumptions. Thus, internal and external debates together contribute to the progress of the apocalyptic tradition, as the topoi of the tradition are revised and reinterpreted in light of the advances and failures of previous generations.

The internal and external conflicts that constitute the apocalyptic tradition were studied in regard to two types of form, namely, propositional logic and mythic narrative. Drawing on Paul Ricoeur's conception of myth as "a vast field of experimentation . . . of playing with hypotheses," chapter 2 examined the ways in which eschatological myths are employed to resolve the contradiction posed by the problem of evil in a monotheistic belief system, and to impose a teleological structure upon the human experience of time. Exploring the implications of Ricoeur's maxim, "The symbol gives rise to thought," I demonstrated how the cosmological myth of the Christian Apocalypse was rationalized into propositional form in the arguments of early Christian apologists, who disputed cosmological questions with pagan philosophers as they competed with other mystery cults offering their own salvific revelations. In propositional form, the topoi of Christian eschatology condense the mythic conceptions of time and evil into their 'rational' essence: "Time must have a stop," and "Evil is or will be justified in the ultimate destiny of the cosmos." These fundamental agreements formed the basis for arguments internal to the apocalyptic tradition. The process of rationalization continued as the implications of the propositions were developed; discourse on each of the eschatological topoi exhibited a characteristic internal logic following certain identifiable patterns, discussed under the headings of theodicy and chronology.

The examination of the topos of evil focused on philosophical debates over the problem of theodicy. Monotheistic arguments about evil and the debates over rational theodicies share certain characteristics of legal argument: as they are essentially concerned with establishing or denying divine justice, they have tended to cluster around the stasis points of forensic rhetoric. The defense of theism based on the stasis of fact declares the phenomenal unreality of evil. Defenses based on the stasis of definition seek to redefine the divine attributes, such as omnipotence or benevolence, and thereby to eliminate the apparent contradiction posed by the existence of evil. The Christian eschatological myth was regarded as a defense of theism based upon the third stasis of quality, one that offers the narrative of the Apocalypse as a "morally sufficient reason" for the divine sufferance of evil. Finally, the stasis of jurisdiction characterizes all theistic arguments that place God beyond human standards of judgment, and deny human beings the right to question the purposes of the Deity. Although theological solutions to the problem of evil can combine and recombine these defenses in a variety of ways, eschatological narratives provide a powerful temporal frame for understanding the problem, and hence have remained perennially attractive to audiences who cannot resist the attempt to imagine the End that will justify the means (that is, the divine permission of death, sin, and suffering).

The topos of time was examined through John Angus Campbell's concept of epochal rhetoric. Epochal symbolism, according to Campbell, constructs cosmic and social time into "an era so marked by a strategic, stylized symbolism that it divides history into a 'before' and 'after' "; such symbolism springs from the "tensional field" of history created by the universal awareness of mortality.[5] The problem of theodicy is linked to that of temporality, since the phenomenal experience of death is perceived as an evil that requires explanation. Christian eschatology, a unique form of temporal symbolism offering a mythical solution to the problem of evil, thus appears as one type of response to what Campbell terms the "ultimate exigence." The motives that prompted the development of Christian epochal symbolism were illuminated by a study of early Christian chronologies, which attempted to codify the eschatological myth into a sequential representation of cosmic time from Genesis to Revelation. Drawing on the work of historian Richard Landes, I argued that the epochal symbolism of the World Week, which ordered history into a sequence of thousand-year periods mirroring the seven days of creation, dominated early Christian attempts at chronological calculation, and that the apocalyptic implications of this symbolism are evident in the attempts of orthodox church historians to produce timetables of history that would suppress millennial expectations by postponing the world's End for some centuries. The first articulation of the Christian rhetorical epoch was thus conceived in the literal sense of the Greek word *epoché*, that is, a suspension of judgment: the early Christians were forced to develop a symbolic mode of historical self-understanding that could account for the unexpected delay of the Last Judgment.

The primitive Christian rationalization of eschatological disappointment established a rhetorical pattern that has been re-enacted by countless apocalyptic sects and movements. The pattern is based on a temporal paradox: the declaration of the End of time calls a community of believers into being; the community then strives to redefine its place in universal history as it confronts its own unexpected historical continuance. Every apocalyptic sect that has survived the failure of its predictions has done so through a process of symbolic negotiation in which its initial epochal formulations are reconstructed into a more durable form of historical self-definition, as the original declaration of the imminent End comes to mark a foundational moment in the institutional narrative of the sect or church. The discourse of patristic chronographers such as Hippolytus and Lactantius demonstrated that the epochal definitions intended to explain the postponement of the final Judgment contained inherent apocalyptic implications insofar as they endowed certain years or dates with transcendent historical meaning. For this reason, apocalyptic speculations upon the topos of time have tended to adopt the mathematical logic of the countdown, as interpreters deduced conclusions about the End from the chronological premises of sacred history and supported their claims with numerological proofs.

All mythic narratives of the origins and destiny of humanity must present themselves as authoritative to the extent that they lay claim to human allegiance and serve as norms for conduct. Hence it is necessary to consider a third topos in apocalyptic rhetoric, that of authority. Arguments on the topos of authority follow certain patterns, which were explicated in terms of Max Weber's typology of legitimation. Weber identified three essential types of authority: rational, traditional, and charismatic. These categories can be viewed as descriptive of the rhetorical strategies employed by those who seek to achieve and maintain spiritual as well as political authority. The Christian Scriptures clearly lay claim to charismatic authority, in the sense that they embody a divine gift or revelation. However, from a rhetorical perspective, charisma is best conceived not as a property of the text, but as an attribution by the audience. In the act of endowing the myth of the Last Judgment with charismatic authority, the historical audience attempts to assume the standpoint of the "universal audience," a divine perspective that forecloses the possibility of disagreement. In light of the difficulties that would attend a historical study of the formation of the Christian canon through the differentiation of Scripture and apocrypha, the charismatic sources of prophetic authority were ignored in favor of what Weber termed the "routinization of charisma," the process by which the implications of the authoritative claims of Scripture are discovered and rationalized. Thus, this study of apocalyptic argument did not seek to discover the charismatic grounds of textual authority, but rather the authority of interpretive claims about the text and the legitimation of these claims through rational and traditional arguments.

The discussion of authority concluded with a brief consideration of the political implications of Christian eschatology. The history of certain influential legends of the apocalyptic tradition—the papal Antichrist, the Last World Emperor, the Angelic Pope—demonstrated that mythic symbolism may evolve from the audience's need to understand newly developing structures and institutions of power by placing them within a context of cosmic narrative. The development of imperial and papal versions of the apocalyptic narrative illustrated the historical and potential uses of eschatological symbols for purposes of both legitimation and subversion.

Apocalypse as Dramatic Enactment

From an examination of the topical logic of eschatological speculation, the study moved to a consideration of the dramatistic logic that governs both the apocalyptic myth and the discourse of its interpretation. Application of the theory of dramatism to apocalyptic discourse constitutes the second major innovation of this study. Although many scholars have sought to explain the power of the Apocalypse in regard to the dramatic form of its mythic narrative, the implications of the dramatistic insight have not been systematically pursued. Some few scholars have considered the logical and argumentative form of apocalyptic discourse;[6] but, to my knowledge, there are no scholarly studies that examine apocalyptic argument as itself a form of dramatic enactment. This investigation employed two constructs from the dramatistic theory of Kenneth Burke: the tragic and comic "frames of acceptance" and the "psychology of form." By these means, I sought to examine both the argument of apocalyptic drama and the drama of apocalyptic argument.

The dramatistic perspective brought the investigation of the problems of time and evil to another level of analysis, involving the study of tragedy and comedy not only as literary genres, but also, and most importantly, as symbolic modes for coming to terms with the world. The tragic and comic frames are examples of what Burke denominates in more general terms as frames of "acceptance" and "rejection"; and the human impulse to construct these discursive patterns "starts from the problem of evil. In the face of anguish, injustice, disease, and death one . . . constructs his notion of the universe or history, and shapes attitudes in keeping."[7] The tragic and comic acceptance frames offer different symbolic "solutions" to the problem of evil, and shape human attitudes toward time and history in different ways. This insight was amplified by invoking the aesthetic philosophy of Susanne Langer, who argues that the formal patterns of drama operate "by creating the semblance of a history, and composing its elements into a rhythmic single structure."[8] According to Langer, tragedy and comedy each exhibit distinctive rhythms and modes of emplotment. These features are not mutually exclusive; they may each be found within a given narrative. In fact, to the extent that a symbolic narrative strives for "completion" in its representation of the world, and to widen its perspective to account for the various motives of human action, it will contain elements of both the tragic and comic frames.

The differences between the tragic and comic frames of acceptance, as embodied in their characteristic dramatic constructions of time and evil, can be summarized as follows. The tragic plot conceives of evil in terms of sin or guilt; its mechanism of redemption is victimage, and its plot moves toward the isolation of the evildoer in the "cult of the kill." The comic plot conceives of evil in terms of error, misunderstanding, or ignorance; its mechanism of redemption is recognition, and its plot moves toward exposure of the evildoer's fallibility and his incorporation into society. The tragic rhythm is progressive and cadential, while the rhythm of comedy is episodic; the tragic plot promotes a view of time and human action as predetermined, leading to an inevitable resolution that "is always the turn to an absolute close," while the comic plot portrays time as open-ended by depicting "the upset and recovery of . . . equilibrium."[9] Following Burke and Langer, I concluded that an audience's views of historical time and human agency are shaped in part by the frames of acceptance and the temporal rhythms found within the dramatic representation of history as myth.

Previous interpreters, such as Adela Yarbro Collins, have emphasized the tragic features of the book of Revelation. Collins argued that the function of the Apocalypse is similar to that of Aristotelian tragedy: by projecting conflicts onto a cosmic screen and offering a cathartic resolution of these conflicts, the audience's feelings of fear and resentment are "brought to consciousness and become less threatening."[10] While agreeing with this insight, I sought to expand upon it by pointing to comic elements in the mythic drama of Revelation. The heroes of this drama, the saints of the millennial kingdom who faithfully endure the persecutions of the beast, are comic in that their fortune changes from misery to happiness rather than from happiness to misery. Furthermore, the narrative structure of the drama is one that Aristotle classified as comic: the "double plot," in which the virtuous are rewarded and the evil punished. These comic elements are balanced by the tragic features of the drama: the sense of time as moving to a predetermined conclusion, the catastrophic predictions of the destruction of earthly kingdoms presaged by signs and wonders in the heavens, and the radical duality that separates the servants of Christ from the servants of the beast. By emphasizing the elements of tragedy or comedy, interpreters seeking clues to the meaning of history align their frames of acceptance with the symbols and assumptions associated with the tragic or comic visions.

As interpreted through the tragic frame, the Apocalypse is a closed symbolic system in which each element of the myth signifies a particular historical or political referent. Such an interpretation reduces time to a linear structure of necessity. The comic frame interprets apocalyptic symbolism as open rather than closed, emphasizing the multivalence of symbols and repudiating their simplistic identification with historical referents; in this interpretation, time is structured as cyclical or episodic, and the absolute necessity of history is replaced by an open horizon of possibility. The comic view of time and history probably reached its furthest extension within the Christian tradition in the third-century theology of Origen, whose doctrine of *apocatastasis* posited a cyclical theory of history and denied orthodox teaching on the eternality of hell by teaching that all creatures, even Satan, would ultimately be saved.[11] The tragic view has been taken to its furthest limits time and time again by interpreters predicting an imminent visitation of divine wrath, of whom William Miller is a representative example. To discover how the discourse of interpretation can follow the logic of the tragic and comic frames to such differing extremes, I examined the aesthetic and predictive functions of apocalyptic narrative.

Scholars are agreed that the earliest Christian audiences for the book of Revelation were accustomed to forms of worship that involved the oral reading of prophetic texts.[12] On the most fundamental level of audience response, the text therefore provides an opportunity for mythic enactment in which the audience experiences the emotions of hope and fear through the mimetic representation of history in symbolic form. Following Collins and other historians, such as John Gager, the Apocalypse's resolution of symbolic conflicts can be seen to promote an aesthetic suspension of ordinary time, in which the defeat of the powers of evil and the establishment of the millennial kingdom are experienced by the audience as fleeting realities. Public performance of Revelation thus makes the individual and collective experience of evil more bearable by offering a shared vision of millennial bliss along with a cathartic discharge of emotions. This aesthetic function of the text of the Apocalypse is, however, in constant tension with its predictive function. When read as a prediction of historical events, the prophecy structures history as a tragic drama marked by a sequence of signs that leads inexorably to a predestined catastrophic conclusion. Focusing on the inevitability of prophetic fulfillment, this mode of interpretation postpones the final Judgment to the future (however imminent this future may be), and therefore has the effect of heightening the audience's anticipation. Thus, while the aesthetic experience of Revelation collapses sacred time into the present through a vivid evocation of emotionally charged symbolism, the interpretation of the text as a prediction of events to come emphasizes the distinction between the profane present and the sacred future.[13] The history of apocalyptic interpretation therefore features a continually operating dialectic of the Now and the Not-yet, and oscillates between reading the text as prediction and experiencing it as enactment.

The earliest Christians perceived no contradiction between the aesthetic and predictive modes of understanding the Apocalypse. Interpreting the symbols of the beast and the whore of Babylon as clear representations of the hated Roman power, they expected the destruction of that power within their lifetimes. Yet, while they waited, they took comfort in Revelation's depiction of the blissful world to come and, to some degree, experienced that world as present in communal worship. With the passage of time and the conversion of the empire to Christianity, however, the text became more difficult to interpret as a set of historical predictions: the prophesied End had failed to materialize, and the former Antichrist now convened ecclesiastical councils and used his troops to suppress heresy. As the catharsis of the mythic drama was enacted and re-enacted while the End delayed, the audience's aesthetic experience of this catharsis was altered through repetition. Under these circumstances, the drama of the End came to appear as an allegorical representation of the Church's struggle against its enemies in all ages. The essentially comic nature of the turn toward allegorical modes of interpretation was explicated through an examination of the anti-apocalyptic eschatology of Augustine, whose classic work *The City of God* redefined the Christian rhetorical epoch and articulated a viable historical stance for Christian communities following the failure of their initial expectations.

Augustine's interpretation of the Apocalypse, which came to represent the orthodox position of the institutional church,[14] effectively imposed a comic substructure onto the tragic construction of temporality by maintaining the inscrutability of the divine purpose in the vicissitudes of history. Augustine prohibited any attempt to calculate the times of the End; he undercut the tragic dualism of apocalyptic prophecy by interpreting its conflicts as allegorical representations of ongoing moral struggles within the soul, and by warning his readers against the tendency to project absolute evil onto a demonic scapegoat. The millennial kingdom was interpreted not as a prophecy of a realm yet to be established, but as a parable of the historical church; those who looked for some later fulfillment of the millennial hope were henceforth to be seen as heretics. Finally, Augustine regarded the historical calamities that constitute the traditional apocalyptic signs—wars, apostasy, earthquakes, and the like—as unreliable guides to the progress of divine fulfillment, since these signs are always present. Rather than portents of the End, such calamities were seen as episodic recurrences that humans must face without resort to apocalyptic understanding. Augustine's invocation of the comic perspective is evident in his cautionary warning that believers should be skeptical in evaluating apocalyptic claims, so that "when we fall into a panic over present happenings as if they were the ultimate and extreme of all things, we may not be laughed at by those who have read of more and worse things in the history of the world."[15] Thus the comic interpretation of Revelation qualifies its absolute dualities and neutralizes its predictive function.

The dramatic forms of tragedy and comedy are revealed in the apocalyptic narrative through the discourse of interpretation. These forms are also manifested in the discourse of apocalyptic advocacy, which elaborates the topoi of authority, time, and evil into a propositional logic. The structure of this logic is governed by Burke's psychology of form. According to this view, form is "the creation of an appetite in the mind of the auditor, and the adequate satisfaction of that appetite."[16] The apocalyptic rhetor who seeks to establish conclusions about the End of all things must therefore build the eschatological topoi into lines of argument that both raise and adequately meet audience expectations. Thus, apocalyptic argument as conducted within the tragic frame may be seen as a hypothetical conversation, in which the topoi of authority, time, and evil appear as a series of claims made by rhetors and questions raised by audiences. The topos of evil is the "ultimate exigence" for the argument, the problem that the apocalyptic claim purports to solve. This exigence can be expressed as a question: "How shall we account for our present ills?" The essential claim of tragic apocalypticism, "The End is near," functions as an answer to this query by positing that present ills can best be understood as signs of imminent catastrophe and redemption. As expressed in propositional form, this claim provokes an audience response in the form of demands for the source of the speaker's authority ("Who says so?" or "How do you know?") and for further clarification and proof ("When will it happen?").

Depending upon the presumptions of particular audiences, the topos of authority may require a defense of the authority of the sacred text on which the prediction is based. In cases where the authority of the text is assumed, this topos will be elaborated into a defense of the rhetor's interpretive method. A credulous audience may require little support for the rhetor's interpretive principles, while a sophisticated audience familiar with hermeneutical problems will exact a more rigorous methodological defense from the rhetor. If these expectations are met, the curiosity of the audience is aroused: it will respond to the promise of knowledge about the future with an expectation of further details about the prediction and its exact degree of proximity. To hold the audience's attention, the rhetor must predict a date, or at least a general span of time, which establishes the saliency of the rhetor's predictions for the audience by placing the events of the End within its immediate temporal horizon. The limits of this temporal horizon are defined at the one extreme by the need to capture an audience without exposing the rhetor to the risk of immediate disconfirmation, and at the other extreme by the lifetime of the audience. Within these limits, the rhetor's inventional choices allow varying degrees of proximity and specificity as the prediction is elaborated. With some variations, therefore, argument on the topos of time turns toward a discourse of calculation that satisfies the audience's curiosity about the date and thereby reassures auditors that they can expect personally to see the validation of the rhetor's claims. Arguments on the topos of evil can provide support for the temporal claim, as the calculations on the topos of time are paralleled with a calculus of evil based on the principle that "the night is always darkest just before the dawn." By listing the evils of the world and pyramiding this list into a structure of apocalyptic significance, the rhetor in effect seeks to prove that the night has never been darker and that the dawn can therefore be expected soon. Another variation on the topos of evil that parallels the rhetorical impulse to date specificity is the attempt to personify the demonic principle of Antichrist in a particular historical ruler or public figure. As the implications of the myth are discovered and rationalized in this fashion, the topoi of time and evil are transformed from *themes* of the eschatological narrative into characteristic patterns of reasoning or *lines of argument* that together form a structure of proofs in support of the apocalyptic claim.

The rhetor's choice of answers to the paradigmatic questions of the discourse orients the audience toward the tragic or comic frames. Each answer conditions the expectations of the audience in particular ways; as these expectations are aroused and (sometimes) fulfilled, apocalyptic argument takes on the character of dramatic enactment as rhetors draw the audience into the world of the mythic narrative and assume the attitudes and roles of characters in the cosmic drama. The tragic and comic frames are useful for analyzing this enactment so long as they are viewed not as binary categories of opposition, but as poles on an interpretive continuum that includes a variety of responses. A particular argument may therefore lie somewhere in between the extremes of pure tragedy and pure comedy, as each answer to the essential apocalyptic questions tends toward one or another interpretive frame. With this caveat, the argumentative elaborations of the tragic and comic visions of apocalypse were differentiated by their substantive resolutions of the apocalyptic topoi.

Argument in the tragic frame defines evil in supernatural terms, placing history temporarily in the control of demonic powers that can only be overthrown by catastrophic divine intervention. Such argument structures time by the expectation of a predestined End in the immediate future. Argument in the comic frame defines evil in human terms of ignorance and fallibility, assigning to human beings the task of overcoming the world's ills and thereby ushering in the apocalypse. Comic apocalyptic argument may structure time by postponing the date of the apocalypse, by claiming the date is unknowable, or by employing allegorical interpretation to apply prophecy to history in a way that threatens no disruption of the episodic pattern of historical time. Whether the symbols of prophecy are interpreted as references to distant future events or as allegory, the net effect is the same: the audience is prevented from reading any ultimate historical meaning into the calamities of the present, which are experienced not as signs of an imminent catharsis but as episodic setbacks to the progress of God's people. With regard to substantive content, then, apocalyptic argument in the tragic frame locates the cause of evil in supernatural forces and tends toward the establishment of a date that is fixed and imminent, while argument in the comic frame tends to locate the cause of evil in human error and to postpone the date or render it irrelevant.

The substantive claims of tragic apocalypticism have implications for the practice of argument, relating to the psychology of the audience and the function and purpose of rhetorical discourse. The prediction of a date for the End of all things imparts a dramatic urgency that transforms the audience from a collection of rational judges weighing argumentative claims into spectators and participants in a drama of cosmic redemption. Under the pressure of elapsing time as the predicted date of the End approaches, the audience tends to divide into adherents or sympathizers, on the one hand, and skeptics or detractors on the other. This division can also be seen as a choice between tragic or comic frames: as audience members who accept the apocalyptic claims come to view themselves as actors in a cosmic drama approaching its cathartic conclusion, skeptical members of the audience gleefully await a different sort of ending, a comic denouement in which claims to eschatological certainty will be debunked. The prediction of a date thus has the effect of polarizing the audience for apocalyptic discourse: one side prepares for the final catastrophes with discourse that grows more frenzied and urgent, while the other side views every expression of apocalyptic urgency as an opportunity for further ridicule.

Under these conditions, the primary function of apocalyptic argument in the tragic frame shifts from *persuasion* to *enactment*. The End itself is beyond the capacity of human discourse to hasten or postpone; the deterministic construction of the tragic apocalypse eliminates contingency from history, and ultimately from argument itself. Since the End cannot be postponed through discourse, and since the apocalyptic prophecy predicts that many will reject the message of salvation, arguers tend to lose their concern with convincing an audience; argument becomes a mode of ritual enactment that retraces the pattern of the divine revelation. The rhetor who seeks to persuade an audience of the truth of his or her apocalyptic claims ultimately must fall back upon a retelling of the mythic narrative. At this point, argument devolves into a performative unveiling of the divine Truth, embodied in myth and beyond the reach of rational discourse. As the powerful emotions evoked by the apocalyptic symbols provoke reaction from auditors, their division into believers and skeptics parallels the division of humanity in the Last Judgment. Thus, every apocalyptic sect comes to re-enact the role of the embattled community of saints surrounded by the forces of the beast; and, as the predicted End approaches, apocalyptic rhetors increasingly tend to view their opponents or interlocutors as representatives of demonic forces, consigning them to the "lake of fire . . . into [which] were flung any whose names were not to be found in the roll of the living" (Rev. 20:14–15).

Burke's theory of the tragic and comic frames provides a dramatistic key that unlocks the mysteries of the mythic narrative of the Apocalypse and renders comprehensible the patterns of argument employed by those who interpret the narrative for purposes of prediction and exhortation. When the myth is applied to present events, history itself takes on the temporal structures of tragedy or comedy (depending on which elements of the myth are emphasized). As rhetors define the nature of the cosmic drama and situate themselves within it, they produce discourse that elaborates narrative premises into rational argument. The logic of apocalyptic argument is thus governed by the dramatistic frame within which the discourse is conducted. Although examples of both comic and tragic argument were provided, this study was chiefly concerned with the characteristic patterns of apocalyptic discourse in the tragic frame. To illustrate these patterns, chapters 4 and 5 analyzed the discourse of the nineteenth-century Millerite movement and the twentieth-century author Hal Lindsey.

Millerite Discourse

The Millerite movement provides a paradigmatic example of the formation of a community through the discursive construction and reconstruction of a rhetorical epoch. Chapters 4 and 5 sought to explain the historical and social processes involved in the development of Millerism by showing how the apocalyptic topoi of authority, time, and evil were elaborated into an argumentative system; how this system conditioned the expectations of its audiences; and how it managed to survive the disappointment of these expectations by refashioning the epochal definitions that had prompted its formation. The declaration of the epoch's imminent End in 1843 called forth an audience that anticipated the dramatic conclusion with eager fascination; the failure of the prediction forced this audience to seek an institutional identity that legitimated its existence and provided a coherent "plausibility structure"[17] that rationalized the epoch's extension.

Millerite arguments on the topos of authority were illuminated by considering the places allotted, at different periods of the movement's history, to the three forms of legitimation identified by Max Weber. In Weber's terms, the Millerite system employed rational and traditional legitimations founded in the charismatic authority of Scripture. The ultimate authority for Miller's apocalyptic claim that the world would end in 1843 derived from the Bible. Although authority was fixed in the text, which predicted no definite date for the End, Miller and his followers claimed that such a conclusion could be rationally derived using interpretive principles taken from Scripture itself, such as the maxim that "with the Lord one day is like a thousand years" (II Peter 3:8). While Millerite advocates began by rejecting any pretensions to charismatic authority based on personal revelations, the excitement generated by their highly specific predictions caused some of the movement's adherents to lay claim to "spiritual gifts," including visions, prophecies, and the performance of miracles. These eruptions of charismatic fervor were initially denounced by movement leaders as "fanaticism." In the aftermath of the Great Disappointment, however, a remnant of Miller's followers managed to survive and prosper under the leadership of the visionary prophet Ellen G. White, whose charismatic revelations provided a basis for the apocalyptic movement's institutional identity as the Seventh-day Adventist Church. Charismatic legitimation thus came to play a more prominent role in Adventist discourse as the dates calculated through elaboration upon the topos of time approached and passed; new sources of authority had to be found that would validate the Great Disappointment as an event "of God's own appointment."[18]

Adventist arguments on the topos of time were the constitutive feature of the group's identity. For Miller's opponents as well as his followers, the distinctive characteristic of the movement's discourse was its elaborate structure of rational proofs offered to support a highly specific claim of the world's End in 1843. Most prominent among these proofs were the argument from sign and the argument from chronological calculation. As the year 1843 approached and passed, various attempts at recalculation were made in which the date of the End was extended to the spring of 1844, and finally to October 22 of that year. The initial resistance and final capitulation of the Adventist leadership to these increasingly specific predictions provided support for the theory that the declaration of an imminent conclusion of history creates a formal expectation which requires satisfaction, and that the audience's demand for predictive specificity can (under certain circumstances) force the rhetor to commit to a date as a means of satisfying this expectation. Thus, the selection of an exact date for the world's End was shown to be not merely an argumentative tactic, or a freakish aberration in the history of Biblical interpretation, but the natural functioning of the psychology of the audience, the logical extension of apocalyptic variations on the eschatological topos of time.

The examination of Millerite discourse concluded with a study of the eschatological topos of evil. I argued that Millerism can best be understood as a product of the breakdown of the comic frame that had guided postmillennial reformers in their efforts to rid the world of the evils of slavery and alcohol. The historical affinity of disappointed abolitionists and temperance advocates with the Adventist cause indicates that a primary motive for conversion to apocalyptic belief was the frustration felt by reformers who had exhausted revivalism and rational persuasion as means of achieving their goals. This frustration culminated in a tragic perception of the world's evils as so systemic and numerous as to be incapable of resolution by any merely human measures. Millerite elaboration on this apocalyptic topos was exemplified in the pamphlet *The Groaning Creation*, which attempted a cumulative calculation of the entire extent of corruption and suffering across time and space, reducing the sum of all evils to a single demonic principle requiring divine intervention as its sole remedy. Thus, the comic view of evil as ignorance that could be overcome through rational argument and social reform was replaced by a tragic perception of evil as an "ultimate exigence," resolvable only by a dramatic historical finale in which the righteous would be rewarded and the wicked punished for all eternity.

Millerite discourse drew upon basic premises of American social knowledge, most particularly the generally unquestioned assumption of the Bible's divine authority. While Miller and his followers did succeed in attracting a large following by building on these premises, the failure of their predictions ensured that future preachers of imminent apocalypse would remain minor figures, unable to attract the attention (let alone gain the adherence) of mainstream society. The collective memory of the Adventist debacle added to the stock of social knowledge on the ultimate questions of time and history and defined the rhetorical situation for apocalyptic preachers for generations to come. Until the second half of the twentieth century, proclaiming the imminence of the End was enough to relegate one to the margins of culture.

Hal Lindsey's Apocalypse

Chapter 6 explored the confluence of historical circumstances and rhetorical skill that enabled one prominent contemporary preacher to overcome the stigma attached to apocalyptic doctrines and reach an audience in the tens of millions. To place Hal Lindsey's reformulation of the apocalyptic topoi into its historical context, I examined the rehabilitation of premillennial beliefs among evangelical circles in the decades after the Civil War. The epochal construct by which this rehabilitation was accomplished was the theory of dispensationalism, as popularized in the famous Scofield Reference Bible. As their prophetic predecessors had before them, adherents of this doctrine divided time into a series of ages and placed themselves at the end of the penultimate age, which was to be brought to its close with the inauguration of the millennial kingdom. However, in their effort to dissociate themselves from the Millerite fiasco, dispensationalists rejected all attempts to calculate the times of the End. Despite this rejection, they preserved a heightened awareness of the imminence of the apocalypse by propounding the doctrine of the "secret rapture," the invisible return of Christ for His saints, which would precede the catastrophic conclusion of history. By this means, the expectation of an immediate End of all things was maintained in a fashion that rendered apocalyptic predictions immune to disconfirmation. The sole concession that dispensationalists allowed to the discredited "historicist" school of prophetic interpretation was their interpretation of the travails of the Jewish people, in particular the effort to re-establish their ancestral home in Palestine, as a sign of the conclusion of the church's epoch. The continuing (if sporadic) progress of the Zionist cause ensured that new generations of apocalyptic advocates would never lack historical proofs of the validity of their arguments. With the foundation of the modern state of Israel in 1948, dispensationalists had what they thought was conclusive proof that the End of the age was indeed at hand.

The most significant apocalyptic sign, however, was provided by the invention and use of nuclear weapons at the close of the World War II. The revelation of this horrific new technology propelled humanity into an era that quickly came to be called the "atomic age." That the Bomb heralded an epochal division was evident from the first; the question at issue was how the new epoch was to be understood. The rationalist world view of scientism seemed to have reached its limit with an invention that threatened the ultimate negation of the dreams of technological progress. In the context of the postwar arms race, the "terror of history" (to use Mircea Eliade's phrase[19]) was endowed with a new and concrete meaning. The catastrophic predictions of the tragic apocalypse suddenly acquired a remarkable degree of plausibility, and fundamentalist Christians whose message of impending doom had long been met with ridicule once again found audiences for their arguments.

Hal Lindsey's *The Late Great Planet Earth* was one of many books that employed the historical facts of the nuclear threat and of the new Jewish state as signs of the impending End. Lindsey adroitly incorporated these events, along with others such as the social turmoil of the 1960s and the 1967 Israeli conquest of Jerusalem, into his bestselling apocalyptic narrative. Lindsey's commercial success did not, however, cause any discernible movement or sect to coalesce around his writings, as was the case with William Miller. I argued that this difference is an effect of the privatization of religion in contemporary society, a phenomenon that poses a difficult task to the scholar who seeks to link a particular text with particular behaviors of the audience. Since there is no effective way to measure the degree of conviction in the audiences to Lindsey's writings, I proposed to analyze the text in terms of the "implied audience," the appropriate reader that Lindsey sought to address, and to see what responses the author seeks to prompt in this appropriate reader. Lindsey's development of the topoi of authority, time, and evil effected a transformation in his implied audience, from a state of doubt and fear to a state of faith and hopeful anticipation.

Analysis of Lindsey's arguments about authority revealed a fundamental difference between the audiences for apocalyptic discourse in the mid-nineteenth and late twentieth centuries. Where Miller and his associates could safely assume that their audiences accepted the historical accuracy and divine inspiration of the Bible, Lindsey aimed his message at an audience that, as he himself defines and portrays it, is skeptical, irreligious, and ill-disposed to the acceptance of prophetic teachings. Thus, before he could begin to prove his claim that the imminent End is predicted in Scripture, Lindsey was forced to devote the initial pages of his book to establishing the authoritative grounds on which this primary claim could be based. He attempted to do this by demonstrating the literal accuracy of biblical predictions relating to past events, from the destruction of Jerusalem by the military might of Babylon to the modern establishment of the state of Israel. Once convinced that these events were clearly and literally foretold by the prophets, the implied reader was prepared to grant a hearing to the argument that the End of the world can be expected in his or her lifetime.

Lindsey's authoritative argument is flawed by his failure to acknowledge the crucial importance of interpretation. He falsely claims unanimity among biblical scholars on disputed issues of prophetic exegesis. While this may appear to serve his purpose by securing the authoritative foundation of his argument, such tactics indicate a refusal to address the concerns of the skeptical audience to which Lindsey supposedly aims his discourse. None but the most ignorant of inquiring skeptics could fail to be aware of the fact that the symbols of scriptural prophecy are open to a variety of interpretations. Hence it appears that, to some extent at least, Lindsey's discourse amounts to "preaching to the converted"; that, although he claims to provide good reasons for the acceptance of the Bible's divine authority, in reality he assumes the premises he ostensibly seeks to establish.

This point can be clarified by an examination of the use of sign argument. The effectiveness of the apocalyptic argument from sign rests on its implicit authoritative premise; in other words, such events as wars, earthquakes, and the return of the Jewish people to their ancestral home indicate nothing in and of themselves, but only serve as evidence of the imminence of the End to the extent that the reader already accepts the authority of the scriptural prophecies in which these events are predicted. Both Miller and Lindsey produced arguments that exhibit this form of circularity. Nevertheless, Miller's arguments can be said to be more rational than Lindsey's, given the premises of social knowledge that were available to each. One can hardly fault Miller and his followers for producing arguments that assumed the spiritual authority of the Bible when this assumption was shared by virtually everyone in their society. In contrast, Lindsey's arguments assumed the authority of the Bible at a time when this assumption was itself a principal focus of dispute.

Lindsey's rhetorical skill is most clearly revealed in his elaborations on the topos of time. On this issue, substantive differences are evident between Lindsey's discourse and that of the Adventists. Miller and his followers had resolved this topos into an explicit temporal claim by predicting the End in a specific year and eventually upon a particular date; with the collapse of this claim in the Great Disappointment, all such specific resolutions of the temporal theme in apocalyptic argument were discredited for generations to come. Hence, Lindsey was forced to employ a different line of argument, one which sought to maintain the sense of apocalyptic anticipation without resorting to falsifiable predictions. He managed to avoid the perils of predictive specificity by an artful use of strategic ambiguity. Although his arguments appeared to imply that the year 1988 would inaugurate the prophesied fulfillment of history, Lindsey qualified his assertions in such a

manner as to render them invulnerable to direct refutation. In particular, he proposed a flexible timetable based on an interpretation of the apocalyptic dictum that
"this generation will not pass away until all these things take place" (Mt. 24:34) as
a reference to the contemporary generation that had witnessed the founding of the
Jewish state. The multiple connotations of the term "generation" render it admirably
suited to Lindsey's purposes. While the word appears to imply a particular span of
time within which the fulfillment of prophecy can be expected, this time span has
no definite length. Thus, the audience's desire for specificity was satisfied without
resorting to predictions that could be falsified by the mere fact of time's passage.
In addition to its meaning as a temporal measure, "generation" can also signify the
collective identity of all those alive at a certain time. This allowed Lindsey to
promote a powerful identification with his implied audience, described in his
introduction as the "searching generation." Thus, the term functions as what G.
Thomas Goodnight has called "generational argument":[20] the self-understanding
of those present at a perceived turning point of history was employed as motivation
for acceptance of Lindsey's own construction of the future.

Lindsey's arguments on the topos of evil exemplify the assumptions of tragic
apocalypticism. Like the Millerites, he rejected all purely human solutions to the
world's ills, and drew up a list of the calamities that threaten humanity as evidence
of the looming catastrophe of history. This portion of Lindsey's argument is no-
teworthy for its uncritical adoption of the political demonology of cold war anticommunism, and for the exegetical skill with which the projected nuclear conflict
between the superpowers was translated into biblical terms. His elaborate predictions
of a massive invasion of the Middle East by Soviet and Chinese forces, to be
followed by a nuclear battle of Armageddon, were supported both by interpretations
of obscure scriptural passages and appeals to secular authorities. Though many
scholars have attacked these predictions, they have remained as standard features
of fundamentalist apocalyptic discourse in spite of inaccurate etymology and other
flaws. The persuasive power of Lindsey's catastrophic predictions resides not in
their argumentative validity, but in their ability to evoke the terrors of the nuclear
age, and thereby to function as a rhetorical appeal to fear as a motive for apocalyptic
conversion.

Though there was not a "Lindseyite" movement to parallel the Millerites, the
diffused forms of apocalyptic rhetoric are visible in the discourse of the political
and religious movement known as the New Christian Right. Chapter 7 presented
an analysis of three representatives of this movement. I began with Lindsey's best-
selling manifesto, The 1980s: Countdown to Armageddon, which demonstrated the
power of the tragic apocalypse as a frame for making sense of the evils of the modern
world. While maintaining a pessimistic and fatalistic view of historical destiny, this
text also called believers to active involvement in politics and public life. This
apparent contradiction, characteristic of American fundamentalism during the early
1980s, has puzzled historians and rhetorical critics. I argued that the political
activism of premillennial believers was not inspired by the belief that the prophesied
events of the nuclear Armageddon could be postponed or averted. Rather, the

public stance of Lindsey and his readers is best understood as a form of dramatic enactment, an attempt to define a role in the cosmic drama while awaiting its cathartic conclusion. From the dramatistic perspective, Lindsey's political arguments are perfectly consistent with his pessimistic understanding of history. His endorsement of the movement to bring fundamentalist values into the political sphere embodies all the virtues of the tragic hero, whose struggle is all the more noble because it is hopeless. By supporting conservative political candidates and causes, apocalyptic believers aimed to hold the satanic forces at bay for a brief but significant moment, while history moved "at an ever-accelerating rate of speed into a prophetic countdown."[21]

The study of apocalyptic ideology in the New Christian Right concluded by examining the speeches and writings of two other prominent spokesmen for the movement, Ronald Reagan and Pat Robertson. Their apocalyptic appeals became the subject of an intermittent controversy over "Armageddon theology" in the 1980s, during which the eschatological beliefs of conservative political figures were subjected to public scrutiny and criticism. Notwithstanding the commercial success of Hal Lindsey's publications, and in spite of empirical data indicating that a substantial portion of the American public accepts Lindsey's assertion that nuclear war is foretold in the Bible, the eventual repudiation of the tragic apocalypse by politicians such as Ronald Reagan and Pat Robertson indicates that the American civil religion is ultimately grounded in the comic frame. Though the optimistic view of the future has been called into question by the tragedies of the twentieth century, the American public has shown that it is not ready to abandon the assumption that history's motion is progressive, not degenerative.

Conclusions

This study identified striking similarities between the apocalyptic arguments of the Millerite movement and of Hal Lindsey. In the 1840s and in the 1980s, apocalyptic rhetors were involved in public controversies over differing conceptions of history's ultimate meaning and direction. In both cases, rhetors interpreted a complex of contemporary historical events through the ancient symbolism of Christian eschatology, and succeeded in finding large audiences for their interpretations. Both Hal Lindsey and the Millerites elaborated the three topoi of eschatology—authority, time, and evil—into argumentative systems that accounted for rebuttals and contradictory evidence within the terms of their own logic and thereby were insulated from disconfirmation. Each employed carefully constructed deductive arguments as they attempted to prove their claims that the world's End was to be expected in the mid-nineteenth and late twentieth centuries. Argument from sign played a prominent role in their apocalyptic deductions. The Millerite and the Lindseyite systems of argument were found to be governed by the narrative logic of the tragic drama, which structures time in terms of historical necessity and posits an absolute dualism between divine and demonic forces. Given the fundamental preoccupation of each system, namely, the problem of evil as it appears within the context of cosmic time, it appears that the hypothesis advanced in chapter 1 is amply justified by the evidence: apocalyptic discourse does indeed constitute a symbolic theodicy that operates through its discursive construction of temporality.

Implications

A study of arguments on the perennially recurring issues of eschatology has no alternative but to fall short of completion, since the essential character of this discourse lies in its perpetual announcement and postponement of closure. I have not attempted to answer the ultimate questions of time and evil; rather, I have only sought to examine certain systematic responses to these questions. In selecting particular varieties of apocalyptic discourse for close rhetorical analysis, it has been necessary to skirt some issues that may yet prove fruitful avenues for exploration by rhetoricians. It therefore seems fitting to close this study of the discourse of closure with a reaffirmation of continuity, in which the implications of this study for rhetorical scholarship are addressed and suggestions are offered for future research.

I have identified three topoi as central to the discourse of apocalypse: time, evil, and authority. While my primary concern was to study these three commonplaces as they appear together in the complex argumentative formations that we call apocalyptic, the study of each of these topoi in their own right opens up avenues for further exploration. The proposal that apocalypse is a symbolic theodicy, a mythic and rhetorical solution to the problem of evil as faced by every human society, invites further study of other rhetorical forms and traditions that address this problem. In particular, the suggestion that the classical issues of forensic rhetoric might be useful in disentangling the various strategies of theological argument on one of the most perplexing problems of religious belief will remain tentative until further study can substantiate its utility.[22] With regard to the topos of time, I have examined the apocalyptic solution to the theodicy problem as a particular construction of temporality, or, to use John Angus Campbell's term, an epochal rhetoric, and argued that the peculiar feature of the Christian epoch (in its original formulation before the adoption of the Anno Domini chronology) was its construction with reference to a point of ending rather than of origin. However, the full implications of this argument for a theory of epochal formation will not be apparent until these findings are contextualized by extensive cross-cultural studies of the rhetoric of temporality.[23]

Arguments on the topos of authority were explicated through a comparison of Max Weber's typology of rational, traditional, and charismatic legitimations of authority and Aristotle's division of rhetorical proofs into the categories of logos, ethos, and pathos. This identification proved useful for the analysis of Millerite rhetoric, which I argued relied at various points in the history of the movement on rationality, tradition, and charisma as forms of rhetorical legitimation. Much more work needs to be done, however, to expand the initial insight of a link between

Weberian sociology and Aristotelian rhetoric into a critical tool that can be applied to religious movements and, perhaps, to other social phenomena. Furthermore, although the differences between tragic and comic variations on the topoi of time and evil were discussed at length, this study offered no parallel discussion of the topos of authority. To complete the examination of the apocalyptic topoi as realized through the tragic and comic visions, a more detailed analysis of the comic understanding of authority would seem to be necessary. While space does not permit such an analysis here, some tentative suggestions can be offered that may be confirmed through further research. From the evidence examined so far, it would appear that apocalyptic argument in the tragic frame grounds the authority of its pronouncements in the text of Scripture; that such argument locates the ultimate source of authority in the divinely inspired word, the meaning of which is fixed and determined by a single correct interpretation. Hence, the role of the interpreter in tragic apocalypticism is reduced to the breaking of the divine code. For argument in the comic frame, by contrast, authority is necessarily more mutable and can be refashioned to fit human needs, since the comic awareness of human fallibility requires the denial of all claims to absolute knowledge. The prevalence of allegorical modes of interpretation among those (such as Augustine) who have adopted the comic perspective on the Christian Apocalypse is entirely consistent with this understanding of authority. Though the comic apocalypse may offer Scripture as a source of inspiration, the role of the interpreter in this mode is not to determine a single fixed meaning, but to read the multivalent meanings of the prophetic code in light of one's awareness of the unavoidable fallacies of interpretation. More research must be done on the varieties of apocalyptic experience and on discourse grounded in the comic frame before the characteristically comic articulations of the topos of authority can be fully understood, and before this understanding can be integrated with the rhetorical reading of Weber's typology of legitimation.

On the broadest level of generality, this study of the logic of apocalypticism has implications both for the practice of generic criticism and for future studies of civil religion. At the outset of the study, I noted certain problems that attend the study of rhetorical genres. In defining *genre* as "a group of acts unified by a constellation of forms that recurs in each of its members,"[24] this method of criticism tends to make classification based on form its raison d'etre. The critic's search for significant form results in a formal construct described in three dimensions, the substantive, stylistic, and situational; the rhetorical artifact is observed and explained as a product of stylistic and substantive responses to perceived situational demands. While this model has its virtues, its limitations are serious. Insofar as genre criticism emphasizes discourse as form over discourse as action, it tends to diminish the importance of situation and reduce a dynamic process to a static model; insofar as it makes classification its primary focus, it produces no significant critical argument.[25] These limitations of generic criticism are evident in the scholarly literature on apocalypticism. Relying on generic distinctions that are inevitably problematic, eschatologists have attempted to understand this discourse by categorizing it as premillennial or postmillennial, apocalyptic or prophetic, tragic or comic. This study has not sought to dispense with these critical categories. Rather, it has sought to animate genre by adding a fourth dimension, that of time, to our understanding of discursive form. In the words of Katherine Olson, I have attempted to deepen our understanding of the genres of apocalyptic discourse by "replacing them in the historical flow."[26] The study of the apocalyptic tradition as "an argument extended through time" thus implies that the scope of generic criticism should be enlarged to include both synchronic and diachronic analysis, as a step toward understanding the historical evolution of rhetorical forms.[27]

This enlargement is particularly appropriate and useful for the study of prophetic texts. For, insofar as apocalyptic rhetoric is understood as predictive, it not only reflects the demands of its historical situation; it also creates its own demands and expectations. Prediction involves the rhetor and audience in a complex social dynamic. Therefore, one cannot hope to understand a text by simply noting that it predicts either disaster or a benevolent millennium, and thereby belongs to a class of texts that do this. Rather, viewing rhetoric from a dynamic perspective requires critics to note subtle differentiations in the temporal constructions that render predictions relevant to a given audience. Such constructions foster different sorts of audience expectations and can imply very different normative requirements in the realms of politics and ethics. While this study has been devoted to the elucidation of the dynamics of temporal prediction in specifically religious discourse, more research is required to establish whether the patterns of prophecy identified here are also present in secular discourse that predicts or anticipates the future.

Indeed, the contemporary secularization of apocalyptic discourse has been noted by many critics.[28] Most notably, the rhetoric of the antinuclear and environmental movements has been criticized for its apocalyptic tone.[29] If the identification of apocalyptic patterns in such discourse is supported by further analysis, then perhaps this study will provide a framework within which rhetorical critics can move beyond generic classification into a diagnostic and prescriptive critique of the rhetoric of social movements. As a preliminary attempt at such a critique, I offer these comments on the lessons of the Apocalypse for modern rhetors. This study has shown how audiences may be impelled by the desire for consummation, for narrative closure, for absolute knowledge; how eschatology suffuses our language as an entelechial "principle of perfection"[30] that is manifested in an irrepressible tendency to anticipate conclusions both catastrophic and blissful, and in appeals that naturally tend toward ultimacy. While this tendency in our language probably cannot be extinguished, it may perhaps be curbed or channeled. In this regard, rhetors who seek to motivate audiences with predictions of disaster or millennium (of whatever secular variety) would do well to remember the history of prophetic failure.

All evils, it would seem, have their apocalypse, their revelatory catastrophe, just as every vision of the good society culminates in some utopia or blueprint for an ideal order. Contemporary audiences are surrounded by rhetoric presenting complex scenarios of disaster and salvation that contradict and combine with one another,[31] and face constant appeals to what J. Robert Cox has called the "locus of the irreparable."[32] Rhetors seek to confront us with an apocalypse of AIDS, of

environmental pollution, and (most horrifying of all) of nuclear weapons; technological changes are trumpeted as advances into a new age of progress even as
they figure in our cultural nightmares of destruction. So far, however, it remains
true that though every evil has its apocalypse, every apocalypse has its disappointment. When appeals to the irreparable are overused, they become ineffective; fear
may turn from an incentive for action into fatalism, or threats may appear no longer
credible. Rhetors who seek to ensure the survival and effectiveness of their movements must take care that their discourse does not contain the seeds of apocalyptic
despair, that the inevitable and ordinary disappointment that confronts anyone who
chooses to act politically does not turn into a version of the "Great Disappointment"
experienced by the Millerites. For example, one recent author has discovered the
pattern of apocalyptic frustration in the rhetoric of the ecology movement. Comparing himself and other environmentalists to the misguided followers of William
Miller, Eric Zencey argues:

> It is ironic that the ecology movement, in offering a vision of a sustainable society,
> drew some part of its strength from a mentality that was, by its very nature, not
> sustainable. . . . The Millerites came down from their mountains to re-enter a world
> they had left long before, one whose rhythms in time were alien to them. They
> returned to their communities, where they learned to live without the comfort of a
> known and certain judgment. . . . Theirs is a transition that those of us interested in
> radical ecology might do well to emulate.[33]

Apocalyptic disillusionment may also provide a partial explanation for the failure
of such efforts as the American scientists' movement in the late 1940s. In their
eagerness to control the development and use of nuclear weapons, these rhetors
made a deliberate decision to appeal to fear of atomic destruction as a primary
motive for international control. As one Chicago atomic scientist put it, "Only one
tactic is dependable—the preaching of doom."[34] While the ethical concern of the
would-be prophets of the scientists' movement is laudable, their rhetorical tactics
were, to say the least, shortsighted. As other preachers of doom have learned time
and again, fear is anything but dependable; it is an emotion that cannot be consistently sustained. Furthermore, in employing vivid scenarios of ultimate destruction, the scientists failed to account for the dialectical structure of the apocalyptic
myth, which, as Richard H. Popkin has noted, has historically nurtured visions of
triumph alongside those of catastrophe.[35] Because the images of disaster and the
millennium are inseparably linked, so that catastrophe without redemption is almost
unthinkable, the scientists' appeals to fear had the unintended and ironic effect of
lending support to the arguments of religious fundamentalists who could explain
nuclear destruction as the culmination of the Christian epoch, on the one hand,
and of those who looked to nuclear technology to inaugurate a technological millennium of unimaginable prosperity, on the other.[36]

In this way, the traditional apocalyptic myth provided a theological framework
that absorbed nuclear terror, while its secular analogue provided ideological support
for the commitment of vast economic resources to the development of military and

commercial applications of nuclear power. Thus, the appeal to ultimate fears not only failed to overcome nationalistic impulses and spark a movement to a single world government, as many scientists had hoped;[37] it also contributed in no small measure to the developing logic of the cold war, as those who waited in vain for a new world order to materialize clutched at the policy of deterrence as the sole apparent means by which disaster could be averted and the balance of power preserved. Compounding the error of their predecessors forty years earlier (and in a grimly comic illustration of Karl Marx's famous dictum that history repeats itself, first as tragedy, then as farce), the nuclear freeze movement of the 1980s likewise resorted to apocalyptic fear appeals to mobilize audiences, only to have their strategy neatly coopted by the Reagan administration, which offered the Strategic Defense Initiative as a technological panacea for nuclear anxiety.[38]

Analysis of the nuclear age as an argument formation, a rhetorical epoch structurally similar to the previous era, prompts some observations on the contemporary forms of epochal discourse.[39] Like the Christian rhetorical epoch, the nuclear age was defined and constituted from its inception with reference to a point of ultimate ending that seemed to remain perpetually imminent. Treading a path laid out by the first followers of Jesus and John the Baptist, the scientist-prophets who declared the end of the old order did so out of a real sense of urgency and a conviction that time was short. Just as their predecessors had done, they misjudged in failing to anticipate the endless postponement of the catastrophic judgment. But the nuclear age differs from its religious predecessors in one important respect. As I have shown, the religious visions of the late Hebrew and early Christian prophets juxtaposed images of destruction and salvation; the spectacle of catastrophic destruction in the last days was made tolerable by the millennial promise of a kingdom of perfect justice and eternal life for believers. In the apocalyptic scenarios of the latter-day prophets of doom, however, all hope of redemption is eclipsed.[40] To choose but one among hundreds of examples: Jonathan Schell's influential and controversial *The Fate of the Earth* argues with apocalyptic fervor that "the task is nothing less than to reinvent politics: to reinvent the world." Yet readers of Schell's secular sermon are left with no concrete imagery of a world thus reinvented, nor of modes of persuasion or forms of social life that could accomplish this task. What lingers instead in the mind is his terrifying depiction of a "republic of insects and grass," a world in which the extinction of all human life results in a landscape devoid of meaning.[41]

Indeed, whatever his intentions may have been, Schell's vision is so horrific in its nihilism that it is hardly surprising that competing visions would seek to compensate for it by reasserting the relevance of the archaic religious epoch. Thus, as antinuclear activists emphasized the novelty and the gravity of the threat that confronted the human race, their arguments were subsumed and appropriated by others who insisted on a redemptive meaning to history that could account even for what seemed to some to be history's ultimate negation, an ever-present prospect of human extinction. The secular doomsayers were, in turn, further alarmed by the increasing credibility of preachers who assimilated technological scenarios of catastrophe into the religious narrative; as rumors circulated about the apocalyptic beliefs of those in power, their own apocalyptic fears increased, as did the stridency of their rhetoric. Thus the arguments and the fears of fundamentalists and secular prophets in the nuclear age fed upon each other, as each epochal rhetoric strove for dominance by offering competing constructions of public time implying very different notions of human choice and destiny.

This study has shown that apocalyptic myth functions in our culture as a well of metaphor, a subterranean spring of symbolic resources drawn upon by those who seek to define and construct their own historical epoch, and that this well of metaphor is capable of sustaining attitudes toward history that range from political passivity to triumphalist nationalism. The book of Revelation has been employed in the service of diverse ideologies, by imperial monarchists and by revolutionary communists; its powerful images have provided a symbolic ground for the religious pretensions of state power as well as for the critique of such pretensions. But, whether it is employed in the service of power or in the critique of power, the recurring fallacy of apocalyptic eschatology seems to rest in a human tendency to identify the particular with the ultimate; to identify this or that nation or ruler as an embodiment of ultimate evil or divine righteousness, this or that moment in time as the inception of ultimate catastrophe or millennial bliss. In the hope that this book may help to provide a corrective (if not a cure) to this tendency, I will close with a final meditation on the contemporary significance of apocalyptic myth.

A Last Judgment: The Tragic and Comic Visions in the Nuclear Age

As I have demonstrated, the apocalyptic argument from sign takes on a different character when it is shown to be inherently circular, and when one recalls that the same signs—wars, earthquakes, famines, evil in high places—have always been offered as grounds to support the same claim, which has never materialized. In view of the fact that apocalyptic believers through the ages have demonstrated adherence to their tenets strong enough to withstand repeated and unequivocal disconfirmations, exposing this recurring use of sign argument as fallacious may well be a useless effort. The apocalyptic well of rhetorical invention is apparently inexhaustible; the unshakable beliefs of the dogmatist will always find expression in new arguments or revised versions of the old. As Jacques Derrida notes, the effort to demystify the discourse of apocalypse thus becomes an interminable task, one that can all too easily degenerate into an exercise of ritual debunking. Yet my purpose in the preceding chapters has not been simply to expose the perennially reappearing fallacies of apocalyptic argument. Rather, the close attention to the reasoning and advocacy of eschatological discourse was pursued in the spirit of Burke's comic frame, which "in making man a student of himself, makes it possible for him to 'transcend' occasions when he has been tricked or cheated, since he can readily put such discouragements in his 'assets' column, under the head of 'experience.' "[42] What comic lesson, then, can be derived from the experience of those who have failed in their attempt to read the signs of the times?

From the fact that the signs of the End have always been with us, we might conclude that the signs are endowed with meaning only by an interpretive fallacy of circularity; that there is no End, no final vantage point from which Truth will be revealed, that eschatology, the quest for ultimate meaning, is itself a fallacy. We might therefore be impelled to identify with the deconstructive mission of Derrida, who announces: "I have come to tell you this, there is not, there never has been, there never will be an apocalypse, the apocalypse deceives, disappoints." Derrida seeks to proclaim the "end of the end, the end of ends."[43] Recognizing an inconsistency in his own discourse, which seeks to declare the end of all discourse that declares the end, Derrida attempts to salvage his position by claiming, "I intended to analyze a genre rather than practice it, and even where I would practice it, to do so with this ironic kind . . . of clause wherein I tried to show that this clause never belonged to the genre itself." Nevertheless, as he admits, "every language on the apocalypse is also apocalyptic and cannot be excluded from its object."[44] Derrida is thus forced to re-enact the apocalyptic drama even as he attempts to bring down the curtain, illustrating yet again the persistence of a discourse that has survived every declaration of absolute closure. In the face of such persistence, critics are fully justified in remaining skeptical about attempts to declare an end to declarations of the End. One can go further and say that Derrida's attempt demonstrates that apocalypse is a discourse that is inherently self-refuting, one that bespeaks continuity with every utterance of closure. For the declaration of ending cannot be accomplished except by a language act of speech or of writing, connected in time to a seemingly endless series of other such acts, a series implying a continuity denied by the words themselves.

Those who search for a transcendent lesson, an understanding of the Apocalypse as offering something more to humanity than a revelation of deception and disappointment, must take another tack. The omnipresence of apocalyptic signs throughout history might be interpreted as a clue that the End has been misunderstood. Perhaps, just as the apocalyptic signs have always been with us, the End itself has always been present, though unrecognized; perhaps the End is always near, if not as an absolute closure to temporality and history then as a normative standard against which our actions may be measured. To be sure, this amounts to a redefinition of the Apocalypse as essentially concerned not with temporality, but with ethics. Franz Kafka's cryptic assessment of the eschatological vision seems to point in this direction: "Only our concept of time makes it possible for us to speak of the Day of Judgment by that name; in reality it is a summary court in perpetual session."[45]

This reinterpretation of the Last Judgment may seem audacious to those wishing to preserve the myth of the Christian Apocalypse as a literal expression of historical teleology. From this perspective, Kafka's ethical understanding of the Judgment appears similar to Rudolf Bultmann's program of "demythologization," in which the transcendent value of the Christian teaching is preserved by divorcing it from its archaic mode of expression in myth. However, my purpose is not simply to endorse Bultmann's method of "bargaining with modernity,"[46] which, as Paul Tillich has argued, ignores the inescapable fact that "religious language is and always must be mythological." The problem is not the mythological character of Revelation; rather, it is that any interpretation of the myth (whether by skeptics or by dogmatists) that reduces it to literal and factual content inevitably distorts the deliberately metaphorical language of prophecy. Hence, following Tillich, I argue that one "should speak not of demythologization, but of deliteralization, which means not taking the symbols as literal expressions of events in time and space."[47] So understood, the Apocalypse offers not a prediction of history's final conclusion, but a narrative representation of an End that remains as an ethical ground for judgment though it is not in principle attainable within history. In this reading, the proper answer to the question, "When will the Last Judgment occur?" is not "In 1843," or "In the year 2000"; for all such answers deny the truly ultimate significance of the Apocalypse and are destined to reveal, with the passage of time, their misapprehension of its message. Only an answer that questions the fundamentally tragic assumptions on which the apocalyptic question is based can prevent the Apocalypse from being rendered irrelevant and thereby preserve its ultimate significance. The proper reply to the question, then, is "It has already occurred; it is always about to occur; it is here now and always has been." In the terminology of this study, this represents a shift from a tragic to a comic interpretation of the Apocalypse, from a literal and predictive reading to a figurative reading that protects the relevance of the text by asserting the primacy of ethical significance over historical content.[48]

The argument for a comic reading of the Apocalypse paradoxically finds support from the modern apocalyptic sign that is most frequently taken as evidence for the tragic interpretation, namely, the threat of nuclear destruction. The recently acquired human capacity to end all life on earth does appear to many as a tragic sign of a catastrophic conclusion of history. Yet one must ask whether the tragic apocalypse might be a self-fulfilling prophecy; whether the logic of a purely historicist eschatology may not, in the end, contribute to the realization of the End it predicts. This point can be illuminated with reference to Eliade's study of cosmological solutions to the eschatological problem. Eliade identifies the "terror of history" as the recurring motive that drives humanity's ongoing attempt to negate time through ritual and historical action. The nuclear threat has transformed this motive by adding a technological basis for fear that, in its concrete literality, surpasses the ancient archetypal terror. If Eliade is correct in arguing that the epochal myths of a culture represent its attempts to overcome this terror by ordering the life of humanity into a sequence that is intelligible through, and enacted in, its rituals and its history, then we may well wonder whether the widespread acceptance of the tragic apocalyptic vision does not prepare citizens of militarized industrial states to enact the drama of cosmic destruction in the modern theater of war. In just this fashion Adolf Hitler's lifelong fascination with the Wagnerian mythos culminated in his own *Götterdämmerung*, a fiery drama of cosmic catastrophe played out in the rubble of Berlin with the armies of the world as supporting cast. More recently, author A. G. Mojtabai visited Amarillo, Texas, home of the final assembly plant for all nuclear weapons manufactured in the United States, and found the inhabitants of that city employing apocalyptic doctrines to reconcile themselves to the imminent destruction of the world in a nuclear firestorm.[49]

Such absolutist conceptions of history have been effectively critiqued in Hans Blumenberg's summary of the ethical implications of Christian and secular eschatologies. Arguing for a philosophy of history rooted in what I have called the comic frame, Blumenberg defends the concept of modernity and the idea of progress against all forms of eschatological dogmatism:

> If there were an immanent final goal of history, then those who believe they know it and claim to promote its attainment would be legitimized in using all the others who do not know it and cannot promote it as mere means. Infinite progress does make each present relative to its future, but at the same time it renders every absolute claim untenable. The idea of progress corresponds more than anything else to the only regulative principle that can make history humanly bearable, which is that all dealings must be so constituted that through them people do not become mere means.[50]

Whether nuclear weapons are justified by the purely secular logic of deterrence theory or by the religious logic of the Apocalypse, there can be no doubt that such weapons do hold all humanity hostage as a means to an ultimate end. To translate Blumenberg's ethical insight into dramatistic terms: If history is to be understood as a cosmic drama, then there is legitimate cause for concern that the interpretation of this drama as tragedy might itself have tragic consequences. Barry Brummett poses the question concisely: "Can our world still afford this venerable symbolic remedy for humanity's misfortune?"[51]

While I share Brummett's concern, I cannot but wonder whether the question as posed is naive. As this study concludes, my response to his query is twofold: No, we cannot afford the venerable symbolic remedy of the tragic apocalypse, but neither can we simply eliminate it. For it is hardly possible to conceive of a way to extirpate a vision of humanity's ultimate destiny that has survived for thousands of years through every imaginable disconfirmation. We are thus left with a paradox: on the one hand, critics are justified in concluding on ethical grounds that humanity in the nuclear age cannot afford the tragic apocalypse, while on the other hand, the study of apocalyptic argument leads to the conclusion that its stratagems are endless, and not susceptible to negation through rational criticism. It is my contention that the comic vision may enable humanity to escape from this critical double bind. For, as I argued in chapter 3, the drama of Revelation is not reducible to either tragedy or comedy, but holds these two forms in perpetually creative tension. The comic vision is thus available as a resource for critique, one that provides a textual basis for criticizing the apocalyptic mentality from within its own foundational assumptions. If this critique is to be successful, it must acknowledge that our experience of history includes radical ruptures and discontinuities that only the tragic vision can account for successfully. But if the tragic vision allows us to recognize events such as Hiroshima and Auschwitz as rents in the fabric of history, it is the comic perspective that enables us to mend these rents and continue to build lives and communities in the face of unimaginable horror.

It would appear, then, that an adequate grasp of the human eschatological dilemma in the nuclear age requires a dialectical understanding, and perhaps a synthesis, of the tragic and comic perspectives. A poetic expression of this necessity can be found in one of the seminal texts of modern literature, Samuel Beckett's *Waiting for Godot*. Written three years after the events of Hiroshima and Nagasaki, this play was dubbed by its author as a "tragicomedy in two acts." The drama depicts two tramps, Vladimir and Estragon, passing the time as they wait to keep an appointment with "Godot," a figure who never appears and of whose very existence the tramps are uncertain. While they wait they encounter Pozzo and Lucky, a master and his slave, and witness the slave subjected to cruel abuse. Twice, toward the end of each act, a young boy appears with the same message from Godot: "Mr. Godot told me to tell you he won't come this evening but surely tomorrow." In each case the message heightens anticipation but only leads to further disappointment. That the figure of Godot represents the eschatological hope of the ages, the appearance of God within history, is evident from the play's repeated references to Christian Scripture, and in particular from the rambling speech given by the slave Lucky when his master orders him to think aloud for the amusement of the tramps.

> Given the existence . . . of a personal God quaquaquaqua with white beard qua-
> quaquaqua outside time without extension who from the heights of divine apathia
> divine athambia divine aphasia loves us dearly with some exceptions for reasons
> unknown but time will tell and suffers like the divine Miranda with those who for
> reasons unknown but time will tell are plunged in torment plunged in fire whose
> fire flames if that continues and who can doubt it will fire the firmament that is to
> say blast hell to heaven.[52]

Toward the end of the second act, the young messenger associates Godot with the "personal God" of Lucky's speech by asserting, under questioning by Vladimir and Estragon, that the long-awaited figure has a white beard. As if to ensure that the audience gets the point, the playwright depicts the tramps in the depths of a despair that can only be termed religious:

> VLADIMIR: We'll hang ourselves to-morrow. (*Pause.*)
>   Unless Godot comes.
>
> ESTRAGON: And if he comes?
>
> VLADIMIR: We'll be saved.[53]

Beckett's play is, perhaps, the paradigmatic representation of eschatological expectation in the modern era. In this ultimate reductio ad absurdum of the apocalyptic drama, all action is reduced to waiting for that which never comes, all emotion dwindles to a hopeful anticipation that the characters cling to the more fiercely as their disappointment grows ever more certain. As the two tramps await the arrival of Godot to redeem them from nihilistic despair, they pass the time with songs, with speeches, with antic horseplay that smacks of vaudeville; these efforts occupy their attention for a time but prove unsatisfactory as substitutes for the redemption they seek. Tragedy and comedy collapse into each other as each attempt to stave off despair provokes laughter that dies away into the silence of the void. *Waiting for Godot* expresses a tragicomic vision in that it simultaneously asserts the necessity and the futility of hope.

It is possible to admire the unflinching courage of Beckett's existential vision without endorsing it as a solution to humanity's eschatological dilemma. Indeed, the bleakness of this vision makes it particularly unsuitable for the masses of humanity, who are unlikely to accept its depiction of an open horizon for human action as a void that people scramble to fill with any meaning that promises to postpone the pain of existence. Other artists have expressed the fusion of tragedy and comedy in very different ways.[54] My concern here is only to note the implications of this fusion for the dramatistic theory of apocalypse. Considered as "attitudes toward the world, ways of coming to terms with its triumphs and vicissitudes,"[55] tragedy and comedy are incomplete without each other; especially in the nuclear age, some form of understanding that acknowledges the applicability of both the tragic and comic frames may be necessary for our survival.

While acknowledging the humor inherent in tragic attempts to declare the End with repetitive finality, I wish to stress the essential nobility of the quest for eschatological meaning over and against its absurdity. Admittedly, it may be difficult for the critic to perceive the grandeur of the apocalyptic vision in view of the historical record of the failed predictions it has spawned, which taken together appear as a vast joke on human pretensions to absolute knowledge; and the effort is made doubly difficult by our contemporary nuclear predicament, in the context of which the joke seems no longer humorous, but perhaps deadly in its implications. But if the catastrophic vision is to be prevented from becoming a reality, it may be necessary to recover anew the meaning of revelation as uncovering, to remember that apocalypse signifies not only closure, but also disclosure. As theologian David Tracy puts it, "Apocalyptic challenges . . . any purely 'private' understanding of the Christian event by forcing a recognition of the genuinely public, the political and historical character of all Christian self-understanding"; it challenges us "to face the reality of the really new, the *novum*, and the future breaking in and exploding every complacency,"[56] including the complacency of tragic dogmatism. In the same vein, Gordon Kaufman's *Theology for a Nuclear Age* urges theologians "to enter into the most radical kind of deconstruction and reconstruction of the traditions they have inherited."[57] This book has attempted to make a contribution to the task of exploding the complacency of those who assert the tragic predetermination of history, by employing a rhetorical methodology for both deconstruction and reconstruction of the apocalyptic tradition. If the challenge offered by Tracy and Kaufman—indeed, by the Apocalypse itself—is to be met, rhetoricians must join with theologians, and with all who seek a way out of our current predicament, in reminding humanity that every End is an opportunity for a new beginning.

Waco and Beyond

This book has focused on apocalyptic doctrines as they move, or attempt to move, into the mainstream of public discourse. In keeping with this emphasis, I have deliberately avoided discussion of violence in apocalyptic sects and movements. While violence is hardly an unprecedented feature in the history of apocalypticism, the remarkable religious freedom accorded such groups in the United States has made bloody clashes with the state relatively rare. However, the fiery end of the Branch Davidian sect members near Waco, Texas, seems to require some comment, in view of the historical link of this group to others examined in this study, and in view of the impact of events of March–April 1993 on public awareness of apocalypticism. The tragedy at Waco is likely to have an impact on the way we—scholars and the general public—study and think about apocalyptic sects and movements for some time. As the millennial year 2000 draws near, it is worth pausing to absorb the lessons of this symbolic drama.

As this book goes to press, the flood of post-Waco commentary has subsided to a trickle. A formal investigation into the facts of the case and its handling by various government agencies has been launched; in due time its findings will be reported and relegated to the back pages. Except for the occasional human-interest story on survivors in the aftermath, news of the Branch Davidians' mini-Armageddon has disappeared from our newspapers and television screens. Whatever the results of the investigation, the central puzzle will probably remain: Could the tragedy at Waco have been avoided, or was it the inevitable conclusion to a deliberate search for martyrdom? Some who interpreted the crisis for media audiences treated it as a sort of auto-da-fé, the public burning of a heretic on live national television. Other self-styled "cult experts" and "millennial experts" went so far as to claim that if the government had simply consulted specialists with credentials resembling their own, the violent ending could have been prevented. I do not intend to second-guess official decisions; there are still too many facts to be sorted out, and the mercurial nature of eschatological belief is such that it is questionable whether anyone's advice could have saved the lives of those who died in the siege of Ranch Apocalypse. Nevertheless, some of the central themes of this book are visible in the story of David Koresh and his followers, and may yet help to explain their motivations.

In the days following the original raid on the Branch Davidian compound, reporters unraveling the sect's tangled history observed that it had splintered off from the Seventh-day Adventist Church during the 1930s, under the leadership of Bulgarian-born church-school teacher Victor Houteff. Most went on to note statements by Adventist leaders dissociating the church from Koresh's group, and took pains to distinguish Seventh-day Adventism, a respected Christian denomination, from the bizarre teachings and practices of the Branch Davidians. Few took any notice of the original roots of Seventh-day Adventism in the Millerite movement, or reflected on the different lessons drawn from the book of Revelation by the followers of David Koresh and those of his spiritual ancestor, William Miller. It is understandable that modern Adventist leaders would not care to acknowledge their relationship to the Branch Davidians; after all, both Kouteff and Koresh had been "disfellowshipped" from the Seventh-day Adventist church for their heretical teachings and unorthodox lifestyles, and Millerites and Seventh-day Adventists were accustomed to await Armageddon with prayer rather than with deadly arsenals. Yet the story that concluded in the ashes of Ranch Apocalypse did not begin in Texas. The lineage of the Branch Davidians can be traced from the Millerites of the 1830s, through the Seventh-day Adventists, to the Davidian sect founded by Houteff in Depression-era Los Angeles.

In the dynamic mutations of doctrine through generations of religious leadership, we may perceive an age-old pattern governing the formation of apocalyptic communities. It is a dialectical process of community-building and critique, in which eschatological myth inspires a group to withdraw from society or from a church in anticipation of a coming Judgment, only to find that the preaching of imminent doom leads unexpectedly to prosperity and formal establishment of yet another church, which may in turn spawn its own dissident prophets, and so on ad infinitum. When the Millerite preacher Charles Fitch urged his audiences in 1843 to "COME OUT OF BABYLON" and dissociate themselves from their churches, he surely never anticipated that those who heard his sermon would themselves found a church that would endure for a century and a half. Still less could he have imagined that new prophets would arise one day to condemn the leadership of this church as apostate and wicked, predicting an imminent cleansing of Adventist leadership and forming a new congregation from disaffected members of the old. Thus, when seen in historical context, the story of the Branch Davidians shows how a millennial group can grow into an accepted denomination and splinter again, moving from the margins of culture to the center and back to the margins. Similarly, the Mormon Church has transformed itself from a fringe cult at odds with state authority to a bastion of respectability whose leaders are periodically forced to take action against certain Latter-day Saints led astray by their fascination with the Latter Days.[1]

Whether the volatile blend of apocalyptic expectation and messianic delusion that characterized David Koresh's teaching could ever have stabilized into a more respectable institutional form is debatable. Understanding the appeal of Koresh's rhetoric, and the possible directions it might have taken if federal agents had not interrupted its trajectory, is a complex task made doubly difficult by the fact of his literal demonization in the media.[2] One fragment of this peculiar biblical exegesis seems particularly ripe for analysis in terms of religious argument: his oft-quoted statement that "If the Bible is true, then I'm Christ."[3] We can only speculate as to what worlds of inarticulate assumptions and beliefs are packed into this phrase; we have lost our chance to reconstruct the unspoken chain of reasoning that warrants the move from the grounds of biblical verity to the conclusion of Koresh's divinity. The Branch Davidians who died in the fire at Ranch Apocalypse are now forever silenced, and unable to explain by what combination of argument and charismatic ethos they were persuaded to follow their messiah to a fiery death. Yet if we truly seek to understand their actions, it is incumbent upon us to take their beliefs seriously, and not to dismiss them with the easy cant of the "cult experts" who are so quick to assert the "brainwashing" of those who choose martyrdom. Indeed, we would do well to realize that labelling a religious group as a "cult" is itself a rhetorical act that functions to exclude it as beyond the pale—and thus to legitimate its victimization in what might otherwise be seen as an assault on religious freedom.[4]

One final aspect of the Branch Davidian debacle is worth considering here: the apocalyptic drama as media spectacle. Throughout this book I have argued that the myth of the Apocalypse is continually reenacted in the histories of its audiences, and attempted to explain differences and variations in the scripts for the End as a function of interpretive and rhetorical choices linked with the tragic and comic frames. The dramatistic approach seems particularly appropriate in this case, for never has the apocalyptic drama been played out before a wider audience. There is ample evidence to indicate that David Koresh's own apocalyptic script could only have taken the form of tragedy. Yet little reflection is required to conclude that we need to examine the role of the media as shapers of this drama, and not merely its passive transmitters. It is clear that the presence of reporters and television cameras had a profound effect on the progress of the siege as well as on its eventual outcome. Consider: it is highly probable that the decision to proceed with the original raid was hastened by the publication of a critical exposé of the Branch Davidians in a local newspaper; the sect and the FBI spent considerable time negotiating over Koresh's demand for access to the news media; the encampment of the international press corps near the compound for the entire duration of the siege ensured that the story would remain in the public eye, thus embarrassing government officials and increasing the pressure to bring the siege to a speedy conclusion; media representatives began to bid for film and television rights to the story before it was even concluded. Under such constant media scrutiny, it is easy to see how the judgment of both sides became warped.

Imagine the predicament of a man who believes he is the Messiah, the Lord of the Universe, but who is unable to attract the attention, let alone command the worship, of any but a small group of followers. Paranoid, delusional, convinced the world is out to get him, he preaches that his own martyrdom will serve as the trigger for history's grand finale. How would such a person react to the appearance of hundreds of heavily armed officers on his doorstep—and to the concentrated attention of reporters and television cameras? The show of force would likely confirm his delusions of persecution, while the media attention would fuel his grandiose sense of self-importance. David Koresh always had a flair for the dramatic, but his mesmerizing preaching had found no audience outside his circle of disciples. Now the spotlight was on him, and his stage was the world. He must have been in his element: his prophecy of martyrdom was coming true, and his words were reaching the widest audience he could ever have hoped for. If Koresh's proofs of his own divinity failed to persuade, this too was a fulfillment of prophecy: for like Jesus, Koresh the Lamb was destined to be rejected and scorned by all except his chosen few. In this way, law enforcement officials, the press, and television viewers all acted out the roles scripted for them in Koresh's apocalyptic tragedy.

The unblinking eye of the media made it inevitable that government decisions would be guided by dramatic considerations. The longer the siege dragged on, the more inadvertently comical it became; as officials attempted one negotiating strategy after another, their efforts seemed increasingly ludicrous, and the tragedy was transformed into a farce that, it seemed, could go on indefinitely.[5] In the end, the government's actions were probably motivated by the same sense of an ending that governs the logic of apocalyptic drama: the need to control the script by seizing the initiative and seeking some form of narrative closure. When the saga finally concluded in a fiery inferno, carried live by all the television networks, the television critic for the New York Times reviewed the drama for its entertainment value, expressing in his title the overwhelming consensus of the viewing audience: "As TV, Drama in Waco Had a Grim Inevitability."[6]

There is no shortage of messiahs and prophets in the world; no gift of prophecy is necessary to predict that as the millennium approaches we will see more religious groups who are willing to martyr themselves to validate their faith in an imminent End of history. The next time the apocalyptic drama plays out on the stage of the world media, however, it will be useful to remember that there are numerous possible endings to its story, and not all of them require bloodshed. If we recall that our history's end has not yet been written, and that we ourselves are its co-authors, then perhaps we will come to see that no ending is inevitable, and that the saving bliss of catastrophe is a luxury we can ill afford.

Notes

CHAPTER 1

1. One of the earlier and most notable of such efforts is the "Commission on the Year 2000," sponsored by the American Academy of Arts and Sciences in the mid-1960s. For reports of this group's deliberations, see Daniel Bell, ed., *Toward the Year 2000*; for a sample of some of the more provocative futurological speculation undertaken under its auspices, see Herman J. Kahn and Anthony J. Wiener, *The Year 2000*.

2. An influential literary example of utopian speculation employing the millennial date is Edward Bellamy's nineteenth-century classic *Looking Backward*. A more recent, and less optimistic, assessment of our future was offered by the pop singer Prince, whose 1983 hit song "1999" featured these anticipatory lyrics: "Two thousand zero zero, party's over, Whoops! out of time / Tonight we're going to party like it's nineteen ninety-nine." Most recently, German director Wim Wenders' 1991 film "Until the End of the World" depicted fin-de-siècle expectations in a context of technologically induced alienation and despair. A thoughtful overview of fin-de-siècle culture through the centuries, combined with an astonishingly thorough survey of contemporary trends, may be found in Hillel Schwartz, *Century's End: A Cultural History of the Fin de Siècle from the 990s through the 1990s*.

3. For a fundamentalist Christian perspective on the times, see Pat Robertson, *The New Millennium*. The widely publicized New Age predictions of a so-called Harmonic Convergence in 1987 involved a timetable for cosmic rebirth that would extend over the transition into the next millennium, ending in 2012. R. Gustav Niebuhr provides an overview of recent religious trends in his article "Millennium Fever: Prophets Proliferate, The End Is Near," *Wall Street Journal*, 5 December 1989, A1, A5.

4. Among the numerous recent works on Nostradamus is John Hogue, *Nostradamus and the Millennium: Predictions of the Future*; see also V. J. Hewitt and Peter Lorie, *Nostradamus: The End of the Millennium*.

5. For some applications of rhetoric in biblical interpretation, see Amos Wilder, *Early Christian Rhetoric: The Language of the Gospel*; George Kennedy, *New Testament Interpretation through Rhetorical Criticism*; Martin Warner, ed., *The Bible as Rhetoric: Studies in Biblical Persuasion and Credibility*; and Northrop Frye, *The Great Code: The Bible and Literature*. A good introduction to rhetoric as a method of inquiry in the social sciences is John S. Nelson with Allan Megill and Donald N. McCloskey, eds., *The Rhetoric of the*

Human Sciences: Language and Argument in Scholarship and Public Affairs. Examples of the use of rhetoric in literary criticism are numerous. The controversial deconstructionist critic Paul de Man has been one of the most influential leaders of this trend; see his *Blindness and Insight: Essays in the Rhetoric of Contemporary Criticism,* and *The Rhetoric of Romanticism.*

6. A spirited argument against those who attack rhetoric as deceptive or limit its scope to the study of compositional techniques, coupled with an able account of the history of rhetorical theory, may be found in Brian Vickers, *In Defence of Rhetoric.* Vickers' study includes a thoughtful discussion of the misuses of rhetoric by de Man (see note 5 above).

7. Margaret D. Zulick, "The Agon of Jeremiah: On the Dialogic Invention of Prophetic Ethos," 126.

8. By this I mean that the subjects of rhetorical inquiry may properly include the ethical and political functions of aesthetic forms; the artistic and the ethical dimensions of political discourse; and the political and artistic implications of ethical philosophy. This description of rhetoric's status in relation to other disciplines follows that of Aristotle, whose immensely influential *Rhetoric* describes it as "an offshoot of dialectical and ethical studies," intrinsically related to politics (I.2.1356a); see Richard McKeon, ed., *The Basic Works of Aristotle,* 1330. I am also indebted to Thomas B. Farrell's thoughtful discussion of the aesthetics of rhetoric in "Rhetorical Resemblance: Paradoxes of a Practical Art."

9. A systematic treatment of this view of rhetoric can be found in Kenneth Burke, *A Rhetoric of Motives.*

10. See, for example, Amos Wilder, "The Rhetoric of Ancient and Modern Apocalyptic"; Michael Barkun, *Disaster and the Millennium.*

11. Mircea Eliade's examination of the myths of ending and cosmic decline in various religious traditions leads him in *Myth and Reality* to distinguish "primitive," Hindu, and Greek eschatologies from Judeo-Christian conceptions. See especially chapter 14, "Eschatology and Cosmogony." According to Eliade, the significant innovation of Jewish and Christian eschatology is the abandonment of "the circular Time of the Eternal Return" in favor of "linear and irreversible Time," in which eschatology represents the "triumph of a Sacred History" (65). An early Christian expression of a linear view of time, accompanied by an attack on cyclical doctrines of cosmic repetition, can be found in Augustine, *The City of God* XII. 20–21. A complete discussion of the difference between Western and non-Western eschatologies would require many volumes. In chapter 2 of this study, I will offer a conceptual framework for such a discussion grounded in social knowledge theory and the classical topoi. Of necessity, however, this study must bracket the issue of cross-cultural comparison, and opts instead to examine how rhetors and audiences in nineteenth-and twentieth-century America have adopted and applied the Christian eschatology as embodied in Revelation and other canonical texts. Those wishing to examine ultimate conceptions of time and history in pre-Christian and non-Western traditions may consult the following sources: Harald A. T. Reiche provides a survey of Greco-Roman traditions of decline and end in "The Archaic Heritage: Myths of Decline and End in Antiquity," in *Visions of Apocalypse: End or Rebirth?* ed. Saul Friedlander, Gerald Horton, Leo Marx, and Eugene Skolnikoff. An Icelandic version of the Norse myth of Ragnarok appears in *The Prose Edda of Snorri Sturlson,* trans. Jean I. Young. Hindu mythologies of decline and end are well treated in Wendy Doniger O'Flaherty, *The Origins of Evil in Hindu Mythology,* especially pp. 35–45. For discussions of Buddhist mythology regarding cosmic decline and the ultimate end of humankind, see Winston L. King, "Eschatology: Christian and Buddhist"; R. Pannikar, "The Destiny of

Technological Civilization: An Ancient Buddhist Legend *Romavisaya*"; and E. Zurcher, "Prince Moonlight: Messianism and Eschatology in Early Medieval Chinese Buddhism."

12. *Plato's Statesman*, 273c–73e, trans. J. B. Skemp, 152.

13. A variety of usages are included for *eschatos* in Liddell and Scott's Greek lexicon. Homer used the word in a spatial sense: "farthest, uttermost, extreme." A second sense is of degree, including the meanings "uttermost, highest." Another sense is temporal: "last, finally, in the end" (*A Greek-English Lexicon*, 9th ed., s.v. *eschatos*).

14. Professional eschatologists have used a wide variety of terms in their study of apocalypse. The doctrines studied here have been examined by different scholars under the rubrics of eschatology, apocalyptic, messianism, millennialism, millenarianism, chiliasm, etc., with these terms often employed interchangeably without regard to usage in other scholarship. The above definitions, which will be elaborated in the chapters that follow, are adopted from Bernard McGinn, *Visions of the End: Apocalyptic Traditions in the Middle Ages*, 3–4. For a detailed discussion of terminology and definitions in apocalyptic studies, see the appendix to Richard Landes' essay "Lest the Millennium Be Fulfilled: Apocalyptic Expectations and the Pattern of Western Chronography 100–800 CE," in *The Use and Abuse of Eschatology in the Middle Ages*, 205–9.

The confusion of terms among scholars has been compounded by the (often indiscriminate) secularized use of "apocalypse" as a literary or political genre. This study seeks to avoid and even reverse the trivialization of the concept cautioned against by Amos Wilder:

> [W]ith alleged apocalyptic vision and writing it is still very much a question whether, in fact, everything is at stake, because it is very human to vociferate apocalyptically when something that we prize is taken away from us, whether a baby rattle or a bank account, whether our sense of class or national pride, or our sense of how things should be generally. The true apocalyptic seizure is something different from apoplexy! The rhetoric in either case may be dynamic, ultrarational, and even purple. But one should be able to tell the difference between the tantrums of a romantic who cannot bring the world to heel and the impersonal voice which springs out of the crucible where the world is made and unmade." ("The Rhetoric of Ancient and Modern Apocalyptic," 440)

To this I need only add that this study is not concerned only with the voice that "springs out of the crucible," but will define apocalyptic discourse in such a way as to include the interpretation of such utterances.

15. Hofstader writes that for exponents of the paranoid style,

> History *is* a conspiracy, set in motion by demonic forces of almost transcendent power, and what is felt to be needed to defeat it is not the usual methods of political give-and-take, but an all-out crusade. The paranoid spokesman sees the fate of this conspiracy in apocalyptic terms—he traffics in the birth and death of whole worlds, whole political orders, whole systems of human values. . . . Time is forever just running out. Like religious millenarians, he expresses the anxiety of those who are living in the last days and he is sometimes disposed to set a date for the apocalypse. (Richard Hofstader, *The Paranoid Style in American Politics and Other Essays*, 29–30)

16. See Earl Creps, "The Conspiracy Argument as Rhetorical Genre." Robert Bellah provides support for Creps's view in his essay "Evil and the American Ethos," in *Sanctions for Evil*, ed. Nevitt Sanford and Craig Comstock, eds., 177–191.

17. See Norman Cohn, *The Pursuit of the Millennium*, rev. ed., 15.

18. For a rhetorical analysis of such use of apocalyptic and conspiracy argument, see John C. Heald, "Apocalyptic Rhetoric: Agents of the Antichrist from the French to the British."

19. Ernst Käsemann, "The Beginnings of Christian Theology," 17.

20. McGinn, *Visions of the End*, 94–101, 168–79.

21. See Robin Bruce Barnes, *Prophecy and Gnosis: Apocalypticism in the Wake of the German Reformation*.

22. Among the numerous studies of apocalypticism in the English Reformation are Bryan W. Ball, *A Great Expectation: Eschatological Thought in English Protestantism to 1660*; P. G. Rogers, *The Fifth Monarchy Men*; Paul Christianson, *Reformers and Babylon: English Apocalyptic Visions from the Reformation to the Eve of the Civil War*.

23. Grace Halsell, *Prophecy and Politics: Militant Evangelists on the Road to Nuclear War*.

24. Ray C. Petry, *Christian Eschatology and Social Thought*, 13–14.

25. Robert Jay Lifton, "The Image of the End of the World: A Psychohistorical View," in *Visions of Apocalypse*, ed. Friedlander et al., 151–70. Jung's examination of the Apocalypse is contained in *Answer to Job*, trans. R. F. C. Hull, 142–203; see especially p. 183.

26. See Petry, *Christian Eschatology and Social Thought*; also Gordon D. Kaufman, *Theology for a Nuclear Age*.

27. Frank Kermode, *The Sense of an Ending*.

28. Paul Hanson, *The Dawn of Apocalyptic*; Nathan O. Hatch, *The Sacred Cause of Liberty: Republican Thought and the Millennium in Revolutionary New England*.

29. Frank Kermode, "Apocalypse and the Modern," in *Visions of Apocalypse*, ed. Friedlander et al., 86.

30. E. J. Hobsbawm, *Primitive Rebels: Studies in Archaic Forms of Social Movement in the 19th and 20th Centuries*; Peter Worsley, *The Trumpet Shall Sound*. Hobsbawm's study is exclusively devoted to revolutionary millennialism among Italian peasants, particularly the "Lazzarettiani" of the 1870s, and is therefore limited in scope. Worsley gives much attention to non-Western groups such as the well-known "cargo cults" of the Pacific and other colonized regions, as does Vittorio Lanternari's *The Religions of the Oppressed: A Study of Modern Messianic Cults*. The relationship of colonialism and theft of land to apocalyptic and millenarian sects among "primitive" peoples is well demonstrated by such examples as the late nineteenth-century Native American "Ghost Dance" movement. Models of apocalypticism based on such movements, however, tend to be somewhat misleading when applied in modern contexts.

31. Hobsbawm, *Primitive Rebels*, 71.

32. The original edition of Cohn's *Pursuit of the Millennium* (London: Secker & Warburg, 1957) offers the most detailed application of psychoanalytic theory to apocalypticism. Here Cohn argues that those who seek an adequate explanation of millennial movements

> cannot afford to ignore the psychic content of the phantasies which have inspired them. All these phantasies are precisely such as are commonly found in individual cases of paranoia. The megalomaniac view of oneself as the elect, wholly good, abominably persecuted yet assured of ultimate triumph; the attribution of gigantic and demonic powers to the adversary; the refusal to accept the ineluctable limitations and imperfections of human existence, such as transience, dissension, conflict,

fallibility whether intellectual or moral; the obsession with inerrable prophecies—these attitudes are symptoms which together constitute the unmistakable syndrome of paranoia. But a paranoiac delusion does not cease to be so because it is shared by so many individuals, nor yet because those individuals have real and ample grounds for regarding themselves as victims of oppression." (1st ed., 309)

While I find this interpretation quite persuasive, critics should be exceedingly cautious in applying modern clinical concepts to patients long dead (and beyond the reach of clinical study). In this regard, it is interesting to note that in the revised edition of *The Pursuit of the Millennium* (London: Oxford University Press, 1980) Cohn has muted, if not abandoned entirely, his emphasis on psychoanalytic interpretation. The above passage has been excised from this edition, along with others that employ psychoanalytic theory to develop Cohn's controversial comparison of medieval apocalyptic sects with twentieth-century totalitarian and revolutionary movements. Unless otherwise specified, all citations are from the revised edition.

33. Critiquing Cohn and other proponents of psychological explanations of millennialism, anthropologist Kenelm Burridge comments: "There is little doubt that many a millenarian movement could accurately be described as a 'psychological reaction to cultural inadequacy'. . . . Yet if statements such as these are not merely variations of the propositions 'it is, therefore it is or must be,' or simply shorthand characterizations, it is not easy to see in what ways they carry a meaning that is not obvious at the outset." See *New Heaven New Earth: A Study of Millenarian Activities*, 121. Burridge classifies the various explanations of apocalypticism into four categories: "psycho-physiological," "ethnographic" (or historical and particularist), Marxist, and "Hegelian" (or idealist). Burridge's critique of apocalyptic scholarship contains helpful insights but requires revision in light of more recent efforts. Basing his anthropological analysis on data from India, Polynesia, and Native American tribes, Burridge goes on to offer a typical pattern of millenarian movements as proceeding from "old rules [to] no rules [to] new rules" (166, 170). This typology may accurately characterize the non-Western groups Burridge examines, and has been applied with some success to Millerism by Jonathan Butler (see his essay "The Making of a New Order: Millerism and the Origins of Seventh-Day Adventism"). However, it remains unclear for the present what application Burridge's typology might have to today's apparently widespread apocalyptic beliefs, which do not appear to be on the verge of crystallizing into a new order.

34. Norman Cohn, *The Pursuit of the Millennium*, 285–86.

35. Michael Barkun, *Disaster and the Millennium*, 128, 60, 208. Barkun does acknowledge that disaster is "a necessary but hardly a sufficient condition [of apocalyptic movements]." Among the additional factors he cites as necessary are: "multiple rather than single disasters; a body of ideas or doctrines of a millenarian cast must be readily available; a charismatic figure must be present to shape those doctrines in response to disaster; and the disaster area itself must be relatively homogeneous and insulated" (6). The second and third of these conditions are clearly issues for rhetorical analysis. Barkun's recent book, *Crucible of the Millennium*, attempts to repair the gaps in his earlier theory by emphasizing the distinction between "natural disasters and those caused by human actions" (ix). Barkun acknowledges the importance of canons of rationality (19–20), but fails to pursue the implications of this insight. Concluding his work with an analysis of "the apocalyptic mood 1960–85," he argues that the events of the traumatic sixties "suggest that 'disaster' functions as a mental construct which can be linked not only to observable death and destruction but

to events that symbolize loss of control and meaning" (153–54). To which this critic responds, "Exactly"—and proposes to begin, rather than conclude, an analysis with this insight. In Barkun's favor, it must be said that *Crucible of the Millennium* is a competent and useful historical study of early nineteenth century millennialism and utopianism, with an excellent demographic analysis of the Millerite and other movements that will be useful to rhetorical critics.

36. This phrase is borrowed from Ernest Bormann's essay, "Fetching Good Out of Evil: A Rhetorical Use of Calamity."

37. For an outline of this theory as applied to apocalyptic movements, see David F. Aberle, "A Note on Relative Deprivation Theory as Applied to Millenarian and Other Cult Movements"; for an application of the theory to early Christian apocalypticism, see Adela Yarbro Collins, *Crisis and Catharsis: The Power of the Apocalypse*, 84 and elsewhere.

38. Aberle, "A Note on Relative Deprivation Theory," 209.

39. Ernest R. Sandeen, "The 'Little Tradition' and the Form of Modern Millenarianism," 169.

40. The classic statement of this position on the linguistic and symbolic foundations of social status is Peter Berger and Thomas Luckmann's *The Social Construction of Reality*; see especially the discussion of the constitution of institutional realities and individual roles through "an objectified stock of knowledge common to a collectivity of actors" (73–74) on pp. 72–79. A more extended treatment of the communicative origins of social order can be found in Hugh Dalziel Duncan, *Communication and Social Order*. An initial attempt to develop this position into a sociology of argument is Charles W. Kneupper, "Rhetoric, Argument, and Social Reality: A Social Constructivist View."

41. See Robert Jay Lifton, "The Image of the End of the World: A Psychohistorical View," in *Visions of Apocalypse*, ed. Friedlander et al.

42. Barry Brummett, "Using Apocalyptic Discourse to Exploit Audience Commitments through 'Transfer,' " 59.

43. Ronald F. Reid, "Apocalypticism and Typology: Rhetorical Dimensions of a Symbolical Reality," 237.

44. Reid seems to point to the medieval era as such a period, claiming that apocalyptic was in eclipse during the Middle Ages; but studies by McGinn, Reeves, and others have conclusively shown that apocalyptic discourse was widespread from the sixth to the sixteenth centuries. Reid argues, "During the Middle Ages, when millenarianism was not popular, its few adherents were drawn mostly from the poor, the weak, and those who were outside the mainstream of Christian thought" ("Apocalypticism and Typology," 237). For histories and critical discussions of significant texts and traditions of popular and learned apocalypticism in the medieval period, see McGinn, *Visions of the End*; also Marjorie Reeves, *The Influence of Prophecy in the Later Middle Ages*. In a provocative essay, historian Richard Landes argues that the terminology through which historians study the past causes them to ignore evidence of apocalyptic beliefs: "[W]e modern historians too often overlook or trivialize the fact that those 'medieval' men were living not in the Middle Ages, in their own minds at least, but at the very end of the Last one" ("Lest the Millennium Be Fulfilled," 204–5).

45. For medieval sources, see McGinn, *Visions of the End*, and other studies as noted above. Ball's *A Great Expectation* is only one of many studies of English apocalypticism in the sixteenth century. For more detailed documentation and discussion of the significance of apocalypticism's move into mainstream thought in the twentieth century, I refer the reader to William Martin, "Waiting for the End: The Growing Interest in Apocalyptic Prophecy."

46. The inherent circularity of such explanations is noted by Burridge (see above). Howard Kaminsky also addresses this issue: "If we bear in mind the kind of causative factors that [scholars have considered]—anxiety, sense of deprivation, social suffering, etc.—we must admit that in no single case is it even remotely possible to deduce the movement from any single factor, any group of factors, or any definable degree of intensity of such factors. All such efforts lead directly to the circle: X is alleged to be necessary for the movement, but the only way we know that X is present is that a movement has come into being" ("The Problem of Explanation," in Thrupp, ed., *Millennial Dreams in Action*, 216).

47. In his essay "A Rhetorical Interpretation of History," John Angus Campbell argues that death is the ultimate anomaly: in the common recognition of mortality, "we confront an exigence beyond the capacity of any symbolism whatever ultimately to assuage" (236). On pages 240–46, Campbell discusses the "structural weaknesses of cosmological symbolism." See chapter 2 for further discussion of these issues.

48. An exception is Barry Brummett's recent study *Contemporary Apocalyptic Rhetoric*, which does analyze apocalyptic as an argument form. However, Brummett follows most other historians and sociologists in assuming that the audience for apocalyptic is predisposed to acceptance of its claims. By focusing on the study of texts and failing systematically to examine behavioral responses to them, he inadvertently slights the active role of the audience: "I will be concerned largely with the texts of apocalyptic rhetoric and from them deduce how an audience that *would* be swayed by a given text *is* swayed. . . . Apocalyptic . . . offers itself, and those who have need of it come to it" (30).

49. Adela Yarbro Collins, *Crisis and Catharsis: The Power of the Apocalypse*, 84.

50. In the first (1957) edition of *The Pursuit of the Millennium*, subtitled *Revolutionary Messianism in Medieval and Reformation Europe and its Bearing on Modern Totalitarian Movements*. As noted above, this argument has largely disappeared from the revised edition (1980), which is subtitled *Revolutionary Millenarians and Mystical Anarchists of the Middle Ages*.

51. Ruth Bloch, *Visionary Republic: Millennial Themes in American Thought, 1756–1800*, xi–xii.

52. These terms refer to the temporal position of the second coming of Christ: either before or after the millennial kingdom, a thousand-year period of peace, prosperity, and holiness. Premillennialism holds that the return of Christ would precede and actually inaugurate the millennium, while postmillennialism advocates a temporal scheme in which Christ's physical return would follow the millennium, conceived in more spiritualized terms as a time when God's rule over the earth would be progressively established through missionary activity. For a discussion of these terms and their history, see James West Davidson's *The Logic of Millennial Thought*, 28–29 and passim; for an evaluation of the doctrines in the context of other theological interpretations of the millennium, see Robert G. Clouse, ed., *The Meaning of the Millennium: Four Views*.

53. See, for example, Timothy Weber, *Living in the Shadow of the Second Coming: American Premillennialism, 1875–1982*, 13–14 and passim.

54. For the standard historian's distinction between pre- and postmillennialism, see Alan Heimert, *Religion and the American Mind*, 66 and passim. Ernest Tuveson argues the same thesis using different terminology in *Redeemer Nation: The Idea of America's Millennial Role*. The most detailed critique of received accounts of the social significance of pre- and postmillennialism is found in Davidson, *The Logic of Millennial Thought*, 31–34. For another version of the controversy and a summary of recent attacks on scholarship using this typology,

see James M. Moorhead, "Between Progress and Apocalypse: A Reassessment of Millennialism in American Religious Thought, 1800–1880"; also "Searching for the Millennium in America." Here Moorhead argues that in the nineteenth century, "Those who watched for an imminent Second Coming often supported the same evangelical and benevolent endeavors for which their postmillennial counterparts labored" (21).

55. For a detailed examination of Robertson's political theology, see Stephen O'Leary and Michael McFarland, "The Political Use of Mythic Discourse: Prophetic Interpretation in Pat Robertson's Presidential Campaign." Robertson's interpretation of biblical apocalyptic shifted considerably from 1980 through 1988; the synthesis he effects is unique and, as O'Leary and McFarland argue, a response to the peculiar rhetorical exegencies of a presidential campaign. Falwell's active participation in American politics in the 1980s is rooted in a different scheme of prophetic interpretation, essentially similar to Lindsey's, which is discussed at length in chapters 6 and 7 of this study. A defense of an activist premillennialist position on prophecy and politics, authored by two professors at Falwell's Liberty University, can be found in Ed Dobson and Ed Hindson, "Apocalypse Now? What Fundamentalists Believe about the End of the World."

56. Tom D. Daniels, Richard J. Jensen, and Allen Lichtenstein, "Resolving the Paradox in Politicized Christian Fundamentalism."

57. For an account of the classical roots of this debate, see Ernst Cassirer, *The Myth of the State*, especially chapter 3. In *Language and Myth* Cassirer sets forth his own theory of the mythic origins of language and logic. Suzanne Langer's introduction summarizes Cassirer's view:

> [L]anguage, man's prime instrument of reason, reflects his mythmaking tendency more than his rationalizing tendency. Language, the symbolization of thought, exhibits two entirely different modes of thought. [The mind] expresses itself in different forms, one of which is discursive logic, the other creative imagination. . . . Myth never breaks out of the magic circle of its figurative ideas. It reaches religious and poetic heights; but the gulf between its conceptions and those of science never narrows. . . . But language, born in that same magic circle, has the power to break its bounds; language takes us from the mythmaking phase of human mentality to the phase of logical thought. (viii–x)

From this evolutionary perspective, language is seen to act as the bridge between myth and logic, as the means by which logos is brought out of mythos. The present essay will provide support for this view by examining the discourse of theodicy and apocalypse as a product of the ratiocination of myth. It should be noted at the outset, however, that such an evolutionary perspective is not meant to imply that logic supersedes myth, or that the two are opposed in any simple fashion. This study follows the lead of Hans Blumenberg, who cautions against such a teleological bias in his critique of Cassirer:

> The classical "disinformation" that is contained in the formula 'from mythos to logos' and that still lies innocently dormant in Plato's indecision between myth and logos is complete where the philosopher recognizes in myth only the identity of the objects for which he believes he has found the definitive mode of treatment. The mischief of that obvious historical formula lies in the fact that it does not permit one to recognize in myth itself one of the modes of accomplishment of logos.

See *Work on Myth*, 27. While logic has historically been used as a mode of critique, to debunk the claims of myth, such an opposition is only one of the possible ways of conceiving this relationship. The present study seeks to examine apocalyptic as an argument formation in order to demonstrate an alternative conception, in which rational and mythic thought are functionally intertwined and mutually supportive of each other.

58. For examples of recent uses of time as a dimension of rhetorical analysis, see the work of Michael Leff, particularly "Textual Criticism: The Legacy of G. P. Mohrmann"; "Rhetorical Timing in Lincoln's House Divided Speech"; and "Dimensions of Temporality in Lincoln's Second Inaugural." Other perspectives on, and uses of, time and temporality in rhetorical theory and criticism are to be found in Thomas B. Farrell, "Knowledge in Time: Toward an Extension of Rhetorical Form"; Edwin Black, "Electing Time"; and Thomas S. Frentz, "Rhetorical Conversation, Time, and Moral Action."

59. Cited in J. Robert Cox, "The Fulfillment of Time: King's 'I Have a Dream' Speech (August 28, 1963)," 183.

60. Cox, "The Fulfillment of Time," 200–204.

61. Ernest R. Sandeen, "The 'Little Tradition' and the Form of Modern Millenarianism," 167.

62. Barry Brummett, "Premillennial Apocalyptic as a Rhetorical Genre," 85. It might be said in Brummett's defense that he has restricted his argument to discussion of premillennial apocalyptic, and has not attempted to define all apocalyptic discourse as a genre. This still begs the question as to whether any genre can be studied and understood without reference to the other discourses to which it is related. Here I follow McGinn, who argues that "the content of apocalyptic eschatologies (the plural is surely more accurate) expresses a pattern of beliefs about time and eternity that are too complex to be reduced to any single essential notion. . . . [A]pocalypticism should always be seen as a genus that includes a number of species" (*Visions of the End*, 10). Brummett seeks to address the deficiencies of his earlier work on the subject in his recent book, *Contemporary Apocalyptic Rhetoric*. Here, he examines premillennialism and postmillennialism as subgenres of apocalypse, seeking to "strike a proper balance between describing what is commonly true of all examples of the discourse and still accounting for wide and inevitable variations" (23). However, I am not persuaded that Brummett's theoretical perspective can successfully measure the varieties of apocalyptic experience. As a critical method (at least as practiced by Brummett) genre theory seems unable to provide a coherent account of the dynamic social processes that *generate* variations in religious discourse. Thus, he argues that "[A]pocalyptic is remarkably similar across its many texts, at least within the broad categories of premillennial and postmillennial discourse. [It] does not vary itself as much as do many other genres to fit the varying audiences of the moment" (30). That this view is overly simplistic will be shown in chapters 4 and 5, where I link changes in the style and substance of Millerite discourse to the shifting demands and expectations of its audiences.

Finally, a serious defect in the generic approach is that the ahistoric nature of generic labels can actually hinder understanding. For example, Brummett claims in his 1984 essay that the book of Revelation (dating from the late first century CE) is an example of premillennial apocalypse, when "premillennialism" was not articulated as a theory of apocalyptic interpretation until the late eighteenth and early nineteenth centuries. Since (as I will argue in chapter 3) the ambiguity of the mythic symbols of the Apocalypse is exactly what allowed pre- and postmillennialism to develop as competing schools of interpretation, such generic labeling must inevitably distort critical perceptions of the original scriptural texts.

63. For a useful summary of this controversy, see John J. Collins, *The Apocalyptic Imagination: An Introduction to the Jewish Matrix of Christianity*, especially chapter 1. *Semeia* 14 (1979) [published as *Apocalypse: The Morphology of a Genre*, ed. John J. Collins] is devoted to a study by the Society for Biblical Literature Genres Project that surveys texts from 250 BCE–250 CE in an attempt to demonstrate generic coherence. A later issue of the same journal seeks to take up where the earlier project left off; see Adela Yarbro Collins, ed., "Early Christian Apocalypticism: Genre and Social Setting," *Semeia* 36 (1986). Of particular interest in this issue are David Hellholm's criticisms of the standard view of apocalyptic genre and his attempt to create a detailed system for analyzing communicative levels in the Apocalypse. See Hellholm, "The Problem of Apocalyptic Genre and the Apocalypse of John"; also the response by David E. Aune, "The Apocalypse of John and the Problem of Genre."

64. A typical list of generic features may be found in Klaus Koch, "What is Apocalyptic? An Attempt at a Literary Definition."

65. See David Hill, *New Testament Prophecy*, ch. 3. Hill's distinction, a commonplace of biblical criticism, is taken from Gerhard von Rad, *Theology of the Old Testament*, vol. 2, 303. Hanson (*The Dawn of Apocalyptic*, 4–10) critiques such simplistic applications of generic theory, viewing prophecy and apocalyptic as sociological phenomena rather than as literary genres. Hanson argues that much of the dispute over genre is rooted in terminology and confusion of definitions, and that critics should not be too quick to link apocalypse as a literary genre with the discourse of apocalyptic movements. (See also Collins, *The Apocalyptic Imagination*, 9–11.) In the third chapter of this study I shall propose that Christian eschatology has inspired "tragic" and "comic" interpretations that may be seen as analogous, if not exactly equivalent, to "apocalyptic eschatology" and "prophetic eschatology" as defined by Hanson.

66. This discussion is based on Stephen C. Pepper's *World Hypotheses*. Pepper argues that critical methods are based in "world hypotheses" that are founded in and identifiable by their root metaphors, or basic understandings about the nature of the universe. These "world hypotheses" in turn dictate the critic's perception of reality and acceptance or rejection of evidence. The four primary world hypotheses in Pepper's schema are formism, mechanism, contextualism, and organicism. For a discussion and critique of these root metaphors as found in and applied to rhetorical criticism, see B. L. Ware, "Theories of Rhetorical Criticism as Argument," especially ch. 3, "The Paradoxical World of Formistic Criticism," and ch. 4, "The Wide, Wide World of Contextualist Criticism."

67. See Pepper, *World Hypotheses*, 232–79; Ware, "Theories of Rhetorical Criticism as Argument," 208–300.

68. Pepper, *World Hypotheses*, 232.

69. While the concept of topoi is central to the rhetorical tradition, no consensus has as yet appeared among rhetorical scholars regarding the proper definition and application of topical theory. For some recent treatments of the issue, see: Donovan J. Ochs, "Aristotle's Concept of the Formal Topics"; Karl R. Wallace, "Topoi and the Problem of Invention"; Michael Leff and Dean E. Hewes, "Topical Invention and Group Communication: Toward a Sociology of Inference"; Carolyn R. Miller, "Fields of Argument and Special Topoi"; and Michael Leff, "Topical Invention and Metaphoric Interaction." As Leff notes, "The term 'topic' is notoriously ambiguous, and even in its technical uses, its meaning ranges from recurrent themes appearing in a certain kind of discourse to abstract patterns of inference" ("Topical Invention and Metaphoric Interaction," 220). This study will use the term in both

of these senses: authority, time, and evil are treated as recurring themes or "commonplaces" in apocalyptic discourse, while the demonstration of common structures of reasoning and argument on these themes will illustrate the conception of topoi as patterns of thought and inference. Chapters 2 and 3 will develop in detail a theory of topoi as social knowledge propositions operating in discourse according to Burke's psychology of form, and attempt to illustrate the process of topical invention as a product of interaction between rhetor and audience.

70. McGinn, *Visions of the End*, 10.

71. Sandeen, "The 'Little Tradition' and the Form of Modern Millenarianism," 166–68.

72. Millerite newspapers were published in a number of cities in the United State, including Boston, New York, Philadelphia, and Cincinatti. Circulation figures indicate print runs of 10,000 for daily editions of the *Midnight Cry* in New York, 5,000 for weekly editions of *Signs of the Times* in Boston, and editions of thirty and fifty thousand for irregular issues of the *Philadelphia Alarm*, between 1840 and 1844. See Leroy Edwin Froom, *The Prophetic Faith of Our Fathers*, vol. 4, 624–25. Whitney Cross estimates in *The Burned-over District: The Social and Intellectual History of Enthusiastic Religion in Upstate New York, 1800–1850* that the movement had about 50,000 followers at its peak in 1843–1844, (287). In *The Miller Heresy, Millennialism, and American Culture*, Ruth Doan notes shifting estimates of the Millerite population ranging from ten thousand to a million, but adds that the difficulty of distinguishing between followers and interested or sympathetic observers of the movement makes such calculation problematic (4–5). Doan's study thoroughly documents the public controversy caused by Millerite advocacy. According to Paul Boyer (*When Time Shall Be No More: Prophecy Belief in Modern American Culture*, 5–6), there were twenty-eight million copies of Hal Lindsey's *The Late Great Planet Earth* in print by 1990 (after twenty years of publication), while Lindsey's *The 1980's: Countdown to Armageddon* appeared on the New York Times bestseller list for many weeks in 1980. Precise sales figures are not released by the publisher, but numerous printed reports confirm Lindsey's status as the single best-selling author in America during the period from the 1970s through the mid-1980s. For an account of public controversy over apocalyptic theology in the 1980s, see O'Leary and McFarland, "The Political Use of Mythic Discourse."

73. Thomas Farrell, "Knowledge in Time," 124.

74. See, for example, Ruth Bloch, *Visionary Republic*; Ernest Tuveson, *Redeemer Nation: The Idea of America's Millennial Role*; and Nathan Hatch, *The Sacred Cause of Liberty*.

75. James M. Moorhead, "Searching for the Millennium in America," 25.

76. See above. Two other useful histories are Whitney Cross's *The Burned-over District* and David Rowe's *Thunder and Trumpets: Millerites and Dissenting Religion in Upstate New York, 1800–1850*. While these studies offer excellent accounts (Rowe's is a detailed study of the Millerite movement, while Cross examines Millerism in the context of other religious currents), both are restricted in their geographical scope and do not systematically address the broad issues of rationality and public controversy that are the focus of my analysis.

CHAPTER 2

1. See Lloyd F. Bitzer, "The Rhetorical Situation."

2. Michael Leff, "Topical Invention and Metaphoric Interaction," 215. The discussion that follows owes much to Leff's conceptions of the topoi as developed here and in two other essays: "The Topics of Argumentative Invention in Latin Rhetorical Theory from Cicero to Boethius," and "Topical Invention and Group Communication."

3. Paul Ricoeur, "Evil, a Challenge to Philosophy and Theology," 69.

4. Leff, "Topical Invention and Metaphoric Interaction," 220.

5. Richard M. Weaver, *Language Is Sermonic*, 208.

6. Frank D'Angelo, "The Evolution of the Analytic Topoi: A Speculative Inquiry," 51. For another thoughtful overview of topical theory see Karl R. Wallace, "*Topoi* and the Problem of Invention."

7. Thomas B. Farrell, "Knowledge in Time," 125.

8. Farrell, "Knowledge in Time," 126.

9. *Rhetoric* 1358a.13–15, 18–22, trans. W. Rhys Roberts, in *The Basic Works of Aristotle*, ed. Richard McKeon, 1334.

10. Though there is some disagreement among contemporary argumentation scholars over this issue, most would agree to define an "argument field" as a domain or specialized practice of argument formed by shared assumptions and normative standards, such as law, mathematics, etc. See Stephen Toulmin, *The Uses of Argument*, 14–15, 36–37; Leff and Hewes, "Topical Invention and Group Communication," 776; also Carolyn R. Miller, "Fields of Argument and Special Topoi," 147–58.

11. *Rhetoric* 1391b–93a, in McKeon, ed., *The Basic Works of Aristotle*, 1409–12.

12. Leff suggests a possible link between this categorical notion and the etymological sense of topos as place, whereby the common topoi "function as containers for special topics" ("Topical Invention and Metaphoric Interaction," 221, n. 15.

13. See Thomas B. Farrell, "Knowledge, Consensus, and Rhetorical Theory"; also "Social Knowledge II."

14. *Topica* 100a.18–20, trans. by W. A. Pickard-Cambridge, in McKeon, *The Basic Works of Aristotle*, 188.

15. *Rhetoric* 1396b.22, in McKeon, *The Basic Works of Aristotle*, 1419. Whereas Aristotle here defines the *topoi* as classes or types of enthymemes, elsewhere he seems to indicate that they are elements or constituent parts. Whether such confusion is the result of mistranslation or Aristotle's own lack of clarity is a question that must be left aside here.

16. Kathleen Hall Jamieson, *Eloquence in an Electronic Age*, 18.

17. See Thomas M. Conley, "The Enthymeme in Perspective"; also Leff, "Topical Invention and Metaphoric Interaction," 221.

18. *Rhetoric* 1362b.30; 1364a.23–30, in McKeon, *The Basic Works of Aristotle*, 1348.

19. Leff, "Topical Invention and Metaphoric Interaction," 222.

20. Kenneth Burke, *Attitudes toward History*, 336.

21. Glenn Tinder, "Eschatology and Politics," 313. I follow Tinder in characterizing this view as "positivistic," a term that I take to describe a philosophic perspective (traceable from Kant and Hume to the Vienna school) that rejects as meaningless all metaphysical statements, or any statement not derived through formal scientific method and subject to the principle of verifiability.

22. This approach is fully in accord with Kenneth Burke's notion of "Logology," which considers theology "as a kind of verbal 'grace' that perfects nature. . . . Logology involves only *empirical* considerations about our nature as the symbol-using animal" (Kenneth Burke, "Theology and Logology," 153). For a similar resolution of this problem, see John Angus

Campbell's treatment of the "universal audience" in his essay "A Rhetorical Interpretation of History": " 'Universal audience'... is a term I use in an empirical and historical sense. By the term I mean that a mode of symbolization embodying a universal standpoint actually emerged in history. I am making no metaphysical claim about an 'audience' that 'exists' as an entity apart from the symbols which articulate it" (253).

23. Tinder, "Eschatology and Politics," 313.

24. Peter J. Marston, "Rhetorical Forms and Functions of Cosmological Argument," 32.

25. Marston, "Rhetorical Forms and Functions of Cosmological Argument," 16.

26. Burke's notion of "terministic screens" is developed in his essay of that title in *Language as Symbolic Action*, 44–62. For a discussion of cosmologies as terministic screens, see Marston, "Rhetorical Forms and Functions of Cosmological Argument," 54–56.

27. Burke, *A Rhetoric of Motives*, 13. Burke follows this thought with a speculative proposal for a study in comparative eschatology and character (16):

> Surely, it would not take much to distinguish between the character of a person who foresaw a world ending "not with a bang but a whimper," and one who feared some mighty holocaust. . . . Or contrast the medieval imagery of the mighty burning with many modern scientists' pale preference for the "heat death," according to the principle of . . . entropy, whereby the earlier potency of matter must finally dwindle into a universal, uniform impotence. [In their choice of such visions,] People would spontaneously classify themselves; for by reason of the "scene-agent" ratio the individual can identify himself with the character of a surrounding situation, translating one into terms of the other; hence a shift to a grander order, the shift from thoughts of one's own individual end to thoughts of a universal end, would still contrive to portray the character of the individual, even while acquiring greater resonance and scope and enabling men to transcend too local a view of themselves.

This book is offered as a sort of prolegomenon to such a full-scale study.

28. An obvious question here is the extent to which cultural conditioning prevents or enables the volitional shifting between such conceptual maps or transcendence strategies. If individuals are thoroughly "indoctrinated" with the precepts of a particular culture or group, their volitional possibilities may indeed be limited. At certain times and places in history, however (such as the late Roman Empire and twentieth-century California), critics may note a phenomenon of a "marketplace" of religious and cosmic ideas, in which transcendent systems vie with one another to offer strategies for living. The religious "consumer" in San Francisco or Santa Monica can, and often does, sample a variety of doctrines sequentially and simultaneously, including semiorthodox "hybrid" versions of traditional faiths, Sufism, a variety of Buddhisms (Tibetan, Japanese, Burmese, Mahayana, Hinayana, Zen, Vipassana, tantric, etc.,), beliefs in "channeling" of spirits, crystals, UFOs and past lives, secularized transcendence such as that provided by EST, and more alternatives too numerous to list. This situation was probably very like what prevailed in Rome as the empire began to absorb territories containing a variety of sects, faiths, mystery cults, and philosophical schools, each offering their own cosmological doctrines and transcendent strategies, while members of the Roman upper class dabbled with different cults and initiation rites. It was of course in this context that Christianity acquired its initial following by offering apocalyptic eschatology as a transcendent solution to the cosmological question. For a study of the mystery religions

of classical antiquity, see Walter Burkert, *Ancient Mystery Cults*; for an incisive analysis of religious culture in twentieth-century California, see Shiva Naipaul, *Journey to Nowhere*.

29. Immanuel Kant, *Critique of Pure Reason*, trans. J. M. D. Meiklejohn; see especially p. 228, "On the Transition from Rational Psychology to Cosmology," and subsequent pages for Kant's discussion of the transcendental antinomies or "Antithetic of Pure Reason" (238). The "First Conflict of the Transcendental Ideas" analyzed here is argued out dialectically on pages 241–45.

30. The second, third, and fourth antinomies are respectively concerned with substance and composition, causality and freedom, and the existence of "an absolutely necessary being." This last antinomy aims to represent arguments supporting the ontological proof of the existence of God, which is based on the concept of "necessary existence." For a lengthier discussion of Kant's attack on rational theology, see Justus Hartnack, *Kant's Theory of Knowledge*.

31. Kant, *Critique of Pure Reason*, 241.

32. Kant, *Critique of Pure Reason*, 233. Kant continues:

Take, for example, the series *m, n, o,* in which *n* is given as conditioned in relation to *m,* but at the same time as the condition of *o,* and let the series proceed upwards from the conditioned *n* to *m* (*l, k, i,* etc.) and also downward from condition n to the conditioned *o* (*p, q, r,* etc.)—I must presuppose the former series, to be able to consider *n* as given, and *n* is according to reason (the totality of conditions) possible only by means of that series. But its possibility does not rest on the following series *o, p, q, r,* which for this reason cannot be regarded as given, but only as capable of being given. . . . I shall term the synthesis on the side of the conditions—from that nearest to the given phenomenon up to the more remote—*regressive;* that which proceeds on the side of the conditioned, from the immediate consequence to the more remote, I shall call the *progressive* synthesis. The former proceeds *in antecedentia,* the latter *in consequentia.* The cosmological ideas are therefore occupied with the totality of the regressive synthesis, and proceed *in antecedentia,* not *in consequentia.* When the latter takes place, it is an arbitrary and not a necessary problem of pure reason; for we require, for the complete understanding of what is given in a phenomenon, not the consequences which succeed, but the grounds or principles which precede.

33. See note 32 above.

34. See, for example, Marston's analysis of argument that assumes a finite cosmos, and the resulting depiction of policy choices in terms of an "era of limits" in Jeremy Rifkin's *Entropy* and in former California governor Jerry Brown's State of the State address (Marston, "Rhetorical Forms and Functions of Cosmological Argument," 210–18).

35. An extended meditation on this topic quite similar to Kant's in its dialectical form is to be found in Augustine's *The City of God* XII.16–21. One might even say, judging from the popularity of cosmological myth and speculation, that indifference to this question is a relatively rare response.

36. In the Second Division, Kant distinguishes the transcendental dialectic from the transcendental analytic in terms of interest to rhetoricians. Kant abandons Aristotle's notion of rhetorical and dialectical discourse as concerned with the probable: "Dialectic [is] in general a logic of appearance. This does not signify a doctrine of *probability*; for probability is truth, only cognized upon insufficient grounds, and though the information it gives us is

imperfect, it is not therefore deceitful" (186). Dialectic is attacked because it "leads us, in disregard of all the warnings of criticism, completely beyond the empirical employment of the categories, and deludes us with the chimera of an extension of the sphere of *pure understanding*" (188). After such an attack, it need hardly be added that rhetoric was beneath Kant's notice. The dialectic is not, however, merely an instrument for deception. Kant concludes this section on a more affirmative note: "There is therefore a natural and una-voidable dialectic of pure reason—not that in which the bungler, from want of the requisite knowledge, involves himself, nor that which the sophist devises for the purpose of misleading, but that which is an inseparable adjunct of human reason, and which, even after its illusion have [sic] been exposed, does not cease to deceive, and continually to lead reason into momentary errors, which it becomes necessary continually to remove" (189). Kant's im-placable dismantling of the transcendental dialectic through the application of the tran-scendental analytic is thus never final, but a perennial Sisyphean task, like Freud's reclaiming of consciousness from the unconscious. In this passage, the dialectic seems somewhat tamed, like an imperfectly trained dog, man's best friend and "inseparable adjunct," that must be kept on a short leash lest it persist in its habit of straying where it does not belong and leaving messes that the philosopher must continually clean up.

37. Kant, *Critique of Pure Reason*, 277.

38. Kant, *Critique of Pure Reason*, 283–84.

39. Donald Wilcox, *The Measure of Times Past: Pre-Newtonian Chronologies and the Rhetoric of Relative Time*, 32.

40. See Kant, *Critique of Pure Reason*, 156–61, for "the Ground of the Division of all Objects into Phenomena and Noumena," and for the rationale that forbids the application of the categories and intuitions to noumenal reality. The argument is summarized in Hart-nack, *Kant's Theory of Knowledge*, 89–90. Wilcox (*The Measure of Times Past*, 31–35) notes that this division is Kant's solution to the problem of Cartesian dualism. The theological consequences of Descartes' solution are noted by Eric Voegelin: "An ego that doubts and desires to go beyond itself is not the creator of itself but requires a creator and maintainer of its doubting existence, and that cause is the 'God' who appears in the analyses of the *Third Meditation* and the *Principles*" ("Quod Deus Dicitur," in *Trajectories in the Study of Religion*, ed. Ray Hart, 4). According to Kant's argument, Descartes' error lay in under-standing the self or perceiving ego as a noumenal reality. For Kant, the self (like time and space) is a primary intuition and necessary condition of perception, not an empirical fact, and thus cannot be used to extrapolate into the noumenal realm.

41. Walter R. Fisher, *Human Communication as Narration: Toward a Philosophy of Reason, Value, and Action*, xi.

42. David Carr, *Time, Narrative, and History*, 65.

43. See the section "Narrative Rationality as a Rhetorical Logic," in Fisher, *Human Communication as Narration*, 47–48. Kant might agree to classify narrative as a rhetorical logic, but would nevertheless dismiss all such logics along with dialectic.

44. The appeal to the empirical should not disguise the fact that this analysis itself attempts to enact a strategy of transcendence by locating meaning within developments in the history of ideas, and placing this history into a wider context, thus retracing the path of Hegel's critique of Kant. The Kantian conflict between the transcendent analytic and the transcendent dialectic, and the dismissal of cosmological and theological proofs (a dismissal that can never be final due to the inherently self-deceptive nature of dialectical thought—see note 36 above) is surmounted by Hegel's recognition of "the so-called proofs for the

existence of God as descriptions and analyses of the process of the *Geist* itself. . . . The rising of thought beyond the sensual, the thought transcending the finite into the infinite, the leap that is made by breaking from the series of the sensual into the supersensual, all this is thought itself, the transition is *only thought itself*." (Hegel, *Enzyklopaedie* 1830 §50, quoted in Voegelin, "Quod Deus Dicitur," *Trajectories in the Study of Religion*, 4.)

45. Carr, *Time, Narrative, and History*, 47. The contrast with the argument in note 32 above, in which Kant privileges the terminology of series and sequence as the definitive model of cosmic time, could hardly be more striking. To those who argue that the temporal structure of narrative is merely a "fiction" that human beings impose on external events that are themselves orderless, Carr replies: "All this confuses the issue, because, as these theorists very well know, what stories and histories represent or depict is not purely physical events but human experiences, actions, and sufferings, including the human activity of projecting meaning onto or finding meaning in physical or other events. Thus the physical world does find its way into stories, but always as back-drop or sphere of operations for human activity. . . . [H]uman reality . . . is being construed [by these theorists] according to the model of the ticking clock" (19–20). In Kenneth Burke's terms, time is construed in terms of "motion" rather than of "action." See *Language as Symbolic Action*, 53.

46. Kermode, *The Sense of an Ending*, 7. As Carr notes, Kermode's use of the term "fictive" seems to place him in the camp of those who view narrative form as something arbitrarily imposed on events in the "real" world (*Time, Narrative, and History*, 13).

47. Kenneth Burke, "Psychology and Form," in *Counter-Statement*, 31.

48. Carr, *Time, Narrative, and History*, 183, 185. Note that the strategic ambiguity of Carr's use of the plural voice represents a significant attenuation of the force of his qualification. This strategy is evident on page 183, where Carr specifically addresses the issue of cultural relativity:

> These arguments against the universality and 'transcultural necessity' of the narrative conception of time are perhaps less than convincing. . . . In a sense they can never be fully convincing to *us* because *we* are asked to admit the reality of a way of construing and living in time which is alien to us. At the same time the considerations introduced by these arguments are important enough to make us cautious about asserting the universality of narrative time. When we say, then, that historical narrative is just an extension of historical existence, and that historical existence is the social counterpart of the individual's way of experiencing and acting in time, *we* are asserting this about *ourselves*, not necessarily about everyone. Who, then, are *we*? Perhaps just that community that recognizes itself as sharing a certain conception of and a certain way of living in time, and recognizes that in this it differs or may differ from other communities past, present, or future.

By arguing that the community is constituted through recognition of a common temporal conception, Carr is able both to have his cake and eat it: even as he *appears* to answer the question, Who are we?, his reply obscures the issue of what community or communities serve as a referent for the plural pronoun (so that the reader is unsure whether *we* refers to Western societies, or the human community, or simply readers of Carr's book, or whether the temporal conception that constitutes the community can be *any* conception, or only that conception that Carr has helped his readers to recognize). One cannot help but recall Stephen Pepper's comment about the contextualist critic (*World Hypotheses*, p. 252): "If you ask him, 'Then how do you know that your analysis of experience is true of all experience?'

he replies, 'I don't.' " If you ask further, 'Then you admit your analysis is false?' he replies, 'Catch me if you can.' "

49. Mircea Eliade, *Myth and Reality*, 54–74.

50. Eliade, *Myth and Reality*, 61–62.

51. Eliade, *The Myth of the Eternal Return or, Cosmos and History*, 112–26.

52. Eliade, *The Myth of the Eternal Return*, 119–20. See the beginning of chapter 1 of the present study for Plato's version of the myth in the *Politicus*.

53. Augustine, *The City of God* XII.14, 487–88.

54. *Advent Herald*, 6 November 1844, 1. Published in Boston by J. V. Himes; available through the courtesy of the Orrin Roe Jenks Collection of Adventual Materials, Aurora University, Aurora, Illinois.

55. The opposition of these antinomic temporal structures should not obscure the fact that both the linear and cyclical conceptions are in their own ways, as Eliade puts it, strategies for overcoming the "terror of history" through the "annulment of time." This is clear enough in the passage from Augustine cited above, but perhaps requires reiteration in the case of the cyclical cosmologies. Eliade's comments on the Greek version of the cyclical cosmos will serve as another indication of the differing weights assumed by historical events according to the changes in one's conception of time:

> [T]he myth of eternal repetition, as reinterpreted by Greek speculation, has the meaning of a supreme attempt toward the 'staticization' of becoming, toward annulling the irreversibility of time. If all moments and all situations of the cosmos are repeated *ad infinitum*, their evanescence is, in the last analysis, patent; *sub specie infinitatis*, all moments and all situations remain stationary and thus acquire the ontological order of the archetype. Hence, among all the forms of becoming, historical becoming too is saturated with being. From the point of view of eternal repetition, historical events are transformed into categories and thus regain the ontological order they possessed in the horizon of archaic spirituality. (*The Myth of the Eternal Return*, 123).

56. For amplification of this point, see Ramsay MacMullen, *Christianizing the Roman Empire*, 10–42.

57. "[W]here does one look for justice when the central authority of the state no longer protects against bandits? Where does one look for cosmic order when the ceremonies of renewal have been performed regularly and the Nile does not rise as it should: or, as in Sumer, when the Euphrates changes its course and the life-giving ditches are empty? Where is one to look for social or cosmic order during the 'time of troubles,' the period of total disruption and chaos, common to all civilizations?" (Campbell, "A Rhetorical Interpretation of History," 241).

58. For a discussion of these circumstances, see Campbell, "A Rhetorical Interpretation of History," 245–46.

59. An example of such an introduction of scientific cosmology into the social knowledge base is Stephen Hawking's best-seller *A Brief History of Time*, which has recently been made into a popular film.

60. The topic could be expressed in many ways; this phrase is Gunnar Boklund's, from his article "Time Must Have a Stop: Apocalyptic Thought and Expression in the Twentieth Century."

61. Paul Ricoeur, *The Symbolism of Evil*, 11.

62. Carr, *Time, Narrative, and History*, 163.

63. See Carr, *Time, Narrative, and History*, 88–89.

64. Campbell terms this rhetorical situation the "tensional field" that forms the ground of history: "When the awareness of life against death is expressed in strategic, stylized symbols, history . . . is manifest as a shared field of tension" ("A Rhetorical Interpretation of History," 235).

65. Lloyd Bitzer, "The Rhetorical Situation," 6.

66. Campbell, "A Rhetorical Interpretation of History," 236.

67. Ricoeur, "Evil, a Challenge to Philosophy and Theology," in *Trajectories in the Study of Religion*, 73–74.

68. For a discussion of the modernist program of the developing social sciences from Kant onwards as an attempt to construct a rational, secular theodicy, see Ernest Becker, *The Structure of Evil*. In spite of its title, the word "evil" is rarely employed in Becker's analysis, which rejects the theological baggage of this term and turns instead to the terminology of sociology and psychology. With evil reduced to "alienation," Becker's modernist terminology can only define "the demonic nature of social evil in our time" as the result of our failure "to introduce critical reason into the realm of human affairs" (142)—an explanation that I, at least, find stunningly inadequate as an explanation of Hiroshima and the Holocaust, neither of which receives so much as a mention in Becker's index. For discussion of the inability of both traditional theology and modern social science to account for these and other examples of modern evils, see Jeffrey Burton Russell, *The Prince of Darkness: Radical Evil and the Power of Good in History*, particularly chapter 16, "Auschwitz and Hiroshima"; also Jim Garrison, *The Darkness of God: Theology after Hiroshima*.

69. Ricoeur, *The Symbolism of Evil*, 236–37.

70. Max Weber provides support for this view in *The Sociology of Religion*, where he discusses the process by which "religious faith developed into an assertion of intellectual propositions which were products of ratiocination," and finds that the Pauline epistles, which played a key role in this development, were aimed at a "group of urban proselytes who were accustomed to meditating on the conditions of salvation and who were to some degree conversant with Jewish and Greek casuistry." Trans. Ephraim Fischoff, 192–93.

71. Claude Levi-Strauss, *Structural Anthropology*, trans. Claire Jacobson and Brooke Grundfest Schoepf, 229.

72. Peter Berger, *The Sacred Canopy: Elements of a Sociological Theory of Religion*, 53.

73. "[T]he more [religious] development tends toward the conception of a transcendental unitary god who is universal, the more there arises the problem of how the extraordinary power of such a god may be reconciled with the imperfection of the world that he has created and rules over." Weber, *The Sociology of Religion*, trans. Ephraim Fischoff, 139.

74. David Hume, *Dialogues Concerning Natural Religion*, part X, 66. Readers familiar with the literature on theodicy will recognize that there are many ways in which the problem can be stated. In the book *The Problem of Evil*, M. B. Ahern notes that the "problem of evil" is actually multiple, and divides the study of theodicy into three separate categories: (1) the general problem (as stated by Hume) of whether the existence of God is compatible with *any* evil; (2) the specific abstract problems of whether the existence of God is compatible with each *possible* specific kind of evil; (3) the specific concrete problems of whether the existence of God is compatible with each *actually occurring* instance of evil. In Ahern's terms, my analysis focuses on the general problem of evil (although I do touch upon the

specific versions of the problem, and would argue that the argument presented here has implications for these versions also); hence, I have chosen to ignore the traditional theological distinctions between "moral evil" and "natural evil." For a discussion of these distinctions, see John Hick, *Evil and the God of Love*, 12–13.

75. H. J. McCloskey, "God and Evil," in *God and Evil*, ed. Nelson Pike, 61.

76. Alvin Plantinga, *God and Other Minds*, 116; Nelson Pike, "Hume on Evil," in *God and Evil*, 85–102.

77. Toulmin, *The Uses of Argument*, 98–100.

78. Pike, "Hume on Evil," 88.

79. For discussion of this point, see Robert Richman, "The Argument from Evil," and Douglas Langston, "The Argument from Evil: Reply to Professor Richman."

80. C. S. Lewis, *God in the Dock: Essays on Theology and Ethics*. Also see Richman, "The Argument from Evil," for an explicit invocation of the trial analogy:

> Suppose that someone has killed a fellow human being. He is not to be absolved of moral (or legal) guilt simply on the ground that there may be sufficient excusing conditions for his act, or on the ground that his mother (or his attorney) claim that there *must* be such conditions. Of course, we must survey the standard excusing conditions for homicide, and see whether one of them, or some other special circumstance, is operative in the given case. If no sufficient excusing condition can be specified, then the claim that the killing is not blameworthy is simply unwarranted. Of course, this procedure does not *prove* that a sufficient excusing condition does not exist. But this is unimportant, since supplying such a proof would be a logical impossibility. The point . . . is that if we are to avoid moral scepticism, the burden of proof must be on the defender of one who has committed or permitted a morally reprehensible act to specify the morally sufficient reasons for the act. . . . If there is . . . [a God], he is *prima facie* blameworthy for permitting . . . evil. We may grant the possibility of there being morally sufficient reasons for his doing so. But the burden of proof is on the theist to tell us what these reasons are. (209–10)

Richman acknowledges the impossibility of proving Pike's proposition but still argues, by a forensic analogy, for the moral culpability of the creator until a successful defense / theodicy has been offered. He thus ignores the question of what it would take to establish sufficiency; while standard excusing conditions for homicide may be available in the courtroom, we have no such standard excuses for creating a universe containing evil! Or, rather, the standard excuses are generally found insufficient by philosophers. Richman presumably would reject mythic narrative as a solution to the problem, as Hume does in the argument cited below.

81. Cicero, *De Inventione* I.8.10, trans. H. M. Hubbell, 21–23.

82. Jeanne R. Fahnestock and Marie J. Secor, "Grounds for Argument: Stasis Theory and the Topoi," 135–46, 137. These authors note that rhetorical theorists have offered differing accounts of the number of stases and their specific designations. For example, the fourth stasis of jurisdiction was abandoned by Cicero in his later works because of its inapplicability in Roman legal procedure (138). In addition to their utility for the analysis and invention of forensic argument, the questions of stasis theory have also been developed by some scholars into stock issues for the analysis of policy propositions. Susan Kline's essay "Toward a Contemporary Linguistic Interpretation of the Concept of Stasis" provides some support for these efforts to utilize the stases for the understanding of everyday argument in

an essay that grounds stasis theory in the communicative philosophies of Austin, Searle, and Habermas.

83. On the hierarchical organization of stasis questions, see Fahnestock and Secor, "Grounds for Argument: Stasis Theory and the Topoi," 138. These authors give the Abscam case as an example:

> The first collision of charge and denial occurred at the stasis of fact: "You took the money" / "I did not take the money." Here the preponderance of evidence in the form of video tapes moved the issue to the stasis of definition: "You took a bribe" / 'I took evidence for my investigation." As the bargaining proceeded, the defendants lost this issue, so ground was shifted to the third stasis of quality where we can characterize the prosecution as maintaining: "You deserve censure for an act particularly reprehensible in a public official," and the defense mitigating this evaluation of the crime by answering: "I do not deserve such severe censure because I did not do what those who bribed me asked me to do." The final plea in the fourth stasis turns to the nature of the legal case itself and the jurisdiction of the court, the prosecution maintaining the propriety of the investigation and indictment, the defense claiming entrapment and appealing judgment to a higher court. Whether or not the investigation constituted entrapment is, of course, a question that takes us down to the stasis of definition again, and the two sides will continue to chase each other up and down the stases and in and out of the courts until the appeal process is exhausted. (139)

84. See Mary Baker Eddy, *Science and Health with Key to the Scriptures*, 205, 71, 480.

85. *The City of God*, trans. Henry Bettenson, 473. Another version of this argument appears in book VII, ch. 12, of Augustine's *Confessions*: "We must conclude that if things are deprived of all good, they cease altogether to be; and this means that as long as they are, they are good. Therefore, whatever is, is good; and evil, the origin of which I was trying to find, is not a substance, because if it were a substance, it would be good. . . . For you [God] evil does not exist, and not only for you but for the whole of your creation as well." *Confessions*, trans. R. S. Pine-Coffin, 148. Those seeking more detailed treatment of Augustine's theodicy may consult G. R. Evans, *Augustine on Evil*.

86. Kenneth Burke, *The Rhetoric of Religion*, 86–93.

87. *Confessions* VII.3, trans. R. S. Pine-Coffin, 136.

88. Alvin Plantinga, "The Free Will Defence," 106.

89. The free will defense has been subjected to rigorous attack on this point by Mackie, Flew, and others. I shall not attempt to review these arguments here, since to do so would take this essay far afield into a discussion of human freedom and divine omnipotence. Those wishing to pursue this line of inquiry will find extensive references and an overview of the arguments in the final chapter of Hick's *Evil and the God of Love*.

90. Hick, *Evil and the God of Love*, 350, 363–64.

91. Kant, "On the Failure of All Attempted Philosophical Theodicies," trans. Michel Despland, in Despland, *Kant on History and Religion*, 283.

92. Stanley Hauerwas and David Burrell, "From System to Story: An Alternative Pattern for Rationality in Ethics," in Stanley Hauerwas, *Truthfulness and Tragedy: An Alternative Pattern for Rationality in Ethics*, 32. I disagree with Hauerwas and Burrell's

implication that narrative is not an explanation; I would say that narrative offers an explanation of a different order.

93. Irenaeus, *Against Heresies*, trans. Alexander Roberts and James Donaldson, in *The Ante-Nicene Fathers*, vol. I, 561.

94. By coherence I mean narrative probability, the perception that a story "hangs together," in the specific sense of its "argumentative or structural coherence" (Fisher, *Human Communication as Narration*, 47).

95. Pat Robertson, quoted in William Martin, "Waiting for the End," 34.

96. David Hume, *Dialogues Concerning Natural Religion*, 67–68.

97. Fyodor Dostoevsky, "Rebellion," from *The Brothers Karamazov*, trans. Constance Garnett, 226–27.

98. Antony Flew, *God: A Critical Enquiry*, 49.

99. Walter R. Fisher, *Human Communication as Narration: Toward a Philosophy of Reason, Value, and Action*, 62–64; Alasdair MacIntyre, *After Virtue: A Study in Moral Theory*, 144–45, 216.

100. Max Weber, *The Sociology of Religion*, trans. Ephraim Fischoff, 139–40, 112–15.

101. Donald Wilcox, *The Measure of Times Past: Pre-Newtonian Chronologies and the Rhetoric of Relative Time*, especially 12–13.

102. Wilcox, *The Measure of Times Past*, 4.

103. David Landes, *Revolution in Time: Clocks and the Making of the Modern World*, 33.

104. See *Encyclopaedia Britannica*, 1985 ed., s.v. *Calendar*.

105. Campbell, "A Rhetorical Interpretation of History," 229.

106. See Hans Blumenberg, *The Legitimacy of the Modern Age*, trans. Robert M. Wallace, 467.

107. Campbell, "A Rhetorical Interpretation of History," 235–36.

108. Eliade, *Myth and Reality*, 54–76; *The Myth of the Eternal Return*, 112–37. For the significance of this attitude toward history see especially 118–19.

109. As Blumenberg notes, the significant innovation of modern scientific rationalism and its progressive view of history is that it reversed this traditional assumption of myth. Attacking Karl Lowith's thesis (as proposed in *Meaning in History*) that the idea of progress is but a secularized version of Christian eschatology, Blumenberg argues in *The Legitimacy of the Modern Age* for an understanding of the idea of progress as essentially autonomous, bearing a resemblance to earlier eschatological doctrines not through an identity of substance but from the fact that successive epochal symbolisms must "reoccupy the territory" of those that precede them (37–50, particularly page 46). "The constancy of language [from Christianity to the modern, 'progressive' epoch] is an index of a constant function for consciousness but not of an identity of content" (87).

110. Blumenberg, *The Legitimacy of the Modern Age*, 468. Though I find this argument to be correct in its essentials, I take this opportunity to specify that Blumenberg's account fails to grasp the earthly nature of millennial expectation, that is, its emphasis on the restoration of the material world and the tangible enjoyments by the elect of the benefits of the kingdom (as in the passage from Irenaeus cited above). Though the ultimate result is the same, the negation of history, the question is whether this negation is accomplished by the symbolic routes of devaluation or of perfection; that is, whether history is to be seen only as being overturned by divine action, or as (to some degree) sanctified through its status

as the scene within which divine action takes place. The concept of a millennial or messianic reign *on earth* appears to preserve some value in the historical process, even though this reign is itself understood as the final End, or telos, of history.

111. Yonina Talmon, "Millenarism," in *International Encyclopedia of the Social Sciences*, ed. D. L. Sills, 349–62, 362.

112. M. Werner, in *The Formation of Christian Dogma*, argues that the delay of Christ's return was the central problem of the early church. See also Albert Schweitzer, *The Quest of the Historical Jesus*.

113. The phrase "realized eschatology" is taken from C. H. Dodd, who argued this thesis in his 1938 book *History and the Gospel*. For a concise explanation of Dodd's notion, see the entries for Dodd and "Eschatology" in *The Oxford Dictionary of the Christian Church*, ed. Frank L. Cross, 410, 462.

114. Bruce J. Malina, "Christ and Time: Swiss or Mediterranean?" 5. The principal target of this essay is Oscar Cullmann's *Christ and Time: The Primitive Christian Conception of Time and History*, trans. Floyd Filson, which argues that "Revelation and salvation take place along the course of an ascending time line. Here the strictly straight line conception of time in the NT must be defined as over against the Greek cyclical conception" (32). In Cullmann's view, this linear conception implies a developed future consciousness. Against this position, Malina claims that "There surely is no expressed concern for the future in the Synoptic story line. And it would appear that the same holds for the entire N[ew] T[estament] since any time description consisting of this age and a rather proximate age to come has no room for a future *of the sort we speak of*" [emphasis added]. Here he seems to be guilty of the very offense for which he indicts Cullmann, in that he argues that New Testament texts lack consciousness of a future when what he really means is that they lack a *modern American consciousness* of a future—a point I will readily concede. Ultimately, however, Cullmann and Malina both attempt to minimize the significance of future expectation and emphasize the importance of Christ's incarnation and resurrection as the decisive events of salvation history (see Cullman's *Christ and Time*, 88–90).

115. Malina, "Christ and Time," 13.

116. Malina, "Christ and Time," 10 (emphasis added).

117. See especially Aristotle's discussion of the temporal orientations of forensic, deliberative, and epideictic rhetoric in *Rhetoric* I.3. For a discussion of the ubiquity of rhetorical education in the Hellenized Near East during the period in question, see James L. Kinneavy, *Greek Rhetorical Origins of Christian Faith*, 80–91; also George Kennedy, *New Testament Interpretation through Rhetorical Criticism*, 8–10. I do not claim that Greek philosophical ideas about time were identical to those of the earliest Christians, but simply that the diffusion of these ideas was widespread. The influence of Greek philosophical categories on early Christian doctrine is especially evident in John's gospel, where the philosophic principle of the Logos is adapted for Christian purposes.

118. Malina, "Christ and Time," 9.

119. Among the key texts that Malina gives little or no attention are the entire Apocalypse, the second letter of Peter, and Paul's second Thessalonian letter. 2 Peter 3:3–5 gives evidence of a strategy of inoculation against the ridicule to which the early Christians were subjected due to the failure of their public predictions of Christ's return: "First of all you must understand this, that scoffers will come in the last days with scoffing, following their own passions and saying, 'Where is the promise of his coming? For ever since the fathers fell asleep, all things have continued as they were since the beginning of creation.'" As I

will show in subsequent chapters, this text has historically served as an argumentative resource for apocalyptic sects by transforming the taunts of opponents into further evidence for the proximity of the End. In 2 Thessalonians 2:1–3, Paul cautions against apocalyptic excitement in terms that make clear that the expectation of a future, imminent End was widespread in the community and shared by Paul himself: "Now concerning the coming of our Lord Jesus Christ and our assembling to meet him, we beg you, brethren, not to be quickly shaken in mind or excited, either by spirit or by word, or by letter purporting to be from us, to the effect that the day of the Lord has come. Let no one deceive you in any way; for that day will not come, unless the rebellion comes first, and the man of lawlessness is revealed." For a study presenting considerable evidence of future-oriented apocalypticism among the Thessalonian community and a cogent rhetorical analysis of the Pauline letters, see Robert Jewett, *The Thessalonian Correspondence*.

120. Malina, "Christ and Time: Swiss or Mediterranean?" 15. In like fashion, Malina interprets Jesus' statements in the New Testament that "Tomorrow will be anxious for itself," and "Let the day's own trouble be sufficient for the day" (Mt. 6:34) as already embodying social knowledge propositions of Mediterrenean society (p. 6), an interpretation that would rob these sayings of any novelty and remove altogether the point of their articulation.

121. See the discussion of Augustine in chapter 3 of this study.

122. Donald Wilcox is somewhat more generous than Malina in his assessment of the awareness of chronology in the Mediterranean world of late antiquity in *The Measure of Times Past* (see especially chapter 4, "The Time of the Œcumene"). Whereas Malina argues that Mediterranean "peasants" (a term that he seems to apply indiscriminately to all early Christians) did not calculate in linear chronological sequences because they lacked the "modern" conceptual categories that would have enabled them to do so, Wilcox claims that Hellenic historians did not use such calculations because they were more concerned with thematic unity, which "did not demand that events be represented as part of a strict chronological series" (118). In essence, however, Wilcox is close to Malina's position in that he generally regards ancient chronologies as founded on an unsophisticated notion of episodic, relative time. Extensive evidence of chronological sophistication among Christian authors of the patristic period, from the second century CE onward, is presented in Richard Landes, "Lest the Millennium Be Fulfilled." Such sophistication cannot of course be attributed to the temporal conceptions of Jesus and the first generation of disciples, but it seems unlikely that a developed sense of chronology could have arisen so quickly if the early Christians were as bound to a present orientation as Malina claims.

123. Landes, "Lest the Millennium Be Fulfilled," 142, n. 17.

124. Quoted in Landes, "Lest the Millennium Be Fulfilled," 141–42.

125. Landes, "Lest the Millennium Be Fulfilled," 142.

126. Quoted in Landes, "Lest the Millennium Be Fulfilled," 145. Such precise calculations apparently contradict Malina's thesis that abstract calendrical time did not exist for Mediterranean societies. Malina dismisses the significance of the concept of the millennial or "world week," along with the Greek philosophical conception fo the "Great Year" (a cosmic cycle of 36,000 solar years), first by claiming that each of these conceptions "is rooted in process focused on the present," then by arguing that "both the Great Year and the World Week were based on the sort of abstract speculation and mathematical demonstration which present-oriented . . . traditional people found as unreal as a dream" ("Christ and Time," 13, n. 25). There seems to be a marked inconsistency here: whereas Malina initially claims that abstract speculation and mathematical demonstrations of temporal conceptions were "social

inventions and skills that *did not exist*" (10, emphasis added) at that time, he later concedes that these existed but *had no reality* for these ancient societies, since the products of such speculation "belonged to the imaginary realm of possibilities" (13). To this argument, I respond that though such speculations are indeed imaginary, their influence on human beings is no less real for that.

127. Landes, "Lest the Millennium Be Fulfilled," 146.

128. Lactantius, *Divine Institutes* VII. 14, trans. Bernard McGinn, in *Apocalyptic Spirituality*, ed. McGinn, 55.

129. *Divine Institutes* VII. 25, in *Apocalyptic Spirituality*, ed. McGinn, 76.

130. Landes, "Lest the Millennium Be Fulfilled," 148.

131. See note 105, above.

132. The adoption of this figure as the basis of an open-ended chronology moved Western historiography closer to the absolute time line of Newtonian science. This did not mean, however, that years calculated in Annus Domini could not be given apocalyptic significance by skillful exegetes. Among the numerous dates proposed for the End of the world after the adoption of A.D. chronology were the years 1000 and 1260. See Henri Focillon, *The Year 1000*; McGinn, *Visions of the End*, 89–90, 160–61. Focillon's account of the "terrors" that attended the passing of the first millennium of Christianity has been accepted by many journalistic writers but rejected by most historians. For a persuasive argument against the received historian's account, and in favor of the apocalyptic significance accorded to the year 1000, see Richard Landes, "The Terrible Hopes of the Millennium: Europe and the Year 1000."

133. Landes, "Lest the Millennium Be Fulfilled," 141.

134. Wilcox notes in passing the significance of apocalypticism as a contextual factor in chronological calculation (129–30, 138–39), but fails to pursue the point or to realize the inherent dangers of chronological calculation from the viewpoint of church authorities anxious to suppress apocalyptic excitement.

135. For example, Wilcox claims that "Augustine's interest in the temporal order of events required no absolute dating system; the generational one sufficed for his purposes . . . since it was closer to the personal reality that gave time meaning" (*The Measure of Times Past*, 128). As Landes notes, however, the temporal categories that Augustine employs in the *The City of God* can only be understood in the context of that book's polemical purpose: "Augustine's remarks . . . clearly addressed a lively and highly informed audience of eschatological computists" ("Lest the Millennium Be Fulfilled," 156; see chapter 3 of this study for further discussion of Augustine's anti-apocalyptic polemic). Similarly, in his discussion of the medieval historian Gregory of Tours, Wilcox identifies a supposed error in Gregory's calculation of the age of the world and observes that, given this error, "neither the copyist [of the maunuscript] nor his subsequent readers could have thought the actual linear sequence of great importance" (139). In fact, as Landes shows (170, n. 134) Gregory's calculation is correct, and the "error" is a product of misreading by modern historians. Landes cites a manuscript from Cologne, circa 798–799, which places the history of the author's present on the time line of Annus Mundi and betrays exactly the concern with linear sequence that Wilcox denies: "From the beginning of the world until this thirty-first year of the reign of Charles the King—the same year in which he received a third of the population of Saxony as guests [hostages], and in which messengers from Greece came to offer him the imperium— there are 5998 years according to the Hebrew verity transmitted by Jerome . . . and from the incarnation of the Lord there are 798 years. And whomever this does not please, let him

sweat and read and calculate it better" (trans. Landes, 189). In the context of the still-prevalent theory of the millennial World Week, the year 5998 had obvious apocalyptic overtones; the author challenges those displeased by the implication that the End was near to exert the same effort and come up with an alternate calculation.

136. Wilcox, *The Measure of Times Past*, 138.

137. Liddell and Scott, *A Greek-English Lexicon*, s.v. *epoché*. Blumenberg draws attention to this etymology in *The Legitimacy of the Modern Age*, 258, 459.

138. For an extended study that examines the human tendency to order time into symbolic patterns that encourage the numerological logic of the countdown, see Hillel Schwartz, *Century's End*.

139. See reference to Max Weber in note 70 above for a discussion of the level of ratiocination in the Pauline letters as a response to the demands of an educated urban audience accustomed to "casuistry" in the Jewish and Hellenic traditions of cosmological speculation. Also see Acts 17:18–34 for a dramatic narrative of Paul arguing for the Christian religion among the philosophical schools of Athens.

140. The division of authority into legal, traditional, and charismatic types can be found at various places in Weber's sociology. I quote here from the essay "Politics as a Vocation," translated by H. H. Gerth and C. Wright Mills, 78–79.

141. For a discussion of the use of the term *charisma* in sociological, historical, and religious studies since Weber, I refer the reader to Charles F. Keyes, "Charisma: From Social Life to Sacred Biography." Among the types of charisma discussed by Keyes are the charisma of office and the charisma of gnosis or secret knowledge. The problem of charismatic authority is examined at some length in pages 8–13.

142. Richard Weaver provides support for the view that charisma is not a quality that inheres in a leader or in a text, but is generated by the "common consent" of the audience (*Language Is Sermonic*, 106). To consider charisma as an intrinsic property of either the prophet or the prophetic text would implicitly be to propose criteria for the acceptance or rejection of individual revelations as authentic. For an excellent study employing the dialogic theory of Mikhail Bakhtin to illuminate the social construction of prophetic authority, see Margaret D. Zulick, "The Agon of Jeremiah: On the Dialogic Invention of Prophetic Ethos."

143. In support of this claim I refer the reader to Walter R. Fisher's essay "Toward a Logic of Good Reasons." Fisher argues that "any evaluative system is circular," since "Evaluation inherently involves tautology" (377). Charisma is not only an analytic and descriptive term, but an evaluative term akin to Robert Pirsig's "Quality" (see *Zen and the Art of Motorcycle Maintenance*), which eludes precise definition, or which can only be defined in circular fashion. This is so because what constitutes charisma is precisely the quality of being able to move an audience, so that the presence of this quality in a prophet or textually embodied prophecy can only be determined through an audience's recognition of charisma as it allows itself to be moved. In the same fashion, Pirsig argues that attempts to define Quality must ultimately reduce to some vague statement such as, You know it when you see it (201, 203).

144. Campbell, "A Rhetorical Interpretation of History," 251. The universal audience has been debated by rhetorical scholars since it was first introduced as a construct in rhetorical theory by Chaim Perelman and L. Olbrechts-Tyteca in *The New Rhetoric*. So far as I am aware, Campbell is the only scholar explicitly to pursue Perelman's suggestive linking of the theory of the universal audience to the Judeo-Christian notion of a deity that is both universal and personal. This link is implicitly reinforced by Ray's comparison of Perelman's term with

Kant's categorical imperative and Rousseau's general will, and by Scult's attempt to make the universal audience serve the function of a ground for rhetorical ethics. All of these formulations may be viewed as attempts to rationalize a basis for ethics that serves a "transcendent" purpose formerly accomplished by religion. See John W. Ray, "Perelman's Universal Audience"; Allen Scult, "Perelman's Universal Audience: One Perspective," and also "A Note on the Range and Utility of the Universal Audience." Campbell specifically disavows any metaphysical pretensions that might be read into the link he identifies between Perelman's theory and the epochal insight of Judeo-Christian culture: " 'Universal audience' . . . is a term I use in an empirical and historical sense. By the term I mean that a mode of symbolization embodying a universal standpoint actually emerged in history. I am making no metaphysical claim about an 'audience' that 'exists' as an entity apart from the symbols which articulate it" (253).

145. This formulation is actually Edwin Black's interpretation of Aristotle. See the fourth chapter of *Rhetorical Criticism: A Study in Method.*

146. See Campbell, "A Rhetorical Interpretation of History," 256: "[A] full disclosure of the universal audience never occurs in human experience. Nor in principle can it. History can only move within its constitutive symbols and the symbols which constitute it reveal it to be an in-between."

147. In the case of Revelation, the debate over its inclusion in the canon of Scripture raged as late as the fifth century CE. See McGinn, *Visions of the End*, 12; also J. N. D. Kelly, *Early Christian Doctrines*, 479. For discussion of the *Epistle of Barnabas* and other noncanonical texts, see Landes, "Lest the Millennium Be Fulfilled."

148. The classic study of revolutionary popular apocalypticism in the medieval era is Norman Cohn's *The Pursuit of the Millennium* (see chapter 1 for a brief discussion of Cohn's argument).

149. Quoted in Phyllis Bird, *The Bible as the Church's Book*, 44. Those interested in the impact of the Reformation on shifting conceptions of the authority of Scripture and the role of interpretation may consult Robert Grant and David Tracy, *A Short History of the Interpretation of the Bible*; see also J. K. S. Reid, *The Authority of Scripture.*

150. For a discussion of the dangers of subjectivism in biblical interpretation, see Reid, *The Authority of Scripture*, 80–81, 96–102.

151. On typology as a method of interpretation and as a strategy of argument, see Ronald Reid, "Apocalypticism and Typology"; also Sacvan Bercovitch, ed., *Typology and Early American Literature.* For an evangelical discussion of typological interpretation, see Patrick Fairbairn, *The Typology of Scripture.*

152. Bernard McGinn has examined the earliest roots and some later flowerings of this legend in *Visions of the End* and elsewhere: as this book goes to press, I eagerly await McGinn's forthcoming *Antichrist through the Ages.* For more detailed discussion of the origins and complex political uses of these traditions, see McGinn, "Angel Pope and Papal Antichrist." For extensive evidence of the complete dominance of the papal Antichrist legend (even to the point of declaring the identification an article of faith) in post-Reformation England, and of its influence on Puritan thinkers in America, see Christopher Hill, *Antichrist in Seventeenth-Century England.*

153. See Robin Bruce Barnes, *Prophecy and Gnosis: Apocalypticism in the Wake of the German Reformation.*

154. See McGinn, *Visions of the End*, 70–76, 84.

155. See McGinn, *Visions of the End*, 88–93.

156. See the twelfth-century *Play of Antichrist,* trans. J. Wright, for a dramatic representation of the Last Emperor legend that includes a scathing attack on the papacy. McGinn notes that this play "appears to have been composed about 1160 at the court of Frederick [Barbarossa]" (*Visions of the End,* 117–21). The clash of apocalyptic traditions is even more vivid in a set of popular prophecies current in the mid-thirteenth century, in which the pope and Emperor Frederick II are depicted as hurling apocalyptic prophecies against each other (quoted in *Visions of the End,* 170):

The Emperor to the Pope:

> The fates warn, the stars teach, and so do the flights of birds
> That I will soon be the hammer of the world.
> Rome, a long time wavering, having committed various errors,
> Will collapse and cease to be the capital of the world.

The Pope to the Emperor:

> Yor reputation relates, Scripture teaches, and your sins announce
> That you will have a short life and eternal punishment.

157. *Visions of the End,* 186–87, 187.

158. For a thoughtful analysis of the development and radical anti-authoritarian uses of apocalyptic traditions from the late medieval era through the Reformation, see Barnes, *Prophecy and Gnosis,* 24–44 and passim.

159. A brief but useful discussion of the influence of the Last Emperor legend and other apocalyptic traditions on European literature and culture can be found in Frank Kermode, "Apocalypse and the Modern," 88–93.

160. On scriptural hermeneutics in the Middle Ages, see Grant and Tracy, A *Short History of the Interpretation of the Bible,* 85–87.

161. This account is based in part on Hans Frei, *The Eclipse of Biblical Narrative,* 26–30, 37. For another discussion of the connection between the Reformation and literal-historical interpretations of the Bible, see Barnes, *Prophecy and Gnosis,* 30–59.

162. The impact of Enlightenment rationalism upon doctrines of scriptural interpretation, and in particular upon apocalypticism, is documented in Theodore Dwight Bozeman, *Protestants in an Age of Science: The Baconian Ideal and Antebellum American Religious Thought,* 119–24, 144–59; see also Jack B. Rogers and Donald K. McKim, *The Authority and Interpretation of the Bible: An Historical Approach,* 200–369. As Bozeman notes, the nineteenth-century synthesis of theology and Enlightenment rationality was a precarious one, founded not in Lockean empiricism but in Francis Bacon's inductive scientific method. In this regard, it is worth noting that some historians have claimed that Bacon's program for the advancement of learning was itself influenced by apocalyptic beliefs and expectations (see Barnes, *Prophecy and Gnosis,* 26–28).

163. Charles Hodge, *Systematic Theology* (1874), quoted in Timothy Weber, "The Two-Edged Sword: The Fundamentalist Use of the Bible," 106.

164. Quoted in George Marsden, "Everyone One's Own Interpreter? The Bible, Science, and Authority in Mid-Nineteenth-Century America," 90.

165. Marsden, "Everyone One's Own Interpreter?," 90–95; Timothy Weber, "The Two-Edged Sword," 105–10, 115.

166. See Bozeman, *Protestants in an Age of Science,* for a discussion of the ways in

which Protestant theologians used evidence from the natural sciences, especially geology, to prove the literal truth of scriptural prophecies (119–24).

CHAPTER 3

1. McGinn, *Visions of the End*, 3, 5.

2. For a recent contribution to this dialogue, see Robert C. Rowland's "On Mythic Criticism," and the accompanying replies to Rowland's critique by Martha Solomon, Michael Osborn, Barry Brummett, and Janice Hocker Rushing.

3. For an account of these debates, see Ernst Cassirer, *The Myth of the State*, especially ch. 3; also Lawrence J. Hatab, *Myth and Philosophy: A Contest of Truths*.

4. Han Blumenberg, *Work on Myth*, trans. Robert M. Wallace, 27.

5. Translator's footnote, *Work on Myth*, 112.

6. For discussion of the pre-Christian elements in the mythic narrative of Revelation, see Adela Yarbro Collins, *The Combat Myth in the Book of Revelation*. For a discussion of the way in which the symbols of Revelation revise and synthesize elements of the Danielic apocalypse, see John Gager, *Kingdom and Community: The Social World of Early Christianity*, 51–54.

7. Blumenberg, *Work on Myth*, 118.

8. Northrop Frye, *The Anatomy of Criticism*, 141.

9. For a summary of attempts by biblical scholars to determine the text's literary unity and integrity, see Bernard McGinn's essay "Revelation," in *The Literary Guide to the Bible*, ed. Robert Alter and Frank Kermode, 523–41, especially 524–25. An extended analysis of the internal symbolism and formal construction of the text may be found in Austin Farrer's *A Rebirth of Images: The Making of St John's Apocalypse*. I have chosen here to focus on apocalyptic interpretation rather than the text of the Apocalypse itself. Those seeking a thorough analysis of Revelation in its social and political matrix by a New Testament scholar trained in rhetorical criticism should consult Elisabeth Schüssler Fiorenza's *Revelation: Vision of a Just World*.

10. M. H. Pope, "Seven, Seventh, Seventy," in *The Interpreter's Dictionary of the Bible*, vol. 4, ed. George Arthur Buttrick, 294–95. On the significance of the patterns of seven in the Apocalypse, see Farrer, *A Rebirth of Images*, 36–90; also Bernard McGinn, "Revelation," 525.

11. Elisabeth Schüssler Fiorenza, *The Book of Revelation: Justice and Judgment*, 166.

12. See John Wick Bowman, "The Revelation to John: Its Dramatic Structure and Message."

13. See Gager, *Kingdom and Community*, 56; also Adela Yarbro Collins, *Crisis and Catharsis: The Power of the Apocalypse*, 144. For an extended analysis of the Apocalypse that considers its oral presentation as essential to an understanding of the text, see David L. Barr, "The Apocalypse of John as Oral Enactment."

14. Collins, *Crisis and Catharsis*, 152–53.

15. Aristotle, *Poetics* 1453a 10–35, trans. Ingram Bywater, in *The Basic Works of Aristotle*, ed. Richard McKeon, 1467.

16. Northrop Frye, *Anatomy of Criticism*, 185.

17. John Dominic Crossan, *Raid on the Articulate: Comic Eschatology in Jesus and Borges*, 22.

18. Critics who seek to apply theories of tragedy and comedy to the various texts of the Christian canon quickly find that these texts weave tragic and comic themes into a complex pattern that defies easy classification. While the tragic theme of predestined suffering and sacrifice may appear to dominate, many scholars have found a contrapuntal comic rhythm in Christian historical narrative. Wylie Sypher, for example, concludes that "the drama of the [Christian] struggle, death and rising—Gethsemane, Calvary, and Easter—actually belongs in the comic rather than the tragic domain." See Wylie Sypher, *Comedy*, 220; Northrop Frye, *Anatomy of Criticism*, 185 and passim; and M. Conrad Hyers, *The Comic Vision and the Christian Faith*, 156–57.

19. Kenneth Burke, *Attitudes toward History*, 3.

20. Susanne K. Langer, *Feeling and Form*, 326.

21. Kenneth Burke, "Myth, Poetry, and Philosophy," in *Language as Symbolic Action*, 398.

22. Hugh Dalziel Duncan, *Communication and Social Order*, 403.

23. Langer, *Feeling and Form*, 352.

24. Burke, *The Rhetoric of Religion*, 4.

25. Langer, *Feeling and Form*, 358.

26. Langer, *Feeling and Form*, 331.

27. Langer, *Feeling and Form*, 351.

28. See Bowman, "The Revelation to John: Its Dramatic Structure and Message."

29. Quoted in Crossan, *Raid on the Articulate*, 16–17. Crossan's concept of "comic eschatology" anticipates many of the insights of this study. Other precedents for the application of tragedy and comedy to biblical texts can be found in Dan Otto Via, *The Parables: Their Literary and Existential Dimension*, 96–176; and J. Cheryl Exum, ed., *Tragedy and Comedy in the Bible*. In this volume, see in particular Edwin M. Good, "Apocalyptic as Comedy: The Book of Daniel." These authors provide valuable insight into dramatic aspects of Biblical texts, and into eschatological dimensions of the parables and Jesus' discourse as presented in the gospels, but do not discuss the text of Revelation.

30. Gager, *Kingdom and Community*, 55.

31. Gager, *Kingdom and Community*, 52.

32. Elizabeth Schüssler Fiorenza, *The Book of Revelation: Justice and Judgment*, 168.

33. See David Barr, "The Apocalypse of John as Oral Enactment." Barr argues, "As an enacted story the Apocalypse has the power to bring into existence that reality which it portrays, to transform the finite province of meaning into the paramount reality of those who worship. It becomes a charter story that establishes a new world in which God triumphs over evil through the death of Jesus and the suffering of his followers. Because the Kingdom of God *is* his true worship, the very enactment of the Apocalypse establishes that Kingdom in this world" (256).

34. For accounts of such disputes in American theology during the colonial era, see James West Davidson, *The Logic of Millennial Thought*.

35. A good introduction to the teachings of Origen and his followers can be found in J. N. D. Kelly, *Early Christian Doctrines*, rev. ed. (San Francisco: Harper & Row, 1978), 68–74. For discussion of the Alexandrian school's impact on apocalyptic interpretation, see McGinn, *Visions of the End*, 25–27.

36. *Visions of the End*, 27, 103. Tyconius' work is unfortunately lost to us; however, it exerted a powerful influence on the scriptural hermeneutics of Augustine and many other theologians of the late patristic and medieval periods.

37. Augustine, *The City of God* 18.53.838.

38. Augustine, *The City of God* 20.1.896.

39. Augustine, *The City of God* 20.2.896.

40. Augustine, *The City of God* 20.9.914.

41. Augustine, *The City of God* 20.9.915.

42. Augustine, *The City of God* 20.9.915.

43. Augustine, *The City of God* 20.17.929.

44. Augustine, "To Heysichius, On the End of the World" (Letter 199), in *Writings of Saint Augustine*, vol. 12, trans. Sister Wilfrid Parsons, 384.

45. The tension between the tragic and comic frames in Augustine's philosophy of history is illuminated in Augustine's discussion of original sin in *The City of God* 13.14: "[F]rom the misuse of free will there started a chain of disasters: mankind is led from that original perversion, a kind of corruption right at the root, right up to the disaster of the second death, which has no end. Only those who are set free through God's grace escape from this calamitous sequence" (523). The "second death" is a reference to Revelation 20:14, in which the dragon, the beast, and their servants are cast into the eternal lake of fire. The event of the Fall leads, by a predestined sequence, to this tragic judgment. For the recipients of grace, however, the chain of calamities is broken; history retains its tragic structure, but the substructure of the comic frame is available to the saints, who are freed by grace and no longer bound to the tragic fate.

46. Augustine, Letter 199 "To Heysichius,"in *Writings of Saint Augustine*, 387.

47. Kenneth Burke, "Psychology and Form," in *Counter-Statement*, 31.

48. Hal Lindsey with C. C. Carlson, *The Late Great Planet Earth*, 40.

49. This danger will not, of course, disappear when a less immediate date for the End is proposed; but once a movement or sect is formed, the apparent disconfirmation of prophecy can easily be rationalized. For discussion of the mechanisms of such group rationalization, see *When Prophecy Fails*, by Leon Festinger, Henry W. Riecken, and Stanley Schachter.

50. Edgar Whisenant, *88 Reasons Why the Rapture Will Be in 1988*, 3–5.

51. *The Late Great Planet Earth*, 43.

52. The best discussion of the Antichrist legend in the Middle Ages can be found in McGinn, *Visions of the End*. See also Wilhelm Bousset, *The Antichrist Legend*.

53. McGinn, *Visions of the End*, 175–76. The argument parallels that of an anonymous broadside from Chicago in the mid-1980s. Paul Boyer cites a number of identical attempts to calculate the numerical value of the names and titles of various historical figures (*When Time Shall Be No More*, 65, 276). Other recent variations on the papal Antichrist argument may be found in the pamphlets distributed around the United States by followers of the renegade and paranoid evangelist Tony Alamo: "The Pope's Secret," and "Did You Know That the Pope and Ronald Reagan Are a Couple of Antichrist Devils and They Are Selling Us All Down the Drain?"

54. See William M. Alnor, *Soothsayers of the Second Advent*, 19–27.

55. For an example of such a "comic jeremiad" see the inaugural speech to Pat Robertson's 1988 presidential campaign, which O'Leary and McFarland discuss at length in "The Political Use of Mythic Discourse."

56. J. Robert Cox, "The Die is Cast: Topical and Ontological Dimensions of the Locus of the Irreparable." Cox seems mainly concerned with the irreparable consequences of human choice, with that realm of decision making that seeks to avert catastrophe. The tragic apocalyptic vision looks forward to catastrophe as a given, and situates human choice within

a cosmological narrative, in which the conclusion is not affected by the individual's decision. An old American hymn from the shape-note tradition ("The Great Day," circa 1859), expresses this juxtaposition of tragic fatalism with individual choice: "I've a long time heard that there will be a judgment, / That there will be a judgment in that day. . . . / I've a long time heard that the sun will be darkened, . . . / I've a long time heard that the earth will be burning, . . . / O the earth will be burning in that day, / Oh! Sinner, where will you stand in that day?" (*The Original Sacred Harp*, 567).

57. The word "exclusively" indicates that the vocabulary of sacrifice can never be entirely purged from Christianity; but there is nevertheless a way in which its tragic sacrificial insight can be "comicalized" with an optimistic view of human nature. This line of argument would hold that Christ's sacrifice did indeed redeem humanity, but that our current state of sin and guilt is due to our ignorance of, or failure to see good reasons to accept, this sacrifice. Therefore, all we need do to redeem humanity from sin is to confront people with their ignorance and give them good reasons to accept salvation. This view necessarily rejects the strict predestination of Calvinist theology and moves toward what Jonathan Edwards denounced as Arminianism, the belief that all human beings have the freedom to choose salvation through the sacrifice of Christ. Such a comic, "liberal" interpretation is quite compatible with even the more fundamentalist versions of Christianity as they attempt to present their message through the agencies of modern media. I recall in particular an episode in which Ben Kingsley of *The 700 Club* urged the unconverted viewers of that television show to follow him in reciting a short confessional prayer—and then told the audience that, having recited the prayer, they were saved! Calvin and Edwards must certainly have been spinning in their graves.

58. James H. Moorhead, "The Erosion of Postmillennialism in American Religious Thought, 1865–1925."

59. Loraine Boettner, "Postmillennialism," in *The Meaning of the Millennium: Four Views*, ed. Robert G. Clouse, 125.

60. Jonathan Edwards' complex eschatology is well represented in *The Works of Jonathan Edwards*, vol. 5, *Apocalyptic Writings*, ed. Stephen J. Stein.

61. Eliphalet Nott, "A Sermon Preached before the General Assembly of the Presbyterian Church . . . May 19, 1806," quoted in Leroy Edwin Froom, *The Prophetic Faith of Our Fathers*, vol. 4, 89. Emphasis in original.

62. Quoted in J. F. Maclear, "The Republic and the Millennium," in *The Religion of the Republic*, ed. Elwyn A. Smith, 191.

63. Quoted in Paul E. Johnson, *A Shopkeeper's Millennium*, 109.

64. For a summary of these movements and their theological basis, see William G. McLoughlin, *Revivals, Awakenings, and Reform: An Essay on Religion and Social Change in America, 1607–1977*.

65. Shirley Jackson Case, *The Millennial Hope*, 229–30.

66. Even the most purely rational "proofs" of the end of the world, to the extent that they are believed and taken as fact, cannot fail to produce an emotional reaction; for such "information" is not neutral, but belongs to that class of facts that we cannot help being moved by (you have cancer, you are pregnant, a hurricane is coming, the missiles have left the silos). Such emotions are bound to increase as the event approaches, and though the predicted event itself may be spurious, the emotions aroused by anticipation are no less real for that.

67. Jacques Derrida, "Of an Apocalyptic Tone Recently Adopted in Philosophy," trans.

John Leavey, Jr., 84. The paradoxical purpose of Derrida's essay is to announce the apocalypse of apocalypticism; that is to say, the ultimate end of all programs and philosophies that purport to reveal the ultimate End, "the end of the end, the end of ends" (81). The irony of this position is not lost on Derrida, who announces: "I intended to analyze a genre rather than practice it, and even when I would practice it, to do so with this ironic kind [genre] of clause wherein I tried to show that this clause never belonged to the genre itself; nevertheless, . . . every language on the apocalypse is also apocalyptic and cannot be excluded from its object" (90). For further discussion of Derrida's ideas on apocalypse see chapter 8.

68. On contingency as a feature of rhetoric, see Thomas Farrell, "The Tradition of Rhetoric and the Philosophy of Communication," 167–70.

69. Randall A. Lake's essay "The Implied Arguer" provides a schema that may clarify this discussion of ritualistic argument. Lake proposes a continuum "between instrumental and consummatory acts, that is, acts that are means to other ends and acts that are ends in themselves, respectively. The former require an audience that must be convinced to take subsequent action to achieve the desired end-state, while the latter do not depend on such subsequent acts for their efficacy, and, therefore, could conceivably dispense with audiences altogether" (71). In Lake's terms, apocalyptic argument in the tragic mode tends to lose its "instrumental" character and move toward the "consummatory" pole of the rhetoric–ritual continuum.

70. A. Cheree Carlson, "Gandhi and the Comic Frame: 'Ad Bellum Purificandum.' "

71. Carlson, "Gandhi and the Comic Frame," 453.

72. For a discussion of the various conceptions of "freedom" in Western religious and philosophical speculation, and of their implications for the constitution of historical narratives, see Richard McKeon, "Freedom and History," in *Freedom and History and Other Essays*, ed. Zahava McKeon.

73. For further discussion of this issue, see chapter 7).

CHAPTER 4

1. H. Richard Niebuhr, *The Kingdom of God in America*, 105.

2. Ruth Alden Doan, "Millerism and Evangelical Culture," in *The Disappointed: Millerism and Millenarianism in the Nineteenth Century*, 121.

3. P. Gerard Damsteegt, *Foundations of the Seventh-Day Adventist Message and Mission*, 10.

4. The history of these movements is entertainingly told in Alice Felt Tyler's *Freedom's Ferment*.

5. Charles Finney, quoted in Paul E. Johnson, *A Shopkeeper's Millennium: Society and Revivals in Rochester, New York, 1815–1837*, 109.

6. Damsteegt, *Foundations*, 9.

7. William G. McLoughlin, *Revivals, Awakenings, and Reform: An Essay on Religion and Social Change in America, 1607–1977*, 123. Such ecstatic emotionalism was frowned upon by the mainstream churches. Lyman Beecher and some of his colleagues arranged to meet Finney in 1827 in an effort to persuade him to abandon these practices. Finney and his fellow revivalists agreed to discourage "audible groaning, boisterous shouting, fainting, and other convulsions," but refused to abandon the use of such techniques as the "anxious bench" and all-night prayer meetings. See McLoughlin, 124.

8. Charles Finney, cited in William G. McLoughlin, *Modern Revivalism: Charles Grandison Finney to Billy Graham*, 91.

9. Charles G. Finney, *Lectures on Revivals of Religion*.

10. Quoted in Johnson, *Shopkeeper's Millennium*, 110–11.

11. See Johnson, *Shopkeeper's Millennium*, 113–14. In 1832, Weld switched from the temperance cause to that of abolition, and went on to become one of the most active preachers for the antislavery movement.

12. For discussion of the role played by Weld and the Tappan family of philanthropists, see Whitney Cross, *The Burned-over District*, 217–19 and passim. Further evidence and more detailed discussion of the growth of the abolitionist movement and its relationship to revivalism can be found in John Hammond, *The Politics of Benevolence: Revival Religion and American Voting Behavior*.

13. See Damsteegt, *Foundations*, 12, and Cross, *The Burned-over District*, 258–61. Cross gives a brief though useful discussion of the bitter schism of 1837 in the Presbyterian church, caused by the ascendancy of "ultraists" (see note 15 below) in the national governing body. In this church, it was in part the revivalists' methods themselves that were at issue.

14. Cross, *The Burned-over District*, 224–25.

15. Cross uses the term "ultraism" to discuss the historical cycle of revivalism in *The Burned-over District*, pages 252–58. He defines ultraism as "the state of religious emotionalism immediately preceding heterodoxy" and describes it as "a combination of activities, personalities, and attitudes creating a condition of society which could foster experimental doctrines" (173).

16. Cross, *The Burned-over District*, 257.

17. Quoted in Hammond, *The Politics of Benevolence*, 102.

18. Bernard Weisberger, *They Gathered at the River: The Story of the Great Revivalists and Their Impact on Religion in America*, 150.

19. Cross, *The Burned-over District*, 271.

20. For example, the fortunes of the Tappan family, donors of substantial sums to temperance and antislavery societies, and whose donations supported Oberlin College (founded by Finney's wing of the revival movement), were nearly dissolved in the events of 1837. See Cross, *The Burned-over District*, 273.

21. *The Signs of the Times, or the Moral Meaning of our Present Commercial Difficulties, A Sermon Preached in St. Paul's Church, Philadelphia, Pennsylvania on Sunday Evening Nov. 17, 1839 by Rev. N. T. Bent, AM*, 19. This pamphlet, along with almost all of the original Millerite newspapers and periodicals quoted in this and the next chapter, may be located in the Orrin Roe Jenks Collection of Adventual Materials at Aurora University in Aurora, Illinois. I wish to reiterate my thanks to historian David T. Arthur, curator of the Jenks collection, for his assistance with these materials.

22. Jonathan Butler, "From Millerism to Seventh-day Adventism: 'Boundlessness to Consolidation,' " 51.

23. "We have no purpose to distract the churches with any new inventions, or to get ourselves a name by starting another sect among the followers of the Lamb. We . . . [do not] seek to demolish their organizations, nor build new ones of our own; but simply to express our convictions like Christians, with the reasons for entertaining them which have persuaded us to understand the word and promises . . . of our Lord." From the *Report of the General Conference of Christians Expecting the Advent of Our Lord Jesus Christ, Held in Boston Oct. 14, 1840*, 14–15. See note 36 below.

24. Ruth Alden Doan, *The Miller Heresy, Millennialism, and American Culture*, 21. Doan comes closer than any previous scholar to a rhetorical examination of the public controversy over Millerism.

25. William Milles, *Views of the Prophecies and Prophetic Chronology, Selected from Manuscripts of William Miller, with a Memoir of His Life*, 11–12.

26. Robert Gale, *The Urgent Voice: The Story of William Miller*, 37.

27. See David L. Rowe, *Thunder and Trumpets: Millerites and Dissenting Religion in Upstate New York, 1800–1850*, 17.

28. William Miller, *Evidences from Scripture and History of the Second Coming of Christ about the Year* A.D. *1843: Exhibited in a Course of Lectures*, 221–22.

29. Quoted in Froom, *Prophetic Faith*, 509.

30. Rowe, *Thunder and Trumpets*, 21.

31. Quoted Froom, *Prophetic Faith*, 501.

32. Anonymous letter to William Miller, quoted in Rowe, *Thunder and Trumpets*, 24.

33. For a complete list of Millerite newspapers and periodicals containing circulation figures and dates of publication, see Le Roy Edwin Froom, *The Prophetic Faith of Our Fathers*, vol. 4, 624–25.

34. Froom lists sixteen such conferences in *Prophetic Faith*, 555–59. The enumeration of twenty-six General Conferences is based on a list compiled by David T. Arthur (personal communication). Froom notes: "These General Conferences were the unifying, directing, driving force of the expanding Advent Movement, the crystallizing and authorizing bodies, and the source of the formal published 'Addresses to the Public,' presenting the united Millerite case before the World. Because of their . . . representative character, they therefore constitute the most authoritative declarations of the movement" (*Prophetic Faith*, 556). In addition to those listed as "General Conferences," Froom notes that over 120 local conferences were held between January 1842 and October 1844. Seven such local gatherings are noted in Canada; others were held as far west as Ohio, Indiana, and Michigan (557).

35. See Frances D. Nichol, *The Midnight Cry*, 81; also Clyde E. Hewitt, *Midnight and Morning*, 92–93.

36. Henry Dana Ward, "History and Doctrine of the Millennium," from the *Report of the General Conference of Christians Expecting the Advent of Our Lord Jesus Christ, Held in Boston Oct. 14, 1840*, 42. Although this pamphlet contains 174 pages, each of the manifestoes and lectures it contains is numbered separately. Hence, the page numbers given for the various citations from the "Report" (hereafter referred to as *Report . . . 1840*) do not reflect their actual sequence in the volume as published.

37. *Report . . . 1840*, 14–15.

38. See David T. Arthur, "Joshua V. Himes and the Cause of Adventism," in *The Disappointed*, ed. Numbers and Butler, 38, 42.

39. See Ronald Graybill, "The Abolitionist-Millerite Connection," in *The Disappointed*, ed. Numbers and Butler, 139–52. With the exception of Angelina Grimké Weld (whose involvement with Millerism after her marriage to Theodore Weld remained a private affair), all those named here were active in their public advocacy of Millerism.

40. See pages 9–12 of *Proceedings of the Second Session of the General Conference of Christians Expecting the Advent of Our Lord Jesus Christ, Held in Lowell, Ms. [Massachusetts], June 15, 16, 17, 1841* (Second Advent Tracts, no. 8). The copy of this document in the Jenks Collection of Adventual Materials at Aurora University is without a cover and gives no evidence of a publisher, but advertisements in other Millerite publications indicate

that it was, like the first *Report*, published by Joshua Himes from the Boston office of the *Signs of the Times* newspaper.

41. Joshua V. Himes, letter to William Miller, June 26, 1841; quoted in Nichol, *Midnight Cry*, 87. Emphasis in the original text.

42. Resolutions of the "Boston Second Advent Conference," reprinted in *Signs of the Times*, 1 June 1842, 69.

43. Damsteegt, *Foundations*, 37. Damsteegt does not quote the document in which this argument is advanced, but cites an editorial, 'Midnight Cry,' in *Signs of the Times*, 15 June 1842.

44. See Froom, *The Prophetic Faith of Our Fathers*, 448.

45. Cross, *Burned-over District*, 287. Other sources confirm this estimate. William Miller offers a calculation of the number of Adventist leaders and followers in his 1845 publication *Mr. Miller's Apology and Defence*: "I should think that about two hundred ministers embraced my views, in all the different parts of the United States and Canada; and that there have been about five hundred public lecturers. . . . In nearly a thousand places Advent congregations have been raised up, numbering, as near as I can estimate, some fifty thousand believers" (22). These figures are confirmed by modern historical scholarship. The most thorough recent attempt to calculate the numerical strength of Millerism is to be found in David L. Rowe, "Millerites: A Shadow Portrait," in *The Disappointed*, ed. Numbers and Butler, 1–16. Rowe argues that the size of the movement is impossible to calculate with any precision, since beliefs cannot be measured apart from public activity, while "many orthodox Christians accepted Miller's tenets and used millenarian-like rhetoric without ever joining the Adventist movement" (4). With this caveat, Rowe proceeds to extrapolate from textual sources by hypothesizing an average size of Millerite meetings and multiplying this average by the number of communities in which Millerite activity is known to have flourished. By these methods, he concludes that "the total number of Millerites would not have been under 25,000—and may well have approached [50,000]."

46. See note 28 above.

47. *Signs of the Times*, 9 November 1842, 61.

48. William Miller, *Mr. Miller's Apology and Defence*, 24. While this equivocal discussion was obviously composed with the benefit of hindsight, it nevertheless reflects a certain degree of hesitancy that characterized Miller's predictions—though not those of his followers—during the period of the movement's ascendancy.

49. Quoted in Rowe, *Thunder and Trumpets*, 121.

50. Quoted in Rowe, *Thunder and Trumpets*, 121.

51. Quoted in Damsteegt, *Foundations*, 37.

52. Charles Fitch, *Come Out of Her, My People: A Sermon*, 9. Emphasis in original text.

53. Charles Fitch, *Come Out of Her, My People*, 11, 14.

54. See Doan, *The Miller Heresy, Millennialism, and American Culture*, 124–25; also David T. Arthur, "Millerism," in *The Rise of Adventism: Religion and Society in Mid-Nineteenth Century America*, ed. Edwin W. Gaustad, 169–71.

55. For an account of the various attempts to explain the failure of prophecy, see Froom, *Prophetic Faith*, 797–809.

56. *The Advent Herald*, 21 August 1844, quoted in Froom, *Prophetic Faith*, 812.

57. Joseph Bates, 1847, quoted in Froom, *Prophetic Faith*, 812.

58. Editorial, *Advent Herald and Signs of the Times Reporter*, 30 October 1844, 93.

59. "Behold, the Bridegroom cometh!" Anonymous, *Advent Herald and Signs of the Times Reporter*, 16 October 1844, 85.

60. "Bro. Miller's Letter, On the Seventh Month," *Advent Herald and Signs of the Times Reporter*, 16 October 1844, 88.

61. Many of the widespread and still current stories about Millerite excesses, such as the claim that they donned white "ascension robes" and waited on tops of mountains for the Lord's return, or that New England insane asylums were filled with people whose Adventist zeal led them into derangement, have been ably refuted by Nichol in *The Midnight Cry*. There is no doubt, however, that some Adventists placed themselves in precarious situations as a result of their certainty that they would soon have no need of purely earthly provisions. Adventist Luther Boutelle's memoir provides but one of many accounts of such doings: "Crops were left unharvested, their owners expecting never to want what they had raised. Men paid up their debts. Many sold their property to help others pay their debts, who could not have done so themselves. Beef cattle were slaughtered and distributed among the poor" (reprinted in *The Disappointed*, ed. Numbers and Butler, 209). Ronald Graybill discusses the case of the Massachusetts Millerite Ezekiel Hale, Jr., who spent a good portion of his wealth in support of the Adventist cause and distributed the rest to his more skeptical children. After the Great Disappointment he went to court in an effort to recover his property. See "The Abolitionist-Millerite Connection," 143.

62. Memoir of Hiram Edson, reprinted in the appendix to *The Disappointed*, ed. Numbers and Butler, 215.

63. See Festinger, et al., *When Prophecy Fails*, 193–229, for a discussion of the effects of such a disconfirmation on a modern American sect. In attempting to place this sect in a historical context, however, Festinger makes a curious error in regard to the Millerites: "The disconfirmation of October 22 brought about the collapse of Millerism. . . . By the late spring of 1845 it had virtually disappeared" (22–23). The authors are apparently unaware of the relationship of Millerism to Seventh-Day Adventism; and such an error is all the more surprising in that the subsequent history of the Adventists seems to provide support for their theory.

64. Two doctrines in particular that the later Adventists introduced were the "sabbatarian" teaching that the Sabbath should be celebrated on the seventh day (Saturday), and "annihilationism," the teaching that God would destroy the souls of unrepentant sinners rather than torment them throughout eternity in hell. While these doctrines are not a concern of the present study, a complete rhetorical history of the transformation of Millerism into Seventh-Day Adventism would certainly require attention to their development in the later revelations and teachings of the woman usually considered the founder of the Seventh-Day Adventist Church, Ellen G. White. Born Ellen Harmon, she converted to Miller's premillennialism with her sister and her parents in the early 1840s after hearing him lecture in a church in Portland, Maine. She and her family were "disfellowshipped" from their home church for adhering to Miller's teachings. Shortly after the Great Disappointment, in December, 1844, she received her first vision, "in which was portrayed the travels of the advent people on their way to the city of God" (Froom, *Prophetic Faith*, 979). Her visions and messages on the developing Adventist faith, which continued until her death in 1915, were concerned with a range of subjects, including "health, education, temperance, evangelism, sane finance. . . . The influence of these messages . . . confirmed the faith of the Sabbatarian Adventists in their Bible-founded . . . mission, [and] steered them away from the numerous time settings that caused repeated setbacks to other groups" (Froom, *Prophetic Faith*, 985,

995). More information on Ellen White and later doctrinal developments in Seventh-Day Adventism can be found in Jonathan M. Butler, "The Making of a New Order: Millerism and the Origins of Seventh-day Adventism," in *The Disappointed*, ed. Numbers and Butler, 189–208; Gary Land, ed., *Adventism in America: A History*, particularly Godfrey T. Anderson, "Sectarianism and Organization, 1846–1864," 36–65.

65. The reinterpretation of prophetic fulfillment turned on the meaning of the passage from Daniel that Miller had emphasized: "Unto two thousand three hundred days: then shall the sanctuary be cleansed." Whereas Miller had assumed that the cleansing of the sanctuary referred to the earthly Second Coming, later Adventists interpreted this passage as referring to an invisible sanctuary in heaven which Christ had entered to prepare for His final advent: "Thus those who followed the light of the prophetic scriptures saw that, instead of coming to the earth at the termination of the 2300 days in 1844, Christ then entered the most holy place of the heavenly sanctuary to perform the closing work of atonement preparatory to His coming." Ellen G. White, *The Great Controversy* (1888), reprinted under the title *Cosmic Conflict*, 373. See also Froom, *Prophetic Faith*, 895–99: "So it was that what had seemed like the greatest *disappointment* of all time was now seen as indeed one of the most remarkable fulfillments of all prophetic history—a movement of God's own *appointment*, despite its human limitations and misconceptions" (895).

CHAPTER 5

1. Quoted in J. N. Loughborough, *Rise and Progress of the Seventh-Day Adventists*, 33.

2. Quoted in Clara Endicott Sears, *Days of Delusion: A Strange Bit of History*, 117.

3. See Nichol, *Midnight Cry*, 84.

4. Quoted in Hewitt, *Midnight and Morning*, 127.

5. See Froom, *The Prophetic Faith of Our Fathers*, vol. 4, 477.

6. Quoted in Nichol, *Midnight Cry*, 120.

7. Such arguments sometimes dissented from key features of the Millerite system while accepting its basic premises, as when Henry Dana Ward continued to publish letters in the *Signs of the Times* that rejected not only Miller's 1843 date but also the very assumption that the date of the End could be known, while at the same time agreeing that the End was imminent. See *Signs of the Times*, 1 December 1841, 135–36. One Millerite writer acknowledges the diversity of positions held within the movement: "The advocates of Christ's soon coming again, are in some things apparently much disagreed, in the very outset. . . . They differ in their theories of the advent seriously. They differ widely in their principles and manner of interpreting many prophecies." (*Signs of the Times*, 15 March 1841, 189). The writer goes on to argue that these "discrepancies of opinion" are "no strange affair, but just what should have been expected under such circumstances."

8. William Miller, letter to Truman Hendryx, 26 March 1832. Reprinted in Sylvester Bliss, *Memoirs of William Miller*, 102.

9. Josiah Litch, "Protest," in *Signs of the Times*, 20 September 1843, 38.

10. "Letter from Wm. Miller," *Signs of the Times*, 8 November 1843, 97.

11. Josiah Litch, "Address to the Clergy," *Signs of the Times*, 1 January 1842, 152.

12. The contributions of Scripture and the history of its interpretation can be considered premises of "social knowledge" as Farrell defines this term: "conceptions of symbolic rela-

tionships among problems, persons, interests, and actions, which imply (when accepted) certain notions of preferable public behavior" ("Knowledge, Consensus, and Rhetorical Theory," 4).

13. William Miller, "Rules of Interpretation," in *Views of the Prophecies and Prophetic Chronology*, 20–21.

14. From *Sketches of the Christian Life and Public Labors of William Miller*, ed. James White, 287–89.

15. See Froom, *Prophetic Faith*, 507, for another such account.

16. Miller, quoted in Froom, *Prophetic Faith*, 479.

17. Miller, quoted in Froom, *Prophetic Faith*, 489.

18. Some of these calculations appear on the famous and colorful "1843 Chart" that was lithographed and used at camp meetings (reproduced in *The Disappointed*, ed Numbers and Butler). It is difficult to know how many members of Miller's audiences followed his proofs through step by step, but the impact of the chart on the audiences at the meetings is attested by eyewitness accounts. See Sears, *Days of Delusion*, 108–9.

19. According to the *Encyclopaedia Britannica*, Usher's calculation of the age of the world through Biblical texts appeared in his *Annales Veteris et Novi Testamenti* (1650–54), and was "inserted by some unknown authority" into the margins of editions of the Authorized Version (s.v. *Usher, James, Encyclopaedia Brittanica*, 11th ed.).

20. Anonymous, "Objections to Calculating the Prophetic Times Considered," *Signs of the Times*, 26 April 1843, 59.

21. William Miller, "The Great Sabbath," *Signs of the Times*, 15 January 1842, 156.

22. Anonymous, *Advent Herald*, 16 October 1844, 86.

23. *Report . . . 1840*, 2–3.

24. *Report . . . 1840*, 4.

25. *Signs of the Times*, 29 June 1842, 101.

26. F. G. Brown, "The Safe Position," *Advent Herald*, 15 January 1845, 177.

27. F. G. Brown, "The Safe Position," 177–78.

28. "Address to the Public. Confession of the Adventists—Defence of their Course—Their Position," 30. This essay is unsigned, but was published in the *Supplement to the Advent Herald*, vol. 8, dated December 4, 1844, ed. Joshua Himes, Sylvester Bliss, and Apollos Hale. The copy of this pamphlet in the Jenks Collection at Aurora University contains a contemporary margin note on the first page of the essay that appears to identify Bliss as the author. As an extended apology for the movement this document deserves further study in its own right; space considerations, however, prevent more than a brief reference here.

29. Quoted in Ronald Graybill, "The Abolitionist-Millerite Connection," in *The Disappointed*, ed. Numbers and Butler, 139.

30. Cross, *Burned-over District*, 317.

31. "E.C.C.," "A Voice from Slave Land," *The Advent Message to the Daughters of Zion*, 35.

32. Miller, *Evidences from Scripture and History*, 205.

33. Rowe, *Thunder and Trumpets*, 116.

34. Quoted in Rowe, *Thunder and Trumpets*, 116.

35. B. Mathias, *The Groaning Creation: or, The Miseries and Liabilities of the Present Life, and the Hopes of the Other: A Sermon for the Times*, 3.

36. Mathias, *The Groaning Creation*, 14–15.

37. Mathias, *The Groaning Creation*, 19, 20–22.

38. Mathias, *The Groaning Creation*, 22.

39. The distinction between repetitive and progressive form is drawn from Kenneth Burke, *Counter-Statement*, 124–25. Repetitive form Burke defines as "the consistent maintaining of a principle under new guises." Progressive form Burke divides into "syllogistic progression," which is "the form of a perfectly conducted argument, conducted step by step," while "qualitative progression" puts the audience into "a state of mind which another state of mind can appropriately follow." The argument analyzed here employs both syllogistic and qualitative progression: the author deductively argues for the culpability of all humanity and the incompleteness of every human remedy, and this consciousness of guilt and sin prepares the audience for the redemptive solution, the millennium.

40. Mathias, *The Groaning Creation*, 24.

41. Mathias, *The Groaning Creation*, 24, 25.

42. Mathias, *The Groaning Creation*, 32, 41.

43. Mathias, *The Groaning Creation*, 42.

44. Mathias, *The Groaning Creation*, 9.

45. See Charles Finney's letter to Theodore Weld, quoted in Hammond, *The Politics of Benevolence*, 102. Another example of this dramatic sense of tragic foreboding can be found in an 1859 article in the *American Theological Review*: "The plot of the world's great drama has long been thickening: but everything indicates that its denouement is at hand. . . . Already we hear the roll of the drum, the clangor of the trumpet, and the shout of captains, concentrating and marshalling the hosts" (quoted in James Moorhead, *American Apocalypse: Yankee Protestants and the Civil War 1860–1869*, 18–19).

46. "Reflections on the Destiny of Human Society," anonymous editorial in *Advent Herald*, 30 October 1844, 95–96.

47. Cross, *The Burned-over District*, 320.

48. Farrell, "Knowledge, Consensus, and Rhetorical Theory," 4.

49. Ernest R. Sandeen, *The Roots of Fundamentalism: British and American Millenarianism, 1800–1930*, 54–55.

50. Mark Noll, "Misreading the Signs of the Times," 10-I.

51. See Jonathan Butler, "The Making of a New Order": "[The Millerites'] millennial failures . . . escalated the novelty to eccentricity, the avant-gardism to affectation" (195). I do not claim that Miller's arguments did not seem eccentric to his contemporaries, but merely that they were credible enough to attract the attention of a fairly large portion of the public, and that one effect of the Great Disappointment was to ensure that no specific prediction of the End could ever again attain such credibility.

CHAPTER 6

1. See Ernest R. Sandeen, *The Roots of Fundamentalism*, as well as Timothy Weber, *Living in the Shadow of the Second Coming*.

2. On the notion of audience as implied in the text, see Edwin Black, "The Second Persona."

3. Brookes was the principle leader of the Niagara Conference, which met annually from 1878 to 1901 and which attracted ministers, theologians, and interested lay persons from a number of denominations. Also during this period, Moody's Northfield Conferences "changed the character of American Protestantism" by giving millenarians "a nationally

prominent platform from which to teach and an extraordinary opportunity to establish themselves as prominent, reputable Protestant leaders" (Sandeen, *Roots of Fundamentalism,* 172, 175).

4. Weber, *Living in the Shadow of the Second Coming,* 16.

5. Arno Gaebelein, quoted in Weber, *Living in the Shadow of the Second Coming,* 48.

6. Robert Speer, *The Second Coming of Christ* (New York, 1903), quoted in Weber, *Living in the Shadow of the Second Coming,* 58.

7. Weber, *Living in the Shadow of the Second Coming,* 45–46, 48.

8. C. I. Scofield, "Rightly Dividing the Word of Truth," in *The First Scofield Reference Bible,* 1572.

9. Sandeen, *Roots of Fundamentalism,* 67.

10. Weber, *Living in the Shadow of the Second Coming,* 21.

11. Although the conflicts between "pretribulationists," "midtribulationists," and "post-tribulationists" have been severe, with those who hold to one or another system of prophetic timing often denouncing their fellows with a rancor reserved for agents of Antichrist, the parameters of the present study prohibit a full examination of these issues. For discussion of the historical roots of such disputes, see Sandeen, *Roots of Fundamentalism,* 215–21 and passim. A recent restatement of post-tribulationist exegesis can be found in Jim McKeever, *Christians Will Go through the Tribulation.* For an attack on posttribulationism by an eminent modern premillennialist, see John F. Walvoord, *The Blessed Hope and the Tribulation.*

12. Both Weber and Sandeen discuss the fear of death as a motivation for belief in the rapture. See *Living in the Shadow of the Second Coming,* 229; *Roots of Fundamentalism,* 211. Surveying modern premillennialist literature to determine the degree to which this theme is emphasized, I have found further evidence of the denial of death as a motive. See, for example, Hal Lindsey's *The Rapture:* "The truly electrifying fact is that many of you who are reading this will experience this mystery. You will never know what it is to die physically" (43).

13. Weber, *Living in the Shadow of the Second Coming,* 238.

14. Through most of Christian history, the typological interpretation of the church as the "spiritual Israel" and inheritor of the Jewish prophetic covenant had prevailed. In the context of this interpretation, the notion of a literal restoration of the Jews to Palestine had little meaning; attention to the role of the Jews in last-day events tended to conceive of the Jews' restoration as a conversion, and focused on their eventual acceptance of Jesus as the Messiah. Joachim of Fiore, the influential Italian abbot whose eschatological vision of history "changed the course of Christian apocalypticism" (McGinn, *Visions of the End,* 126), probably drew on an older tradition when in the eleventh century he predicted the conversion of the Jews as one of the penultimate events of the final age (see McGinn's translation from Joachim's *Expositio in Apocalypsim,* in *Visions of the End,* 134). The theme has entered into the English language as a proverbial representation of an ultimate, and presumably unknowable, conclusion of history. Andrew Marvell's famous poem "To His Coy Mistress" invokes the legend of the Jews' conversion as a synecdoche for the End of time itself: "Had we but World enough, and Time, / This coyness Lady were no crime. / . . . I would / Love you ten years before the Flood: / And you should if you please refuse / Till the Conversion of the Jews." The effect is of the poet pleading with the beloved not to put him off until doomsday, or kingdom come.

15. See G. F. Cox, "Return of the Jews," *Signs of the Times*, 1 June 1842. Cox attempted to prove that the prophecies of the Jewish restoration to Palestine had all been fulfilled "when the Jews returned from Babylon, after the fall of the Chaldean or Assyrian empire," and, therefore, that *"no return of the Jews, as a nation, to the land of Palestine, is promised in the Scriptures, other than what has already taken place"* (67). To admit otherwise would have been to consent to a postponement of the apocalypse until political conditions allowed such a restoration, a prospect so distant in the 1840s as to be nearly unimaginable.

16. William E. Blackstone, an associate of D. L. Moody and the author of a popular book entitled *Jesus is Coming*, may serve as an example of the curious relationship that existed between Zionism and American premillennialism. In the early 1890s, Blackstone drew attention to the plight of Russian Jews suffering under czarist pogroms by drawing up a memorial document on their behalf which advocating a restoration to Palestine. This document was signed by a number of prominent Americans, including the Chief Justice of the United States Supreme Court and prominent members of the House and Senate, and was sent to President Benjamin Harrison in 1891. Blackstone maintained a correspondence with Theodore Herzl, the founder of modern Zionism; when Herzl wavered on the question of whether the proposed Jewish state's location should be in Palestine or elsewhere, "Blackstone sent him a marked copy of the Old Testament, showing, in typical premillennialist fashion, those passages which indicated that the Jews must return to the Holy Land" (Weber, *Living in the Shadow of the Second Coming*, 139–40). A Zionist Conference that convened in Philadelphis in 1918 praised this staunch premillennialist as a "Father of Zionism"; in 1956, a forest was dedicated to his memory by the citizens of Israel. Far from being an anomaly, Blackstone's support of the Jewish state was but an early example of a tradition of association between American dispensationalists and Zionists that has continued through the decades down to the present. The widely reported friendship between American premillennialist Jerry Falwell and Israeli prime minister Menachem Begin, who reportedly telephoned Falwell to enlist support from American fundamentalists for Israel's 1982 invasion of Lebanon, is a recent example of the political and ideological alliance between Zionism and fundamentalism. For extensive discussion of this alliance, see Grace Halsell, *Prophecy and Politics*.

17. Compare the NEB translation: "On that day the heavens will disappear with a great rushing sound, the elements will disintegrate in flames, and the earth with all that is in it will be laid bare."

18. Ray C. Petry, *Christian Eschatology and Social Thought*, 13–14.

19. For an expert sociological analysis of the causes and consequences of the privatization of religion in contemporary industrial culture, see Thomas Luckmann, *The Invisible Religion*, particularly pp. 103–14. An insightful discussion of the effects of these developments on American communal and religious life can be found in Robert N. Bellah, et al., *Habits of the Heart*, 220–24.

20. Edwin Black, "The Second Persona," 112.

21. Quoted in Jonathan Kirsch, "Hal Lindsey," 31.

22. *The Late Great Planet Earth*, vii.

23. *The Late Great Planet Earth*, vii–viii.

24. Kirsch, "Hal Lindsey," 31.

25. *The Late Great Planet Earth*, 2.

26. *The Late Great Planet Earth*, 7.

27. *The Late Great Planet Earth*, 7.

28. *The Late Great Planet Earth*, 8.

29. *The Late Great Planet Earth*, 9, 10, 16.

30. *The Late Great Planet Earth*, 18.

31. *The Late Great Planet Earth*, 19, 21, 31.

32. *The Late Great Planet Earth*, 40. This passage is a quotation from John Cumming, *The Destiny of Nations* (1864).

33. *The Late Great Planet Earth*, 32.

34. *The Late Great Planet Earth*, 32, 33.

35. *The Late Great Planet Earth*, 34, 37.

36. *The Late Great Planet Earth*, 41.

37. *The Late Great Planet Earth*, 42, 44, 47.

38. This passage is quoted as it appears on page 43 of *The Late Great Planet Earth* (italics are Lindsey's). As noted above, Lindsey shifts between different biblical translations as his purpose dictates. Lest this fact confuse my readers, I reiterate that when I perform my own examination and analysis of particular scriptural passages, I am using the NEB; in dealing with other authors' interpretations of scripture, I use whatever translation they employ. Hence, chapters 4 and 5 of this study rely on the original King James translation, since this was used exclusively by the Millerites.

39. *The Late Great Planet Earth*, 43.

40. *Webster's New World Dictionary*, 2d ed., s.v. *generation*.

41. G. Thomas Goodnight, "Generational Argument," in *Argumentation: Across the Lines of Discipline*, ed. Frans H. van Eemeren, Rob Grootendorst, J. Anthony Blair, Charles A. Willard, 134.

42. *The 1980's: Countdown to Armageddon*, 162.

43. *The 1980's: Countdown to Armageddon*, 163.

44. *The Late Great Planet Earth*, 46.

45. This implication is not lost on Lindsey, who acknowledges that the presence of the Islamic shrine constitutes a "major problem barring the construction of a third Temple," but argues "Obstacle or no obstacle, it is certain that the Temple will be rebuilt. Prophecy demands it" (*The Late Great Planet Earth*, 45). There is considerable evidence to support Lindsey's claim that certain circles in Israel are preparing to reinstitute temple worship. For further discussion of this issue, and of the documented links between fundamentalist Christians in the United States and Jewish terrorists who have attempted to destroy the Islamic shrine, see Halsell, *Prophecy and Politics*, 96–116.

46. *The Late Great Planet Earth*, 52.

47. Adela Yarbro Collins, "Reading the Book of Revelation in the Twentieth Century," 234.

48. The First Scofield Reference Bible, 883.

49. Whatever critics might think of the present political implications of this identification, there is no doubt that it has a long history. Bernard McGinn translates a thirteenth-century text of the English Franciscan Roger Bacon that interprets the prophecy of Gog and Magog as a reference to Scythia; see *Visions of the End*, 157.

50. *The Late Great Planet Earth*, 53, 54.

51. *The Late Great Planet Earth*, 54, 55.

52. *The Late Great Planet Earth*, 56, 57, 58, 59.

53. *The Late Great Planet Earth*, 53.

54. Larry L. Walker, "How the NIV Made Use of New Light on the Hebrew Text," in *The NIV: The Making of a Contemporary Translation*, ed. Kenneth L. Barker, 100.

55. Quoted in Vernon Grounds, "Prophetic Speculation and Public Policy," 6. Grounds' article appeared in the *ESA Parley*, a newsletter published in Washington D.C. by Evangelicals for Social Action.

56. Quoted in J. Barton Payne, *Encyclopedia of Biblical Prophecy: The Complete Guide to Scriptural Predictions and their Fulfillment*, 367.

57. John B. Taylor, *Ezekiel: An Introduction and Commentary*, 243.

58. *The Late Great Planet Earth*, 70.

59. See McGinn, "Moslems, Mongols, and the Last Days," ch. 18 in *Visions of the End*, for evidence of this fear in medieval apocalypticism.

60. *Webster's New World Dictionary*, 2d ed., s.v. *yellow peril*.

61. *The Late Great Planet Earth*, 75.

62. Aristotle, *Poetics* 1452a, trans. G. M. A. Grube, 20.

63. *The Late Great Planet Earth*, 71.

64. Hal Lindsey, *There's a New World Coming*, 141.

65. *The Late Great Planet Earth*, 73–74.

66. *The Late Great Planet Earth*, 83, 84, 86.

67. *The Late Great Planet Earth*, 89, 90, 91.

68. *The Late Great Planet Earth*, 101, 118.

69. *The Late Great Planet Earth*, 119, 111.

70. *The Late Great Planet Earth*, 117.

71. See chapter 4, note 52.

72. *The Late Great Planet Earth*, 126, 127.

73. This phrase is borrowed from J. Michael Hogan, "Apocalyptic Pornography and the Nuclear Freeze: A Defense of the Public."

74. *The Late Great Planet Earth*, 163–64.

75. *The Late Great Planet Earth*, 133–34.

76. *The Late Great Planet Earth*, 135, 139.

77. *The Late Great Planet Earth*, 139.

78. *The Late Great Planet Earth*, 140, 141, 145.

79. Lindsey writes: "A fearful thing is predicted as occurring at the time of the Red Army's destruction. God says, 'I will send fire on Magog [Russia] and upon those who dwell securely [false hope] in the coastlands [various continents]...' (Ezekiel 39:6 Amplified). According to this, Russia, as well as many countries who thought they were secure under Antichrist's protection, will have fire fall upon them.... [T]his could be a direct judgment from God, or God could allow the various countries to launch a nuclear exchange of ballistic missiles upon each other" (*The Late Great Planet Earth*, 150). The interpolations are Lindsey's.

80. *The Late Great Planet Earth*, 151, 152, 154.

81. *The Late Great Planet Earth*, 156–57.

82. *The Late Great Planet Earth*, 145.

83. *The Late Great Planet Earth*, 163.

84. *The Late Great Planet Earth*, 171, 173.

85. *The Late Great Planet Earth*, 174, 175.

86. *The Late Great Planet Earth*, 176.

87. *The Late Great Planet Earth,* 177.

88. Public Agenda Foundation, *Voter Options on Nuclear Arms Policy,* 40, table 26. For a discussion of these data, see Andrew J. Weigert, "Christian Eschatological Identities and the Nuclear Context."

89. *The Late Great Planet Earth,* 40.

90. See William G. McLoughlin, *Revivals, Awakenings, and Reform: An Essay on Religion and Social Change in America, 1607–1977,* 193–216.

91. McLoughlin, *Revivals, Awakenings, and Reform,* 212.

CHAPTER 7

1. See *Living in the Shadow of the Second Coming,* 237–38.

2. Tom D. Daniels, Richard J. Jensen, and Allen Lichtenstein, "Resolving the Paradox in Politicized Christian Fundamentalism," 248.

3. For a sample of such coverage, see *The New Republic's* cover story on "America's Ayatollahs," 29 September 1986. The bepuzzlement of the authors (liberal pundits all) in confronting the more recondite features of fundamentalist eschatology and political theology is typical of the press accounts of the period.

4. *The 1980's: Countdown to Armageddon,* 4, 6.

5. *The 1980's: Countdown to Armageddon,* 106, 68.

6. *The 1980's: Countdown to Armageddon,* 131, 132.

7. *The 1980's: Countdown to Armageddon,* 154.

8. *The 1980's: Countdown to Armageddon,* 157.

9. *The 1980's: Countdown to Armageddon,* 154.

10. Quoted in Robert Scheer, *With Enough Shovels: Reagan, Bush, and Nuclear War,* 66.

11. *The Late Great Planet Earth,* 43; *The 1980's: Countdown to Armageddon,* 163.

12. Quoted in Frances Fitzgerald, *Cities on a Hill,* 128,164.

13. *The 1980's: Countdown to Armageddon,* 158.

14. Conrad Hyers, *And God Created Laughter,* 115.

15. Ronald Reagan, "Televised Nationwide Address on Behalf of Senator Barry Gold-water," 27 October 1964, reprinted in *Speaking My Mind: Selected Speeches,* 22–36, 36.

16. Kurt Ritter, "Reagan's 1964 TV Speech for Goldwater: Millennial Themes in American Political Rhetoric," 68.

17. This stump speech from the 1964 Goldwater campaign is reprinted in *A Time for Choosing: The Speeches of Ronald Reagan, 1961–1982,* ed. Alfred Balitzer and Gerald M. Bonetto, 57; the editors incorrectly identify the text with the October 27, 1964 televised address referred to above. The texts have some similarities but are not identical. My thanks to Kurt Ritter for his assistance with this portion of my research.

18. "Remarks at the Annual Convention of the National Association of Evangelicals in Orlando, Florida, March 8, 1983," in *Public Papers of the Presidents of the United States: Ronald Reagan 1983, Book I—January 1 to July 1, 1983,* 362–63.

19. For an incisive analysis of the speech, see G. Thomas Goodnight, "Ronald Reagan's Re-formulation of the Rhetoric of War: Analysis of the 'Zero Option,' 'Evil Empire,' and 'Star Wars' Addresses."

20. Quoted in Jim Castelli, "The Environmental Gospel According to James Watt," *Chicago Tribune*, 25 October 1981, B2.

21. Replying to a question from a student in a public forum at Harvard University, Weinberger said, "I have read the Book of Revelation and, yes, I believe the world is going to end—by an act of God, I hope—but every day I think that time is running out" (quoted in Robert Scheer. *With Enough Shovels*, xi).

22. Quoted in Ronnie Dugger, "Does Reagan Expect a Nuclear Armageddon?" *Washington Post*, 8 April 1984, C1.

23. Similar statements, reported from a number of individuals and forums, are reprinted in Grace Halsell, *Prophecy and Politics*, 43–49. Of greatest interest is a somewhat unreliable account (based on memories of a 1971 conversation) by James Mills, President Pro Tem of the California State Senate while Reagan was governor. Mills reports that at a state dinner, Reagan remarked to him:

> Everything is falling into place. It can't be too long now. Ezekiel says that fire and brimstone will be rained upon the enemies of God's people. That must mean that they'll be destroyed by nuclear weapons. They exist now, and they never did in the past. Ezekiel tells us that Gog, the nation that will lead all of the other powers of darkness against Israel, will come out of the north. Biblical scholars have been saying for generations that Gog must be Russia. What other powerful nation is to the north of Israel? None. But it didn't seem to make sense before the Russian revolution, when Russia was a Christian country. Now it does, now that Russia has become communistic and atheistic, now that Russia has set itself against God. Now it fits the description of Gog perfectly. (James Mills, "The Serious Implications of a 1971 Conversation with Ronald Reagan," 140–41, 258; excerpts in Halsell, *Prophecy and Politics*, 45)

24. For a discussion of Robison's views, see Martin Gardner, "Giving God a Hand."

25. See Dugger, above, and also: "Reagan and Mondale Urged to Reject 'Armageddon' Idea," *San Francisco Chronicle*, 24 October 1984; "President urged to Repudiate View That Nuclear War Is Near," *San Jose Mercury News*, 25 October 1984, 8A; "Reckoning with Armageddon," *New York Times*, 25 October 1984. A transcript of the press conference held on the West Coast was published by Washington Research Institute under the title *Armageddon Theology and Presidential Decision-Making: Religious Leaders' Concern*.

26. The documentary was produced and narrated by Joe Cuomo of WBAI in New York City and broadcast by public radio stations throughout the nation in the fall of 1984. Transcript provided by the Christic Institute, Washington, D.C., 1984. Ellingwood's testimony is confirmed by an independent source. In his book *Reagan Inside Out*, a laudatory biography of the president aimed at the evangelical community, Bob Slosser (well known in Christian fundamentalist circles for his books authored with Pat Robertson and other religious leaders) documents Reagan's longstanding interest in prophetic eschatology (13–19). The book also includes a curious account of a meeting held in the California governor's mansion in October 1970 with Ronald and Nancy Reagan, Herb Ellingwood, entertainer Pat Boone and his wife Shirley, and evangelists Harald Bredesen and George Otis. According to both Bredesen and Otis, topics of conversation included the prophetic significance of the 1967 Six- Day War and the Israeli capture of Jerusalem, as well as other apocalyptic signs. One of these signs, as told by Harald Bredesen, is of obvious significance: "Just before Jesus Christ comes back, there will be 'a vast resurgence of charismatic happenings. And in that

day, both leaders and people will be Spirit-filled and Spirit-empowered on a scale hitherto unknown' " (*Reagan Inside Out*, 18). The meeting culminated, according to George Otis, in a prayer session that included a visitation of the Holy Spirit and a prophecy of Reagan's future destiny. In view of its obvious relevance to the topic of this study, I present here an excerpt from George Otis's account as retold by Bob Slosser:

> [T]hey stood, holding hands, eyes closed. . . . "I was just sort of praying from the head," Otis said. "I was saying those things you'd expect—you know, thanking the Lord for the Reagans, their hospitality, and that sort of thing."
>
> That went on for ten or fifteen seconds, and then it changed. "Everything shifted from my head to the spirit—*the* Spirit," Otis recalled. "The Holy Spirit came upon me and I knew it. In fact, I was embarrassed. There was this pulsing in my arm. And my hand—the one holding Governor Reagan's hand—was shaking. . . . It wasn't a wild swinging or anything like that. But it was a definite, pulsing shaking. And I made a great physical effort to stop it— but I couldn't."
>
> As this was going on, the content of Otis' prayer changed completely. His voice remained essentially the same, although the words came much more steadily and intently. They spoke specifically to Ronald Reagan and referred to him as "My son." They recognized his role as leader of a state that was indeed the size of many nations. His "labor" was described as "pleasing."
>
> The foyer was absolutely still and silent. The only sound was George's voice. Everyone's eyes were closed.
>
> "If you walk uprightly before Me, you will reside at 1600 Pennsylvania Avenue."
>
> The words ended. The silence held for three or four seconds. Eyes began to open, and the seven rather sheepishly let go of hands.
>
> Reagan took a deep breath and turned and looked into Otis' face. All he said was a very audible "Well!" It was almost as though he were exhaling.
>
> Otis was struck by the calm expression on Reagan's face. "I was really concerned about how he might have taken it all," George remembered. "But the expression on his face was kind, wholesome— a receptive look, you know. It was not gushy or sentimental or any of that. He just said, 'Well,' and that was that. We all said good-bye, and we left." (*Reagan Inside Out*, 14–15)

In view of the fact that this is a thirdhand account, based on a thirteen-year old memory, Otis' story must be taken with a considerable grain of skepticism. Yet, though the story's veracity as historical fact may be doubted, it is nevertheless significant as a narrative designed to appeal to Slosser's evangelical readers by illustrating Mr. Reagan's degree of comfort with prayer in the evangelical style. Thus, whether the account is true or not, it reinforces my point that a significant element in Reagan's success was his ability to speak the language of fundamentalists and evangelicals without alarming those closer to the political and religious center. Though Otis's story was published during the 1984 election campaign, it was universally ignored in the secular press; one can hardly resist wondering, however, what liberals would have made of this tale had they featured it in their apocalyptic polemics.

27. The complete text of the question and Reagan's response is as follows:

Q. In the Jerusalem Post you were quoted—and I don't know if the quote was accurate—as saying that this generation might see Armageddon, that a lot of the Biblical prophecies are sort of being played out today, or could be—[*inaudible*].

The President. Where was that?

Q. In the Jerusalem Post. And I was going to say, is this really true? Do you believe that?

The President. I've never done that publicly. I have talked here, and then I wrote people, because some theologians quite some time ago were telling me, calling attention to the fact that theologians have been studying the ancient prophecies— What would portend the coming of Armageddon?—and have said that never, in the time between the prophecies up till now has there ever been a time in which so many of the prophecies are coming together. There have been times in the past when people thought the end of the world was coming, and so forth, but never anything like this.

And one of them, the first one who ever broached this to me—and I won't use his name; I don't have permission to. He probably would give it, but I'm not going to ask—had held a meeting with the then head of the German Government, years ago when the war was over, and did not know that his hobby was theology. And he asked this theologian what did he think was the next great news event, worldwide. And the theologian, very wisely, said, "Well, I think that you're asking that question in case you've had a thought along that line." And he did. It was about the prophecies and so forth.

So, no. I've talked conversationally about that.

Q. You've mused on it. You've considered it.

The President. [*Laughing*] Not to the extent of throwing up my hands and saying, "Well, it's all over." No. I think whichever generation and at whatever time, when the time comes, the generation that is there, I think will have to go on doing what they believe is right.

Q. Even if it comes?

The President. Yes. ("Interview with Gary Clifford and Patricia Ryan of People Magazine, December 6, 1983," in *Public Papers of the Presidents of the United States: Ronald Reagan 1983, Book II—July 2 to December 31, 1983* (Washington, D.C.: U.S. Government Printing Office, 1985), 1714–15)

The anecdote of the "theologian" and the "head of the German Government" is retold in Slosser, *Reagan Inside Out,* 16. Here Mr. Reagan identifies the individuals as evangelist Billy Graham and German Chancellor Konrad Adenauer.

28. The text of the question and the relevant portions of Mr. Reagan's reply, are as follows:

Mr. Kalb. Mr. President, I'd like to pick up this Armageddon theme. You've been quoted as saying that you do believe, deep down, that we are heading for some kind of biblical Armageddon. Your Pentagon and your secretary of defense have plans for the United States to fight and prevail in a nuclear war. Do you feel that we are now heading perhaps, for some kind of nuclear Armageddon? And do you feel that this country and this world could survive that kind of calamity?

The President. Mr. Kalb, I think what has been hailed as something I'm supposedly, as president, discussing as principle is the recall of just some philosophical discussions with people who are interested in the same things; and that is the prophecies down through the years, the biblical prophecies of what would portend the coming of Armageddon, and so forth, and the fact that a number of theologians

for the last decade or more have believed that this was true, that the prophecies
mean that Armageddon is a thousand years away or day after tomorrow. So, I have
never seriously warned and said we must plan according to Armageddon.

Now, with regard to having to say whether we would try to survive in the event
of a nuclear war, of course we would. But let me also point out that to several
parliaments around the world, in Europe and in Asia, I have made a statement to
each one of them, and I'll repeat it here: A nuclear war cannot be won and must
never be fought. And that is why we are maintaining a deterrent and trying to achieve
a deterrent capacity to where no one would believe that they could start such a war
and escape with limited damage. ("Debate Between the President and Former Vice
President Walter F. Mondale in Kansas City, Missouri, October 21, 1984," in
*Public Papers of the Presidents of the United States: Ronald Reagan 1984, Book II—
June 30 to December 31, 1984*, 1601)

29. For a sober and dispassionate assessment of Reagan's fascination with astrology and
psychic phenomena as well as apocalypticism, see Garry Wills, *Reagan's America: Innocents
at Home*, 196–98; also *Under God: Religion and American Politics*, 144–51.

30. Ed Dobson and Ed Hindson, "Apocalypse Now? What Fundamentalists Believe
about the End of the World," 16, 22. These men were co- authors of Jerry Falwell's *The
Fundamentalist Phenomenon*; at the time this essay was published, Dobson was vice-president
of student affairs, and Hindson was professor of religion, at Falwell's Liberty University.
The document is of considerable interest both as an example of religious apologia and as a
rationale for apocalyptic politics.

31. Charles Colson, *Kingdoms in Conflict*, 18. The first quoted paragraph is essentially
a verbatim transcript of Reagan's words in a 1971 conversation with James Mills, President
Pro Tem of the California State Senate while Reagan was governor, as quoted above (note
23).

32. Compare this excerpt from an early fifth-century dialogue by the Christian historian
and hagiographer Sulpicius Severus: "There is no doubt that Antichrist, conceived by an
evil spirit, has already been born. He is now a child and will take over the empire when he
comes of age" (quoted in McGinn, *Visions of the End*, 52).

33. "Pat Robertson's Perspective," *700 Club Newsletter*, February–March 1980, reprinted in *All in the Name of the Bible*, ed. Hassan Haddad and Donald Wagner, 121.

34. Robertson, quoted in Jimmy Swaggart, "The Coming Kingdom: You Cannot Have
a Kingdom Until You Have a King," 4–5.

35. The term "civil religion" has been prominent in sociological discussions of religion
in American life since Robert Bellah coined the phrase in his 1967 essay "Civil Religion in
America." The best discussion of the utility and the limitations of this concept as a rhetorical
construct can be found in Roderick P. Hart's study *The Political Pulpit*. For a recent
presentation of a number of scholarly views on the topic, see Leroy Rouner, ed., *Civil
Religion and Political Theology*. As the term is used here, it refers to "a rhetorical model of
religion that fuses or blurs religion and state so that implicitly or explicitly, one supports
and strengthens the other through the interweaving of value systems" (O'Leary and Mc-
Farland, "The Political Use of Mythic Discourse," 451, n. 25).

36. Robertson, "A New Vision for America," 17 September 1986, Washington D.C.,
paragraphs 20–21, 52. Speech text provided by "Americans for Robertson."

37. Swaggart, "The Coming Kingdom," 5, 12.

38. Charles Pack, "Pat Robertson Says vs. What the Bible Says," 1.

39. The conference was the West Coast Prophecy Conference, held at the Sheraton Inn in Anaheim, California, December 1986. A published version of Constance Cumbey's attack on Robertson, which purports to trace his supposed links to various New Age groups, may be found in the chapter titled, "A Secret Kingdom?" in her book *A Planned Deception: The Staging of a New Age Messiah*, 147–83. Cumbey has continued to denounce Robertson in various speeches on the prophecy circuit and in her own newsletter, *New Age Monitor*. According to Cumbey in 1987, Robertson responded to these attacks by threatening her with a lawsuit; the outcome of the dispute is unknown.

40. I queried Charles Taylor, the host of this conference, author of *World War III and the Destiny of America* and editor of *Bible Prophecy News*, on the topic of SDI. He responded by arguing that "Star Wars" (as he termed it) was necessary since, according to prophecy, there would be a certain number of people who would convert to Christianity during the Tribulation, and SDI was needed to ensure the survival of this chosen few during the predicted nuclear holocaust.

41. See Wayne King, "The Record of Pat Robertson on Religion and Government," *New York Times* 27 December 1987, 20. In addition, CBS reporter Leslie Stahl questioned Robertson about his Armageddon beliefs on "Face the Nation" the Sunday before the New Hampshire primary. There Robertson indicated explicitly that, though the return of Christ was inevitable, it would not follow a nuclear holocaust: "I not only don't believe it's inevitable; I don't believe we are going to see it. And I will do everything in my power to keep it from happening" ("Face the Nation," transcript provided by CBS News, Washington D.C.: 14 February 1988, 5).

42. Edgar C. Whisenant, *88 Reasons Why the Rapture Will Be in 1988*, 56.

43. O'Leary and McFarland, "The Political Use of Mythic Discourse," 448.

44. See Hart, *The Political Pulpit*, 43–53 and passim. To borrow a phrase from Nathan O. Hatch (see the next note), the statements that caused trouble for both Reagan and Robertson might be seen as expressions of "uncivil millennialism."

45. Nathan O. Hatch, "The Origins of Civil Millennialism in America: New England Clergymen, War with France, and the Revolution," 408–9.

46. Hatch, "The Origins of Civil Millennialism in America," 409.

47. Ernest Tuveson, *Redeemer Nation: The Idea of America's Millennial Role*.

48. Charles Taylor, "G-O-G," *Bible Prophecy News*, July 1985, 4.

49. Zola Levitt, *The Levitt Letter*, 1 January 1990, 1.

50. Hal Lindsey, "Soviets Still Masters of Deceit," *Countdown*, June 1990, 1.

51. Quoted in Roy Rivenburg, "Is the End Still Near?" *Los Angeles Times* 30 July 1992, E2.

52. Hal Lindsey and Chuck Missler, *The Magog Factor*, 39, 41, 44.

53. The effect of the Persian Gulf conflict of 1990–1991 on religious speculation about Armageddon was reported in a number of sources. See Russell Chandler, "Persian Gulf Conflict Stirs Predictions of Final Conflict," *Los Angeles Times*, 20 September 1990, A5; Joe Feuerherd, "Author: Gulf War Beginning of Endtimes," *National Catholic Reporter*, 1 February 1991, 10; John Elson, "Apocalypse Now?" *Time*, 11 February 1991; Edwin Yamauchi, "Armageddon, Oil and the Middle East Crisis," *Christianity Today*, 29 April 1991, 50–51.

54. Hal Lindsey, "The Hidden Dangers of Peace," *Countdown*, May 1991, 1, 6–7. The complex relationship of American religious fundamentalism to the political cause of

conservatism is evident in Lindsey's conclusion that "It is the obligation of every Christian and every American to fight and forestall this drive to create a New World Order" (7).

55. Anonymous, "Soviet Union Still Threat," *Countdown*, March 1990, 24.

56. Walvoord and Walvoord, *Armageddon, Oil, and the Middle East Crisis*, rev. ed., 228.

57. See William M. Alnor, *Soothsayers of the Second Advent*, 22–24.

CHAPTER 8

1. Jacques Derrida, "Of an Apocalyptic Tone Recently Adopted in Philosophy," trans. John P. Leavey, Jr., 89.

2. Kenneth Burke, "Theology and Logology," 153.

3. Alasdair MacIntyre, *Whose Justice? Which Rationality?* 12.

4. See Thomas B. Farrell, "Knowledge, Consensus, and Rhetorical Theory," and also "Social Knowledge II."

5. Campbell, "A Rhetorical Interpretation of History," 229, 235–36.

6. E.g., Barry Brummett, "Premillennial Apocalypse as a Rhetorical Genre," and *Contemporary Apocalyptic Rhetoric*; Ronald Reid, "Apocalypticism and Typology: Rhetorical Dimensions of a Symbolical Reality." As discussed in chapter 1, these studies are marred by overly simplistic application of generic theory (Brummett) and by historical inaccuracies (Reid). For a study by a historian who examines apocalypticism in terms of logic and argument, see James West Davidson, *The Logic of Millennial Thought*.

7. Kenneth Burke, *Attitudes Toward History*, 3.

8. Susanne K. Langer, *Feeling and Form*, 326.

9. Langer, *Feeling and Form*, 351, 331.

10. Adela Yarbro Collins, *Crisis and Catharsis*, 152.

11. See J. N. D. Kelly, *Early Christian Doctrines*, 473–74. Origen's system depended on a heavily allegorical reading of Scripture, consistent with the comic frame of interpretation as discussed in this study. His teachings had many adherents but were condemned as heretical by a series of ecumenical councils, notably the Second Council of Constantinople in 553.

12. See David Barr, "The Apocalypse of John as Oral Enactment"; also John Gager, *Kingdom and Community*, 56.

13. The notion of sacred and profane time is drawn from Mircea Eliade, *The Sacred and the Profane*, trans. Willard R. Trask, 68–113, esp. p. 104.

14. See R. A. Markus, *Saeculum: History and Society in the Theology of St. Augustine*.

15. Augustine, Letter 199 "To Heysichius," in *Writings of Saint Augustine*, vol. 12, 387.

16. Burke, "Psychology and Form," in *Counter-Statement*, 31.

17. For a discussion of religious communities as plausibility structures, see Peter Berger, *The Sacred Canopy*, 78–79, 124–25.

18. See chapter 4, note 65.

19. See Mircea Eliade, *The Myth of the Eternal Return*, 149–54.

20. See G. Thomas Goodnight, "Generational Argument," in *Argumentation: Across the Lines of Discipline*, 129–44.

21. Lindsey, *The 1980s: Countdown to Armageddon*, xii.

22. Accordingly, I propose that arguments on the problem of evil within the Western religious traditions should be the subject of detailed study with the intention of discovering the applicability or inapplicability of the forensic stases. Such examinations should extend from the popular level, exemplified in such recent texts as Harold S. Kushner's *When Bad Things Happen to Good People* to the level of expert theological argumentation as embodied in the philosophical texts of authors such as Augustine, Leibniz, and John Hick. For a sample of Augustine's attempts to grapple with the problem, see book VII of the *Confessions*, as well as the essay on "Divine Providence and the Problem of Evil" (De Ordine), in *Writings of Saint Augustine*, trans. Robert P. Russell, vol. 1. For a classic attempt at a rational philosophical theodicy within the framework of theistic belief (later hilariously lampooned in Voltaire's *Candide*), see G. W. Leibniz, *Theodicy*. For an overview of the theological and philosophical debate and an attempt at its resolution, see John Hick, *Evil and the God of Love*.

23. In particular, it may be useful to contrast epochal discourse that constructs time with reference to the expectation of a prophetic future with discourse grounded in the past as embodied in both myth and historical memory. By comparing the rhetoric of temporality in the Christian tradition to its analogues in other religions and cosmological systems, future scholarship in rhetoric and comparative religion may reveal important insights into the nature of socially constructed time. For a recent study that provides an excellent contribution to this line of research, see Randall A. Lake, "Between Myth and History: Enacting Time in Native American Protest Rhetoric."

24. Karlyn Kohrs Campbell and Kathleen Hall Jamieson, "Form and Genre in Rhetorical Criticism: An Introduction," in *Form and Genre: Shaping Rhetorical Action*, ed. Campbell and Jamieson, 20.

25. For amplification on this point, see Wayne Brockriede, "Rhetorical Criticism as Argument."

26. Katherine Olson, "Completing the Picture: Replacing Generic Embodiments in the Historical Flow."

27. See Thomas B. Farrell, "Knowledge in Time: Toward an Extension of Rhetorical Form," 123–53.

28. See James V. Schall, "Apocalypse as a Secular Enterprise"; Barry Brummett, "Popular Economic Apocalyptic: The Case of Ravi Batra"; Harold Mixon and Mary Frances HopKins, "Apocalypticism in Secular Public Discourse: A Proposed Theory."

29. See J. Michael Hogan, "Apocalyptic Pornography and the Nuclear Freeze: A Defense of the Public"; Eric Zencey, "Apocalypse and Ecology."

30. On the principle of perfection, see Kenneth Burke, "Definition of Man," in *Language as Symbolic Action*, 17–18.

31. For a variety of scientific versions of eschatology, see: Richard Morris, *The End of the World*; Harvey Brooks, "Technology- Related Catastrophes: Myth and Reality," and Robert S. Morison, "Biological Eschatology," both in *Visions of Apocalypse*, ed. Friedlander et al.

32. See J. Robert Cox, "The Die is Cast: Topical and Ontological Dimensions of the Locus of the Irreparable."

33. Zencey, "Apocalypse and Ecology," 54–57.

34. Quoted in Paul Boyer, *By the Bomb's Early Light: American Thought and Culture at the Dawn of the Atomic Age*, 70.

35. Richard H. Popkin, "The Triumphant Apocalypse and the Catastrophic Apocalypse," in *Nuclear Weapons and the Future of Humanity*, ed. Avner Cohen and Steven Lee.

36. The dawn of the nuclear age was greeted by scores of secular pronouncements that were clearly of an eschatological character. Scientists and reporters vied with each other to imagine the benefits of the peaceful use of atomic power; many predicted revolutionary changes in all aspects of society and in human nature itself. Norman Cousins' meditation in *Modern Man is Obsolete* is typical of such rhetoric:

> Man now has it within his grasp to emancipate himself economically. If he wills
> it, he is in a position to redirect his competitive impulses; he can take the step from
> competitive man to co-operative man. He has at last unlocked enough of the earth's
> secrets to provide for his needs on a world scale. The same atomic and electrical
> energy that can destroy a continent can also usher in an age of economic sufficiency.
> It need no longer be a question as to which peoples shall prosper and which shall
> be deprived. There are resources enough and power enough for all. (14–15)

37. For discussion of the rhetorical failure of the scientists' movement, see Boyer, *By the Bomb's Early Light*, 47–106. The most complete account is that found in Alice Kimball Smith, *A Peril and a Hope: The Scientists' Movement in America 1945–47*.

38. See Rebecca S. Bjork, "Reagan and the Nuclear Freeze: 'Star Wars' as a Rhetorical Strategy"; Janice Hocker Rushing, "Ronald Reagan's 'Star Wars' Address: Mythic Containment of Technical Reasoning."

39. See G. Thomas Goodnight, "The Nuclear Age as an Argument Formation," paper presented at the Conference on Methodologies of Survival, Dubrovnik, Yugoslavia, June 1987.

40. For an expanded argument on this point, see Karl Jaspers's *The Atom Bomb and the Future of Man*, which attempts to think through the ethical implications of the nuclear peril as an eschatological novelty. Jaspers argues: "In the past there have been imaginative notions of the world's end; its imminent expectation for their generation was the ethically and religiously effective error of John the Baptist, Jesus, and the first Christians. But now we face the real possibility of such an end. The possible reality which we must henceforth reckon with . . . is no longer a fictitious end of the world. It is no world's end at all, but the extinction of life on the surface of the planet" (4).

41. Jonathan Schell, *The Fate of the Earth*, 226. Schell's "republic of insects and grass" is perhaps the most thorough realization of what Kenneth Burke calls the reduction of symbolic *action* to nonsymbolic *motion*. See Burke's article on "Dramatism" in *The International Encyclopedia of the Social Sciences*, vol. 7, 447.

42. Burke, *Attitudes toward History*, 171.

43. Derrida, "Of an Apocalyptic Tone," 95, 81.

44. Derrida, "Of an Apocalyptic Tone," 91.

45. Franz Kafka, "Reflections on Sin, Pain, Hope, and the True Way," trans. Willa and Edwin Muir, 169.

46. This aptly coined phrase is taken from Peter Berger, *The Heretical Imperative: Contemporary Possibilities of Religious Affirmation*, 90.

47. Paul Tillich, *A History of Christian Thought*, 524.

48. This does not imply an absolute rejection of teleology. For an expanded argument on this point, see Amos Wilder's *Eschatology and Ethics in the Teaching of Jesus*: "The

conception of the Judgment and the supernatural rewards, including the Kingdom, stand to Jesus and to the community as *representations*, with full validity and credibility, indeed, of the unprophesiable, unimaginable but certain, God-determined future. This future and God's action in it lend immense weight and urgency to their present moral responsibility. Yet this temporal imminence of God is but a function of his spiritual imminence, and it is this latter which really determines conduct. . . . The radical character of Jesus' ethics does not spring from the shortness of time but from the new relation to God in the time of salvation. The sanction for it is not the sanction of imminent supernatural retributions—except formally—but the appeal to the God-enlightened moral discernment recognizing the nature and will of God and inferring consequences (thence eschatologically dramatized)." (161).

49. A. G. Mojtabai, *Blessed Assurance: At Home with the Bomb in Amarillo, Texas.*

50. Hans Blumenberg, *The Legitimacy of the Modern Age,* trans. Robert M. Wallace, 35.

51. Barry Brummett, "Premillennial Apocalypse as a Rhetorical Genre," 93.

52. Samuel Beckett, *Waiting for Godot,* 29.

53. Beckett, *Waiting for Godot,* 61.

54. Two films that unite the tragic and comic visions in their representations of radical evil in twentieth-century history are Stanley Kubrick's *Dr. Strangelove,* which savagely satirizes the military as it depicts total nuclear destruction, and Lina Wertmuller's *Seven Beauties,* a black comedy set in part in a Nazi death camp. Both films successfully confront the tragic reality of evil by employing comic forms.

55. The words are Robert Martin's. See chapter 3, note 29.

56. David Tracy, *The Analogical Imagination: Christian Theology and the Culture of Pluralism,* 265–66.

57. Gordon Kaufman, *Theology for a Nuclear Age,* 13.

EPILOGUE

1. "Mormon Church Purges Survivalists," United Press International Newswire, 30 November 1992, 19:39:16 GMT.

2. Examples of Koresh's demonization are numerous; I will cite only one here. *Time's* cover story of 3 May 1993 superimposed a quote from Revelation over Koresh's face engulfed in flames: "His name was Death, and Hell followed with him" (Rev. 6:8).

3. This quotation appeared in many places. See "4 Federal Agents Die in Shootout While Trying to Seize Cult Leader," *New York Times,* 1 March 1993, A1, A11.

4. Religious freedom, of course, is limited by the criminal law, and I do not mean to excuse any illegal actions committed by Koresh and his followers. Yet to this day it remains unclear what these actions may have been, or whether these allegations, if true, constituted sufficient justification—in a strictly legal sense—for the initial raid on the compound. (It is necessary to stress that the firearms stockpiled by the Branch Davidians were all acquired legally.) Furthermore, whether or not one believes the government's actions were justified, the remarkable inability of officials to offer a coherent rationale for either the initial raid or the subsequent assault on the compound with tanks and tear gas was a valid cause for concern. I am not arguing that the government acted wrongly; my point is simply that the widespread acceptance of the term "cult" as a frame for these events has functioned to prevent

both government officials and the general public from raising issues and questions that might reasonably be applied to this case. Once the immolation of the Branch Davidians has been neatly pigeonholed as "another Jonestown," those Americans who expressed their approval of the assault in numerous national opinion polls could remain untroubled by the legal and constitutional issues.

5. Surely one of the most bizarre episodes in the tragedy was the FBI's attempt to blast Koresh and his followers into submission by bombarding their compound at all hours with a selection of music ranging from Nancy Sinatra's "These Boots Are Made For Walkin' " to ancient ritual chants of Tibetan monks. Such moments provided comic relief from the main thrust of the tragic action, similar to the gravedigger's soliloquy in *Hamlet*. When the pop music critic for the *New York Times* weighed in with his review of the government's musical choices, the reduction of psychological warfare to media spectacle was complete. See Jon Pareles, "It's Got a Beat and You Can Surrender to It," *New York Times*, 28 March 1993, E2.

6. Walter Goodman, "As TV, Drama in Waco Had a Grim Inevitability," *New York Times*, 20 April 1993, B1, B4. A brief sampling of other articles that I drew upon to write this epilogue follows: Scott Pendleton, "Media Plays Controversial Role in FBI-Cult Standoff in Waco," *Christian Science Monitor*, 15 March 1993, 3; Gustav Niebuhr, "Sect is Marked by Schisms and Dire Predictions," *Washington Post*, 1 March 1993, A1; Gustav Niebuhr, "Other Davidians Say Texas Cult is Giving Them a Bad Name,' *Washington Post*, 21 March 1993, A18; Neal Stephenson, "Blind Secularism," *New York Times*, 23 April 1993, A19; Michael Kelly, "After Waco's Inferno, an Inquisition That Insists on Rational Answers,' *New York Times*, 25 April 1993, E3; "Adventists Disavow Waco Cult," *Christian Century*, 17 March 1993, 285.

Bibliography

Aberle, David F. "A Note on Relative Deprivation Theory as Applied to Millenarian and Other Cult Movements." In *Millennial Dreams in Action: Studies in Revolutionary Religious Movements*, ed. Sylvia Thrupp, 209–14. New York: Schocken Books, 1970.

Ackerman, Robert John. *Religion as Critique*. Amherst: University of Massachusetts Press, 1985.

"Address to the Public. Confession of the Adventists—Defence of their Course—Their Position." In *Supplement to the Advent Herald*, vol. 8. Boston: Joshua V. Himes, December 4, 1844.

Ahern, M. B. *The Problem of Evil*. New York: Schocken Books, 1971.

Allan, Graham. "A Theory of Millennialism: The Irvingite Movement as an Illustration." *British Journal of Sociology* 25 (1974): 296–311.

Alnor, William M. *Soothsayers of the Second Advent*. Old Tappan, N.J.: Fleming H. Revell Co., 1989.

Anderson, Godfrey T. "Sectarianism and Organization, 1846–1864." In *Adventism: A History*, ed. Gary Land, 36–65. Grand Rapids, Minn.: William B. Eerdmans, 1986.

Andrews, Valerie, Robert Bosnak, and Karen Walter Goodwin, eds. *Facing Apocalypse*. Dallas, Tex.: Spring Publications, 1987.

Aristotle. *Poetics*. In *The Basic Works of Aristotle*, ed. Richard McKeon, trans. Ingram Bywater. New York: Random House, 1941.

———. *Poetics*. Trans. G. M. A. Grube. Indianapolis, Ind.: Bobbs-Merrill, 1958.

———. *Rhetoric*. In *The Basic Works of Aristotle*, ed. Richard McKeon, trans. W. Rhys Roberts. New York: Random House, 1941.

———. *Topica*. In *The Basic Works of Aristotle*, ed. Richard McKeon, trans. W. A. Pickard-Cambridge. New York: Random House, 1941.

Arthur, David T. "Joshua V. Himes and the Cause of Adventism." In *The Disappointed: Millerism and Millenarianism in the Nineteenth Century*, ed. Ronald L. Numbers and Jonathan M. Butler, 36–58. Bloomington: Indiana University Press, 1987.

———. "Millerism." In *The Rise of Adventism: Religion and Society in Mid-Nineteenth Century America*, ed. Edwin S. Gaustad. 154–72. New York: Harper & Row, 1974.

Augustine. *The City of God*. Trans. H. Bettenson. New York: Penguin Books, 1972.

———. *Confessions*. Trans. R. S. Pine-Coffin. London: Penguin Books, 1961.

———. "Divine Providence and the Problem of Evil" (De Ordine). Trans. Robert P. Russell. In *Writings of Saint Augustine*, vol. 1. New York: Cima Publishing, 1948.

———. "To Heysichius, On the End of the World" (Letter 199). Trans. Sister Wilfred Parsons. In *Writings of Saint Augustine*, vol. 12, 356–401. New York: Fathers of the Church, Inc., 1955.

Aune, David E. "The Apocalypse of John and the Problem of Genre." *Semeia* 36 (1986): 65–96.

Ball, Bryan W. *A Great Expectation: Eschatological Thought in English Protestantism to 1660*. Leiden, The Netherlands: E. J. Brill, 1975.

Barkun, Michael. *Crucible of the Millennium*. Syracuse, NY: Syracuse University Press, 1986.

———. *Disaster and the Millennium*. New Haven: Yale University Press, 1974.

Barnes, Robin Bruce. *Prophecy and Gnosis: Apocalypticism in the Wake of the German Reformation*. Stanford, Calif.: Stanford University Press, 1988.

Barr, David L. "The Apocalypse of John as Oral Enactment." *Interpretation* 40 (1986): 243–56.

Becker, Ernst. *The Structure of Evil*. New York: Macmillan, 1968.

Beckett, Samuel. *Waiting for Godot*. New York: Grove Press, 1982.

Bell, Daniel, ed. *Toward the Year 2000*. Boston: Houghton Mifflin, 1968.

Bellah, Robert. *Beyond Belief: Essays on Religion in a Post-Traditional World*. New York: Harper & Row, 1970.

———. "Civil Religion in America." *Daedalus* 96 (1967): 1–21.

———. "Evil and the American Ethos." In *Sanctions for Evil*, ed. Nevitt Sanford and Craig Comstock, 177–91. San Francisco: Jossey-Bass Inc., 1971.

Bellah, Robert N., Richard Madsen, William M. Sullivan, Ann Swidler, and Steven M. Tipton. *Habits of the Heart: Individualism and Commitment in American Life*. New York: Harper & Row, 1985.

Bellamy, Edward. *Looking Backward*. New York: New American Library, 1960.

Bender, John, and David E. Wellbery, eds. *Chronotypes: The Construction of Time*. Stanford, Calif.: Stanford University Press, 1991.

Bent, N. T. *The Signs of the Times, or the Moral Meaning of Our Present Commercial Difficulties, A Sermon Preached in St. Paul's Church, Philadelphia, Pennsylvania, on Sunday Evening Nov. 17, 1839*... Philadelphia: William Stavely & Co., 1839.

Bercovitch, Sacvan. *The American Jeremiad*. Madison: University of Wisconsin Press, 1975.

———, ed. *Typology and Early American Literature*. Amherst, Mass.: University of Massachusetts Press, 1972.

Berger, Peter. "Christian Faith and the Social Comedy." In *Holy Laughter: Essays on Religion in the Comic Perspective*, ed. M. Conrad Hyers, 123–33. New York: Seabury Press, 1969.

———. *The Heretical Imperative: Contemporary Possibilities of Religious Affirmation*. New York: Doubleday- Anchor, 1979.

———. *The Sacred Canopy: Elements of a Sociological Theory of Religion*. New York: Doubleday-Anchor, 1969.

Berger, Peter, and Thomas Luckmann. *The Social Construction of Reality*. New York: Doubleday-Anchor, 1967.

Bird, Phyllis. *The Bible as the Church's Book*. Philadelphia, Pa.: Westminster Press, 1982.

Bitzer, Lloyd F. "The Rhetorical Situation." *Philosophy and Rhetoric* 1 (1968): 1–14.

Bjork, Rebecca S. "Reagan and the Nuclear Freeze: 'Star Wars' as a Rhetorical Strategy." *Journal of the American Forensic Association* 24 (1988): 181–92.

Black, Edwin. "Electing Time." *Quarterly Journal of Speech* 59 (1973): 125–29.

———. *Rhetorical Criticism: A Study in Method.* New York: Macmillan, 1965.

———. "The Second Persona." *Quarterly Journal of Speech* 56 (1970): 110–19.

Bliss, Sylvester, ed. *Memoirs of William Miller.* Boston: Joshua V. Himes, 1853.

Bloch, Ruth. *Visionary Republic: Millennial Themes in American Thought, 1756–1800.* Cambridge, England: Cambridge University Press, 1985.

Blumenberg, Hans. *The Legitimacy of the Modern Age.* Trans. Robert M. Wallace. Cambridge: Massachusetts Institute of Technology Press, 1985.

———. *Work on Myth.* Trans. Robert M. Wallace. Cambridge: Massachusetts Institute of Technology Press, 1985.

Blumenthal, Sidney. "The Religious Right and Republicans." In *Piety and Politics: Evangelicals and Fundamentalists Confront the World,* ed. Richard John Neuhaus and Michael Cromartie, 269–86. Washington, D.C.: Ethics and Public Policy Center, 1987.

Boettner, Loraine. "Postmillennialism." In *The Meaning of the Millennium: Four Views,* ed. Robert Clouse, 117–41. Downers Grove, Ill.: Intervarsity Press, 1977.

Boklund, Gunnar. "Time Must Have a Stop: Apocalyptic Thought and Expression in the Twentieth Century." *Denver Quarterly* 2 (1967): 69–98.

Bormann, Ernest. "Fetching Good Out of Evil: A Rhetorical Use of Calamity." *Quarterly Journal of Speech* 53 (1977): 130–39.

Bousset, Wilhelm. *The Antichrist Legend.* London: Hutchinson, 1896.

Bowman, John Wick. "The Revelation to John: Its Dramatic Structure and Message." *Interpretation* 9 (1955): 436–53.

Boyer, Paul. *By the Bomb's Early Light: American Thought and Culture at the Dawn of the Atomic Age.* New York: Pantheon Books, 1985.

———. *When Time Shall Be No More: Prophecy Belief in Contemporary American Culture.* Cambridge, Mass.: The Belknap Press of Harvard University Press, 1992.

Bozeman, Theodore Dwight. *Protestants in an Age of Science: The Baconian Ideal and Antebellum American Religious Thought.* Chapel Hill: University of North Carolina Press, 1977.

Brockriede, Wayne. "Rhetorical Criticism as Argument." *Quarterly Journal of Speech* 60 (1974): 165–74.

Bromley, David G., and Anson Shupe, ed. *New Christian Politics.* Macon, Ga.: Mercer University Press, 1984.

Brooks, Harvey. "Technology-Related Catastrophes: Myth and Reality." In *Visions of Apocalypse: End or Rebirth?* ed. Saul Friedlander, Gerald Horton, Leo Marx and Eugene Skolnikoff, 109–136. New York: Holmes & Meier, 1985.

Brown, Norman O. "Apocalypse: The Place of Mystery in the Life of the Mind." In *Interpretation: The Poetry of Meaning,* ed. Stanley Romaine Hopper and David L. Miller, 7–13. New York: Harcourt, Brace, & World, 1967.

———. "The Apocalypse of Islam." In *Facing Apocalypse,* ed. Valerie Andrews, Robert Bosnak, and Karen Walter Goodwin, 138–62. Dallas, Tex.: Spring Publications, 1987.

———. *Closing Time.* New York: Random House, 1973.

———. *Life Against Death: The Psychoanalytical Meaning of History.* Middletown, Conn.: Wesleyan University Press, 1959.

———. *Love's Body.* New York: Random House, 1966.

Bruce, Steve. *The Rise and Fall of the New Christian Right: Conservative Protestant Politics in America 1978–1988*. Oxford: Clarendon Press, 1988.

Brummett, Barry. *Contemporary Apocalyptic Rhetoric*. New York: Praeger Publishers, 1991.

———. "Popular Economic Apocalyptic: The Case of Ravi Batra." *Journal of Popular Culture* 24 (1990): 153–64.

———. "Premillennial Apocalypse as a Rhetorical Genre." *Central States Speech Journal* 35 (1984): 84–93.

———. "Using Apocalyptic Discourse to Exploit Audience Commitments through 'Transfer.' " *Southern Speech Communication Journal* 54 (1988): 58–73.

Burke, Kenneth. *Attitudes toward History*. Berkeley: University of California Press, 1984.

———. *Counter-Statement*. Berkeley: University of California Press, 1968.

———. "Dramatism." In *The International Encyclopedia of the Social Sciences*, vol. 7, ed. David L. Sills, 445–51. New York: Macmillan, 1968.

———. *Language as Symbolic Action*. Berkeley: University of California Press, 1966.

———. *Permanence and Change: An Anatomy of Purpose*. 3d ed. Berkeley: University of California Press, 1984.

———. *The Philosophy of Literary Form*. 3d ed. Berkeley: University of California Press, 1973.

———. *A Rhetoric of Motives*. Berkeley: University of California Press, 1969.

———. *The Rhetoric of Religion*. Berkeley: University of California Press, 1970.

———. "Theology and Logology." *Kenyon Review* 1 (New Series) (Winter 1979): 151–85.

Burkert, Walter. *Ancient Mystery Cults*. Cambridge, Mass.: Harvard University Press, 1987.

Burridge, Kenelm. *New Heaven New Earth: A Study of Millenarian Activities*. Oxford: Basil Blackwell, 1969.

Butler, Jonathan. "From Millerism to Seventh- Day Adventism: 'Boundlessness to Consolidation.' " *Church History* 55 (1986): 50–64.

Butler, Jonathan M. "Adventism and the American Experience." In *The Rise of Adventism: Religion and Society in Mid-Nineteenth Century America*, ed. Edwin S. Gaustad, 173–206. New York: Harper & Row, 1974.

———. "The Making of a New Order: Millerism and the Origins of Seventh-Day Adventism." In *The Disappointed: Millerism and Millenarianism in the Nineteenth Century*, ed. Ronald L. Numbers and Jonathan M. Butler, 189–208. Bloomington: Indiana University Press, 1987.

Campbell, John Angus. "A Rhetorical Interpretation of History." *Rhetorica* 2 (1984): 227–66.

Campbell, Karlyn Kohrs, and Kathleen Hall Jamieson, eds. *Form and Genre: Shaping Rhetorical Action*. Annandale, Va.: Speech Communication Association, n.d.

Carlson, A. Cheree. "Gandhi and the Comic Frame: 'Ad Bellum Purificandum.' " *Quarterly Journal of Speech* 72 (1986): 446–55.

Carr, David. *Time, Narrative, and History*. Bloomington: Indiana University Press, 1986.

Case, Shirley Jackson. *The Millennial Hope*. Chicago: University of Chicago Press, 1918.

Cassirer, Ernst. *Language and Myth*. Trans. Suzanne Langer. New York: Dover Publications, 1946.

———. *The Myth of the State*. New Haven: Yale University Press, 1946.

———. *The Philosophy of Symbolic Forms*. Vol. 2, *Mythical Thought*. Trans. Ralph Manheim. New Haven: Yale University Press, 1955.

Castelli, Jim. "The Environmental Gospel According to James Watt." *Chicago Tribune*, 25 October 1981, B2.

Chandler, Ralph Clark. "The Wicked Shall Not Bear Rule: The Fundamentalist Heritage of the New Christian Right." In *New Christian Politics*, ed. David G. Bromley and Anson Shupe, 41–58. Macon, Ga.: Mercer University Press, 1984.

Chandler, Russell. "Persian Gulf Crisis Stirs Predictions of Final Conflict." *Los Angeles Times*, 20 September 1990, A5.

Charles, R. H. *A Critical History of the Doctrine of a Future Life*. 2d ed. London: Adam & Charles Black, 1913.

Christianson, Paul. *Reformers and Babylon: English Apocalyptic Visions from the Reformation to the Eve of the Civil War*. Toronto: University of Toronto Press, 1978.

Cicero. *De Inventione*. Trans. H. M. Hubbell. Cambridge, Mass.: Harvard University Press, 1949.

Clouse, Robert, ed. *The Meaning of the Millennium: Four Views*. Downers Grove, Ill.: Intervarsity Press, 1977.

———. "The New Christian Right, America, and the Kingdom of God." *Christian Scholars Review* 12 (1983): 3–16.

Cohn, Norman. *The Pursuit of the Millennium: Revolutionary Messianism in Medieval and Reformation Europe and Its Bearing on Modern Totalitarian Movement*. London: Secker & Warburg, 1957.

———. *The Pursuit of the Millennium: Revolutionary Millenarians and Mystical Anarchists of the Middle Ages*. Rev. ed. New York: Oxford University Press, 1980.

Collins, Adela Yarbro. *The Combat Myth in the Book of Revelation*. Missoula, Mont.: Scholars Press, 1976.

———. *Crisis and Catharsis: The Power of the Apocalypse*. Philadelphia: Westminster Press, 1984.

———, ed. "Early Christian Apocalypticism: Genre and Social Setting." *Semeia* 36 (1986).

———. "Reading the Book of Revelation in the Twentieth Century." *Interpretation* 40 (1986): 229–42.

Collins, John J., ed. "Apocalypse: The Morphology of a Genre." *Semeia* 14 (1979).

———. "Apocalyptic Eschatology as the Transcendence of Death." In *Visionaries and their Apocalypses*, ed. Paul D. Hanson, 61–84. Philadelphia: Fortress Press, 1983.

———. *The Apocalyptic Imagination: An Introduction to the Jewish Matrix of Christianity*. New York: Crossroad Publishing, 1987.

Colson, Charles. *Kingdoms in Conflict*. New York and Grand Rapids, Mich.: William Morrow and Zondervan Publishing, 1987.

Conley, Thomas M. "The Enthymeme in Perspective." *Quarterly Journal of Speech* 70 (1984): 168–87.

Conover, Pamela. "The Mobilization of the New Right: A Test of Various Explanations." *Western Political Quarterly* 36 (1983): 632–49.

Cousins, Norman. *Modern Man Is Obsolete*. New York: Viking Press, 1945.

Cox, Harvey. *Religion in the Secular City*. New York: Simon & Schuster, 1984.

Cox, J. Robert. "The Die Is Cast: Topical and Ontological Dimensions of the Locus of the Irreparable." *Quarterly Journal of Speech* 68 (1982): 227–39.

———. "The Fulfillment of Time: King's 'I Have a Dream' Speech (August 28, 1963)." In *Texts in Context: Critical Dialogues on Significant Episodes in American Political Rhetoric*, ed. Michael C. Leff and Fred J. Kauffeld, 181–204. Davis, Calif.: Hermagoras Press.

Crawford, Alan. *Thunder on the Right: The "New Right" and the Politics of Resentment.* New York: Pantheon Books, 1980.

Creps, Earl G. "The Conspiracy Argument as Rhetorical Genre." Ph.D. dissertation, Northwestern University, 1980.

Cross, F. L., ed. *The Oxford Dictionary of the Christian Church.* London: Oxford University Press, 1958.

Cross, Whitney. *The Burned-over District: The Social and Intellectual History of Enthusiastic Religion in Upstate New York, 1800–1850.* Ithaca, N.Y.: Cornell University Press, 1950.

Crossan, John Dominic. *Raid on the Articulate: Comic Eschatology in Jesus and Borges.* Philadelphia: Fortress Press, 1976.

Cullman, Oscar. *Christ and Time: The Primitive Christian Conception of Time and History.* Trans. Floyd Filson. Philadelphia: Westminster Press, 1950.

Cumbey, Constance. *A Planned Deception: The Staging of a New Age Messiah.* East Detroit, Mich.: Pointe Publishers, 1985.

Cuomo, Joe, producer. "Ronald Reagan and the Prophecy of Armageddon." Radio documentary. Transcript provided by the Christic Institute. Washington, D.C.: Christic Institute, October 1984.

Curry, George E. "Is Reagan Arming for Real Armageddon?" *Chicago Tribune,* 11 October 1984, 1A, 43A.

Damsteegt, P. Gerard. *Foundations of the Seventh-Day Adventist Message and Mission.* Grand Rapids, Mich.: William B. Eerdmans, 1977.

D'Angelo, Frank. "The Evolution of the Analytic Topoi: A Speculative Inquiry." In *Essays on Classical Rhetoric and Modern Discourse,* ed. Robert J. Connors, Lisa Ede, and Andrea Lunsford, 50–68. Carbondale: Southern Illinois University Press, 1984.

Daniélou, Jean. *The Lord of History.* Trans. Nigel Abercrombie. London: Longmans, 1958.

Daniels, Tom D., Richard J. Jensen, and Allen Lichtenstein. "Resolving the Paradox in Politicized Christian Fundamentalism." *Western Journal of Speech Communication* 29 (1985): 248–66.

Dart, John. "Sect Leader Continues to Spread Word Despite Uproar Over Forecasts." *Los Angeles Times,* 23 February 1991, F16.

Davidson, James West. *The Logic of Millennial Thought.* New Haven: Yale University Press, 1977.

de Man, Paul. *Blindness and Insight: Essays in the Rhetoric of Contemporary Criticism.* New York: Oxford University Press, 1971.

———. *The Rhetoric of Romanticism.* New York: Columbia University Press, 1984.

Derrida, Jacques. "No Apocalypse, Not Now (full speed ahead, seven missiles, seven missives)." Trans. Catherine Porter and Philip Lewis. *Diacritics* 14 (1984): 20–31.

———. "Of an Apocalyptic Tone Recently Adopted in Philosophy." Trans. John Leavey, Jr. *Semeia* 23 (1982): 63–98.

Despland, Michel. *Kant on History and Religion.* Montreal: McGill–Queen's Unitersity Press, 1973.

Doan, Ruth Alden. *The Miller Heresy, Millennialism, and American Culture.* Philadelphia: Temple University Press, 1987.

———. "Millerism and Evangelical Culture." In *The Disappointed: Millerism and Millenarianism in the Nineteenth Century,* ed. Ronald L. Numbers and Jonathan M. Butler, 118–38. Bloomington: Indiana University Press, 1987.

Dobson, Ed, and Ed Hindson. "Apocalypse Now? What Fundamentalists Believe about the End of the World." *Policy Review* 38 (1986): 16–23.

Dodd, C. H. *History and the Gospel.* New York: Charles Scribner's Sons, 1938.

Dostoevsky, Fyodor. *The Brothers Karamazov.* Trans. Constance Garnett, ed. Ralph E. Matlaw. New York: W. W. Norton & Co., 1976.

Doty, William G. *Mythography: The Study of Myths and Rituals.* University: University of Alabama Press, 1986.

Dugger, Ronnie. "Does Reagan Expect a Nuclear Armageddon?" *Washington Post,* 8 April 1984, C1.

Duncan, Hugh Dalziel. *Communication and Social Order.* London: Oxford University Press, 1962.

E.C.C. "A Voice from Slave Land." *Advent Message to the Daughters of Zion,* September, 1844, 35.

Eddy, Mary Baker. *Science and Health with Key to the Scriptures.* Authorized ed. Boston: Published by the Trustees under the will of Mary Baker G. Eddy, 1934.

Edwards, Jonathan. *The Works of Jonathan Edwards.* Vol. 5, *Apocalyptic Writings,* ed. Stephen J. Stein. New Haven: Yale University Press, 1977.

Eliade, Mircea. *Myth and Reality.* Trans. Willard R. Trask. New York: Harper & Row, 1963.

———. *The Myth of the Eternal Return or, Cosmos and History.* Trans. Willard R. Trask. Princeton: Princeton University Press, 1971.

———. *The Sacred and the Profane.* Trans. Willard R. Trask. New York: Harcourt Brace, Jovanovich, 1959.

Elson, John. "Apocalypse Now?" *Time,* 11 February 1991, 88.

Exum, J. Cheryl, ed. *Tragedy and Comedy in the Bible.* Decatur, Ga.: Scholars Press, 1985.

Fahnestock, Jeanne R., and Marie J. Secor. "Grounds for Argument: Stasis Theory and the Topoi." In *Argument in Transition: Proceedings of the Third Summer Conference on Argumentation,* ed. David Zarefsky, Malcolm Sillars, and Jack Rhodes, 135–46. Annandale, Va.: Speech Communication Association, 1983.

Fairbairn, Patrick. *The Typology of Scripture, Viewed in Connection with the Whole Series of the Divine Dispensations.* 2 vols. New York: Funk & Wagnalls, 1911.

Falwell, Jerry. *Nuclear War and the Second Coming of Jesus Christ.* Lynchburg, Va.: Old Time Gospel Hour, n.d.

Falwell, Jerry, with Ed Dobson and Ed Hindson. *The Fundamentalist Phenomenon.* New York: Doubleday, 1981.

Farrell, Thomas B. "Knowledge, Consensus, and Rhetorical Theory." *Quarterly Journal of Speech* 62 (1976): 1–14.

———. "Knowledge in Time: Toward an Extension of Rhetorical Form." In *Advances in Argumentation Theory and Research,* ed. J. Robert Cox and Charles Arthur Willard, 123–53. Carbondale: Southern Illinois University Press, 1982.

———. "Rhetorical Resemblance: Paradoxes of a Practical Art." *Quarterly Journal of Speech* 72 (1986): 1–19.

———. "Social Knowledge II." *Quarterly Journal of Speech* 64 (1978): 329–34.

———. "The Tradition of Rhetoric and the Philosophy of Communication." *Communication* 7 (1983): 151–80.

Farrer, Austin. *A Rebirth of Images: The Making of St John's Apocalypse.* Westminster, England: Dacre Press, 1949.

Festinger, Leon, Henry W. Riecken, and Stanley Schachter. *When Prophecy Fails*. New York: Harper Torchbooks, 1964.

Feurherd, Joe. "Author: Gulf War Beginning of Endtimes." *National Catholic Reporter*, 1 February 1991, 10.

Finney, Charles. *Lectures on Revivals of Religion*. New York, 1835.

Fisher, Walter R. "Genre: Concepts and Applications in Rhetorical Criticism." *Western Journal of Speech Communication* 44 (1980): 288–299.

———. *Human Communication as Narration: Toward a Philosophy of Reason, Value, and Action*. Columbia: University of South Carolina Press, 1987.

———. "Toward a Logic of Good Reasons." *Quarterly Journal of Speech* 64 (1978): 376–84.

Fitch, Charles. *Come Out of Her, My People: A Sermon*. Rochester, N.Y.: J. V. Himes, 1843.

FitzGerald, Frances. *Cities on a Hill*. New York: Simon & Schuster, 1987.

Flew, Antony. *God: A Critical Inquiry*. La Salle, Ill.: Open Court Publishing, 1984.

Focillon, Henri. *The Year 1000*. Trans. Fred D. Wieck. New York: Frederick Ungar Publishing, 1969.

Fraser, J. T. *Of Time, Passion, and Knowledge*. 2nd ed. Princeton, N.J.: Princeton University Press, 1990.

Frei, Hans W. *The Eclipse of Biblical Narrative*. New Haven, Conn.: Yale University Press, 1974.

Frentz, Thomas. "Rhetorical Conversation, Time, and Moral Action." *Quarterly Journal of Speech* 71 (1985): 1–18.

Friedlander, Saul, Gerald Horton, Leo Marx, and Eugene Skolnikoff, ed. *Visions of Apocalypse: End or Rebirth?* New York: Holmes & Meier, 1985.

Froom, Leroy Edwin. *The Prophetic Faith of Our Fathers*. Vol. 4. Washington, D.C.: Review & Herald Press, 1954.

Frye, Northrop. *Anatomy of Criticism*. New York: Atheneum, 1968.

———. *The Great Code: The Bible and Literature*. San Diego, Calif.: Harcourt, Brace, Jovanovich, 1983.

Gager, John. *Kingdom and Community: the Social World of Early Christianity*. Englewood Cliffs, N.J.: Prentice-Hall, 1975.

Gale, Robert. *The Urgent Voice: The Story of William Miller*. Washington, D.C.: Review & Herald Publishing Association, 1975.

Gardner, Martin. "Giving God a Hand." *New York Review of Books*, 13 August 1987, 17–23.

Garrison, Jim. *The Darkness of God: Theology after Hiroshima*. Grand Rapids, Mich.: William B. Eerdmans, 1982.

Good, Edwin M. "Apocalyptic as Comedy: The Book of Daniel." In *Tragedy and Comedy in the Bible*, ed. J. Cheryl Exum, 41–70. Decatur, Ga.: Scholars Press, 1985.

Goodnight, G. Thomas. "Argumentation in the Nuclear Age." *Journal of the American Forensic Association* 24 (1988): 141–43.

———. "Generational Argument." In *Argumentation: Across the Lines of Discipline*, ed. Frans H. van Eemeren, Rob Grootendorst, J. Anthony Blair and Charles A. Willard, 129–44. Dordrecht-Holland: Foris Publications, 1987.

———. "The Nuclear Age as an Argument Formation." Paper presented at the Conference on Methodologies of Survival, Dubrovnik, Yugoslavia, June 1987.

—————. "Ronald Reagan's Re-formulation of the Rhetoric of War: Analysis of the 'Zero Option,' 'Evil Empire,' and 'Star Wars' Addresses." *Quarterly Journal of Speech* 72 (1986): 390–414.

Grant, Robert M., and David Tracy. *A Short History of the Interpretation of the Bible*. Rev. ed. Philadelphia: Fortress Press, 1984.

Graybill, Ronald. "The Abolitionist-Millerite Connection." In *The Disappointed: Millerism and Millenarianism in the Nineteenth Century*, ed. Ronald L. Numbers and Jonathan M. Butler, 139–52. Bloomington, Ind.: Indiana University Press, 1987.

A Greek–English Lexicon. Ed. George Liddell and Robert Scott. 9th ed. Oxford: Clarendon Press, 1961.

Grounds, Vernon. "Eschatology: Cutting the Nerve of Christian Social Concern." *ESA Parley* 4 (January 1987).

—————. "Prophecy and Pessimism." *ESA Parley* 4 (October 1987).

—————. "Prophetic Speculation and Public Policy." *ESA Parley* 4 (April 1987).

—————. "The Purpose of Prophecy." *ESA Parley* 4 (July 1987).

Haddad, Hassan, and Donald Wagner, ed. *All in the Name of the Bible*. Brattleboro, Vt.: Amana Books, 1986.

Halsell, Grace. *Prophecy and Politics: Militant Evangelists on the Road to Nuclear War*. Westport, Conn.: Lawrence Hill, 1986.

Hammond, John. *The Politics of Benevolence: Revival Religion and American Voting Behavior*. Norwood, N.J.: Ablex Publishing, 1979.

Hanson, Paul D. "Apocalyptic Consciousness." *Harvard Divinity Bulletin* (April-May 1984): 4–6, 14.

—————. *The Dawn of Apocalyptic*. Philadelphia: Fortress Press, 1975.

Harrison, Frank R. "Epistemic Frames and Eschatological Stories." In *The Return of the Millennium*, ed. Joseph Bettis and S. K. Johannesen. 59–85. Barrytown, N.Y.: New ERA Books, 1984.

Harrison, J. F. C. *The Second Coming: Popular Millenarianism, 1780–1850*. New Brunswick, N.J.: Rutgers University Press, 1979.

Hart, Roderick P. *The Political Pulpit*. West Lafayette, Ind.: Purdue University Press, 1977.

Hartnack, Justus. *Kant's Theory of Knowledge*. Trans. M. Holmes Hartshorne. New York: Harcourt, Brace, & World, 1967.

Hatab, Lawrence J. *Myth and Philosophy: A Contest of Truths*. La Salle, Ill.: Open Court Publishing, 1990.

Hatch, Nathan O. *The Sacred Cause of Liberty: Republican Thought and the Millennium in Revolutionary New England*. New Haven, Conn.: Yale University Press, 1977.

—————. "The Origins of Civil Millennialism in America: New England Clergymen, War with France, and the Revolution." *William and Mary Quarterly* 31 (1974): 407–30.

Hatch, Nathan, and Mark Noll, ed. *The Bible in America: Essays in Cultural History*. New York: Oxford University Press, 1982.

Hauerwas, Stanley, and David Burrell. "From System to Story: An Alternative Pattern for Rationality in Ethics." In *Truthfullness and Tragedy: An Alternative Pattern for Rationality in Ethics*. Notre Dame, Ind.: University of Notre Dame Press, 1977.

Hawking, Stephen. *A Brief History of Time*. Toronto: Bantam Books, 1987.

Heald, John C. "Apocalyptic Rhetoric: Agents of the Antichrist from the French to the British." *Today's Speech* 23 (1975): 33–37.

Heath, Robert L. "Kenneth Burke on Form." *Quarterly Journal of Speech* 65 (1979): 392–404.

Heimert, Alan. *Religion and the American Mind*. Cambridge, Mass.: Harvard University Press, 1966.

Hellholm, David. "The Problem of Apocalyptic Genre and the Apocalypse of John." *Semeia* 36 (1986): 13–64.

Herbers, John. "Armageddon View Prompts a Debate." *New York Times*, national ed., 24 October 1984, A1.

Hewitt, Clyde E. *Midnight and Morning*. Charlotte, N.C.: Venture Books, 1983.

Hewitt, V. J., and Peter Lorie. *Nostradamus: The End of the Millennium*. New York: Simon & Schuster, 1991.

Hick, John. *Evil and the God of Love*. Rev. ed. San Francisco: Harper & Row, 1978.

Hill, Christopher. *Antichrist in Seventeenth-Century England*. Rev. ed. London: Verso, 1990.

Hill, David. *New Testament Prophecy*. Atlanta, Ga.: John Knox Press, 1979.

Hobsbawm, E. J. *Primitive Rebels: Studies in Archaic Forms of Social Movement in the 19th and 20th Centuries*. New York: W.W. Norton., 1959.

Hofstader, Richard. *The Paranoid Style in American Politics and Other Essays*. Chicago: University of Chicago Press, 1979.

Hogan, J. Michael. "Apocalyptic Pornography and the Nuclear Freeze: A Defense of the Public." In *Argument and Critical Practices: Proceedings of the Fifth SCA / AFA Conference on Argumentation*, ed. Joseph Wenzel, 541–48. Annandale, Va.: Speech Communication Association, 1987.

Hogue, John. *Nostradamus and the Millennium: Predictions of the Future*. London: Bloomsbury, 1987.

Horsfeld, Peter G. *Religious Television: The American Experience*. New York: Longman, 1984.

Hume, David. *Dialogues Concerning Natural Religions*. New York: Hafner Press, 1948.

Hyers, M. Conrad. *And God Created Laughter*. Atlanta: John Knox Press, 1987.

————. *The Comic Vision and the Christian Faith*. New York: Pilgrim Press, 1981.

————. "The Dialectic of the Sacred and the Comic." In *Holy Laughter: Essays on Religion in the Comic Perspective*, ed. M. Conrad Hyers, 208–40. New York: Seabury Press, 1969.

Irenaeus. *Against Heresies*. Trans. Alexander Roberts and W. H. Rambaut. In *The Ante-Nicene Fathers*, vol. 1, rev. ed., ed. Alexander Roberts and James Donaldson. 309–567. Buffalo, N.Y.: Christian Literature Publishing, 1886.

Jamieson, Kathleen Hall. *Eloquence in an Electronic Age: The Transformation of Political Speechmaking*. New York: Oxford University Press, 1988.

Jaspers, Karl. *The Atom Bomb and the Future of Man*. Trans. E. B. Ashton. Chicago: University of Chicago Press, 1961.

Jenks, Gregory C. *The Origins and Early Development of the Antichrist Myth*. New York: Walter de Gruyter, 1991.

Jewett, Robert. "Coming to Terms with the Doom Boom." *Quarterly Review* 4 (Fall 1984): 9–22.

————. *Jesus against the Rapture: Seven Unexpected Prophecies*. Philadelphia: Westminster Press, 1979.

————. *The Thessalonian Correspondence*. Philadelphia: Fortress Press, 1986.

Johnson, Paul E. *A Shopkeeper's Millennium: Society and Revivals in Rochester, N.Y.,*
    1815–1837. New York: Hill and Wang, 1978.
Jung, C. G. *Answer to Job.* Trans. R. F. C. Hull. Cleveland, Ohio: World Publishing Co.,
    1960.
Kafka, Franz. "Reflections on Sin, Pain, Hope, and the True Way." Trans. Willa and
    Edwin Muir. In *The Great Wall of China: Stories and Reflections,* 162–84. New York:
    Schocken Books, 1970.
Kahn, Herman J., and Anthony J. Wiener. *The Year 2000.* New York: Macmillan, 1967.
Kaminsky, Howard. "The Problem of Explanation." In *Millennial Dreams in Action: Studios
    in Revolutionary Religious Movements.* New York: Schocken Books, 1970.
Kant, Immanuel. *Critique of Pure Reason.* Trans. J. M. D. Meiklejohn. New York: Colonial
    Press, 1900.
———. "On the Failure of All Attempted Philosophical Theodicies." Trans. Michel Desp-
    land. In Despland, *Kant on History and Religion,* 283–97. Montreal: McGill-Queen's
    University Press, 1973.
Käsemann, Ernst. "The Beginnings of Christian Theology." In *Apocalypticism,* ed. R. W.
    Funk, 17–46. New York: Herder & Herder, 1969.
Kaufman, Gordon. *Theology for a Nuclear Age.* Manchester, Eng.: Manchester University
    Press, 1985.
Kelly, J. N. D. *Early Christian Doctrines.* Rev. ed. New York: Harper & Row, 1978.
Kennedy, George. *New Testament Interpretation through Rhetorical Criticism.* Chapel Hill:
    University of North Carolina Press, 1984.
Kermode, Frank. "Apocalypse and the Modern." In *Visions of Apocalypse: End or Rebirth?,*
    ed. Saul Friedlander, Gerald Horton, Leo Marx, and Eugene Skolnikoff, 84–106. New
    York: Holmes & Meier, 1985.
———. *The Sense of an Ending.* New York: Oxford University Press, 1967.
Keyes, Charles F. "Charisma: From Social Life to Sacred Biography." *Journal of the Amer-
    ican Academy of Religion Thematic Studies* 48 (1982): 1–22.
King, Wayne. "The Record of Pat Robertson on Religion and Government." *New York
    Times,* national ed., 27 December 1987, 20.
King, Winston L. "Eschatology: Christian and Buddhist." *Religion* 16 (1986): 169–85.
Kinneavy, James L. *Greek Rhetorical Origins of the Christian Faith.* New York: Oxford
    University Press, 1987.
Kirsch, Jonathan. "Hal Lindsey." *Publisher's Weekly,* 14 March 1977, 30–32.
Klemm, David E. "The Rhetoric of Theological Argument." In *The Rhetoric of the Human
    Sciences,* ed. John S. Nelson, Alan Megill, and Donald N. McCloskey, 276–97. Madison:
    University of Wisconsin Press, 1987.
Kline, Susan. "Toward a Contemporary Linguistic Interpretation of the Concept of Stasis."
    Journal of the American Forensic Association 16 (1979): 95–103.
Kneupper, Charles W. "Rhetoric, Argument, and Social Reality: A Social Constructivist
    View." *Journal of the American Forensic Association* 1980 (16): 173–81.
Koch, Klaus. "What is Apocalyptic? An Attempt at a Preliminary Definition." In *Vision-
    aries and Their Apocalypses,* ed. Paul D. Hanson, 16–36. Philadelphia: Fortress Press,
    1983.
Kolenkow, Anitra Bingham. "The Fall of the Temple and the Coming of the End: The
    Spectrum and Process of Apocalyptic Argument in 2 Baruch and Other Authors." In

Society of Biblical Literature 1982 Seminar Papers, ed. Kent Harold Richards, 243–50. Chico, Calif.: Scholars Press, 1982.

Kushner, Harold S. *When Bad Things Happen to Good People.* New York: Avon Books, 1981.

Lactantius. *Divine Institutes,* book VII. Trans. Bernard McGinn. In *Apocalyptic Spirituality,* ed. Bernard McGinn, 17–80. New York: Paulist Press, 1979.

Lake, Randall A. "Between Myth and History: Enacting Time in Native American Protest Rhetoric." *Quarterly Journal of Speech* 77 (1991): 123–51.

———. "The Implied Arguer." In *Argumentation Theory and the Rhetoric of Assent,* ed. David Cratis Williams and Michael David Hazen, 69–90. Tuscaloosa: University of Alabama Press, 1990.

Lalonde, Peter. *One World under Antichrist.* Eugene, Oreg.: Harvest House, 1991.

Land, Gary, ed. *Adventism: A History.* Grand Rapids, Mich.: William B. Eerdmans, 1986.

Landes, David. *Revolution in Time: Clocks and the Making of the Modern World.* Cambridge, Mass.: Harvard University Press, 1983.

Landes, Richard. "Lest the Millennium Be Fulfilled: Apocalyptic Expectations and the Pattern of Western Chronography 100–800 CE." In *The Use and Abuse of Eschatology in the Middle Ages,* ed. Werner Verbeke, Daniel Verhelst and Andries Welkenhuysen, 137–211. Leuven, The Netherlands: Leuven University Press, 1988.

———. "The Terrible Hopes of the Millennium: Europe and the Year 1000." Paper presented at the conference on "Christendom and Its Discontents," at the Center for Medieval and Renaissance Studies, University of California, Los Angeles, January, 1991.

Langer, Susanne K. *Feeling and Form.* New York: Charles Scribner's Sons, 1953.

Langston, Douglas. "The Argument from Evil: Reply to Professor Richman." *Religious Studies* 16 (1980): 103–13.

Lanternari, Vittorio. *The Religions of the Oppressed: A Study of Modern Messianic Cults.* Trans. Lisa Sergio. New York: Alfred A. Knopf, 1965.

Lattin, Don. "Critics Ask Whether Reagan Takes Armageddon as Gospel." *San Francisco Examiner,* 25 October 1984, A4.

———. "Time is Ripe for Prophets of Doom, Group Warns." San Francisco Chronicle, 2 March 1992, A3.

Lavery, David. "The Audition of History and the Vocation of Man: Reflections on Extinction and Human Destiny." *Michigan Quarterly Review* 14 (1985): 345–67.

Leff, Michael. "Dimensions of Temporality in Lincoln's Second Inaugural." *Communication Reports* 1 (1988): 26–31.

———. "Rhetorical Timing in Lincoln's House Divided Speech." *The Van Zelst Lecture in Communication.* Evanston, Ill.: Northwestern University, 1983.

———. "Textual Criticism: The Legacy of G. P. Mohrmann." *Quarterly Journal of Speech* 72 (1986): 377–89.

———. "The Topics of Argumentative Invention in Latin Rhetorical Theory from Cicero to Boethius." *Rhetorica* 1 (1983): 23–44.

———. "Topical Invention and Metaphoric Interaction." *Southern Speech Communication Journal* 48 (1983): 214–28.

Leff, Michael, and Dean E. Hewes. "Topical Invention and Group Communication: Toward a Sociology of Inference." In *Dimensions of Argument: Proceedings of the Second Summer Conference on Argumentation,* ed. George Ziegelmueller and Jack Rhodes, 770–89. Annandale, Va.: Speech Communication Association, 1981.

Leibniz, G. W. *Theodicy*, ed. Austin Farrer. Trans. E. M. Huggard. La Salle, Ill.: Open Court Publishing Co., 1985.

Lévi-Strauss, Claude. *Structural Anthropology*. Trans. Claire Jacobson and Brooke Grundfest Schoepf. New York: Basic Books, 1963.

Levitt, Zola. *The Levitt Letter*, 1 January 1990.

Lewis, C. S. *God in the Dock: Essays on Theology and Ethics*. Grand Rapids, Mich.: Eerdmans, 1970.

Lienesch, Michael. "The Role of Political Millennialism in Early American Nationalism." *Western Political Quarterly* 36 (1983): 445–65.

Lifton, Robert Jay. "The Image of the End of the World: A Psychohistorical View." In *Visions of Apocalypse: End or Rebirth*, eds. Saul Friedlander, Gerald Horton, Leo Marx, and Eugene Skolnikoff, 151–70. New York: Holmes & Meier, 1985.

Lifton, Robert Jay, and Charles B. Strozier. "Waiting for Armageddon." *New York Times Book Review*, 12 August 1990, 1, 24–25.

Lindsell, Harold. *The Armageddon Spectre*. Westchester, Ill.: Crossways Books, 1984.

———. *The Late Great Planet Earth*. New York: Bantam, 1973.

———. *The Liberation of Planet Earth*. Grand Rapids, Mich.: Zondervan, 1974.

Lindsey, Hal. *The 1980's: Countdown to Armageddon*. New York: Bantam, 1981.

———. *The Rapture*. New York: Bantam, 1983.

———. *The Road to Holocaust*. New York: Bantam, 1989.

———. *There's a New World Coming*. Irvine, CA: Harvest House Publishers, 1973.

Lindsey, Hal, and C. C. Carlson. *Satan Is Alive and Well on Planet Earth*. New York: Bantam, 1974.

Lindsey, Hal, and Chuck Missler. *The Magog Factor*. Palos Verdes, Calif.: Hal Lindsey Ministries, 1992.

Loughborough, J. N. *Rise and Progress of the Seventh-Day Adventists*. Battle Creek, Mich.: General Conference Association, 1892.

Löwith, Karl. *Meaning in History*. Chicago: University of Chicago Press, 1949.

Luckman, Thomas. "The Constitution of Human Life in Time." In *Chronotypes: The Construction of Time*, eds. John Bender and David E. Wellbery, 151–66. Stanford, Calif.: Stanford University Press, 1991.

———. *The Invisible Religion: The Problem of Religion in Modern Society*. New York: Macmillan, 1967.

MacIntyre, Alasdair. *After Virtue: A Study in Moral Theory*. Rev. ed. Notre Dame, Ind.: University of Notre Dame Press, 1984.

———. *Whose Justice? Which Rationality?* Notre Dame, Ind.: University of Notre Dame Press, 1988.

Mackie, J. L. "Evil and Omnipotence." In *The Philosophy of Religion*, ed. Basil Mitchell, 92–104. London: Oxford University Press, 1971.

Maclear, J. F. "The Republic and the Millennium." In *The Religion of the Republic*, ed. Elwyn A. Smith, 183–216. Philadelphia: Fortress Press, 1971.

MacMullen, Ramsay. *Christianizing the Roman Empire*. New Haven, Conn.: Yale University Press, 1984.

Malina, Bruce J. "Christ and Time: Swiss or Mediterranean?" *Catholic Biblical Quarterly* 51 (1989): 1–31.

Markus, R. A. *Saeculum: History and Society in the Theology of St. Augustine*. Rev. ed. Cambridge, Eng.: University Press, 1988.

Marsden, George. "Everyone One's Own Interpreter? The Bible, Science, and Authority in Mid-Nineteenth-Century America." In *The Bible in America: Essays in Cultural History*, ed. Nathan O. Hatch and Mark Noll, 79–100. New York: Oxford University Press, 1982.

———. *Fundamentalism and American Culture*. New York: Oxford University Press, 1980.

Marston, Peter J. "Rhetorical Forms and Functions of Cosmological Argument." Ph.D. dissertation, University of Southern California, 1987.

Martin, William. "Waiting for the End: The Growing Interest in Apocalyptic Prophecy." *Atlantic* (June 1982): 31–37.

Mathias, B. *The Groaning Creation: or, The Miseries and Liabilities of the Present Life, and the Hopes of the Other: A Sermon for the Times*. 4th ed. New York: Published by the author, 1848.

Mavrodes, George. "The Problem of Evil as a Rhetorical Problem." *Philosophy and Rhetoric* 1 (1968): 91–102.

McCloskey, H. J. "God and Evil." In *God and Evil*, ed. Nelson Pike. Englewood Cliffs, N.J.: Prentice-Hall, 1964.

McGinn, Bernard. "Angel Pope and Papal Antichrist." *Church History* 47 (1978): 30–47.

———. "Revelation." In *The Literary Guide to the Bible*, ed. Robert Alter and Frank Kermode, 523–41. Cambridge, Mass.: Harvard University Press, 1987.

———. *Visions of the End: Apocalyptic Traditions in the Middle Ages*. New York: Columbia University Press, 1979.

———, ed. *Apocalyptic Spirituality*. New York: Paulist Press, 1979.

McKeever, Jim. *Christians Will Go through the Tribulation*. Medford, Oreg.: Omega Publications, 1980.

McKeon, Richard. *Freedom and History and other Essays*. Ed. Zahava McKeon. Chicago: University of Chicago Press, 1990.

McLoughlin, William G. *Modern Revivalism: Charles Grandison Finney to Billy Graham*. New York: Ronald Press, 1959.

———. *Revivals, Awakenings, and Reform: An Essay on Religion and Social Change in America, 1607–1977*. Chicago: University of Chicago Press, 1978.

Miller, Carolyn R. "Fields of Argument and Special Topoi." In *Argument in Transition: Proceedings of the Third Summer Conference on Argumentation*, ed. David Zarefsky, Malcolm Sillars, and Jack Rhodes. 147–58. Annandale, Va.: Speech Communication Association, 1983.

Miller, William. *Evidences from Scripture and History of the Second Coming of Christ about the Year A.D. 1843: Exhibited in a Course of Lectures*. Troy, N.Y.: Kemble & Hooper, 1836.

———. *Mr. Miller's Apology and Defence*. Boston: J. V. Himes, 1845.

———. *Views of the Prophecies and Prophetic Chronology, Selected from Manuscripts of William Miller, with a Memoir of His Life*. Boston: Joshua V. Himes, 1842.

Mixon, Harold, and Mary Frances HopKins. "Apocalypticism in Secular Public Discourse: A Proposed Theory." *Central States Speech Journal* 39 (1988): 244–57.

Mojtabai, A. G. *Blessed Assurance: At Home with the Bomb in Amarillo, Texas*. Albuquerque: University of New Mexico Press, 1986.

Moorhead, James H. *American Apocalypse: Yankee Protestants and the Civil War 1860–1869*. New Haven, Conn.: Yale University Press, 1978.

————. "Between Progress and Apocalypse: A Reassessment of Millennialism in American Religious Thought, 1800–1880." *Journal of American History* 71 (1984): 524–42.

————. "The Erosion of Postmillennialism in American Religious Thought, 1865–1925." *Church History* 53 (1984): 61–77.

————. "Searching for the Millennium in America." *Princeton Seminary Bulletin* 8 (1987): 17–33.

Morison, Robert S. "Biological Eschatology." In *Visions of Apocalypse: End or Rebirth?*, ed. Saul Friedlander, Gerald Horton, Leo Marx, and Eugene Skolnikoff. 137–150. New York: Holmes & Meier, 1985.

Morris, Richard. *The End of the World*. Garden City, N.Y.: Doubleday-Anchor, 1980.

Naipaul, Shiva. *Journey to Nowhere*. London: Penguin Books, 1981.

Nelson, John S., with Allan Megill and Donald N. McCloskey, eds. *The Rhetoric of the Human Sciences: Language and Argument in Scholarship and Public Affairs*. Madison: University of Wisconsin Press, 1987.

Neuhaus, Richard John, and Michael Cromartie, eds. *Piety and Politics: Evangelicals and Fundamentalists Confront the World*. Washington, D.C.: Ethics and Public Policy Center, 1987.

Nichol, Frances D. *The Midnight Cry*. Washington, D.C.: Review & Herald Publishing Association, 1945.

Niebuhr, H. Richard. *The Kingdom of God in America*. Middletown, Conn.: Wesleyan University Press, 1988.

Niebuhr, R. Gustav. "Millennium Fever: Prophets Proliferate, The End Is Near." *Wall Street Journal*, 5 December 1989, A1, A5.

Noll, Mark. "Misreading the Signs of the Times." *Christianity Today*, 6 February 1987, 10.

Numbers, Ronald L., and Jonathan M. Butler, eds. *The Disappointed: Millerism and Millenarianism in the Nineteenth Century*. Bloomington: Indiana University Press, 1987.

Ochs, Donovan J. "Aristotle's Concept of the Formal Topics." *Speech Monographs* 36 (1969): 419–25.

O'Flaherty, Wendy Doniger. *The Origins of Evil in Hindu Mythology*. Berkeley: University of California Press, 1976.

————. *Other People's Myths*. New York: Macmillan, 1988.

O'Leary, Stephen D., and Michael McFarland. "The Political Use of Mythic Discourse: Prophetic Interpretation in Pat Robertson's Presidential Campaign." *Quarterly Journal of Speech* 75 (1989): 433–52.

Olson, Kathryn M. "Completing the Picture: Replacing Generic Embodiments in the Historical Flow." Paper presented at the annual convention of the Speech Communication Association, Chicago November, 1990.

Ostling, Richard N. "Armageddon and the End Times: Prophecies of the Last Days Surface as a Campaign Issue." *Time*, 5 November 1984, 73.

Overholt, Thomas. *Channels of Prophecy: The Social Dynamics of Prophetic Activity*. Minneapolis: Fortress Press, 1989.

Pack, Charles. "Pat Robertson Says vs. What the Bible Says." *Prophecy*, November 1986, 1.

Pannikar, R. "The Destiny of Technological Civilization: An Ancient Buddhist Legend Romavisaya." *Alternatives* 10 (1984):237–53.

Payne, J. Barton. *Encyclopedia of Biblical Prophecy: The Complete Guide to Scriptural Predictions and their Fulfillment*. Grand Rapids, Mich.: Baker Book House, 1973.

Pepper, Stephen P. *World Hypotheses*. Berkeley: University of California Press, 1970.

Percy, Walker. "Notes for a Novel about the End of the World." In *The Message in the Bottle*, 101–18. New York: Farrar, Straus & Giroux, 1978.

Perelman, Chaim, and L. Olbrechts-Tyteca. *The New Rhetoric: A Treatise on Argumentation*. Trans. John Wilkinson and Purcell Weaver. Notre Dame, Ind.: University of Notre Dame Press, 1969.

Petry, Ray C. *Christian Eschatology and Social Thought*. New York: Abingdon Press, 1956.

Pike, Nelson. "Hume on Evil." In *God and Evil*, ed. Nelson Pike, 85–102. Englewood Cliffs, N.J.: Prentice-Hall, 1964.

Pirsig, Robert. *Zen and the Art of Motorcycle Maintenance*. New York: Bantam Books, 1976.

Plantinga, Alvin. "The Free Will Defence." In *The Philosophy of Religion*, ed. Basil Mitchell, 105–20. London: Oxford University Press, 1971.

——. *God and Other Minds*. Ithaca, N.Y.: Cornell University Press, 1967.

Plato. *Statesman*. Trans. J. B. Skemp. Bristol, UK: Bristol Classical Press, 1987.

Pope, M. H. "Seven, Seventh, Seventy." In *The Interpreter's Dictionary of the Bible*, vol. 4, ed. George Arthur Buttrick, 294–95. New York: Abingdon Press, 1962.

Popkin, Richard H. "The Triumphant Apocalypse and the Catastrophic Apocalypse." In *Nuclear Weapons and the Future of Humanity*, ed. Avner Cohen and Steven Lee, 131–50. Totowa, N.J.: Rowman & Allanheld, Publishers, 1986.

Proceedings of the Second Session of the General Conference of Christians Expecting the Advent of Our Lord Jesus Christ, Held in Lowell, Ms., June 15, 16, 17, 1841. Boston: Joshua Himes, n.d.

Public Agenda Foundation. *Voter Options on Nuclear Arms Policy*. New York: Public Agenda Foundation, 1984.

Rad, Gerhard von. *Old Testament Theology*. Vol. 2 Trans. D. M. G. Stacker. New York: Harper, 1965.

Ray, John W. "Perelman's Universal Audience." *Quarterly Journal of Speech* 55 (1978): 361–75.

Reagan, Ronald. "Debate Between the President and Former Vice-President Walter F. Mondale in Kansas City, Missouri, October 21, 1984." In *Public Papers of the Presidents of the United States: Ronald Reagan 1984, Book II—June 30 to December 31, 1984*, 1589–1608. Washington, D.C.: U.S. Government Printing Office, 1987.

——. "Interview with Garry Clifford and Patricia Ryan of People Magazine, December 6, 1983." In *Public Papers of the Presidents of the United States: Ronald Reagan 1983, Book II—July 2 to December 31, 1983*. 1711–17. Washington, D.C.: U.S. Government Printing Office, 1985.

——. "Remarks at the Annual Convention of the National Association of Evangelicals in Orlando, Florida, March 8, 1983." In *Public Papers of the Presidents of the United States: Ronald Reagan 1983, Book I—January 1 to July 1, 1983*, 359–64. Washington, D.C.: U.S. Government Printing Office, 1984.

——. "Televised Nationwide Address on Behalf of Senator Barry Goldwater." 27 October 1964. In *Speaking My Mind: Selected Speeches*, 22–36. New York: Simon & Schuster, 1989.

————. *A Time for Choosing: The Speeches of Ronald Reagan, 1961–1982*, ed. Alfred Balitzer and Gerald M. Bonetto. Chicago: Regnery Gateway, 1983.

Reeves, Marjorie. *The Influence of Prophecy in the Later Middle Ages*. Oxford: Clarendon Press, 1969.

Reiche, Harald A. T. "The Archaic Heritage: Myths of Decline and End in Antiquity." In *Visions of Apocalypse: End or Rebirth?* ed. Saul Friedlander, Gerald Horton, Leo Marx, and Eugene Skolnikoff, 21–43. New York: Holmes & Meier, 1985.

Reid, J. K. S. *The Authority of Scripture: A Study of the Reformation and Post-Reformation Understanding of the Bible*. London: Methuen, 1957.

Reid, Ronald F. "Apocalypticism and Typology: Rhetorical Dimensions of a Symbolic Reality." *Quarterly Journal of Speech* 69 (1983): 229–48.

Report of the General Conference of Christians Expecting the Advent of Our Lord Jesus Christ, Held in Boston Oct. 14, 1840. Boston: Joshua V. Himes, 1842.

Richman, Robert. "The Argument from Evil." *Religious Studies* 4 (1968): 203–11.

Ricoeur, Paul. "Evil, a Challenge to Philosophy and Theology." In *Trajectories in the Study of Religion*, ed. Ray L. Hart, 67–80. Atlanta, Ga.: Scholars Press, 1987.

————. *The Symbolism of Evil*. Trans. Emerson Buchanan. Boston: Beacon Press, 1987.

Ritter, Kurt. "Reagan's 1964 TV Speech for Goldwater: Millennial Themes in American Political Rhetoric." In *Rhetorical Dimensions in Media: A Critical Casebook*, 2d ed., ed. Martin J. Medhurst and Thomas W. Benson, 58–72. Dubuque, Iowa: Kendall / Hunt Publishers, 1991.

Rivenburg, Roy. "Is the End Still Near?" *Los Angeles Times*, 30 July 1992, E1–E3.

Robertson, Pat. "Face the Nation." 14 February 1988, interview. Transcript provided by CBS News.

————. *The New Millennium*. Waco, Tex.: Word, 1990.

————. "A New Vision for America." Speech text provided by "Americans for Robertson." 17 September 1986, Washington, D.C.

————. "Pat Robertson's Perspective." *700 Club Newsletter*, February–March 1980. Reprinted in *All in the Name of the Bible*, ed. Hassan Haddad and Donald Wagner, 121–29. Brattleboro, Vt.: Amana Books, 1986.

Robertson, Pat, and Bob Slosser. *The Secret Kingdom*. Toronto: Bantam Books, 1984.

Rogers, Jack B., and Donald K. McKim. *The Authority and Interpretation of the Bible: An Historical Approach*. New York: Harper & Row, 1979.

Rogers, P. G. *The Fifth Monarchy Men*. London: Oxford University Press, 1966.

Rouner, Leroy, ed. *Civil Religion and Political Theology*. Notre Dame, Ind.: University of Notre Dame Press, 1986.

Rowe, David L. "Millerites: A Shadow Portrait." In *The Disappointed: Millerism and Millenarianism in the Nineteenth Century*, ed. Ronald L. Numbers and Jonathan M. Butler, 1–16. Bloomington, Ind.: Indiana University Press, 1987.

————. *Thunder and Trumpets: Millerites and Dissenting Religion in Upstate New York, 1800–1850*. Chico, Calif.: Scholars Press, 1985.

Rowland, Robert C. "On Mythic Criticism." *Communication Studies* 41 (1990): 101–16.

Rushing, Janice Hocker. "E.T. as Rhetorical Transcendence." *Quarterly Journal of Speech* 71 (1985): 188–203.

————. "Ronald Reagan's "Star Wars" Address: Mythic Containment of Technical Reasoning." *Quarterly Journal of Speech* 72 (1986): 415–33.

Russell, Jeffrey Burton. *The Prince of Darkness: Radical Evil and the Power of Good in History*. Ithaca, N.Y.: Cornell University Press, 1988.

Sandeen, Ernest R. "Millennialism." In *The Rise of Adventism: Religion and Society in Mid-Nineteenth Century America*, ed. Edwin S. Gaustad, 104–18. New York: Harper & Row, 1974.

———. "The 'Little Tradition' and the Form of Modern Millenarianism." *Annual Review of the Social Sciences of Religion* 4 (1980): 165–81.

———. *The Roots of Fundamentalism: British and American Millenarianism, 1800–1930*. Chicago: University of Chicago Press, 1970.

Schall, James V. "Apocalypse as a Secular Enterprise." *Scottish Journal of Theology* 29 (1976): 357–73.

Scheer, Robert. *With Enough Shovels: Reagan, Bush, and Nuclear War*. New York: Random House, 1982.

Schell, Jonathan. *The Fate of the Earth*. New York: Avon Books, 1982.

Schmithals, Walter. *The Apocalyptic Movement*. Trans. John E. Steely. Nashville, Tenn.: Abingdon Press, 1975.

Schüssler Fiorenza, Elisabeth. *The Book of Revolution: Justice and Judgement*. Philadelphia: Fortress Press, 1985.

———. *Revelation: Vision of A Just World*. Minneapolis: Fortress Press, 1991.

Schwartz, Hillel. *Century's End: A Cultural History of the Fin de Siècle from the 990s through the 1900s*. New York: Doubleday, 1990.

———. "The End of the Beginning: Millenarian Studies, 1969–1975." *Religious Studies Review* 2 (July 1976): 1–15.

Schweitzer, Albert. *The Quest of the Historical Jesus*. Trans. W. Montgomery. New York: Macmillan, 1968.

Scofield, C. I. "Rightly Dividing the Word of Truth." In *The First Scofield Reference Bible*, ed. C. I. Scofield, 1567–1605. Westwood, N.J.: Barbour, 1986.

———, ed. *The First Scofield Reference Bible*. Westwood, N.J.: Barbour, 1986.

Scult, Allen. "A Note on the Range and Utility of the Universal Audience." *Journal of the American Forensic Association* 22 (1985): 83–87.

———. "Perelman's Universal Audience: One Perspective." *Central States Speech Journal* 27 (1976): 176–80.

Sears, Clara Endicott. *Days of Delusion: A Strange Bit of History*. Boston: Houghton Mifflin, 1924.

Shaw, Brian J. "Reason, Nostalgia, and Eschatology in the Critical Theory of Max Horkheimer." *Journal of Politics* 47 (1985): 160–81.

Shepperson, George. "The Comparative Study of Millenarian Movements." In *Millennial Dreams in Action: Studies in Revolutionary Religious Movements*, ed. Sylvia Thrupp. New York: Schocken Books, 1970.

Simon, Ulrich E. *The End Is Not Yet: A Study in Christian Eschatology*. Digswell Place, UK: James Nisbet & Co., Ltd.

Slosser, Bob. *Reagan Inside Out*. Waco, Tex.: Word Books, 1984.

Smith, Alice Kimball. *A Peril and a Hope: The Scientists' Movement in America 1945–47*. Rev. ed. Cambridge, Mass.: MIT Press, 1971.

Smith, David E. "Millennial Scholarship in America." *American Quarterly* 17 (1965): 535–49.

Smith, Timothy. "Social Reform." In *The Rise of Adventism: Religion and Society in Mid-*

Nineteenth Century America, ed. Edwin S. Gaustad, 18–29. New York: Harper & Row, 1974.

Steinfels, Peter. "Gulf War Proving Bountiful for some Prophets of Doom." *New York Times,* national ed., 2 February 1991, 1.

Swaggart, Jimmy. "The Coming Kingdom: You Cannot Have a Kingdom Until You Have a King." *The Evangelist,* September 1986, 4–5, 12.

Sypher, Wylie. *Comedy.* New York: Doubleday, 1956.

Talmon, Yonina. "Millenarism." In *International Encyclopedia of the Social Sciences,* ed. D. L. Sills. 349–62. New York: Free Press, 1968.

———. "Pursuit of the Millennium: The Relation Between Religious and Social Change." *Archives Européenes de Sociologie* 3 (1962): 125–48; reprinted in *Reader in Comparative Religion,* ed. William A. Lessa and Evon Z. Vogt, 522–37. 2d ed. New York: Harper & Row, 1965.

Taylor, Charles. "G-O-G." *Bible Prophecy News,* July 1985, 4.

———. *Watch 1988!* Huntington Beach, Calif.: Today in Bible Prophecy, 1988.

———. *Watch 1987!* Huntington Beach, Calif.: Today in Bible Prophecy, 1987.

———. *Watch 1986!* Huntington Beach, Calif.: Today in Bible Prophecy, 1986.

———. *World War III and the Destiny of America.* Nashville, Tenn. Thomas Nelson Publishers, 1979.

Taylor, John B. *Ezekiel: An Introduction and Commentary.* Leicester, England: Inter-Varsity Press, 1969.

Thrupp, Sylvia, ed. *Millennial Dreams in Action: Studies in Revolutionary Religious Movements.* New York: Schocken Books, 1970.

Tillich, Paul. A *History of Christian Thought from Its Judaic and Hellenistic Origins to Existentialism,* 2d ed., ed. Carl E. Braaten. New York: Simon & Schuster, 1968.

Tinder, Glenn. "Eschatology and Politics." *Review of Politics* 27 (1965): 311–33.

Tiryakian, Edward A. "Modernity as an Eschatological Setting: A New Vista for the Study of Religions." *History of Religions* 25 (1986): 378–86.

Toulmin, Stephen. *The Uses of Argument.* Cambridge: Cambridge University Press, 1958.

Tracy, David. *The Analogical Imagination: Christian Theology and the Culture of Pluralism.* New York: Crossroad, 1981.

Tuveson, Ernest. *Redeemer Nation: The Idea of America's Millennial Role.* Chicago: University of Chicago Press, 1966.

Tyler, Alice Felt. *Freedom's Ferment.* New York: Harper & Brothers, 1961.

Ulanov, Barry. "The Rhetoric of Christian Comedy." In *Holy Laughter: Essays on Religion in the Comic Perspective,* ed. M. Conrad Hyers, 103–22. New York: Seabury Press, 1969.

Unamuno, Miguel de. *The Tragic Sense of Life in Men and Nations.* Trans. Anthony Kerrigan. Princeton, N.J.: Princeton University Press, 1972.

Via, Dan Otto. *The Parables: Their Literary and Existential Dimension.* Philadelphia: Fortress Press, 1967.

Vicchio, Stephen. *The Voice from the Whirlwind: The Problem of Evil and the Modern World.* Westminster, Md.: Christian Classics, 1989.

Vickers, Brian. *In Defence of Rhetoric.* Oxford: Clarendon Press, 1988.

Voegelin, Eric. "Quod Deus Dicitur." In *Trajectories in the Study of Religion,* ed. Ray L. Hart, 1–16. Atlanta: Scholar Press, 1987.

Vulliamy, Ed. "End of the World Time Comes—and Goes." *San Francisco Chronicle,* 19 September 1988, A14.

Walker, Larry L. "How the NIV Made Use of New Light on the Hebrew Text." In *The NIV: The Making of a Contemporary Translation*, ed. Kenneth L. Barker, 95–105. Grand Rapids, Mich.: Zondervan, 1986.

Wallace, Karl R. "*Topoi* and the Problem of Invention." *Quarterly Journal of Speech* 58 (1972): 387–95.

Wallace, Robert M. "A Reconciliation of Myth and Rationality." *Humanities* 5 (February 1984): 6–8.

Walvoord, John F. *The Blessed Hope and the Tribulation*. Grand Rapids, Mich.: Zondervan, 1976.

———. *Armageddon, Oil, and the Middle East Crisis*. Rev. ed. Grand Rapids, Mich.: Zondervan, 1990.

Walvoord, John F., and John E. Walvoord. *Armageddon, Oil, and the Middle East Crisis*. Grand Rapids, Mich.: Zondervan, 1980.

Ward, Henry Dana. "History and Doctrine of the Millennium." In *Report of the General Conference of Christians Expecting the Advent of Our Lord Jesus Christ, Held in Boston Oct. 14, 1840*. Boston: Joshua V. Himes, 1842.

Ware, B. L. "Theories of Rhetorical Criticism as Argument." Ph.D. dissertation, University of Kansas, 1974.

Warner, Martin, ed. *The Bible as Rhetoric: Studies in Biblical Persuasion and Credibility*. London: Routledge, 1990.

Washington Research Institute. *Armageddon Theology and Presidential Decision-Making: Religious Leaders' Concern*. San Francisco: Washington Research Institute, 1984.

Weaver, Richard M. *Language is Sermonic*. Baton Rouge: Louisiana State University Press, 1970.

Weber, Max. "Politics as a Vocation." In *From Max Weber: Essays in Sociology*, ed. and trans. H. H. Gerth and C. Wright Mills, 77–28. New York: Oxford University Press, 1946.

———. "Religious Rejections of the World and Their Directions." In *From Max Weber: Essays in Sociology*, ed. and trans. H. H. Gerth and C. Wright Mills, 323–59. New York: Oxford University Press, 1946.

———. *The Sociology of Religion*. Trans. Ephraim Fischoff. Boston: Beacon Press, 1964.

Weber, Timothy. *Living in the Shadow of the Second Coming: American Premillennialism, 1875–1982*. Rev. ed. Chicago: University of Chicago Press, 1987.

———. "The Two-Edged Sword: The Fundamentalist Use of the Bible." In *The Bible in America: Essays in Cultural History*, ed. Nathan O. Hatch and Mark Noll. 101–20. New York: Oxford University Press, 1982.

Weigert, Andrew J. "Christian Eschatological Identities and the Nuclear Context." *Journal for the Scientific Study of Religion* 27 (1988): 175–91.

Weisberger, Bernard. *They Gathered at the River: The Story of the Great Revivalists and Their Impact on Religion in America*. Boston: Little, Brown, 1958.

Werner, Martin. *The Formation of Christian Dogma*. Trans. S. G. F. Brandon. New York: Harper & Brothers, 1957.

Whisenant, Edgar C. *88 Reasons Why the Rapture Will Be in 1988*. Nashville, Tenn.: World Bible Society, 1988.

White, Ellen G. *Cosmic Conflict*. Washington, D.C.: Review and Herald Publishing, 1982. Reprint of *The Great Controversy* (1888).

White, James, ed. *Sketches of the Christian Life and Public Labors of William Miller*. Battle Creek, Mich.: Steam Press, 1875.

Wiesel, Elie. "A Vision of the Apocalypse." *World Literature Today* 58 (1984): 194–97.

Wilcox, Donald. *The Measure of Times Past: Pre-Newtonian Chronologies and the Rhetoric of Relative Time*. Chicago: University of Chicago Press, 1987.

Wilder, Amos. *Early Christian Rhetoric: The Language of the Gospel*. Cambridge, Mass.: Harvard University Press, 1971.

———. *Eschatology and Ethics in the Teaching of Jesus*. Rev. ed. New York: Harper & Brothers, 1950.

———. "The Rhetoric of Ancient and Modern Apocalyptic." *Interpretation* 25 (1971): 436–53.

Wills, Garry. *Reagan's America: Innocents at Home*. Garden City, N.Y.: Doubleday, 1987.

———. *Under God: Religion and American Politics*. New York: Simon & Schuster, 1990.

Wilson, Dwight. *Armageddon Now! The Premillenarian Response to Russia and Israel Since 1917*. 2d ed. Tyler, Tex.: Institute for Christian Economics, 1991.

Worsley, Peter. *The Trumpet Shall Sound*. New York: Schocken Books, 1968.

Wright, J., trans. *The Play of Antichrist*. Toronto: Pontifical Institute of Medieval Studies, 1967.

Wuthnow, Robert. "The Political Rebirth of American Evangelicals." In *The New Christian Right: Mobilization and Legitimation*, ed. Robert C. Liebman and Robert Wuthnow. New York: Aldine Publishing, 1983.

Yamauchi, Edwin. "Armageddon, Oil, and the Middle East Crisis." *Christianity Today*, 29 April 1991, 50–51.

Yoachum, Susan. "President Urged to Repudiate View That Nuclear War Is Near." *San Jose Mercury News*, 25 October 1984, 8A.

Young, Jean I., trans. *The Prose Edda of Snorri Sturlson*. Berkeley: University of California Press, 1966.

Zamora, Lois Parkinson, ed. *The Apocalyptic Vision in America: Interdisciplinary Essays on Myth and Culture*. Bowling Green, Ohio: Bowling Green University Popular Press, 1982.

———. *Writing the Apocalypse*. New York: Cambridge University Press, 1989.

Zencey, Eric. "Apocalypse and Ecology." *North American Review* (June 1988): 54–57.

Zulick, Margaret D. "The Agon of Jeremiah: On the Dialogic Invention of Prophetic Ethos." *Quarterly Journal of Speech* 78 (1992):125–48.

Zurcher. E. "Prince Moonlight: Messianism and Eschatology in Early Medieval Chinese Buddhism." *T-oung Pao* 68 (1982):1–59.

Zygmunt, Joseph F. "Prophetic Failure and Chiliastic Identity: The Case of Jehovah's Witnesses." *American Journal of Sociology* 75 (1970): 926–48.

Index